AF616509

The Quest for Absolute Truth

Encouraging You to STAND UP! So We Can Restore America

Russell A. Newman

CrossBooks™
A Division of LifeWay
1663 Liberty Drive
Bloomington, IN 47403
www.crossbooks.com
Phone: 1-866-879-0502

First published by CrossBooks 7/5/2010

ISBN: 978-1-6150-7257-6 (sc)
ISBN: 978-1-6150-7258-3 (hc)

Library of Congress Control Number: 2010908264

Printed in the United States of America
Bloomington, Indiana

This book is printed on acid-free paper.

I Do Not Choose to Be a Common Man

I do not choose to be a common man. It is my right to be uncommon—if I can.

I seek opportunity—not security. I do not wish to be kept a citizen, humbled and dulled by having the state look after me.

I want to take the calculated risk; to dream and to build, to fail and to succeed.

I refuse to barter incentive for a dole. I prefer the challenges of life to the guaranteed existence; the thrill of fulfillment to the stale calm of utopia.

I will not trade freedom for beneficence nor my dignity for a handout. I will never cower before any master nor bend to any threat.

It is my heritage to stand erect, proud and unafraid; to think and act for myself, enjoy the benefit of my creations and to face the world boldly and say, "This I have done" with my own hand, I am a man. I am an American.

-"My Creed" by Dean Alfange, 1952.

"You Should Read this Book" Sales Pitch (Preface)

Fellow patriotic Americans, I have an urgent message that you need to hear. In a world where up is down, wrong is right, warm weather brings snow and corruption is the only way to play the game, *you* will be the casualty unless the nation is restored. America is playing with fire because to tinker with socialism is to flirt with the death of the Republic. America loves her freedom, but slowly, over time, the politicians that we thought we could trust have desecrated the Christian nation, and the federal government has a death grip of control on every aspect of our lives. If you love your freedom, believe the nation needs to be restored, and if you are concerned enough to Stand Up! for what you believe, then you need to read this book. If you think you can handle the Truth—the whole truth and nothing but the truth—then I dare you to pick this book up and read it from cover to cover.

Every single page in this book is controversial, because the only two topics that are discussed are religion and politics. If you cringed at that last statement, you may not want to read this book because I will demonstrate the following:

- Topics in Theology:
    - God exists.
    - The Bible is Absolute Truth.
    - Christianity is entirely true.
    - All religions that contradict Christianity are false.

- Topics in Politics:
    - Liberal theology is immoral.
    - Liberal politics is immoral.
    - Socialism leads to tyranny (all Nazis were socialists).
    - America breeds atheism.

The above topics are but a peek at the pot we will begin to stir. I must warn that Chapters 14 and 15 may be depressing because they accurately reflect America's depraved state. However, all hope is not lost. The last chapter will be encouraging because there are some simple steps that can lead to profound results. Unlike the results of the 2008 elections, America's "fundamental transformation" is coming, and it will truly be "change you can believe in."

Contents

Introduction

America, Religion, and the Gaping Hole in the Soul

Chapter 1

The State of the Christian Nation

"America was born a Christian nation. America was born to exemplify that devotion to the elements of righteousness which are derived from the revelations of Holy Scripture."

—President Woodrow Wilson[1]

"If we will not prepare to give all that we have and that all that we are to preserve Christian civilization in our land, we shall go to destruction."

—President Franklin D. Roosevelt

The United States and Her Early Beginnings

An Answer that We Cannot Create. The question comes up time and time again, "Is America really a Christian nation?" The answer to this simple question has undoubtedly sparked vigorous debate and has caused many people to contemplate America's purpose, but the answer to this simple question has never been discovered in any opinion, debate or idea of the modern man. Indeed, the modern man cannot answer this question, simply because he did not live during the period when the explorers explored, when the colonies were created, or when America was founded. To truly discover whether America is a Christian nation, we must take a trip back in time to discover the reasons for exploring the New World, the impetus

1 President Woodrow Wilson, "The Bible and Progress" (address, Denver, CO, 1911).

behind creating the colonies and ultimately the purpose for establishing the United States. We need not venture into conjecture; the answer to this simple question was established by our founding fathers hundreds of years before you and I ever stepped foot on the face of the earth.

We begin by seeking out the truth—regardless of where it may lead or what we may find. As seekers of the truth, we realize that our opinion is irrelevant to truth—it always has been. Our opinion of truth is irrelevant simply because truth will continue to be true, regardless of whether we like or agree with that which is true. In our Quest for Absolute Truth, we begin by looking into the reasons America was explored. Then, we will dust off some "inconvenient" charters that establish an underlying motive for the creation of the thirteen original colonies. These charters enable us to peek behind the curtain so that we can discover the truth that revisionist historians wish you never knew.

After examining some of the charters, we will examine our founding fathers and the reasons why America—the greatest nation ever to exist—was birthed. Together, we will answer the question of Christian heritage once and for all. Either America is a Christian nation, or she is not. The answer is extraordinarily important because it will help us grasp the severity of the events that are now unfolding and will help us determine whether America is on a sustainable path or whether she needs restoration. We need answers to some very simple questions such as: "Is America a Christian nation?," "Does it matter if America is a Christian nation?" and "Are Christians doing their part to help restore America?"

The Christian Explorer. Before the United States of America was established, there were thirteen colonies. Before these colonies ever came into existence, the land that these colonies settled had to first be discovered. Thus, we arrive at the beginning, the time when what would be America was first discovered by European explorers. Christopher Columbus is perhaps one of the greatest and best-known explorers in American history, but only part of the story is taught in our schools because revisionist history books conveniently omit the most important fact regarding Columbus's purpose for exploring. In fact, revisionists have left out some of the most important facts about Christopher Columbus, facts that prevent people from understanding who he was and his primary purpose for exploring the New World.

As we bypass the liberal historians, we discover a revealing motive as to why Columbus explored America. We begin by reading an excerpt from his memoir, written in 1504, because it describes the reason why he risked his life to explore a new world. Columbus wrote, "When I left in 1492 to discover a new world, here was the purpose. I was led by the Holy Spirit to carry the message of the Gospel of Jesus Christ to undiscovered lands."[2] (For some crazy reason, I was never taught the entire truth when I was learning about the exploration of America. Perhaps it's because the purpose is so clear and so concise that the liberal historians must omit this excerpt, as there is no possible way to manipulate or distort these words.) Nevertheless, in Columbus's own words, it is revealed that he risked his life to sail across the ocean with the intent to expand the kingdom of God by propagating the Gospel of Jesus Christ.

After North America was discovered, we then look to one of the first documents that were written to establish order (through government). Order needed to be established because previous settlements in the New World had failed due to a lack of government. Thus, in November 1620, the Mayflower Compact was enacted. The compact established the purpose for the first colony as well as the basis on which written laws would enter into the New World.[3] The Mayflower Compact reads: "Having undertaken *for the Glory of God, and Advancement of the Christian Faith*, and the Honour of our King and Country, a Voyage to plant the first Colony in the northern Parts of Virginia …"[4] (I am amending these texts somewhat as I quote them to make them more accessible to a present-day reader.)

The Christian Colonies. Before the Constitution and the Declaration of Independence, we know that there were thirteen original colonies. Many of these colonies drafted documents that would ultimately provide a foundation upon which the colonies would eventually build a government. However, many of the documents explicitly reveal the people's religious convictions as well as the purpose for each colony's existence.[5] Understanding the motive of establishing the colonies will help us put into perspective the Declaration of Independence and the reason for drafting the Constitution.

---

2 Carolyn Powell, *The Beginning and Ending of America: Prophecy Present, Past and Future.* (Baltimore: PublishAmerica, 2005).

3 All About History, "Mayflower Compact – The Common Anchor," http://www.allabouthistory.org/mayflower-compact.htm.

4 Yale Law School, "The Avalon Project: Documents in Law, History and Diplomacy," Lillan Goldman Law Library, http://avalon.law.yale.edu/default.asp (emphasis added).

5 Ibid.

(All quotations in this section were pulled from the Avalon Project from Yale Law School.)

We begin in 1606, with the First Charter of Virginia. Virginia drafted a charter that explicitly reveals a Christian motive: "We, greatly commending, and graciously accepting of, their Desires for the Furtherance of so noble a Work, which may, by the Providence of Almighty God, hereafter tend to the Glory of his Divine Majesty, in propagating of Christian Religion to such People, as yet live in Darkness and miserable Ignorance of the true Knowledge and Worship of God …"

In 1620, the Charter of Massachusetts reveals this colony desired "to advance the in Largement of Christian Religion, to the Glory of God Almighty, as also by that Means to stretch out the Bounds of our Dominions, and to replenish those Deserts with People governed by Laws and Magistrates, for the peaceable Commerce of all …"

In 1632, the Charter of Maryland reveals this colony was "treading in the steps of his Father, being animated with a laudable, and pious Zeal for extending the Christian Religion, and also the Territories of our Empire …"

In 1639, Connecticut drafted the Fundamental Orders to govern their colony. We note that the Fundamental Orders state: "For as much as it hath pleased Almighty God by the wise disposition of his divine providence so to order and dispose of things...to maintain and preserve the liberty and purity of the Gospel of our Lord Jesus which we now profess …"

Also in 1639, New Hampshire established The Agreement of the Settlers which states: "do in the name of Christ and in the sight of God combine ourselves together to erect and set up among us such Government as shall be to our best discerning agreeable to the Will of God professing ourselves Subjects to our Sovereign Lord King Charles according to the Liberties of our English Colony of Massachusetts, and binding of ourselves solemnly by the Grace and Help of Christ and in His Name and fear to submit ourselves to such Godly and Christian Laws as are established in the realm of England to our best Knowledge …"

In 1663, the Charter of North Carolina reveals that their purpose was "being excited with a laudable and pious zeal for the propagation of the Christian faith, and the enlargement of our empire and dominions …"

Also in 1663, the Charter of Rhode Island reveals "and to preserve unto them that liberty, in the true Christian faith and worship of God, which they have sought with so much travail, and with peaceable minds, and loyall subjectione to our royal progenitors and ourselves, to enjoy …"

In 1665, the Charter of Carolina states: "And furthermore, the patronage and advowsons of all the churches and chapels, which, as Christian religion shall increase within the province, territory, isles, and limits aforesaid, shall happen hereafter to be erected; together with license and power to build and found churches, chapels and oratories, in convenient and fit places, within the said bounds and limits; and to cause them to be dedicated and consecrated, according to the ecclesiastical laws of our kingdom of England ..."

In 1681, the Charter for the Providence of Pennsylvania states that it desired to "promote such useful commodities as may be of Benefit to us and Our Dominions, as also to reduce the savage Natives by gentle and just mamlers to the Love of Civil Society and Christian Religion ..."

In 1683, the Fundamental Constitutions for the Providence of East New Jersey states: "that no man shall be admitted a member of the great or common Council, or any other place of public trust, who shall not profess faith in Christ Jesus, and solemnly declare that he doth no ways hold himself obliged in conscience to endeavor alteration in the government, or seeks the turning out of any in it or their ruin or prejudice, either in person or estate, because they are in his opinion heretics, or differ in their judgment from him: Nor by this article is it intended, that any under the notion of this liberty shall allow themselves to avow atheism, irreligiousness, or to practice cursing, swearing, drunkenness, prophaness, whoring, adultery, murdering or any kind of violence, or indulging themselves in stage plays, masks, revels or such like abuses ..."

In 1691, the Charter of Massachusetts Bay states: "Province may be Religiously peaceably and Civilly Governed Protected and Defended so as their good life and orderly Conversation may win the Indians Natives of the Country to the knowledge and obedience of the only true God and Saviour of Mankind and the Christian Faith ..."

In 1701, the Charter of Privileges Granted by William Penn to the Inhabitants of Pennsylvania and Territories states: "AND that all Persons who also profess to believe in Jesus Christ, the Saviour of the World, shall be capable (notwithstanding their other Persuasions and Practices in Point of Conscience and Religion) to serve this Government in any Capacity, both legislatively and executively ..."

A New Nation Is Born. It is an undeniable fact that many of the early colonies drafted documents that explicitly reveal a motive for propagating the Gospel of Jesus Christ. Some of the colonies even required government officials to be

Christian, while others sought to establish and build churches. However, as we know, the colonies would not last forever. In due time, each and every colony would join together to create the United States of America.

But before the Declaration of Independence was signed, the Continental Congress called the people of the colonies to *days of prayer and fasting* so that they might know and understand whether or not they should sign the Declaration of Independence and ultimately provoke a war with England.[6] After days of prayer and fasting, it was agreed it was in the colony's best interest to create a sovereign nation. Thus, a new nation was born.

The Declaration of Independence specifically recognizes the existence of God, but not just any god. The recognition of the Christian God, as we are establishing, was not a matter that was concealed. The colonies expressed devout love and admiration for the Gospel of Jesus Christ, and it was this adherence to the Christian faith that ultimately led to the rights set forth in the Declaration of Independence. It is not an accident that we read, "That all men are created equal; that they are endowed by their Creator with certain unalienable rights; that among these are life, liberty and the pursuit of happiness ..." The founding fathers recognized that they were created by the God of the Christian faith.

After the Revolutionary War was won, America had a new beginning with endless opportunity before her. As America was being established, we need to note some of the people who were heavily involved with her establishment. As we progress through the different categories, it will become obvious that America was founded by Christians and for Christians, so Jesus Christ might be exalted in every area of life. Even the government recognized and had reverence for God.

The Involvement of Preachers. Contrary to revised history, preachers had a tremendous amount of involvement in establishing America and many institutions we know and recognize today. We begin by examining the involvement of preachers with the government. John Leland wrote the introduction of the First Amendment of the Constitution, securing some of the greatest freedoms known to man. Francis Bellamy wrote the Pledge of Allegiance that is recited in the schools all across America.

Second, we look at the many famous colleges and universities that were founded by preachers. Prior to the Civil War, ninety percent of the

6 Dr. Richard Lee, "What Should We Believe? Is America a Christian Nation?" There's Hope Ministries, 1998.

presidents of all the universities and the colleges in America were pastors.[7] We should name a few of the schools that churches started and whose presidents were preachers. Churches started prominent schools such as Brown, Columbia, Dartmouth, Harvard, Princeton, William and Mary, and Yale. All these schools were founded by Christian churches, and their presidents were preachers of the Gospel.[8]

In addition to these schools being founded by preachers of the Gospel, their mission was also to share the Gospel of Jesus Christ to their students. John Harvard stated that the purpose of Harvard University was "that every student be plainly instructed and earnestly pressed to consider well the main ends of his life and studies: to know God and Jesus Christ which is eternal life and therefore to lay Christ in the bottom as the foundation of all knowledge and learning, and see that the Lord only giveth wisdom. To let everyone seriously set himself by prayer in secret to seek Christ Jesus as Lord and Master."[9] The seal of Harvard University reads "Truth for Christ and the Church"; which can still be seen on Harvard's campus today. Columbia University's mission statement reveals a similar purpose as it was founded to ensure that "the chief things that are aimed in this college are to teach and gauge the children to know God and Jesus Christ and to love and serve Him in all sobriety."[10]

These are Christian universities that were started by Christians with the purpose of sharing the Gospel of Jesus Christ. The universities were not alone in this endeavor; the first textbook for public schools was the "New England Primer."[11] Since America began as a Christian nation, it was not controversial to have the Lord's Prayer placed on the cover of our first public school system's textbook. The purpose of this textbook was to teach the alphabet to students in Theological verse:

A. In Adam's fall we sinned all.
B. It's Heaven to find, the Bible's mind.
C. Christ crucified for sinners died.[12]

---

7 Ibid.

8 Ibid.

9 Dr. Richard Lee, "Is America a Christian Nation?" Outreach, Inc., http://www.sermoncentral.com/sermons/is-america-a-christian-nation-richard-lee-sermon-on-america-136316.asp?Page=1.

10 Ibid.

11 Ibid.

12 Ibid.

Is it really a shock that a Christian nation would teach their children about the Lord and Savior Jesus Christ? Let me rephrase the question to shed a different light on the circumstances. If America were truly not a Christian nation, why would the American public school system, and the universities, teach their students about Jesus Christ?

The Currency. Since 1865, each and every time your purchase a good or service, you are using a currency that exalts Jesus Christ. This fact is not hard to discover, because every bill and every coin has "In God We Trust" located somewhere on it. Since the founding fathers were not Muslim, we cannot attribute reverence to Allah. Since the founding fathers were not Jewish, we cannot attribute reverence *solely* to Yahweh (and exclude Christ). We know that Americans, in 1865, were not Hindu because we do not read "In Many Gods We Trust." Even though the currency did not have "In God We Trust" until the late nineteenth century, we can easily conclude that Jesus Christ is given recognition because America, as we are demonstrating, is a Christian nation.

Furthermore, take a look at a one-dollar bill. On the back of the note, there are two circles that flank "ONE." Within these two circles are the seal of the United States of America. Take a look at the back of the seal (the left circle). You will notice a pyramid with one eye at the top that radiates with light. This is the eye of God. The Latin phrase that encircles the pyramid, when translated, reads: "God has smiled upon our beginnings." Once again, this is a direct reference to Jesus Christ, who is all-knowing and has immensely blessed America because she placed faith in Him.

The Courts. We will now examine one of the most revealing Supreme Court cases that undoubtedly recognized the United States of America as a "Christian nation."[13] On February 29, 1892, the Supreme Court decided the case: *Church of the Holy Trinity v. United States.* In the Overview of this case, we learn that the Church of the Holy Trinity contracted with a pastor, who lived in England, to come to the U.S. for employment. Consequently, the church was charged and convicted for violating federal law, which "prevented an employer from contracting with foreign laborers to come to the U.S. for employment."

The church filed a lawsuit to challenge the conviction, arguing that the law did not apply to churches. The court held that "the term 'laborer'

---

13 *Church of the Holy Trinity v. United States,* 143 U.S. 457 (1892).

in the federal statute applied to only cheap unskilled labor, and not to professional occupations, such as ministers and pastors." The Supreme Court ultimately determined "that it would be absurd for the law to apply in this instant" and the church's conviction was reversed.

This was certainly a great victory for the church, but we need to looker deeper into the case to discover why this particular decision was reached. An excerpt from Justice Brewer reveals why the Supreme Court ultimately made a decision in favor of the church. Justice Brewer wrote:

> But beyond all these matters no purpose of action against religion can be imputed to any legislation, state or national, because this is a religious people … [T]he gigantic missionary associations, with general support, [aim] to establish Christian missions in every quarter of the globe. These, and many other matters which might be noticed, add a volume of unofficial declarations to the mass of organic utterances that **this is a Christian nation**. [Emphasis added]

Justice Brewer, in providing the justification for the court's decision, also cited the fact that Christopher Columbus and the colonial charters and grants were for religious purposes that establish Christianity. Justice Brewer recognized the fact that Americans were a Christian people who settled and built a Christian nation. It is because of these facts that the Supreme Court recognized that America was, in fact, a "Christian nation."

We also know that, until recently, the Ten Commandments were proudly displayed throughout the courtrooms in America, as they reflect our moral standards. God established the Ten Commandments so that the people may know and understand the law. Why must we have laws and a penal code? Without an established set of moral laws, it would be impossible to live in a civil society because human nature is inherently sinful. If it were not for justice, law-abiding citizens could not peacefully lay their heads down at night because there would be utter chaos.

America, the Christian nation, recognized this principle from the beginning, but as time has marched forward, America has undergone "fundamental transformation." America was founded on the Judeo-Christian ethic, and we have had blessings unlike any other nation in the world. But what has happened to that Christian nation that started out with such a passion for Christ?

The America We Live in Today

America's Christian Heritage Is Being Erased. Have you ever imagined what it would be like if America were not a Christian nation? To find out what she may look like, all we need to do is look at some of the other nations around the world. If we look to the Middle East, where Muhammad and Allah are exalted, we see where terrorism is the norm—endless executions, car bombs, tortures, and a region of the world where fear runs rampant. If we look to China, we note that freedom is severely suppressed: people are killed for disagreeing with or protesting against the all-powerful government. If we look to Russia, we see how communism has not only been a complete failure, but that it too has oppressed its people. Russia has been known to execute Christians, and there was a time when missionaries risked their lives to smuggle in Bibles.

If we take a look at Europe, we see how socialism has failed and how it is bankrupting their governments and destroying their healthcare industry through universal healthcare (Canada's and the UK's versions have been a costly failure too). If we look to South America or Africa, we see developing nations where people are starving and struggling to make ends meet. Honestly, take a step back and look at a globe. Spin the globe around and look at all the nations of the world. Is there a nation, in all the world, that can rival the United States of America?

The answer is "No, there is not a single nation that can point to blessings anywhere close to those that America has enjoyed." The next question is why? Why have we been so blessed while other nations suffer through terrorism, starvation, and oppression? What makes us different, and why are we so special? To answer this question, let's return to the original topic: Why would a group of people want to establish a Christian nation? No other nation has been founded solely upon the Judeo-Christian ethic. No other nation has centered its *entire existence* upon Jesus Christ.

The answer is simple, but it requires us to crack open the Scriptures. In the Bible we read a great promise for any nation who places faith upon God, "Blessed is the nation whose God is the Lord, the people he chose for his inheritance."[14] Because the early settlers were persecuted by the corrupted Church of England, they desired to risk their lives and leave so that they could have religious freedom, in addition to having an extraordinary opportunity to propagate the Gospel in the new and undiscovered world. Americans wanted to show the world how powerful and great a nation can

14 Psalms 33:12.

become if a nation's fate *is* (present tense) truly placed upon the Rock of Jesus Christ. It's no secret that Jesus was the reason—the very purpose—for America's existence and it is not a *coincidence* that America just happens to be the most blessed nation in the world. Who is more powerful? Who has more wealth? Who has more freedom? Who has the greatest opportunity the world has ever known for life, liberty, and the pursuit of happiness? At least this has been the case for more than 230 years.

Have you picked up a newspaper recently? Have you turned on your television and watched the news? Have you noticed that there has been a crusade to erase our Christian heritage? Does it offend you? The fallout from this liberal crusade has caused America to slowly decline in virtually every aspect our society because Christianity is vanishing. Our financial system has suffered, the housing market has collapsed, morality seems to be irrelevant, our courtrooms no longer proudly display the Ten Commandments, it's socially acceptable to be a homosexual, gay marriage is allowed in some states, the murder of innocent children is now a *choice* a mother can make, our government justifies stealing money from one group to give to another, and the list goes on and on and on.

What has happened to us? How have we made such a dramatic shift? In the beginning, we were a humble nation before God. Now, we are one that is truly arrogant, entitled and, in some cases, blasphemous. We have lost all sense of what it truly means to be "American." We have such an "entitlement" mentality that we no longer understand that freedom is not free and it must not be taken for granted.

America no longer recognizes that freedom is a product of Christianity. It was never a coincidence that the Christian nation happened to have the greatest freedoms ever known to mankind. The inverse of this principle is horrifying because genocides, mass murders, oppressive governments, and tyranny run rampant throughout a nation without God.

Wake Up, Christian! Indeed, America has been undergoing a "fundamental transformation." This change is nothing to be proud of, because it's this *change* that is destroying the blessings that we have received. We are turning against the God who has made us great. It's time to step up, wake up and ultimately STAND UP! Open your eyes, and take note that the Church of Jesus Christ is in a serious backslide. I am about to present to you some statistics that should sink your heart; especially when you reflect on the blood that has been shed to protect and to preserve this great Christian nation. Countless men and women have paid the ultimate price—have given their lives—so that we may enjoy the freedom that we take for granted today. Yet Christians do not seem to care. Christians "fit in" with the rest of society, and they have not been making a difference in the name of Jesus Christ—who is, may I remind you, the King of kings and the Lord of lords. Indeed, our sense of entitlement and our immense blessings have left us complacent, and we, as a nation, no longer feel the need to evangelize.

These are undoubtedly harsh words, but they are supported by statistical data that demonstrate an underlying truth behind them. These statistics need to be studied and digested so that the true meaning and future consequences can be understood if America refuses to redirect her path back to God. Statistics reveal that the Christian Church is facing some serious problems in both adding new members and retaining current members. Church problems include:[15]

1. Evangelical churches have failed to gain an additional *two percent* of the population in the last fifty years.
2. No county in America has a greater percentage of churched persons today than a decade ago.
3. Half of all churches last year did not add *one new member* through "conversion growth."
4. In 1900, there were 27 churches for every 10,000 Americans; in 1950, there were 17 churches for every 10,000 Americans; and in 2004 there were only 11 churches for every 10,000 Americans.

Even more appalling is the fact that North America is the *only* continent where Christianity is *not* growing. Our church attendance is declining at a rate of approximately 10 percent over the past seven years.[16] Declines in church attendance result in a net loss of 48 churches per week or 6.85 every single day—and these statistics do not reflect church loss due to the largest recession since the Great Depression.[17] The statistics may be worse, since unemployment keeps the church from receiving a tithe from members who are not currently employed.

---

15 David A. Wheeler, "Understanding the REAL picture of N. America and the Church," Liberty University, http://bb7.liberty.edu/courses/1/EVAN565_B03_200920/content/_3882188_1/dir_UnderstandingNorthAmerica.zip/index.html.

16 Ibid.

17 Ibid.

The crisis is real, and we must do something soon if we have any desire of reversing these effects and ultimately restoring America to her rightful Christian foundation. Now that some of the data has been presented with respect to church growth—or should I say with respect to church loss—the next question would naturally be "Why?" Why are we losing so many churches? Why is North America, *of all places*, the only continent where Christianity is not growing? It almost seems as if I am dreaming because it does not seem possible for these statistics to be true! Yet each and every time I look around, I am reminded that they are in fact true because there is no way the church could be growing with the news and the events that are taking place today.

To find the reason, we must first begin with examining ourselves. "What have I done to further the Kingdom of Jesus Christ?" Statistically speaking, most Christians have done nothing. "How could this be possible? I attend church when it's convenient, I give when I have extra money and I try to live a moral life ..." Perhaps we have the wrong perspective; the law is the *lowest* standard to which people are allowed to stoop. The law is the absolute minimum, the lowest you are allowed to go without being punished. Instead of trying to skate by according to the minimum standard, we should be actively striving toward greatness or the highest standard. Attending church on Sunday, giving ten percent every time you earn a paycheck, and meeting God's moral standards should be the minimum! Yet we continue to lose 48 churches every single week.

Furthermore, experts believe that virtually all Christians (95–97 percent) live their entire lives without sharing the Gospel with *one person*.[18] This is truly heartbreaking. We have managed to somehow transform from a group of Christians who founded a nation to propagate the Gospel to a group that has lost sight of what it truly means to be a Christian. The title "Christian" was given to those early "believers" because they were truly a reflection of Christ. We understand this because it is clear that the first century Christians were willing to be martyred and persecuted for the faith (crucified, beheaded, boiled alive, etc.). By contrast, we, as twenty-first century Christians, cannot even tell a friend!

How could we possibly justify our refusal to simply share Jesus when we stand before an almighty God to give an account of how we used our spiritual gifts, talents, knowledge, and resources to further the Kingdom of God? (Especially when we know Jesus explicitly told Christians to

---

18 Will McRaney, *The Art of Personal Evangelism*, (Nashville, TN: B&H Publishing Group, 2003), 5.

proclaim the good news.)[19] Honestly, is there any justification for such selfishness? Indeed, refusing to share the Gospel is reduced to selfishness.

We Were Created by God for God. Before we go any farther, we need to understand that our life is a gift from God, along with everything we have, because God owns it all.[20] We were created for God as stated in Revelation 4:11 (NLT), "You created everything, and it is for your pleasure that they exist and were created." Not many people think of life this way because there are a lot of people who expect the government to provide everything from money to loans to good deals on cars to even free healthcare that is paid for by those who are productive as if these products and services were inherent rights!

What rights do we have? What entitlement has God given us? We must have forgotten that God owns everything and that we are mere stewards of that which He has provided. We must have forgotten that not even our bodies belong to us – we were bought with a price. Recall 1 Corinthians 6:19–20, "Do you not know that your body is the temple of the Holy Spirit who is in you, whom you have from God, and *you are not your own?* For you were bought at a price; therefore glorify God in your body and in your spirit, *which are God's*" (NKJV, emphasis added).

Let us not fall into the entitlement trap because it will undoubtedly breed selfishness. Selfishness is not a pretty sight. Who enjoys watching a young child steal and hoard all the toys, leaving the other children with nothing? Selfishness is like the Dead Sea: it has a stench because water does not flow out from the sea. As a result, there is no life in that particular body of water. If you become like the Dead Sea, then you will also experience death—perhaps the death of any love for others, sensitivity to evangelism, or ability to discern.

Jesus taught against selfishness: "I tell you the truth, unless you change and become like little children, you will never enter the kingdom of heaven. Therefore, whoever *humbles* himself like this child is the greatest in the kingdom of heaven" (emphasis added).[21] A humble spirit cannot be selfish. An obedient Christian cannot be selfish. We are to be thankful for what we have and not disgruntled for what we do not have.[22]

---

19 Matthew 28:18–20; Mark 16:15–16; Acts 1:8.

20 Psalms 50:9–12

21 Matthew 18:3–4.

22 Psalms 100:4.

So how do all these topics relate? Let's reverse the approach. Selfishness (ultimately sin) causes something to die. Perhaps we lose our passion for Jesus or stop tithing or stop reading the Bible. Whatever the case may be, selfishness is directly impacting the church because churches are disappearing at an astonishing rate. The contraction of the church reduces the restraint on immorality. As we take a look around, we see immorality everywhere, from corrupt politicians to the television to the radio and even to the church. (Today I read a headline where a denomination—one that professes faith in Jesus Christ—has endorsed homosexuality. How is that possible when God calls it an abomination?)

The shrinking presence of the church gives it a smaller impact on society. Thus, we come to a time where Christianity is rejected by the Christian nation. We come to a time when America is trying to pave a path where "legal" immorality runs rampant. Indeed, the shriveling church and the Christian who refuses to evangelize are not helping to restore America.

The America of Tomorrow

The Power of Fear. Have we done everything within our ability to help restore America? You may not be part of the problem, but 95–97 percent of Christians are certainly not helping, nor are they participating in the solution. A heart that is sensitive to the Gospel should have some fear by this point with respect to being a faithful steward in the use of our talents and resources to grow the Kingdom of God as well as America's future.

There should be fear about the state of the church, the direction our nation is heading, and whether or not we are doing everything we can with the talents, knowledge, and resources we have been given. There should be a fear for our children's and grandchildren's future and whether or not the current generation has frivolously spent away their future. There should be a fear for the loss of our freedoms because they are being stripped away one bill, bailout, stimulus package, and government program at a time. Above all, there should be a fear of what will happen to this nation once God turns His back on us. Read the warnings of the prophets; it can, and will eventually, happen if we do not get our act together![23] How many more times will we, the people of the Christian nation, flippantly disregard and mock the God that made her great?

---

23 Begin with Isaiah, Jeremiah, and Ezekiel.

Is there a solution to this colossal catastrophe? Is there any hope left? I believe that America's best days are ahead of us, but in order to reach the peak, we must first diligently climb out of the valley by actively striving towards restoring America. If we can harness the power of fear, we can channel it to the glory of God. We must understand that not all fear is bad. In fact, fear can serve as an extraordinary tool, and it can have a righteous purpose. King Solomon, the wisest man to ever live, once wrote that "the fear of the LORD is the beginning of wisdom."[24] When God-fearing people truly recognize who God is and the power that He has—oh, how we will fall on our knees and revere Him for the God that He is! Unfortunately, the power of fear is not a secret because we can see how it has been used against us time and time again by our own government.

Congress already understands the power of fear and the fact that fear induces change. Do you remember the fear that we had of a financial collapse in the fall of 2008 and how Congress demanded that we must pass the bailout bill *right now*? We did not even have time to read the bill—"Who cares what it may say? The sky is falling!" How about the "stimulus package" that had to be passed immediately because it was essential for the survival of our economy and small business? Would it matter if the stimulus package, by design, was not intended to spend most of the money until a year later, right before the 2010 elections? Would it matter if the bill was never designed to help small business or the economy? Nevertheless, the bill passed because of the fear that was invoked.

What about that healthcare bill that our government demands must be signed into law right now? "There are uninsured people dying in the streets!" Does it matter that the healthcare bill is not designed to insure all Americans, but that it establishes a foundation for a single-payer system? Indeed, liberals understand the power of fear, and they are using your fear against you. It was not by mere chance that Rahm Emanuel said, "Rule 1: Never allow a crisis go to waste, they are opportunities to do big things."[25] Yes, the bailout bill, stimulus package, and healthcare are all big opportunities to radically transform the nation, but are they constitutional?

Since the 2008 elections, we can see how fear is a powerful emotion that has induced change. We need to understand a simple principle: The entity that inflicts the fear channels the change. Right now the entity that

---

24 Proverbs 9:10.

25 *New York Times,* "Obama Weighs Quick Undoing of Bush Policy," http://www.nytimes.com/2008/11/10/us/politics/10obama.html.

is inflicting the most fear is our own government, but some Christians have forgotten that God is still in control. Romans 13:1 (emphasis added) reads: "Everyone must submit himself to the governing authorities, for *there is no authority except that which God has established.*" However, there are limitations to such obedience and submission. When the government commands worship of idols or kings (Daniel 3:6), forbids preaching of the Gospel (Acts 4–5), or murders children (Exodus 1), then it is the believer's *duty* to disobey.[26]

Are Christians justified in standing up to the government and demanding honesty, transparency, accountability, and morality? The magnitude of our government's involvement with the legal murder of children (what they call abortion), not only in our nation but abroad, justifies the Christian's decision to STAND UP! against the government. The biblical minimum for Christians was trampled upon and was left in the dust long ago. Before any more damage is done, Christians must take a stand, and they must get involved.

Could there be a purpose for God establishing an immoral government that encourages—and forces you to support with tax money—the murder of innocent children? Could there be a purpose in the attempted thrust into the immorality of socialism, where the government will steal from one group to give to another? Could this blasphemous government serve a purpose that will ultimately bring glory to God? Indeed it can. Instead of fearing the government, fear God and the consequences that flow from a failure to restore America, so that He can begin channeling the change.

If there is one thing President Obama had right, it is this: America does need a "fundamental transformation." However, the *change* each of us believes in vastly differs from one to another. Obama is trying to "nudge" America into the immorality of socialism, while I am trying to encourage America to return to her Christian heritage. A return to our Christian heritage is desperately needed.

Harness the Power, Move to Action. This chapter was written to invoke fear so that people will be moved to action. People need to understand that America is a Christian nation, but that Christians have become complacent and too comfortable. Perhaps Christians do not evangelize because they do not understand how true their faith actually is. Perhaps some Christians do not evangelize because they never thought about the consequences

26 Ted Cabal, ed., *The Apologetics Study Bible*, (Nashville, TN: Holman Bible Publishers, 2007), 995.

if the nation revolted against her God. Perhaps some Christians do not evangelize because they do not have the confidence to share. Whatever the reason, we know that virtually all Christians refuse to share their faith.

Thus, we come to the purpose for *The Quest for Absolute Truth*. This book was written to arm the Christian with the knowledge that will bring the confidence to begin evangelizing your family and friends. America is at a crossroads. By the grace of God, we have been given another chance to restore this great Christian nation before she plummets into liberalism and entirely erases her Christian heritage.

I invite you to join me in an exciting journey that will truly reveal the Absolute Truth of the Christian faith. My prayer is that, as a result, you will be encouraged to STAND UP! and make a difference and that, together, we can ultimately help to restore America.

Chapter 2

A Survey of Religion

"What is the meaning of human life, or of organic life altogether? To answer this question at all implies a religion. Is there any sense then, you ask, in putting it? I answer, the man who regards his own life and that of his fellow creatures as meaningless is not merely unfortunate but almost disqualified for life."

— *Albert Einstein*

The Abundance of Religion

A Glimpse into Human History. Throughout history countless religions have sprung up in an attempt to give credit to and worship a higher being. History reveals to us time and time again that mankind has always had a passion—a burning desire—to discover, serve, and worship that higher being. This truth becomes obvious by studying history and discovering that forms of religion existed long before the beginning of recorded history. Recorded history is simply the result of producing written accounts of important dates, events, and knowledge.

Written records of religious beliefs have been discovered as far back as the Sumerian Empire, the civilization that is widely believed to be the oldest among the human race. Remnants that have been discovered from the Sumerian Empire indicate that this civilization had already established major institutions such as a government, an economy, and religion before its written language. Since references to religion can be found in the oldest written records, we know that religion has to predate written history because religious beliefs could not have been documented unless the institution of religion was already established. This principle makes intuitive sense because it would be difficult to document an institution that did not exist. Nevertheless, as the human race grew and new civilizations were created, religion remained an intricate part of daily life.

In fact, religious ideologies can be found in virtually every civilization that has existed. Even today, as we live amid the greatest technological revolution mankind has ever known, religion is still a powerful influence. Although civilizations vastly differ from one another in form of government, culture, language, and values, it is fascinating to note the one similarity—the common denominator—among the civilizations. The one bond that links all people together has been the continual need to establish and maintain some sort of religion. Religion is evident in all societies, both ancient and modern.

Religion has also been one of the most powerful influences upon billions of people, and it has dramatically transformed countless lives. Religion has reformed nations, justified wars, influenced governments, established codes of right and wrong and has been the moral and ethical guide to the decisions many people have made throughout history.

Ordinary and powerful people alike have used religious doctrines to make decisions. Even today, in the twenty-first century, the presence of religion can be seen all throughout our world, whether we are heavily involved or not; just take a look around and notice that most nations have a national religion. Despite the modernization that technology brings, nations still incorporate religion into governments, judicial systems, and basic decision-making processes. This may not be the case in America anymore, but it certainly continues to happen elsewhere.

Before we move on, we need to note one very important fact. Even though the ancient world has slowly transformed into the modern world, religion has left its mark on virtually every society that has come into existence—and will continue to do so, until the end of the age.

The Similarity Between Religions. Most religions that have existed throughout the centuries have very similar objectives and somewhat similar beliefs. Most religions support the belief that there is a higher being who created the universe, is worthy of worship, and offers a better life in some sort of heaven to faithful members after physical death.

The possibility of entering into a luxurious afterlife, that so many aspire to reach, is completely dependent upon a decision that is made while living on earth. Although the method by which a person may obtain acceptance by God differs from religion to religion, the aspirations to reach this eternal state of paradise are analogous with one another.

Most religions also support divine justice of some type, and they believe that eternal punishment is reserved for wicked members of society. The punishment of the wicked occurs in a place commonly referred to as hell. This place of eternal destruction is where the wicked, and those not in compliance with religion, go to encounter the wrath of God for the wrong that they have done during the course of their lives.

Although the concept of hell is popular among many religions, not all religions believe in a place of such torment. Some religions believe that people are reincarnated to a lower or higher life form and that one's current incarnation depends upon how they lived in their previous life. But once people have reached a certain rank or successfully met the moral requirements, then they are able to enter into the ultimate reality of eternal paradise.

The different concepts of reincarnation, heaven, hell, and a final judgment have certainly been influential to different people in different ways, but to what extent? Heaven can offer people an enduring sense of hope where the end justifies the means. Through this concept, people are given encouragement to persevere. They have the ability to dream of a future life in paradise, despite the bad circumstances they may have on earth. Hell, on the other hand, can motivate one to change a lifestyle, accept a belief, or be diligent in becoming a better person. Nobody desires eternal punishment in the degree that most religions teach, but it is, nevertheless, a motivating factor that forces people to consider religion.

Most religions have also established moral, social, and ethical standards that provide guidance through many of the important decisions people make. Religious texts help reinforce the values that people are expected to follow. Religious texts help people make moral and ethical decisions, as mankind's inherent nature is sinful. Most people believe that these standards of morality are a special revelation from God, because they are contrary to human nature and because it seems contradictory for mankind to establish morality when mankind is, by nature, immoral.

This becomes obvious when we look back and discover that we continually teach our children how to be moral, but we do not have to teach them how to be immoral. We never have to teach a child to take a toy from another; that is instinctively done as it is the nature of mankind. However, compliance with God's moral and ethical standards helps people change their ways so that it is possible to enter into Heaven. The "changing of ways" is a gross generalization, but one that will be refined in the following pages.

Religion has also been used to explain the unexplainable. The inability of mankind to fully understand most of what we see as we gaze in the galaxies of the universe can cause one to think deeply about the very purpose life itself (Psalms 8:3–4). Why are we living? What is our purpose? How did we get here? And does it really matter what we do in life?

One thing is for certain: we came into this world with nothing, and we will one day leave this world with nothing. Material possessions are temporary; we know this because we cannot take the mansion, the Mercedes, or the cash in the bank with us. Estate attorneys, who draft wills, have a job for this reason alone – we never see a moving truck following the hearse.[27] This brutal concept of reality has left many people perplexed, and it forces them to cautiously think about the choices they make and ultimately about whether there is a future life that extends beyond the physical life. Where will I go when I die? Is there really a heaven and a hell? And what must I do to get there?

Probably the most common theme in religion is the belief in an afterlife. For some reason, people tend to think that the physical life is not the end; rather, it is the beginning of a long and exciting (or dreadful) eternity. The perception of eternity depends on our view of religion. We know eternal life is a major theme because it is emphasized in countless religions that have existed from the ancient world until the present day, but if each religion is so similar in content, then why are there so many different religions? Does one really have to decide on a religion? How could a person possibly know which religion is right?

The Daunting Task of Deciding. As we reflect on human history and the topic of religion, it is easy to conclude that the many different types of religions that have come into existence throughout history are uniquely different. Some have died out, while others have flourished; but as we look at them today, we still have the same problem: Which one should we believe?

Furthermore, why should one religion be right and exalted above all others? And if there are *right* and *wrong* religions, which one is correct? Wouldn't it take a long time for a person to sit down and thoroughly study each religion, with its origin and beliefs, and to systematically sift through

27 Dave Ramsey, Lesson 6: Buyer Beware, Financial Peace Course.

enough concrete facts and evidence to be able to decide whether each religion merits the trust of intelligent and logical people?

These are all excellent questions that you may have in regard to religion, but these questions must be answered *correctly* in order for you to make an accurate decision. Realistically, most people neither can nor are willing to spend the time needed to sift through the various ideologies, documents, and facts in a *Quest for Absolute Truth*. Therefore, one major purpose of this book is to essentially do the work for you and to present the different types of religion.

Not all religions are similar in doctrine, nor are they equally true; in fact, many have contradictory truth claims. This book will explain, with precision, how they differ from one another. Furthermore, this book will demonstrate that there are right and wrong religions and that historical and scientific evidence, combined with logic, points toward only one answer: the *one true faith*.

We will begin our *Quest for Absolute Truth* by examining four major types of religions. We will look at their basic beliefs and the fundamental doctrines of each major category. Then, in Part One, we will remove the religious ideologies that are contradictory or illogical and those that do not contain sufficient evidence by which to commend themselves to logical and thinking people. Even if you do not believe that Absolute Truth can be found, if you have heard this argument before, or if you are undecided with respect to religion, I challenge you to continue reading because this topic should not be taken lightly. It is not a matter of opinion, it is a matter of *fact* that just happens to hold your eternal well-being in the balance of the decision you make.

How to Search for Truth

The Process of Elimination. Virtually every religion falls into one of four major categories: agnosticism, pantheism, Naturalism, or theism.[28] In the remainder of this chapter, we will establish our objective and the approach the book will take. Then we will briefly categorize the religions and present their foundational doctrines.

Part by Part. The objective of the book is twofold. The first is to present Christianity as the one and only Absolute Truth. The process of

28 Dr. Richard Lee, *What Should We Believe? Why Is Jesus the Only Way to God?* There's Hope Ministries, 1998.

systematically proving Christianity entirely true will consume parts one through three. The second objective is to apply biblical principles and knowledge to today's world. We need to know how modernism leads to liberalism, which leads to immorality, which will ultimately collapse the Republic (if America is not restored) because freedom cannot exist without moral responsibility.

Part One is titled "Eliminate the Obvious." If you have previewed the table of contents, you already know that agnosticism, pantheism, and Naturalism are the three categories that are disproved first. Why would it be beneficial to disprove these religions first? The rationale behind disproving these religions, before revealing Absolute Truth, is because these religions do not accept the premise that one all-powerful God exists. Since there is no common ground (except for the fact that we both exist or that birds can fly), it becomes very difficult to move forward. In fact, nothing meaningful can be accomplished until common ground has been established.

Once agnosticism, pantheism, and Naturalism have been disproved, the common ground that has been established is that none of these religions can contain truth and that God *must* exist. The reason the Bible is not used to disprove agnosticism, pantheism, and Naturalism is that doing so would be similar to defining a word by using the word you are trying to define: it would amount to a circular argument. If it can be demonstrated that these three religious beliefs fail without relying on Christianity, it becomes easier to see the fundamental flaws. The flaws will be that much clearer because we are not employing proofs that agnostics, pantheists, and Naturalists reject, that is, the existence of an all-powerful God. Instead, we will use what they use: logic, evidence, and science. If we speak their language, we have a better chance of being heard and, through the process, have created a platform to present the Gospel.

By discrediting their fundamental presuppositions, we must conclude that their theology is not supported by science, logic, or evidence. By definition, their claim on truth would essentially be reduced to *hope*—wishful or magical thinking—and frankly, hope is not adequate when dealing with an issue of this magnitude. Who would choose to play dice with their own soul? Rational people never gamble with their eternal fate; nor do they intentionally base it on radical and unsupported beliefs.

You may then ask: "Why do so many people believe in that which can be proven to be entirely wrong?" I can suggest three answers:

1. They have a closed or hardened heart, not open to the truth and in fact enslaved to selfishness.
2. Christians have not taken the time to actually share the Absolute Truth with family and friends, the people we supposedly care for and love the most!
3. If the Truth has been shared, it may not have been presented in a logical and convincing manner.

Apologetics is crucial. All Christians need to know what they believe and why they believe it and then be able to defend the faith. Without apologetics, evangelism severely suffers because people will inevitably ask questions about what we believe and why. Is it too much to ask for a logical defense? Absolutely not; this is why the Apostle Peter stressed the importance of being ready to give an account of our convictions and be able to defend the Truth.[29] If we could demonstrate how all other religions can be disproved, then it is *reasonable* to expect people to be more likely to listen when presented with the one and only Absolute Truth.

As we proceed, it will become evident that the book narrows truth down to only one religion. All religions certainly make a claim on truth, but they have conflicting claims, and they send people in different directions. Even though there are many truth claims, only one can be true. Think of spiritual truth as if it were a compass. There are hundreds of degrees on a compass and many different directions of travel, but only one can lead to the desired destination. Some religions may come really close, but they ultimately fail the same as those that lead wildly astray. By definition, truth is narrow and it cannot be all-accepting, just as not all points on a compass can lead to the desired destination.

Part Two begins by making arguments for the existence of God—the necessity of that existence. Once it is demonstrated that God must exist, deism and polytheism are disproved. The remaining chapters present, and establish, the one and only Absolute Truth: Jesus Christ is Lord and through Him, alone, is Salvation possible.

After Christianity is proven to be entirely true, Absolute Truth is then used to disprove the other two major monotheistic religions, Islam and Judaism. The purpose of Part Three is to demonstrate how a defense can be effectively constructed to disprove other religions that are contradictory to Absolute Truth. Since Christianity has been proven to be entirely true, if a contradiction arises, then that particular religion must be false because it

29 1 Peter 3:15; see also Colossians 4:6 and Jude 3.

does not align with what we already know to be entirely true. Furthermore, we will look to see if any contradictions within that particular religion are present. If internal contradictions are present, that religion cannot be true because it would not be *entirely true.* The process can be applied to other religions as well, to disprove Satanism, Unitarianism, Sikhism, angel worship, and so forth.

Part Four is titled "Linking Liberalism to Moral Depravity." There we examine how watered-down doctrine and political correctness have led to a backslide with respect to morality. Lowering moral standards, trying to become "politically correct" and refusing to share the Gospel have ultimately led us to where we are today. Even more appalling is the shocking link between our government and one religion that our government has placed on a pedestal—one that has received special attention and towers over every other. We need to know whether there is truly a separation between church and state and why that separation matters. You may be shocked at what has been discovered.

The book begins to conclude, in Chapter 15, with a presentation of priorities that we inevitably choose. We either prioritize the self, man, or God. Chapter 15 examines the outcomes of each priority, which priority is biblical, and the reasons why. Then the chapter presents seven steps Christians can take in order to restore America and encourages the reader that there is still hope that tomorrow will be better than today.

Understanding how to make a difference is crucial. Unless we can funnel passion and concern to the correct avenues, change will be minimal. The change we are looking for redirects focus to God, and it is nothing short of what people used to call a "revival." America needs to be revived, and a new Great Awakening is upon us because Americans understand that our current path is simply *unsustainable.*

We continue our *Quest for Absolute Truth* by encapsulating all religions into four major categories to simplify the process of elimination and refinement.

The Four Major Categories of Religion

Agnosticism. Agnosticism is the belief that the existence of God, gods, or any other divine being cannot be known. In other words, this belief claims that a god's existence can neither be proved nor disproved. The common response of the agnostic, when asked about God, is, "Maybe God exists, and maybe God doesn't." By this definition, agnostics do not have a concrete belief system because, for them, everything is abstract, in flux, and constantly shifting from one potential idea to another as they consider their options.

The thought process of an agnostic is built on a negative skepticism of intellect. They are uncertain that humans can have absolute knowledge about anything, let alone about whether a higher being exists. Even though agnostics are doubtful, in the future they may be open to the concept of religion if more information becomes available or if they become convinced that sufficient information already exists. Hopefully, through this study, agnostics will have the evidence they need to make a decision so they can transition from not knowing to becoming *absolutely certain* about their beliefs in the existence of a higher being.

Pantheism. Pantheism is a belief system that portrays God as a universal energy and a universal positive force. Pantheists believe that everything in existence—people, animals, trees, the solar systems, the cosmos, and ultimately the entire universe—constitutes unity and that this unity is, in some sense, divine. Pantheism is the belief that "God is *everything*, and everything is *God*."

Since pantheism teaches that God is a universal positive force through which everybody is connected, we are all participating in the same energy. An example of pantheism can be found in the *Star Wars* movies. Remember the positive *force* that helps lead the Jedi knights? The first movie coined the phrase, "May the force be with you." This idea of the force stems from pantheism because there is an overall cosmic goal which the force will accomplish, and all people, whether consciously or subconsciously, contribute and work harmoniously to achieve this overall goal. Pantheists tell us we need to get in touch with our inner selves to release the potential that we have within because we, ourselves, are God.

Naturalism. Naturalism is a broad category that is defined as "the doctrine that the world can be understood in scientific terms without recourse to spiritual or supernatural explanations."[30] Naturalism directly contradicts what theists believe, and it is the basic theory from which many other ideologies derive and ground their beliefs. From Naturalism, we see philosophies such as atheism, communism, socialism, humanism, materialism, Marxism, and (nontheistic) evolutionism flourish because

---

30 Naturalism. Dictionary.com. *Dictionary.com Unabridged.* Random House, Inc. http://dictionary.reference.com/browse/naturalism (accessed: November 7, 2008).

Naturalism teaches (in a nutshell) that "everything you see is all that there is and nothing more"—there is no life after death, no heaven, no hell, and no judgment. Naturalism teaches that the moment a person dies is the same moment in which their soul ceases to exist.

Theism. Theism is the most common type of religion in existence today. Theists believe that there is a higher being that created everything, and that everything belongs to God. Theists are divided into two categories, based on the number of higher beings they believe exist.

Monotheism. Monotheism is the belief in the existence and worship of a single God. There are many branches of monotheism, but they all claim that a single God is all-knowing and all-powerful, that this single God initiated creation, and that everything within the universe belongs to this God. Since the monotheist God is the Creator, the monotheist worships that God alone. Monotheism has the largest number of adherents in the world today, and they include religions such as Christianity, Islam, and Judaism.

Polytheism. Polytheism is the belief that more than one god exists. Polytheists hold a range of different views and beliefs. Some believe that there are many different gods, but that one is supreme. Others believe that different gods exist and that only one should be worshiped at a time. From the basic belief of polytheism spring many religious systems such as Hinduism, Shintoism, and the mythology that was found in ancient Greece.

Part One

Eliminate the Obvious

Chapter 3

Some Say "We Cannot Know Whether God Exists"

"His divine power has given us everything we need for life and godliness through our own knowledge of him who called us by his own glory and goodness."

—2 Peter 1:3

"But if from there you seek the Lord *your God, you will find him if you look for him with all your heart and with all your soul."*

—Deuteronomy 4:29

Agnosticism

The Biggest Question of All. Perhaps the biggest and most complicated questions that people have in life center around the existence of an all-powerful and supernatural being. *Does God really exist? How can I know that God exists? Is there any proof? What is the proof?* These are legitimate questions that need to be answered in order for any person to make an intelligent decision on the subject. People need to know the arguments both for and against God so that they are able to make a decision with confidence.

We are looking for answers to the questions that were just presented. We need to know whether or not there is a God. We need to understand the science, evidence, and logic that accompany each category of religion.

At the same time, we also need to understand that if a particular belief cannot answer the most basic theological questions, then we must move forward and continue searching. As this book will make clear, answers to these basic questions exist. There is actually a significant amount of science, evidence, and logic to rationally support the book's conclusion, but first we must remove the categories of religion that cannot possibly contain Truth. The question now turns to the issue of whether or not agnosticism can possibly contain the Truth that so many seek to discover.

Ironically, agnosticism's foundational belief system automatically disqualifies itself from containing any Absolute Truth. Agnosticism cannot contain truth simply because its foundational doctrine holds that a person does not or cannot know the truth. The agnostic believes that absolute truth cannot be found because there is not enough information to make such a decision.

Before we proceed, we need to establish that there are two different variations of agnosticism: benign and malignant.[31]

Benign Agnosticism. Benign agnosticism is the position that people hold when they do not know enough about religion to make an accurate decision. When asked about God and whether or not He exists, the agnostic may reply with "I don't know enough about God to give an answer" or "I haven't thought enough on the subject" or "I've never considered my options." Benign agnostics are people who have not decided because they feel that they simply do not know enough to make an informed decision, but want to avoid making the wrong decision.

These are your more subtle and friendly agnostics; they do not lash out or provide severe criticism because they do not even have a firm belief system. On what grounds could they criticize? Since these people already acknowledge that they do not know enough on the topic, they tend to be more receptive to the ideas other people present. They are open to other views because they are searching for the answer. To their credit, in their search for the truth, they are willing to contemplate all their options. These agnostics are the easiest type to evangelize because they are already searching and open to suggestions, and they have not yet hardened their hearts.

31 Winfried Corduan, *No Doubt about It* (Nashville, TN: Broadman and Holdman Publishers, 1997), 88.

Malignant Agnosticism. Malignant agnosticism, on the other hand, is the position that some people take after they think they have enough information to piece together the theological puzzle. This group has formed its decision and is adamant that Absolute Truth *cannot* be known. They claim it is impossible to know whether or not there is a God because nobody can prove His existence. The reason that nobody can prove God's existence is because He has not revealed Himself to mankind. This camp is where we find the abrasive and assertive agnostics because they can't stand it when a person claims that Absolute Truth can be known or that there is enough information to make a decision with confidence.

Benign Agnosticism

Big Picture, Little Picture. Benign agnosticism simply states that a person does not know enough about God to make a decision. Benign agnostics either believe that they do not know enough details about God to make a decision or that they do not enough about the overall concept of God to make a decision. In this section we will demonstrate that we do not have to be all-knowing in order to grasp the concept. In order to make an accurate decision, people do not necessarily have to know everything about God; that would be foolish. By piecing the information together from the big and little pictures come together, we can have enough information to construct a finite understanding of the existence of an infinite being and demonstrate that God exists.

Let's consider two quick examples to better explain the idea of the big and little pictures. Let's look at science—more specifically, the time line of the universe and black holes. Although these two examples are within the same field of study, they differ because we have knowledge of them in differing aspects. In the one example (black holes), we understand the overall concept but lack details; in the other (the time line of the universe), we understand the details and lack the big picture.

We Understand the Big Picture. Astronomy is the science that deals with the material universe outside of the Earth's atmosphere. Outside of the Earth's atmosphere are black holes. We know and understand the overall concept of a black hole, but we lack specific details. We understand that a black hole is a point in space where so much mass is concentrated that nothing—not even light—can escape its gravitational pull. We know black holes have the ability to pull massive objects (such as other moons, planets, and even stars) toward them and will eventually compress them to an infinitesimally small point. Amazingly, we know a black hole's effects in various solar systems. One example is that many galaxies harbor black holes at their center and preserve the galaxy as we know it today.[32]

Although we know a lot about the big picture of black holes, we really do not know many of the minute details that would help us understand them better. We do not know what is in or at the center of a black hole or the exact strength of its force or the exact size of its center. Some people believe that black holes may be a passageway into other parts of the universe; others believe they could be a method of time travel or a dead -end in which everything that enters is crushed to a miniscule size. We can speculate with a degree of certainty, but we are speculating.

Although we do not completely understand the details, we understand the overall picture. We do know for a fact that black holes exist, that they pull massive objects toward them, and that their strength is so great that not even light cannot escape. We can study their effects and generally understand what they are and how they work. We cannot know everything about black holes, but that does not mean we should disbelieve in their existence. To do so would be silly and illogical.

We Understand the Little Picture. Creation has always been a source of fascination to mankind, but we are still unable to understand the overall picture: precisely *how* it came into existence or what the landscape of the universe will look like a trillion years from now.

Through scientific research and meticulous study, we have made significant advances in understanding details of creation. We understand how specific parts of the universe behave, as well as the mechanics of life. We know some important details on how stars begin, grow, and eventually die. We know details about the gravitational pull a star produces on objects that are billions of miles away. We understand how the planets in our solar system revolve around the sun and that the moon revolves around Earth. We know that within Earth's atmosphere, life exists. We understand a great deal about life on earth and the complicated biological functions that must occur within cells for life to exist. We know many details about creation, but we lack the overall picture as to specifically *how* everything came into existence and what the cosmological landscape will look like

---

32 Ted Bunn, "Black Holes FAQ List," University of California Berkley, http://cosmology.berkeley.edu/Education/BHfaq.html.

a trillion years from now. We can speculate, but certainly nothing more! (We were not eyewitnesses to these events.)

Even if we give credit to a divine being for initiating creation, we still do not have the overall picture. We cannot know what life will be like a trillion years from now. We cannot know what the universe will look like a trillion years from now. In the vast scheme, we only study and understand very small portions. Since we understand many details surrounding creation but lack the overall concept, are we to believe that creation does not exist? I would hope not, because if you are reading this book, then you must be alive and are an active part of creation.

The Information Is Adequate. Through the two previous examples, we have demonstrated that we do not have to be all-knowing in order to grasp some basic concepts. In one scenario we understand the big picture but lack the specific details of black holes. Although we do not understand the details, it would not be logical to refuse to believe in black holes. In the second example, we understand many details surrounding creation but lack the big picture. The fact that we understand very specific parts of creation and life but do not fully understand the big picture does not imply that we cannot know that life exists.

When we take the big and little pictures and start putting them together, we can see how they connect. We certainly do not have all the details, but we have a pretty good idea of how the two interact and are connected with one another. Likewise, we understand God in the same way. The big picture of God is that He exists; He has a sovereign will that will be accomplished; and God created everything. We also know many details about God. We know that God is all-powerful, eternal, omnipresent, and omniscient and has revealed many other specific details throughout the Scriptures.

When we take these two different types of information and piece them together, we can understand how the details and the big picture begin to fit together. Benign agnostics cannot wait for ever single detail from the big and little pictures before they make a decision because we will never be all-knowing. In Part Two we will analyze many of the specific details that God has provided to understand how they relate to the big picture and, ultimately, prove His existence. As a result, the information we have is adequate.

Malignant Agnosticism

The 'Unprovable' Position. Ironically, the position of malignant agnosticism turns out to be pretty indefensible simply because of the fact that it is impossible to prove a negative on that magnitude (i.e. God does not exist). In order to prove a negative, a person must either be all-knowing or demonstrate that the idea of God is an intrinsically impossible idea. We can say with confidence that nobody is all-knowing and that the idea of God is actually quite possible (as this book will demonstrate). Only when people are all-knowing can they begin to make an effective case against God that is supported with observed (empirical) facts and evidence.

It is also interesting to dig deeper into the core principles of this belief because it is a position that is very similar to atheism. Since atheism is a subcategory of Naturalism, the impossibility of proving a negative will be covered again for emphasis when we get to Chapter 5. Nevertheless, the atheist and the malignant agnostic have a lot in common, and this type of agnosticism can quickly lead to the belief that "God does not exist." Consider the following excerpt:

> The agnostic's agenda invariably is this: to argue that since we cannot know if there is a God, we cannot make reference to God. Agnostics never argue as follows: since we cannot know whether there is a God, let us just assume that there might be. Thus agnosticism becomes atheism in the guise of epistemological humility. Yet agnosticism turns out to be as indefensible as atheism. We still cannot prove a negative. The statement 'It is impossible to know if there is a God' becomes just as impossible to demonstrate as 'There is no God.'[33]

It is important to understand the differences and the parallels between malignant agnosticism and atheism when confronting, and ultimately disproving, the theologies. In order to provide the best defense for the Christian faith, we must first understand the root of their belief system in order to hone in on their presuppositions to determine their credibility. The malignant agnostic is trying to disprove God by stating that we cannot know enough to establish God. But is this position credible? Can it be proven? To answer this question, we turn to the only two methods of

33 Corduan, 88–89.

approach that could prove the negative, "It is impossible to know if there is a God."

You Must Be All-Knowing. One method to disprove the existence of God is to be able to show that *all* possibilities for the existence of God have been exhausted and that no such evidence can be found.[34] This sounds like an excellent idea until we realize that it is not possible. Only when people are able to understand every piece of information that exists throughout the entire universe can they *begin* the process of sifting through that information to try and disprove the existence of God.

What is one characteristic of the human race that we know to be entirely true? Human beings have finite minds! One catastrophic problem with this approach to disproving God is that the human mind is finite and that it would be impossible to gain *all knowledge*. Since humans cannot possibly be all-knowing, we cannot disprove God. The universe that we live in is simply too vast for the human mind to even begin to comprehend. If we cannot even fully explain everything in the world that *we live in* (e.g., Cambrian explosion or the theory of global warming), how much more absurd it would be to claim to know and fully understand the remaining unseen universe?

An Intrinsically Impossible Idea. The second approach to disproving the existence of God is to demonstrate that the idea of an intelligent designer, or an all-powerful God, is intrinsically impossible, ruled out by logic.[35] In this method, the person would have to present an argument proving that a higher being could not have been involved with creation and that a divine intervention could not possibly have happened.

The problem with this argument is that the concept of an intelligent designer is a very logical explanation of the unexplainable. Take, for example, the Cambrian explosion or what set into motion the big bang or the creation of the universe. While scientists can certainly make a claim that an intelligent designer was not involved with these phenomena, they are also constrained by the fact that they cannot deny the possibility of a Creator based upon its feasibility. In fact, the existence of God is entirely possible, and the agnostic cannot disprove this idea. (Chapter 6 will present six scenarios that are simply unexplainable unless God's existence is entered into the equation.)

---

34 Ibid., 83.

35 Ibid., 84.

Attempting to Prove a Negative. The realization that it is impossible to be all-knowing is humbling, but it demonstrates that it is impossible to prove a negative statement such as "There is no God." To accomplish this goal, the agnostic has to systematically *disprove* each and every possible way that God could exist, along with convincing proof and evidence. All possible avenues of approach would have to be covered, and the truth is that we know very little about what lies beyond our galaxy—much less about the entire universe. Of course, we speculate and generate *probable* ideas, but they amount at most to conjecture. Nobody knows for sure.

To put into perspective how hard it would be to prove a negative, consider the following example: I go to the beautiful white beaches of Panama City Beach, Florida. As I look around and marvel at the beauty, I then claim that there is not a blue grain of sand with pink polka dots within any of Panama City's beaches or in all of Panama City.[36] Although I have the ability to make this claim—because we know that anybody can *claim* anything—it does not follow that I have made a truthful or meaningful statement. How could my claim be proven entirely true?

In order for people to entirely prove my claim, they would have to physically inspect each and every grain of sand (with a magnifying glass to be absolutely certain because a grain of sand is pretty small) to be able to conclude that no such grain of sand exists. Even though the process sounds delightful and would be so much fun, the search could not be limited to only the surface because I also said "in all of Panama City."

In real estate, rights of ownership extend above and below the surface. Rights of ownership are categorized as water rights, mineral rights, and air rights.[37] Even though the government does not own all the land in the city, it has jurisdiction over the land that falls within the city limits (both above and below the surface). Since *mineral rights* extend far below the surface, disproving my claim would entail an examination of not only the sand on the ground level, but also each and every single grain of sand that is below the surface—on both private and public beaches.

Since the scenario also calls for an inspection of all sand within the city limits of Panama City, we must also examine all sand in people's shoes, clothes, homes and even in their hair. We cannot forget the sand

36 Panama City is distinguished from Panama City Beach as two different places; the former is the city inland, and the latter is where people vacation. For simplicity, we will refer to the vacation spot as Panama City.

37 Georgia Institute of Real Estate, *Real Estate Dynamics, A Practical Approach to Licensing* (Atlanta: Georgian Institute of Real Estate, 2007), 1.3–1.4.

in the cracks of the streets or even the sand in the sewer system (no grain left behind). Every single grain must be examined because this is what is required when proving a negative statement.

Fortunately, the search for the mysterious blue grain of sand with pink polka dots is not *endless* because it is confined to Panama City Beach city limits. Even though we would have to inspect all sand below the surface, we know that the beach has to end at some point as we dig deeper. We know this because the beach does not continue downward forever; the center of the earth is liquid.

As we come down from the mountain of hope and confront reality, what do you think the chances are that every single grain of sand within the city limits of Panama City can be examined without confusing grains or overlooking *even one*? Is it really possible to accomplish such a task? Does it really seem possible to prove this negative? After all, this claim has limitations; therefore it is possible, even though highly unlikely, that one could keep the sand organized and neither miss nor repeat a grain. Realistically, proving this negative statement is much more feasible than proving that God cannot exist. Think about the difficulties that encompass trying to prove a negative, and you will soon discover that the example I provided seems like an impossible task.

How much more information would we have to know to prove that there is no God? Would we not have to search the farthest corners of the universe to be entirely sure? In order to accomplish this mission, a person would have to know everything about everything just to be able to cover all avenues of approach, but then this crazy thing called *reality* hits us: we're human! We are finite beings and cannot, by definition, be all-knowing. Therefore, it is not logical or credible to make a negative truth claim without being able to back it up with empirical facts. As I mentioned earlier, it is pure speculation, opinion, conjecture or whatever title you prefer, but it is not truth.

Agnosticism Leads to Skepticism. The agnostics, who claim people cannot know anything about God, are really quite comical because of the apparent contradiction of their claim. Agnosticism's conclusion leads to skepticism, which is an impossible position to hold. "Note that I did not say *ought not* to hold it; I said that one *cannot* hold it."[38]

Dr. Corduan does an excellent job explaining how skepticism is an entirely contradictory position to hold. Once people fully understand the

38 Corduan, 36 (emphasis added).

paradox, many will see the absurdity (and the humor) of this position. Dr. Corduan writes:

> Skepticism states that one cannot know anything. Does the person who makes that statement know it or not? If the skeptic thinks that skepticism is true, then it is false. The skeptic argues that we can know at least one thing, namely, that skepticism is true. If the skeptic does not claim that skepticism is true, he or she is not saying anything meaningful.
>
> We must distinguish here between what can be said and what can be affirmed meaningfully. Anything can be said, yet that does not mean that we are affirming anything meaningful in the process. I can say, 'A married bachelor drew a square circle in the sand that was also non-sand,' but that proposition is gibberish. It has no more meaning than the random sounds produced by a six-month-old baby. Skepticism is unaffirmable in the same way. You can say that you cannot know anything, but you cannot affirm it meaningfully. You cannot even think it: as soon as you think it is true, it must also be false. The true skeptic, if there were one, would have to suspend all thoughts, including any thoughts about skepticism, and play the role of a brainless plant.[39]

Bringing the Two Together

The Absurdity of Agnosticism. It is absurd for the agnostic to propose that there is not enough knowledge about God to make an accurate decision, and then turn right back around to claim that there is enough knowledge about God to make a decision against God. Was there enough knowledge or not? That is where the contradiction lies: For in one position agnostics claim that it is impossible to know anything about God (skepticism), while on the other hand they claim to know a whole lot about God, which is the reason why they can confidently make a decision against God.

39 Ibid., 36-37.

Conclusion. Agnosticism leads to absolute skepticism; which is an impossible position. Agnosticism is also unprovable position because people cannot prove this negative statement: "God does not exist." This statement cannot be proven because agnostics must either be all-knowing or must prove God to be an intrinsically impossible idea—neither of which can be done.

Since the overall belief system of agnosticism cannot be proved and it ultimately results in the impossible position of skepticism, it is not a stable belief system. Even though you may not be an agnostic, it is beneficial to know the agnostic's perspective and see that it is an impossible position, so you can share with them the illogical concepts that devastate the theory. Agnosticism is not the answer and is consequently eliminated as a potential candidate for Absolute Truth.

Chapter 4

Some Say "God is a Universal Positive Energy Force"

"One Lord, one faith, one baptism; one God and Father of all, who is over all and through all and in all."

—Ephesians 4:5–6

"For there is one God and one mediator between God and [human beings, Christ Jesus, himself human], who gave himself as a ransom for all [people]."

—1 Timothy 2:5–6

Pantheism

Introducing Pantheism. Pantheism is a belief that was first introduced by John Toland in 1705. When compared to the age of most other religions, pantheism is essentially an infant.[40] Despite its young age, pantheism is a broad category that has gained popularity and includes beliefs such as the New Age movement, Hinduism, Taoism, and some strands of Buddhism.[41]

Pantheism is in a separate category from theism because the pantheist view vastly differs from that of theism—even though pantheists believe

40 *The Catholic Encyclopedia* Vol. 11, "Pantheism," http://www.newadvent.org/cathen/11447b.htm.

41 *The Stanford Encyclopedia of Philosophy,* "Pantheism," http://plato.stanford.edu/archives/fall2008/entries/pantheism/.

in a type or variation of God. Of course the key word is *God* and how it is defined. The basic fundamentals of theism teach that God is *separate* from creation, regardless of whether or not the doctrines of monotheism or polytheism are examined. The pantheists greatly differ from theists because their definition of *God* means something entirely different, and it deviates from the traditional view of God.

Pantheism's Theology. Pantheism is the belief that God is a universal positive force. Pantheists believe that God's existence is comprised of everything, including the world that we live in. They believe that the world we live in is not only a part of God, but that God and the world are one and are so intricately intertwined that it is impossible to tell them apart. Pantheism is best explained with the phrase *God is everything and everything is God.*[42] "According to [this] view, God is the universe itself; *beyond* and *outside* the world He does not exist, but only *in* the world, and all nature is His body. In reality, God is everything, and beside him there is nothing. Thus, making God the Soul of the world..."[43]

Pantheism is a unique concept of God and this is where it differs from theism. When pantheism defines *everything* as God, then *everything* would naturally include you, me, and my dog.[44] Through the use of this definition, it is inevitable that pantheists actually believe that you, my dog, and I are all *God*. We are all the ultimate reality and we (as God) are all working toward one universal cosmic goal. Why must the universe have a cosmic, or ultimate, goal? There is too much fine-tuning and meticulous design for the universe to be considered a *wandering accident* or a *fluke*. Do we (as God) know the overall cosmic goal? Nope; all humans are finite. As finite beings, we cannot predict the cosmic goal one hundred years in advance or even one thousand years in advance (much less millions or billions of years). At this point, all we will say is that since we all are God, but we do not clearly understand what our goal is, we must therefore accomplish the cosmic goal subconsciously.

I know that I keep referring to God as "you, my dog, and I," but we should probably elaborate so that pantheism is not, in any way,

42 Thom Rainer, *The Unexpected Journey: Conversations with people who turned from other beliefs to Jesus* (Grand Rapids, MI: Zondervan, 2005), 160.

43 Wilbur M. Smith, *Therefore Stand: Christian Apologetics* (Grand Rapids, MI: Baker Book House, 1974), 343.

44 We are not being flippant with this definition; instead, we are using a literal application in its most basic form.

misconstrued. Pantheism teaches not only that God includes you, me, and my dog but that God is much, much more. God is actually your house, your car, your bed sheets, the earth, and the shooting star that streaks across the sky. God is the lion in the jungle, the monkey in the tree, and the roach that scurries across your kitchen floor. God is the planets, stars, and galaxies in all the universe. God is *everything!*

Since God is everything and there is an overall cosmic goal, we know that this goal *must* be unknown because not *everything* is always on the same page. We know that the overall goal of the universe is not always on the same page with one another because the criminals are against the law-abiding citizens, the Muslims are against the Jews, the terrorists are against freedom itself, and the Democrats are against the Republicans.

Since we know that different parts of creation are working toward different goals, it only makes sense that the overall cosmic goal is *unknown*. This is brilliant! Think about it: no matter what happens (even if evil destroys everything that is good), the pantheist can always say it was the will of God. There is never any accountability or expectation because this universal *force* accomplishes its goal without us ever knowing the goal. This is also really ironic! *We are God*, yet we do not even know the ultimate cosmic goal. As a result, people wander aimlessly through life, not knowing the ultimate goal, yet are able to affirm that whatever they did was the goal.[45]

The theology of pantheism is similar to the *force* in *Star Wars*. In the movie *Star Wars*, you frequently hear the phrase "May the force be with you," as this universal positive energy helps the Jedi knights accomplish their mission. Nobody really knows the true mission or the outcome, but the Jedi knights have faith that the force will be with them.

This is quite oxymoronic. First, why would the *force* need to be with the Jedi fighters? The Jedi knights *are* the force, but then again, so is the enemy! Essentially, what they are saying is that the force will be with the force, which is like saying, "May you be with yourself." Second, it does not make sense for God to be divided, helping both good and evil. Why would God use His right hand to cut off His left? We now turn to pantheism's attempt to justify the apparent dilemma.

Pantheism's Rationale. The rationale behind claiming that we are God is simple: since you and I are a part of the universe, we must also be God.

45 Contradictions, on multiple levels, are prevalent with this view and will soon be addressed later in the chapter.

We must be God because God is everything, and everything includes all human beings (which includes you and me). Pantheism is not a religion that describes some abstract God that you will one day meet after your death; instead, it proposes that you already know God, even though you might not know or understand it yet.

If there is no *higher being*, then we would be our own source of truth. If we *create* truth, we can determine for ourselves what constitutes morality. No concrete moral law can exist, nor any absolutes with respect to right and wrong; instead, morality *is* as each person *creates* it. Distinguishing right from wrong would be a catastrophe on a global scale because of the simple fact that each person is different. Seriously, if we are all God, then whose standard of morality would be right? Would there be any right or wrong? The pantheist can answer this question only by saying, "Since we all subconsciously work toward a common goal [even though we have no idea what that goal may be] it does not matter how right from wrong is established, because the sovereign will of God—that universal positive energy force—will always be accomplished, regardless of what *we* think, say, or do."

Under pantheism's theology, it seems as if I can pretty much do anything I want and still be within the will of God. The argument that God's will is always accomplished is the only way that the pantheists can make the irrational seem rational. Furthermore, pantheists teach that if you have a problem, you need to get in touch with your inner self to resolve your issue. This can be done through some sort of self-discovery method (e.g., yoga, channeling, or karma) and it enables you to release the powerful potential of God's power from within your own body.[46]

Pantheism has become somewhat popular in recent times because of the limitless freedom and power it gives those who believe. The religion states that you can essentially do whatever you would like because you are ultimately the highest power. Since you have the power, you never have to be burdened with sin, forgiveness, or repentance, because it is you who determines what is moral and immoral.

If you do not agree with the other established systems of morality, you have complete freedom to create your own moral standards as long as you do not violate the laws of the government under which you live. Pantheism also does not burden people with having to search for answers

46 Dr. Richard Lee, "What Should We Believe? Why is Jesus the Only Way to God?" There's Hope Ministries, 1998.

to life's problems through some sort of ancient religion. Their answer is much better: be God and create your own solution!

Another Impossible Position. As we separate ourselves from all the emotion, excitement, and euphoria that pantheism temporarily brings, we need to come back to reality and examine its doctrine. We must separate ourselves from the hype and the feel-good to put distance between our feelings and our decisions. Emotion needs to be separated from this decision because it often takes advantage of us and makes us do things that are not logical. Apart from feelings, our objective is to determine whether or not pantheism holds Absolute Truth.

We now begin our analysis of pantheism and the reasons why it is an impossible position to hold.

God is Mutually Exclusive. Although pantheism is a belief system with apparent diversity and multiplicity, if you take this belief (God is everything, and everything is God) and begin to break it down, you will soon discover that the idea of pantheism is actually self-contradictory. The reason is simply because it uses two terms that are mutually exclusive: an entity is either one or the other. The two mutually exclusive terms we are referring to are *God* and *world* (or whatever you would like to replace *world* with – Joseph, Mary, the sun, solar system, etc.) To understand how these terms are contradictory, we need to define God, so that we have a beginning point.

What are God's attributes? Pantheists believe that God is infinite, eternal, omnipotent, and unchanging; the characteristics we would expect God to have. We know they believe this because pantheists, such as Alan Watts, describe God as an infinite being because God is timeless (eternal), spaceless (omnipresent), and all-knowing (omniscient).[47] We now have a starting point to compare *God* with the *world*.

Let's examine the world we live in to see whether it can have the same characteristics that the pantheists have just attributed to *God*. Is our world infinite or eternal? No; Earth is a finite, limited, and changeable entity. The earth has both a beginning point and an end; scientists and theologians alike agree that it will be destroyed by fire at some point in the future. We also know the world we live in is not unlimited because there is only a limited number of species and natural resources available. When they die out or have been entirely consumed, they are no longer present. We know

47 Alan Watts, *The Supreme Identity* (New York: Random House, 1972), 53–56.

this because dinosaurs have long been extinct; they were not eternal. We also know that we are expected to run out of fossil fuels at some point in the future. Why? The earth is not an unlimited entity.

Is it meaningful to portray *God* as some all-powerful and eternal being, only to turn right around and claim that the earth is also God when we know the earth is not eternal? No; it is not meaningful to claim that God is both infinite and finite at the same time because the terms are mutually exclusive. Just as you can never be both alive and dead at the same time, God cannot be both infinite and finite at the same time.

The contradiction of two mutually exclusive terms is as meaningful as saying that I am both human and nonhuman at the same time or I am both alive and dead at the same time. Either I am human, or I am not. Either I am alive, or I am not. I could never be both at the same time because that is impossible. Likewise, either the earth has the attributes of God, or it does not have the attributes of God—but both statements cannot be true.

This principle holds, regardless of whether we are dealing with people, plants, animals, or even the galaxies because they are all alike with respect to this attribute: they are either infinite or finite. Since we know that they are not eternal (have not always existed), they must be finite (came into existence at a point in time). The state of being infinite is the very characteristic that separates God from creation. So it really does not matter what you compare God with because everything else is limited, finite, and not eternal. If you were to compare God with God then that would also not be meaningful in proving pantheism because God is infinite and pantheism is trying to equate an infinite being with finite creation.

Thus, when we use the characteristics that the pantheists attribute to God and compare them to their own theology, we will discover that pantheism's doctrine soon fails because it is seriously flawed. Since it is obvious that the world we live in is neither eternal nor infinite and the pantheists still consider the world to be God, we have a major contradiction.

Pantheism Is Not Logical. In addition to the contradiction of two mutually exclusive attributes, we also have a severe problem when it comes to logic. If you were God, don't you think you would have known it by now? Why did somebody have to tell, teach, and convince every pantheist that they were God in order for them to believe and convert over to that belief system? The truth is that nobody grows up thinking that they are truly God (an all-powerful, eternal, and infinite being). Even if a child were taught pantheism at an early age, how obvious would it be that people are not God because people are constantly being born and then die (because they are not eternal), have to go to school (because they are not all-knowing), and have to continue eating to stay alive (because they are not infinite and continually require food to sustain life)?

Does it really make sense for an all-knowing God to have to relearn his identity? God would have to relearn his identity with each and every single person, so it appears as if the pantheistic God is quite forgetful, but this does not square with the characteristics that even pantheists attribute to *God*. How does one explain an all-knowing God having to relearn his identity? Would that not be contradictory to the God even pantheists declare is both eternal and all-knowing?

Pantheism contains too many contradictions to be logical. The very root of the idea is illogical, and pantheists appear to be jumping through hoops just to make it seem logical. Logic never needs to be forced in order for something to make sense. It appears as if they are doing the exact opposite, trying to force the illogical into that which is logical.

A House Divided Cannot Stand. Logic would also defy pantheism because of the great principle that "anything that is divided amongst itself cannot stand."[48] Nothing divided can stand because the internal conflict would cause either one side, or both, to eventually self-destruct. Consider the following examples to make the principle clear.

A typical healthy human body produces cells that are required to sustain life; they transfer food, oxygen, and waste to and from their respective places throughout the body. When a body is divided, it is trying to both sustain and destroy life at the same time. The best example I can offer is a virus. The body's sole function in creating cells is to sustain life, while a virus (say, AIDS) is preventing the body from its ability to sustain life. The house is divided, and it cannot stand.

A second example is the division of a nation. A healthy nation is one that harmoniously works together to preserve its presence and function in the world. When a nation becomes divided, it has two different segments that vehemently disagree with and oppose one another. Let's take America during the 1860s, since we are familiar with our Civil War. During that time period, there were two opposing forces, and the nation was divided. The opposing forces resorted to war, and one side was ultimately defeated

48 Kingdom divided cannot stand: Mark 3:24; House divided cannot stand: Mark 3:25.

(in some cases a civil war can devastate a nation so badly that it collapses). The result, in our case, was that the Confederate States of America was defeated.

How do these situations relate to pantheism? The question is now, how can *God* be divided against himself and still stand? If God is everything, then God would be both good and evil. This intuitively means that God would have a severe internal conflict and constantly warring impulses. This internal war will eventually cause one side, or both, to be destroyed because anything divided against itself cannot stand.

When a body fights an internal war, either the virus or the body will win, or else both experience the ultimate defeat of death. (The virus can supersede the life of the person if it is transferred to another host before the virus dies; in that case the virus would win.) When a nation goes to war, either the one side or the other will win, or they will both be defeated (surrender is a form of defeat). How is it that God can be divided when we already know that nothing else can be divided and sustain itself?

It does not make sense for God to be both everything that is good and everything that is evil at the same time because that is a contradiction within itself, and we already know that it is a matter of time before the stronger force will ultimately prevail over the weaker.

The Result of Pantheism. The result of God being divided against himself would prevent God from being endless (infinite) because either good or evil will ultimately prevail, and it is only a matter of time before one overtakes the other; or they implode and both are destroyed. The pantheist God cannot exist because it is not logical for an all-knowing God to have to learn about his deity; it's not a trait that fits within the infinite characteristic that even pantheists attribute to God. The pantheist God cannot exist because it attributes two mutually exclusive traits to God: either God is infinite and eternal or he is not; but never both.

There are entirely too many contradictions and illogical concepts for pantheism to be a belief in which thinking people can confidently place their faith. As a result of our study of the pantheistic doctrine, we are able to confidently disqualify it from its candidacy for Absolute Truth.

Panentheism

A Counter Belief. Since the above arguments are both intuitive and logical, a new belief has arisen to try and escape the apparent contradictions. Please meet panentheism. This belief states that God is a finite being and that God is neither *one with the world* (as pantheism claimed) nor beyond/above the world (as theists claim). This idea simply implies that God is here in the world with us, but never one with or above us. By definition, panentheism propagates a finite God or a God that lacks transcendence (an entity entirely separated from creation).

More Contradictions. If God is finite, then God could not be eternal, all-powerful, all-knowing, all-loving, or unchangeable or display any of the other characteristics that are usually attributed to God. Ironically, when you remove one of God's characteristics, you must remove them all because they are inseparable. The very fact that panentheists have made God finite results in not having God at all. Instead they have an entity that they claim is God, but one that is not capable of being God by any recognizable standard.

Panentheism has apparent contradictions within itself that we need to examine. When you remove the one necessary, independent being that was capable of initiating creation, then the belief is essentially the same as atheism. In fact, if you have a God that is not eternal, then that God must have a beginning point—a point when its potential was actualized and God was created; but this does not make any sense!

If God had a beginning point, then the entity we just referred to as God is really not God because it would also require an external force, an independent being, for its own creation. What you would end up with is one God creating another God, but this is also contradictory because there cannot be two Gods (these are some of the basic principles from the cosmological argument presented in Chapter 6).

If the characteristics of God include infinity, then you cannot have two infinite beings. They would ultimately be the same because they would be *indistinguishable.* For one being to be distinguishable from another, they must first be different from one another. Since the characteristics of God are inseparable, removing any one of them negates divinity; otherwise God would not be infinite. Since the definition of God requires infinity, we would no longer have God. Having one God creating another is an absurd concept because you ultimately end up with one being that is infinite and one that is finite, and now we are back at the traditional view of God, or theism.

The Result of Panentheism. Panentheism had some unintended complications that will certainly give the panentheist's apologist a run for his money! (I would not want to be the one assigned to unravel this mess.) Nevertheless, the reason that panentheism is not logical is because a quick run-through of a cause-and-effect scenario leads you down a very unattractive road; it will ultimately revert back to either atheism or theism. It teeters between the two categories because it is not possible to have a finite God. When a person has denied one of God's intrinsic characteristics, the net result is no God.

The point is that panentheism is not a belief that logical and thinking people can confidently place their faith upon because it is also contradictory. Ironically, the idea of removing even one of God's attributes destroys the entire concept of God, and you will ultimately find yourself in another religion. As a result of their many apparent contradictions, both panentheism and pantheism are removed from their candidacy for Absolute Truth.

Chapter 5

Some Say "Science Proves There Is No God"

"I was a young man with unformed ideas. I threw out queries, suggestions, wondering all the time over everything; and to my astonishment the ideas took like wildfire. People made a religion out of them!"

—Charles Darwin

"The evolutionists seem to know everything about the missing link except the fact that it is still missing."

—G. K. Chesterton

Naturalism

What You See Is What You Get. As mentioned in the second chapter, Naturalism is a broad category that is defined as "the doctrine that the world can be understood in scientific terms without recourse to spiritual or supernatural explanations."[49] A more straightforward representation is provided with the statement that George Gaylord Simpson, an evolutionary biologist, made: "Man is a result of a purposeless and natural process that did not have him in mind."[50] This is the idea that if everything can be explained without God, there is no need to posit God's existence. This

49 Naturalism. Dictionary.com. *Dictionary.com Unabridged.* Random House, Inc. http://dictionary.reference.com/browse/naturalism (accessed: November 7, 2008).

50 Lee Strobel, *Case for a Creator* (Grand Rapids, MI: Zondervan, 2004), 23.

view is confirmed by Philip Johnson, law professor and author of *Darwin on Trial.* Although Johnson is not a supporter of Darwinism, he agrees that "the whole point of Darwinism is to show that there is no need for a supernatural creator, because nature can do the creating by itself."[51]

Since Naturalism teaches that the physical world is the ultimate reality (all that exists), we begin to see how a variety of beliefs ultimately stem from Naturalism's foundation. Atheism, communism, Darwinism, (non-theistic) evolutionism, humanism, materialism, and socialism are subcategories of Naturalism because they all reject the possibility of the spiritual realm in their core ideology. In these beliefs, emphasis is never placed on any type of morality set forth by a higher being; instead the emphasis is placed on the *ego* (self) and on human accomplishment alone; hence the idea of utopia in socialism.

Although Naturalism has been extraordinarily popular in both the United States and other parts of the world, we need to know whether this is a theological perspective that is worthy of being titled Absolute Truth. In this chapter, we will pull back the veil, dig deeper, and expose some of the dirty little secrets about Naturalism that you were not supposed to know. There are some fundamental flaws with Naturalism that need to be presented because many people will unfortunately fall into this category, thinking they have found Truth, when, in reality, they have only fallen into a misguided theological trap. Naturalism has not solved the problem with respect to God; but it can be credited with creating far more uncertainty and raising even more unanswerable questions.

Addressing the Institution of Science. On this note, Christians cannot blithely disregard science because they do not like what is discovered or agree with what is theorized. There was a time in history when a Christian by the name of Galileo was mildly persecuted by the church for claiming that the earth was not the center of the solar system and that the earth revolved around the sun. Even though Galileo's rationale may not have been entirely correct, his overall idea was correct. Instead of completely separating Christianity from science and making premature judgments on people with different ideas, have an open mind. An open mind does not mean that you go off the deep end into accepting every idea on the face of the earth, but it does mean that you first listen without prejudice. An open mind is imperative if one is to *objectively analyze* the facts so that Christians are able to distinguish truth from untruth.

---

51 Phillip E. Johnson, quoted in *World* (July-August 2002).

Science is amoral; it is neither right nor wrong. The use of science by human beings ultimately brings morality into the equation. Science can support an abomination; especially if used to disprove God or aid in abortion. On the other hand, science can also bring glory to God when used to prove the Bible to be entirely true or to prove that God exists. Science can even help us have a deeper understanding of the world that God created. Understanding the complexity of life, and everything around us, brings glory to God when we marvel at His handiwork.

God's handiwork is creation, but the age of creation is a controversial topic among Christians. A few points on this subject need to be made before we proceed. Since God is all-powerful, it would be wise not to limit God. Since God cannot be deceptive; he is not able to "mislead by false appearance."[52] Since the Bible is not all-inclusive and frequently uses metaphors to convey a message, interpretation is sometimes required. Since the greater light to govern the day (perceivably the sun) and the greater light to govern the night (perceivably the moon) were created on the fourth day, it seems highly unlikely for the earth to have had twenty-four hour periods when our time is strictly based upon the existence of the sun. The problem is that the Sun was not established until the fourth day.[53] If you remove the Sun, *time as we know it* would be meaningless!

In addition to the sun not being created until the fourth day, another observation is that the word *day* (Hebrew *yom*) is not limited to twenty-four hour periods; it can refer to a future period of time (such as "in the *day* of the Lord") or it can be used to describe an unspecified period of time in the past ("there was a *day* when ..."). Furthermore, the Apostle Peter demonstrated that *days* are irrelevant to God and that *day* can refer to a much longer period of time than we think: "But, beloved, be not ignorant of this one thing, that one day is with the Lord as a thousand years, and a thousand years as one day."[54]

After making these observations, it is entirely *possible* that the age of the earth could very well be more than six thousand years. The Bible does not explicitly state that the creation event took place over the course of six twenty-four hour periods; it uses a term that is most often, but not always, associated with twenty-four hour periods. Since the Bible

---

52 Deceive. Dictionary.com. *Dictionary.com Unabridged.* Random House, Inc.http://dictionary.reference.com/browse/deceive (accessed: October 22, 2009).

53 Genesis 1:14–19.

54 2 Peter 3:8 KJV.

does not explicitly state the age of the earth, it never makes a definitive pronouncement in regard to the subject.

The point is that nobody knows for sure and this is demonstrated by the fact that Christian theologians have created five theories that attempt to describe the age of creation: the gap theory, flood theory, ideal-time theory, age-day theory, and pictorial-day theory.[55] Since the explicit age of creation remains unanswered by the Bible, it is not possible to draw a definitive conclusion without venturing into speculation. As a result, this book leaves open the possibility that the earth may be billions of years old.

Another problem with dating the earth centers upon the science of geology. It would appear that dinosaurs once roamed the earth. We know this because geologists have found their bones in the ground. When we find bones, we automatically assume that the bones once belonged to a living creature because everything that has bones was once living. All living creatures can have bones, but a creature that never lived cannot have bones. Since God does not deceive, it would only be logical to believe that dinosaurs once lived. The problem is that the dinosaurs' existence is dated to an era of millions upon millions of years ago.

Dating techniques (whether carbon dating or measuring the release of argon gas) are surprisingly accurate techniques. We know the techniques of dating are accurate with artifacts of recent history, so when the process is replicated on another object that is much older, the results are perceived to be accurate when the same method was reproduced. The process would be analogous to counting rings on a ten-year-old tree (whose age we could verify) and then using the exact same method on the sequoias (some of which have lived more than 2,000 years; the oldest tree's age is approximated at 3,148 years).[56] If counting rings to approximate age is accurate with a tree that we can verify, when the same process is used to date an older tree, it would not be unreasonable to suggest the results are fairly accurate. The same principles can be applied to the science of geology when determining age of creation, fossils and/or artifacts that have been excavated.

55 Millard Erickson, *Christian Theology* (Grand Rapids, MI: Baker Academic, 1998), 406-408.

56 Willis Linn Jepson, "The Giant Sequoia," Handbook of Yosemite National Park (1921), http://www.yosemite.ca.us/library/handbook_of_yosemite_national_park/sequoia.html.

Russell's Perspective. Personally, I have a great respect for science because it is very logical and structured. It reminds me of God as He is also logical and He structured the universe to His liking with very precise laws. I have struggled with trying to mix the two entities because it is not commonly held that science parallels with Christianity, but my belief is that *accurate* science can become a great ally to the Christian faith.

After all, "An unbiased look at the history of science shows that modern science is an invention of medieval Christianity, and the greatest breakthroughs in scientific reason have largely been the work of Christians."[57] The list of notable Christian scientists includes Copernicus, Kepler, Galileo, Brahe, Descartes, Boyle, Newton, Leibniz, Gassendi, Pascal, Mersenne, Cuvier, Harvey, Dalton, Faraday, Herschel, Joule, Lyell, Lavoisier, Priestley, Kelvin, Ohm, Ampere, Steno, Pasteur, Maxwell, Planck, and Mendel. A good many were clergymen, some were priests (Gassendi and Mersenne), and some became monks (Mendel) or entered into other religious orders (Pascal).[58]

It is a myth that science is disconnected from God, but the Naturalists have seemingly been successful in this endeavor. I will attempt to demonstrate how the two are intricately intertwined and how they can synergize each other to reach a fresh audience by utilizing science to systematically prove Christianity to be entirely true. I have concluded:

1. God created everything, even science.
2. Since God created science, *accurate* science cannot disprove God.

And:

1. God is Absolute Truth.
2. The purpose of science is to discover truth.
3. Scientific truth *cannot* contradict Absolute Truth.
4. Scientific truth reveals God's handiwork.
5. Marveling at God's handiwork brings glory to God.
6. Bringing glory to God is worship.
7. Science is the worship of God.

---

57 Dinesh D'Souza, *What's So Great about Christianity?* (Washington, D.C.: Regnery Publishing, Inc., 2007), 84.

58 Ibid. 97.

> **Therefore:** If used properly, science can become a powerful tool that reaches a fresh audience, in the propagation of the Gospel of Jesus Christ. If science contradicts Absolute Truth, then that science is incorrect and has some "catching up to do." It is because of these arguments that I believe science can become Christianity's greatest ally as these fields of study partially reveal the incomprehensible glory of none other than Jesus Christ, the King of kings and the Lord of lords.

However, it must be noted that science is neither the ultimate reality nor the final authority. Science should never be placed above the Absolute Truth contained within the Holy Bible. If science contradicts an explicit principle or fact within the Bible, and it cannot possibly be interpreted in any other way, then it is to be disregarded. As we know, there are some gray areas in the Bible, since it is not all-inclusive.[59]

The Bible is not all-inclusive because it only highlights a limited number of specific points and very few people in history; therefore it is not feasible, nor is it necessary, to systematically document each and every fact, person, place, or event that has occurred all throughout history. The most basic functions of the Bible reveal concepts such as these: God exists; He has established a system of morality and justice; the Gospel offers hope; and the Truth enables all people to successfully make it from this life into the life after death. Of course the Bible offers far more than the few concepts listed above, but before the deep theological truths of the Bible can be effectively utilized, the common presuppositions (e.g., God exists) must be accepted.

Science can help in this area. If nothing else, it can demonstrate that Naturalism does not have the answer because science cannot support Naturalism's basic presuppositions, as will be demonstrated in this chapter and in Chapter 6. Before an examination of the science Naturalism uses to support itself, we need to examine the different uses of science.

---

59 Until Genesis 4:16, only four humans are mentioned: Adam, Eve, Cain, and Abel. After Cain killed Abel, he was cursed; but he was worried about *others killing him*. Even more interesting is after his curse, he went out and he "lay with his wife." Where did his wife or the other people come from? God reveals what we *need* to know.

Good Science, Bad Science. We have established science as amoral, but the use of science brings morality into the equation. Science has many uses that can positively impact our lives. Preventing disease, curing cancer, and extending life expectancy through the science of medicine are excellent and moral uses of science. Science can also be used to predict weather patterns, detect deadly storms, and implement sophisticated warning systems. These are beneficial uses of science because they help people by saving lives.

As with anything, science can also be manipulated into that which is immoral. Science that enables a mother to murder her own child while still in the womb is immoral. Murder of the innocent cannot be justified, regardless of how inconvenient or burdensome the child may be. Furthermore, the murder of the innocent is not tolerated in society if the crime has been committed against a person living outside the womb (including infants, children, teenagers, adults, and senior citizens alike). The difference is the womb, but regardless of whether persons are inside or outside the womb, they are *people*, and the murder of innocent *people* is immoral. (Abortion will be covered in more detail in Chapter 14.)

On the same note, science is also immoral if used as blasphemy against God. Blasphemy is "the act of insulting or showing contempt or lack of reverence for God," as well as "the act of claiming the attributes of a deity."[60] With respect to science, the first definition is applicable. Building upon this foundation, any intentional distortion, misrepresentation, or withholding of certain facts to further an agenda against God is immoral. This section will demonstrate that science has been used in all three icons in this chapter in an attempt to hide the truth in order to further an agenda (discussed in Chapter 15).

The intentional act of denying God has some very serious consequences that need to be addressed. The abandonment of God has serious consequences that people need to understand. The next section merely highlights some of Naturalism's consequences before the science Naturalism propagates as Absolute Truth is examined.

Implications of Naturalism

A Perpetual Downward Spiral. In order to follow this theory, we need to get into the mind-set of Naturalists and try to view the world through

---

60 Blasphemy. Dictionary.com. *Dictionary.com Unabridged.* Random House, Inc. http://dictionary.reference.com/browse/blasphemy (accessed: October 19, 2009).

their eyes. Since Naturalism teaches that everything can be understood in scientific terms without recourse to supernatural or spiritual explanations, it automatically implies that the human race was either formed from a lower life form by a series of evolutionary steps or that humanity came into existence by mere chance (more realistically, by accident). Since life is a product of random and natural phenomena, an intelligent designer (who created life for a specific purpose or function) could not possibly exist. If there is no intelligent designer, then there would be no eternal life. The thought of places called heaven and hell would be nothing more than a series of myths created to appease the human mind while living on earth.

No eternal life would mean that there is no divine judgment for right and wrong. If there is no final judgment after death, then people would simply be free to do anything and everything they desire because nobody would *ever* be held accountable for their actions outside the judicial systems of the physical world (which may or may not be just). Essentially, everybody is entitled to do whatever fulfills their every desire, regardless of right and wrong, as long as their decisions fall within the limitations and the laws of the particular judicial system to which they answer.

If there is no higher being to serve, then we would have to conclude that everything we do should be for our own purposes. Prioritizing the self above everything else is the pattern of thought that leads to the concept that "I am God": everything *I* do revolves around *my* needs and *my* interests alone. Of course being your own god doesn't necessarily mean that you fall down on your face and worship yourself or that you expect other people to worship you. Being your own god simply means that the only person you revere and are here to serve is yourself, and that can be accomplished by simply fulfilling your desires first.

The naturalistic overtone is one of great pessimism because there is absolutely nothing to look forward to after death. There is no higher being to delight in or worship, and nothing is regarded as *sacred* or *holy*. Morality is also compromised when it is understood to be an artifact of mere humans (inherently sinful beings). In societies where morality is misconstrued, distorted, or nonexistent, we always find the great tragedies and the oppression of people by the government. Since mankind is inherently sinful, morality must be created by a sinless entity (God). When mankind begins to *play God*, by establishing independent systems of morality, the "train runs off the track." Immorality leads to a perpetual downward spiral into chaos (no concrete standards of right or wrong, no justice, no accountability, and no restraint on evil).

These are some of the ideas and consequences that follow from Naturalism. These are the effects and the results of naturalistic theory, but the problem is that none of the results seem very promising. This is problematic because the implications of Naturalism do not seem right to most people. Something is missing from the picture. The picture is incomplete because people throughout history have always had a compelling desire to search out, find, and worship God. It seems as if the desire is inescapable, and the void is too great to be filled with personal gratification and material possessions. Since Naturalism only recognizes the physical world, but people have a desire for the spiritual, it is easy to see how life becomes unfulfilling, trivial, and meaningless. Our own experience tells us there is no purpose without God.

Naturalism is an extreme outlier when compared to the other theological perspectives on the existence of God. Every other religion recognizes the human desire and need to be spiritually fulfilled. Naturalism is the only category of religion that does not believe in the supernatural or the spiritual, and there are severe consequences. First of all, the entire belief system must be grounded upon science—and science alone. The question now becomes: has science adequately proven the impossibility of the existence of God? The answer is a resounding *no* because the scientists know that they cannot disprove God; it is impossible to prove a negative of that magnitude with a finite mind.

Since Naturalism cannot disprove God, it has tried to demonstrate how God is not needed. Through science, Naturalists have tried to demonstrate how life can be a product of natural phenomena without relying on miracles or the supernatural in any way. Have they succeeded in presenting a scientific, accurate, or logical alternative to reliance on God? This chapter examines the science upon which Naturalism has built its entire faith. The next chapter examines the presuppositions that Naturalists must assume and whether or not these presumptions are logical.

Naturalism's Scientific Icons

Three Is a Charm. In this section we will briefly introduce three of the most basic evolutionary icons. All three of these icons are *essential* because they are the backbone of the naturalistic theory. These icons are *key* because they attempt to explain how life came from something that was not previously alive and how microorganisms eventually evolved into the complex species we see today without recourse to the supernatural. These icons attempt to demonstrate that life is, in fact, a product of natural processes *alone.*

The reason that we will only analyze three of the evolutionary icons is because an all-encompassing argument against each of the icons is not necessary to disprove the theory. An all-out examination is not necessary because it would go beyond the scope of this book and because another book has been entirely devoted to disproving the icons and the science that Naturalism uses as if they were empirical facts.[61]

If it can be demonstrated that science cannot prove how life came into existence, then the entire naturalistic theory has failed what it originally set out to accomplish. If Naturalism is disproved in one area, then it cannot be considered Absolute Truth, for it will have been shown not to be *entirely true.* As a result, only one of these icons needs to fail in order to disqualify Naturalism from its candidacy for Absolute Truth. Disproving only one is also not beneficial, as it could be perceived as a fluke. If three are disproved, then a pattern has developed, and Naturalism's incompetence can be better conveyed.

If you would like to learn about many more inconsistencies of naturalistic evolution, I would strongly recommend reading Dr. Jonathon Wells' book *Icons of Evolution: Why Much of What We Teach About Evolution Is Wrong.* This is an extraordinarily thorough analysis by an expert microbiologist who is actively engaged in the field of study that directly pertains to this topic.

However, in this section, we will merely cite some of the facts presented in Dr. Wells's book, as well as some of the statements he made in his interview with Lee Strobel in *The Case for a Creator.* Dr. Wells and Lee Strobel have significantly contributed to this argument, and we credit them with their expertise as we use their rationale to help illustrate Naturalism's fundamental flaws. The primary objective in analyzing these icons is to determine whether or not they are accurate. Accuracy of the science upon which Naturalism builds its foundation will help us determine whether it is a candidate for Absolute Truth. We begin by examining the icons.

---

61 Dr. Jonathon Wells, *Icons of Evolution* (Washington, D.C.: Regnery Publishing, Inc., 2000).

The Icons of Hope. In this section, three of the ten major icons that are used to support the *entire* naturalistic theory are examined. Even today, these icons are used in textbooks and are portrayed as concrete evidence that is then used to convey to students that God is no longer needed.

1. The Miller Experiment. In 1953, Stanley Miller claimed to artificially produce the building blocks of life by reproducing the atmosphere of the primitive earth. Once the atmosphere was created, Miller was able to create amino acids (the building blocks of life) through electric sparks that simulated lightning strikes. The creation of amino acids was eventually able to develop into more and more complex organisms and eventually into the life forms we know and see today. This is the first icon because the Naturalists use the findings to claim that life was a result of an entirely natural phenomenon that did not need an intelligent designer.[62]

2. Darwin's Tree of Life. After scientists were able to explain how a natural phenomenon could have explained the creation of life, the next logical step would be to explain how the most simplistic organism could have evolved into the complex organisms and the different life forms we see today. The Tree of Life was just the explanation the Naturalists needed; it was a sketch in which Charles Darwin depicted the development of life from a single ancestor. Eventually the tree of life was able to develop into limbs, branches, and twigs that represent the different hierarchies of biological classifications (i.e. species, genus, family, order, class, phylum, and kingdom). The general idea is that as time progressed, life evolved with increasing diversity and complexity. This theory suggests that all life forms are "related through descent from some unknown prototype that lived in the remote past."[63]

3. Ernst Haeckel's Drawings of Embryos. Even though the Naturalists could claim to know how life could have occurred without an intelligent designer and could explain the complexity in organisms we see today from a common ancestor, their evidence was limited at the time Darwin published his Tree of Life. Ernst Haeckel's drawings of embryos provided even more evidence that all living organisms began with an embryo that appeared to be identical to all others. Hence, human embryos appeared to be identical with that of an embryonic fish, salamander, tortoise, chick,

62 Strobel, 19.

63 Ibid., 20.

hog, calf, and rabbit. Since all embryos appeared to be identical in their earliest forms, not only were they virtually indistinguishable, but it was conceivable that this could be further explanation of how all life had the same ancient progenitor.[64]

Fundamentally Flawed

Too Good to Be True? Thus far, everything seems to be going great for the Naturalists. They think that they have finally discovered the evidence they need to prove their case and essentially destroy the concept of *God* altogether. Even though Naturalism goes against thousands of years of human thought, it has made its way to the population and has exploded with popularity, but is it too good to be true? Are we really not accountable to a higher being? Are we really free to do anything we desire as long as we abide by the laws enacted by our government? What about the evidence? Is the evidence without blemish and as credible as the scientists claim?

Surprisingly, the science that is in direct support of Naturalism has some dirty little secrets that you were not supposed to know. The fundamental flaws that will be presented in this chapter are problems that have been known for *years*, yet few people know about them, much less the impact they are having on our children all throughout America's public school systems! You are about to be presented with the facts that could topple Naturalism's empire—but these facts are *meaningless* unless you take them seriously, Stand Up! for truth and ultimately demand that inaccurate, faulty, or fraudulent science be removed from the classroom.

"Don't Ask, Don't Tell"—Dirty Darwin Secrets. It appears as if Naturalism's theories have been gaining momentum and uncovering more and more convincing evidence as each new discovery is made, but sometimes new discoveries can cause you to rethink the positions you hold, especially when you find out that the truth was distorted, secretly covered up, or ignored. The need to reexamine truth becomes even more urgent when we discover that we, as a nation, have not only been misleading countless people to believe in something that is false, but we are forcing students to learn a new religion. Naturalism is a religion (Chapter 15), and it is impossible to prove that God does not exist (Chapter 6). Yet our

64 Ibid., 20–21.

textbooks tell a different story and cause our children to reject the notion of God; just ask Lee Strobel.

In the remaining part of this section, we will examine some of the dirty secrets of the Darwinist theory that the Naturalists are trying to prevent you from knowing—as well as the discrepancies in the two other evolutionary icons—because they *all* contain misleading facts that distort the truth that people desperately need to know. The old adage says, "The truth shall set you free" (John 8:32), but I take it another step and say that knowing the *Absolute Truth* will enable you to free your mind from propaganda so you can decide for yourself what constitutes truth.[65] Knowledge is power, and with the knowledge you are about to learn, you will have the power to prevent yourself and your family and friends from falling into another misguided theological trap as the facts begin to clash against the unsound belief system that the Naturalists have briefly enjoyed. Let's dig deeper and discover why Naturalism is not the answer.

Flaws of the Miller Experiment

Dr. Jonathon Wells encapsulates the truth about the Miller experiment when he says that "the Miller experiment is flat-out misleading or false."[66]

The atmosphere that Miller used when he conducted his experiment was based upon the theories of his doctoral advisor, and the atmosphere he used was consistent with the beliefs of the scientists in that era. Even though nobody knows for sure what the primitive earth's atmosphere was like when life first appeared, the general consensus among scientists is that it was not at all like the one Miller used in his experiment. In fact, there's significant evidence against the hydrogen-rich mixture of methane, ammonia, and water vapor that Miller used.[67]

Since there is no evidence to support the original type of atmosphere used in the experiment (with substantial evidence against his theory), scientists now believe Miller's experiment was not, in any way, an accurate representation of how life began. Some scientists, like Marcel Florkin, abandoned Miller's experiment by the 1970s because new discoveries revealed that there was very little hydrogen in the atmosphere, since it would have escaped into space. Instead, scientists now believe that the

65 Propaganda: the spreading of ideas, information, or rumor for the purpose of helping or injuring an institution, a cause, or a person (merriam-webster.com).

66 Strobel, 37.

67 Ibid.

atmosphere probably consisted of carbon dioxide, nitrogen, and water vapor.[68]

Do you think that the results of Miller's experiment would be compromised by the discovery that it was based on incorrect assumptions about the atmosphere? Absolutely; Miller's results do not, in any way, represent what actually occurred in regard to the creation of life. Furthermore, if scientists began abandoning the Miller experiment in the 1970s, in light of new and more accurate evidence, why do some of our school systems still teach the experiment as if it were fact?

Scientists are now convinced that if the same experiment were replicated using an accurate representation of the earth's early atmosphere, it would not produce the basic building blocks of life: amino acids. Dr. Wells explains that even the most accurate replica of the primitive atmosphere would produce not amino acids but a combination of formaldehyde and cyanide. The combinations that would have resulted from the experiment would have actually killed life instead of creating it![69]

It wouldn't even make sense to use the updated version of the experiment because the combination of the resulting elements are known to be lethal. Dr. Wells makes it clear that "the idea [that] using a realistic atmosphere gets you to the first step in the origin of life is just *laughable*" (emphasis added). In fact, it is not even chemically possible to get the results that the experiment desperately needs in order to put itself in a position to claim that natural processes created life. This is a significant discovery because any naturalistic explanation or theory that goes *beyond this point* is automatically discredited from Absolute Truth because the results are not an accurate representation of the truth. Interestingly enough, the reality is that scientists really have no idea how life began and are unable to describe such a phenomenon without incorporating an intelligent designer into the equation.[70]

You need to stop and ask yourself, "If the experiment were reproduced to correctly reflect the primitive atmosphere, and the results would be lethal to life, how could this experiment remain a foundational building block that Naturalism uses to explain the origin of life?" The correct representation of the facts is that the Miller experiment can no longer constitute Absolute Truth; in fact it never held Absolute Truth because the

---

68 Ibid.

69 Ibid., 38.

70 Gregg Easterbrook, "The New Convergence," Wired, http://www.wired.com/wired/archive/10.12/convergence_pr.html.

experiment was flawed from its conception. The correct, and most logical, answer is that the Miller experiment conclusively fails—defeated by what scientists now believe to be an accurate representation of Earth's primitive atmosphere. Thus, strike one against one of the major foundational building blocks of the Naturalist's theory.

Flaws of Darwin's Tree of Life

One of the most popular and recognizable icons of evolution comes from the sketch that Charles Darwin introduced when he published *The Origin of Species* (1859). As stated earlier, the purpose of the icon was to provide a theory of how simplistic organisms could have *possibly* evolved into the complex organisms we see today and that everything evolved from a common ancestor. The sketch of the Tree of Life has grown in popularity as it is used in countless textbooks and is held by many as Absolute Truth.

The question we must ask ourselves is whether or not Darwin's theory can withstand the scrutiny of the fossil record and whether or not the theory is logically viable. Keep in mind that the proponents of Darwinism are going to fight vigorously against any opposition to their beliefs because "It's their way or the highway," regardless of whether or not they are scientifically accurate.[71] They have an agenda to push and nothing will get in their way (as demonstrated in Chapter 15).

Advocates of Darwinism have even smeared their scientific counterparts—who are also expert scientists—merely because they do not recognize Darwinism as Absolute Truth. There is tremendous pressure for these experts to conform to the Darwinist theory or be labeled as *inferior* simply because they reject what some scientists claim as an empirical fact. Scientists who hold beliefs in the possibility of an intelligent designer are scoffed at and ridiculed more than if they were atheists who happened to disagree.

Does it not seem hypocritical to discriminate against the scientists who oppose Darwinism when our society is *supposedly* one that accepts the beliefs of *all* people, regardless of who they are or what they believe? (Or is this evidence of liberalism's double standard?) Nevertheless, some of the scientists who oppose Darwinism are even considered, by some, to be outcasts in the scientific community. This is a harsh verdict from those *objectively* seeking out the truth. This criticism is a great revelation as to what is going on behind the curtains. The sharp "outspoken and militant"

71 Motive of inaccurate reporting of science revealed in chapter 15.

backlash is a result of the perception that Naturalists thought they were winning the war against religion.[72] They thought their view was more appealing, but it has had the reverse effect: their science is demonstrating the necessity of God's existence, and that is simply unacceptable. It is as if science has metaphorically flicked the Naturalist in the nose (one of the most insulting things one person can do to another). Hence the resort to personal attacks—it is the only way to fight back since science, logic, and evidence are no longer on their side.

Despite the severe criticism against those who deny Darwinism, we should remember that the truth will always remain true, regardless of personal opinion. The facts still need be objectively analyzed in order to determine whether or not Darwinism can be regarded as a credible and logical theory in which intelligent and thinking people can place their faith. All people, whether they hold Darwinist beliefs or not, need to objectively examine the evidence so that they can make their own decisions. We continue our quest as Darwinism will now slip under the microscope as we examine the theory and the thoughts of Charles Darwin when his ideas were published.

Shocking but True! It is shocking to point out the fact that, when Darwin sketched his Tree of Life, he was already aware that the current fossil records failed to support his tree in any way. In fact, the evidence was contradictory to his theory at the time the sketch was made.[73] Despite the overwhelming evidence against his theory, Darwin made the sketch anyway by making the *assumption* that future fossil discoveries would vindicate his claims and that his theory would hold firm.

Now that over one hundred years' worth of fossils have been unearthed and numerous discoveries have been made since his theory was published, we have the luxury of looking back through time to compare his theory to reality—the actual discoveries that were made versus pure speculation.

The Explosion that Destroyed Darwinism. Interestingly enough, the discoveries of fossils that have been made since Darwin's time have reduced his tree to nothing more than an *interesting idea* of how complex organisms might have come into existence. When the fossil record is examined, there is no evidence that remotely suggests that all organisms came from

---

72 Dinesh D'Souza, *What's So Great about Christianity* (Washington, D.C.: Regnery Publishing, Inc., 2007), 21.

73 Strobel, 43.

the same ancient progenitor; in fact the results are quite contrary. The discovery that contradicts Darwin's theory is the Cambrian explosion (also known as the "Biological Big Bang").[74]

The Cambrian explosion was a geological period that began a little more than 540 million years ago. This explosion is a metaphor that describes the sudden appearance of most of the major animal phyla that are alive today, as well as some that are now extinct. Before the Cambrian explosion there were some jellyfish, sponges, and worms, but then *suddenly* a vast multitude of different life forms appear that contradict the Darwinist theory.[75]

After the Cambrian explosion, there are representatives of the arthropods (modern variations are insects and crabs), echinoderms (modern variations are starfish and sea urchins), chordates (modern variations are vertebrates and mammals came much later; but chordates are the major group to which they belong), as well as many others.[76]

The time period in which all these different life forms appear was so sudden that natural modifications could not have possibly occurred in such a brief period of time.[77] The actual time period of the Cambrian explosion spans across 70 to 80 million years. Although this may seem like an extraordinarily lengthy period of time, it's quite brief when compared to the billions of years the earth has been in existence and the billions of years that life is *believed* to have existed on our planet.

When Dr. Wells was interviewed by Lee Strobel in *The Case for a Creator*, he put into context how sudden these changes were. In short, imagine yourself on one goal line of a football field. That goal line represents the first fossil that was discovered. You begin walking and you pass the twenty-yard line, the forty-yard line, and as you enter into the other side's half of the field, all you have seen so far are microscopic, single-celled organisms. Continue walking for eighty-four yards, and you only see these same organisms. Then when you reach the opposing sixteen-yard line, you see some sponges and maybe some jellyfish and worms. Then—boom!—all of a sudden, in a *single stride*, all these other animals appear.

According to Dr. Jonathon Wells, the reason that this discovery is so significant is because it is entirely contrary to the Darwin's Tree of

74 The Cambrian explosion is a period of time (in the fossil record) where we discover a rapid change in history. The changes observed vary from the amount of life that existed to the complexity of life. Before the Cambrian explosion, life was simplistic; after the explosion, most of the major types of animals suddenly appear.

75 Strobel, 43.

76 Ibid., 43–44.

77 Ibid., 44.

Life. Nobody in their right mind can call the Cambrian explosion a branching tree because there was not enough time for any branching to occur. Suddenly, all the classes in the Cambrian explosion appeared, and since so many different types miraculously show up at the same time, it's not even feasible to suggest it resembles Darwin's branching tree. (For detailed discussion of the short time frame and the difficulties it poses to classical evolutionary theory, see discussion in *Icons of Evolution* by Dr. Jonathon Wells or *The Case for a Creator* by Lee Strobel.)

If a naturalistic evolutionary process had "evolved" these life forms in the way that Darwin suggested, it would have taken much longer than the time period (a single stride) in which these organisms were found. Furthermore, these organisms are quite diverse in their appearance – their body types were completely different as they were entirely different organisms. The naturalist cannot explain the discoveries by using the Tree of Life because the evidence that we have today has proven it wrong beyond a shadow of a doubt.

There is no more concrete evidence to justify the Darwinist position than there is evidence to prove the existence of the tooth fairy. Darwinists know that their position is not accurate and that the fossil record does not support their position, yet they continue to cram it down your throat as if it were another universal health care bill!

Even if you acknowledge the fact that every fossil has not yet been found, there is such an overwhelming amount of evidence against his theory that it becomes highly unlikely that we will ever find the supporting evidence Darwin hoped we would find. Scientists have enough well-preserved sedimentary rock and fossils before and after the Cambrian era that would have preserved any of Darwin's supporting fossils, if they existed. Such a discovery is highly unlikely because we can examine that time period and the time periods both before and after the Cambrian explosion. Scientists have well-preserved fossils of even the smallest of organisms (bacteria) that date back 3 billion years; much larger fossils are unlikely to have disappeared and they would not have "slipped through the cracks."[78]

Frankly, the Darwinist theory has failed. It is astonishing to note that Charles Darwin knew that his theory would depend upon the fossils discovered in the future, and this admission reveals that Darwin knew that *he could be entirely wrong.*[79] As new evidence has been discovered, we are

78 Ibid., 45–47.

79 Ibid.

able to conclude that Darwinism does not pass the test of Absolute Truth. There are too many inconsistencies with his theory as the evidence we now have (Cambrian explosion) actually disproves Darwinism entirely. We can now remove the second major naturalistic icon from potential candidates of holding Absolute Truth. Thus, strike two against the major icons we will examine.

The Recurring Question. Only one question remains: If Darwin's Tree of Life has been proven to be false—and even Darwin predicted that it might fail with new fossil discoveries—why is this theory still taught in schools as if it were Absolute Truth?

Blatant Lies with Haeckel's Embryos

Next, we will examine the credibility of Haeckel's embryonic drawings to determine whether or not they actually support Darwinism. Haeckel's embryos are also being used in textbooks as factual evidence in support of Darwinism (a theory that we have just proven to be false). We will look into the discoveries that Dr. Wells (an expert embryologist) found when he was doing his graduate work for his doctorate degree in vertebrate embryology.

While Dr. Wells was doing his graduate work, he began comparing actual photographs of embryos to what Haeckel had drawn. What he noticed will be shocking—especially if you have not heard what the experts have known for years.

Dr. Wells discovered that the actual photographs and the drawings that Haeckel made had an enormous discrepancy. At first, Dr. Wells tried to rationalize his findings by telling himself that textbooks tend to oversimplify things, but as he continued his work, it became more and more bothersome. Dr. Wells ultimately found three major discrepancies with these drawings that should render you speechless as to how they ever made it into our public school system's curriculum.

1. The first problem with the embryos is that the similarities in the early stages were faked (fudged, distorted, misleading—or whatever term you want to use to drive the point home). "Apparently in some cases

Haeckel actually used the same woodcut to print embryos from different classes because he was so confident of his theory that he figured he didn't have to draw them separately. In other cases, he doctored the drawings to make them look more similar than they really are. At any rate, his drawings misrepresent the embryos."[80]

If fact, these discrepancies were first exposed in the late 1860s, and his colleagues accused him of fraud! Think about that for a minute: for almost one hundred and fifty years scientists have willingly and knowingly been propagating a fudged representation of the truth. Even worse, the science was incorrect, and those working with Haeckel accused him of intentionally distorting the truth. Astonishingly, when the problems are brought up, people (like Jay Gould from Harvard) would get upset and complain that this is nothing new—it's no secret to the experts.[81] All the scientists know, but it has somehow managed to slip under the radar, and the public was left out of the loop.

2. The second problem we find is that Haeckel "cherry-picked" his examples and ultimately stacked the deck in his favor when he made his selection of which embryos to draw. Haeckel only shows a few of the seven vertebrate embryos, and he excludes any evidence that would go against his theory. As Dr. Wells explains, in his interview with Lee Strobel:

> His most famous rendition has eight columns. Four are mammals, but they're all placental mammals. There are two other kinds of mammals that he didn't show, which are *different*. The remaining four classes he showed—reptiles, birds, amphibian and fish—happen to be more similar than the ones he omitted. He used a salamander to represent amphibians instead of a frog, which looks very different. So he stacked the deck by picking representatives that came closest to fitting his ideas—and then he went further by faking the similarities.[82]

3. The third and most dramatic problem is that the "early stages" that Haeckel claimed were similar are not even close to the early stages

80 Ibid., 48.

81 Stephen Jay Gould, "Abscheulich! (atrocious!): Haeckel's distortions did not help Darwin," *Natural History* 109 (March 2000): 42–49.

82 Ibid., 49 (italics added).

of development. They were actually the *midpoint* of development. Dr. Wells explains that if you go back to the earlier stages of the embryos, the embryos vastly differ from one another, but Haeckel conveniently omitted these differences and used the midpoint of their development (where they were most similar). Then Haeckel falsely claimed that the midpoint of development was the early stages in his presentation.

This is a significant part in our analysis that must be addressed because Haeckel's failure to present the entire story has enabled Naturalists to use his drawings to support Darwinism. If the actual earliest stages of the embryos were used, then they would have contradicted Darwin's theory because Darwin claimed that embryos are most similar in their early stages.

Once again, if Haeckel's embryonic drawings are false—and they have been proven fraudulent for almost one hundred and fifty years—the recurring question shows up again: Why are the embryos still used in our classrooms and in our textbooks as if they were *factual* evidence that supports Darwinism (which has been proven to be false)? Does it bother you that what we teach our children is wrong and that it actually compels them towards atheism?

We can go ahead and conclude that Haeckel's drawings are completely false. They were never true; his colleagues accused him of fraud many years ago, and the drawings do not at all depict the similarity embryos have in their early stages. A blatant lie has unfortunately been misrepresented as truth in the scientific community and used to propagate a naturalistic perspective of life. The results of our investigation have led us to strike three in the evolutionary icons.

Does Truthful Science Matter? For years, these inconvenient truths have somehow been overlooked (or ignored) by the scientists, textbook publishers, and school systems. Even more tragic, these theories have already been proved false many years ago, but they are still presented in some our children's textbooks as if they were empirical facts. As a result, the truth has not been accurately communicated in our public school systems for decades. What kind of message is being sent to students, and does it alter their religious faith?

These textbooks have a powerful influence on students, and the teachers are forced to teach the material regardless of whether they agree with the content or not. What our kids are taught in school undoubtedly impacts their views on the concept of a living God and whether the idea is even feasible. Once again, if you doubt the impact schools have on the opinions of students, just ask Lee Strobel. Strobel's entire theological faith was molded by the inaccurate science that he was presented in a high school biology class.[83]

I thought America wanted to prevent religious doctrine from being *propagated* in the public school system. I thought that was the issue when the liberal progressives vehemently objected to creationism being taught in school. It appears as if Naturalism has all the characteristics of a religion, but is it actually a religion? If so, why do we allow this religion to be propagated? Chapter 15 establishes Naturalism as a religion, based on self-incriminating evidence, court decisions and through the application of the definition of religion. However, before this issue can be addressed, the major points in this chapter need to be tied together, and Naturalism must be established as *logical* suicide in Chapter 6. In Part Four, the double standard will be exposed.

The Sum of Naturalism's Science. In our examination, we have discovered that the truth has been misrepresented for many years, and it continues to be misrepresented today. Dr. Wells further elaborates as to why all ten of naturalism's icons are wrong in his book, *Icons of Evolution*. This chapter was not designed to be an exhaustive list with detailed explanations of every scientific shortcoming within Naturalism; rather, our goal has been to offer enough information to debar it from being a candidate for Absolute Truth.

Also, keep in mind that the purpose of this argument was not to disprove the concept of evolution in itself. The purpose was to disprove Naturalism, the theory that rejects God. Evolution is a broad topic that incorporates an array of ideas such as macro- and microevolution. We know microevolution is true because it can be demonstrated through the breeding of dogs to specific height, weight, personality, physical traits, and so forth. On the other hand, macroevolution is opinion, speculation, and conjecture. It has not been proven beyond a shadow of a doubt, and this belief is supported by Roger Lewin, an award-winning author and former editor with *Science* and *New Scientist* magazines. Lewin summarized a historic scientific conference on macroevolution: "The central question … was whether the mechanisms underlying microevolution can be extrapolated to explain the phenomenon of macroevolution. At the risk of doing violence

83 Ibid., 19.

to the position of some people at the meeting, the answer can be given as a clear, No."[84]

The Evolution Tangent. Evolution is a sensitive subject to many different people, and—since we do not have sufficient knowledge of the *precise method* by which mankind came into existence or *when*—we will not attempt to give any such explanation. In the Bible, God revealed that He created mankind; that is a fact that cannot be argued, but we also note that God refrained from revealing the method by which humans were created or how long the process took.

Granted, the Bible states mankind was created out of "dust from the ground," but that refers to the origin "You are dust, and to dust you shall return."[85] The Bible seems to reference the final product of mankind before God "breathed into his nostrils the breath of life; and man became a living *soul*."[86] The "soul" is what differentiates mankind from every other living being, however the question of precisely *how* is left unanswered because the Bible does not explicitly reveal the exact method. God could have created mankind in an instant or through the passage of any other time. We also need to note that the universe *was* created out of nothing, but mankind was created out of dust—molecules that already existed. This is a critical point because it implies that mankind came from that which was already created rather than from *nothing*. Furthermore, the Genesis account reveals that God "formed" the man from the dust (Genesis 2:7). Formed in this context could refer to a process by which humankind was created. Just as a potter forms the clay into a final product, God could have formed humankind through a process *if* that is how God chose to create humans (before they were given a soul). It is my opinion that evolution is rejected by Christians because it diminishes human life or contradicts the Bible, but neither appears to be true in my eyes.

God is all-powerful and could have created in any way He desired. If God wanted to evolve His creation and then sanctify mankind as the ultimate creation (mankind was sanctified and without sin before the fall), was God not able to accomplish this objective *if* this was how He wanted to create? I say *if* because we, again, do not know how God created; we only know that He did.

84 Roger Lewin, "Evolutionary Theory Under Fire," *Science* 210 (November 1980).

85 Genesis 2:7; 3:19.

86 Genesis 2:7 KJV (emphasis added).

Undoubtedly, evolution is the fuel that has propelled atheists to reject the concept of God with even more tenacity. Their view is that where evolution begins, Christianity ends—but is this really the case? Darwinism appears to have been defeated by the Cambrian explosion, but does that mean that theistic evolution must also be thrown out? I would say no. Theistic evolution is not an outlandish idea, consider the words of a few *Christian* biologists with respect to evolution. Kenneth Miller writes, "Evolution is as much a fact as anything we know in science."[87] Theodosius Dobzhansky states, "Nothing in biology makes sense except in the light of evolution."[88] These men undoubtedly recognize the power of God, but they also have wisdom as they have refrained from limiting God.

It begins to look as though Naturalists and agnostics may have to retreat and invent some more ideas to rationalize their refusal to accept the obvious fact that God *exists*, He is all-powerful, He could have evolved His creation, and such evolution is not discredited through Scripture. (That statement may be premature because I would not expect the Naturalist, agnostic or pantheist to believe until Chapter 7 when the arguments for God's existence are presented as *necessary*.)

For a moment I digress because covering this topic now will preempt an extreme view in the opposite direction; the view that all science is evil or that science is to be completely rejected. On the contrary, science must not be disregarded without first checking the facts. At the same time science is not the final authority; the Holy Bible is the final authority. I dare to suggest that if we build entirely accurate biblical presuppositions, never waver from them, but objectively analyze science, it will become more and more clear that science can turn out to be a major ally for the Christian faith. Together, the Bible and science can disprove all who come against the faith as accurate science reveals Absolute Truth.

Returning to the Original Topic. As interesting as this topic may be, we must continue to move forward in our *Quest for Absolute Truth.* We will now move from scientific evidence and theory, to whether or not Naturalism is a belief in which logical and thinking people can place their faith.

Recapping this chapter, it has been demonstrated that Naturalism is a belief that attempts to explain everything without recourse to spiritual or supernatural explanation. Naturalism has a very pessimistic tone that will

87 Cited by David Sloan Wilson, *Darwin's Cathedral: Evolution, Religion, and the Nature of Society* (Chicago: University of Chicago Press, 2003), 7.

88 Ibid.

eventually lead to chaos, as there would be no absolutes with respect to morality or judgment. From Naturalism, we see how many popular beliefs take root. However, the facts need to be examined, since opinion, feelings, and popularity do not in themselves constitute an adequate foundation for truth.

The three fundamental icons that Naturalism rests upon were presented, and each was disproved because they either distorted, secretly covered up, or ignored the truth. Sure, the truth may have been inconvenient, but Naturalism's science was entirely wrong. Now that a consistent pattern of appeals to incorrect science is obvious, deceit has opened up *all the beliefs* of Naturalism to much greater scrutiny. Naturalism now has a track record of dishonesty; this fact cannot be denied, justified, or sanctified. Thus far, science cannot prove Naturalism to be true, nor can it disprove God.

I am reminded of a proverb written thousands of years ago:

Truthful lips endure forever,
but a lying tongue lasts only a moment. (Proverbs 12:19)

Chapter 6

Some Say "Logic Proves There is No God"

"In their pride the wicked do not seek him; in all their thoughts there is no room for God."

—Psalms 14:4 (TNIV)

"If you are on the wrong road, progress means doing an about-turn and walking back to the right road; and in that case the man who turns back the soonest is the most progressive man."

—C. S. Lewis

The Logical Fallacy

The Unprovable Position. As we reflect on the previous chapter, it has become obvious that the scientific evidence in support of Naturalism is simply not an accurate representation of the truth. In addition to examining the scientific proof, we must also come to a conclusion on whether Naturalism is logical.

The second major fundamental flaw with Naturalism is that it does not make logical sense to logical people. It is impossible for Naturalists to prove their position beyond a shadow of a doubt. Naturalism is an unprovable position because it is also trying to establish a belief system that grounds itself on attempting to prove a negative.[89] As mentioned in

89 Unprovable. Dictionary.com. *Dictionary.com Unabridged.* Random House, Inc. http://dictionary.reference.com/browse/unprovable (accessed: September 24, 2009).

Chapter 3, proving a negative is virtually *impossible* because of the fact that the Naturalist must either be all-knowing or prove that the existence of God is an intrinsically impossible idea. Neither option is plausible because the existence of God is possible and mankind is physically unable to disprove God's existence because the human mind is finite.

In fact, the existence of God is entirely possible and this chapter is dedicated to demonstrating the necessity of God's existence with a touch logic, a dash of common sense and a pinch of the "inconvenient truth." Indeed, it would be absurd to completely discard a logical explanation (God exists) simply because it does not fit into a *specific agenda* (Naturalism's horrifying motive is presented in Chapter 15).

Simple Questions, No Answers. The Naturalist also has a difficult time answering very basic and simple questions that the theist is able to explain by relying on the existence of a higher being who holds absolute power. The Naturalist struggles with questions such as: How does something come from nothing? How does nothing produce everything? How can non-life produce life? How can randomness produce fine-tuning? How does chaos produce information? How can unconsciousness produce consciousness? How would it be possible to establish right from wrong? Furthermore, *who* would determine right from wrong when all of mankind is inherently sinful?

Historically, Naturalists have looked down upon the theist, but what have Naturalists proven with respect to spiritual answers? If anything, they have proven that they can *change* their theories as fast as technology advances or as often as new discoveries are made, but theists are able to firmly maintain their position. Ironically, science is now starting to prove the theist's position as the pendulum is swinging heavily in favor of God. This change has occurred because scientists may understand the details of how solar systems, galaxies, and life function, but they have yet to explain the overall picture of how they came into existence. In fact, without including *God*, the Naturalist cannot explain the unexplainable!

Let's look at one theory that the Naturalist holds, the big bang theory. According to this theory, the universe expanded from an extremely dense and hot state at a discrete point in time, at which (in this theory) time actually began. Since this explosion, our universe continues to expand today. According to this theory, the universe is not eternal; it had a precise beginning point in which everything was created. The problem with a beginning point is not only that everything was created (came into existence), but also the question of *what* initiated creation. The Naturalist cannot explain *where* the matter came from or what started this chain of events.

From scientific research, we know that matter is neither created nor destroyed (though within stars and in atomic weapons, it can be transformed into energy). The only changes, in regard to matter, are different arrangements of atoms that already exist. Since the initial creation, matter is neither created nor destroyed, only rearranged. Based on this understanding, we can assume there is only so much matter that the universe has to work with, but the question of where it all came from still lingers and has become rather troublesome for the Naturalist. Even more troublesome are the presuppositions on which a Naturalist must rely.

Naturalism's Presuppositions

Understanding the Foundational Beliefs. The naturalistic ideology centers upon some bold and audacious beliefs. These beliefs are not optional; if the presuppositions begin to change, the viewpoint begins to shift and can transform into other views such as deism, agnosticism, or theism. The very essence of Naturalism is found within these fundamental presuppositions:[90]

1. Nothing produces everything.
2. Non-life produces life.
3. Randomness produces fine-tuning.
4. Chaos produces information.
5. Unconsciousness produces consciousness.
6. Non-reason produces reason.

The question is whether these beliefs make logical sense to logical people apart from the concept of an intelligent designer. Essentially, is it really possible for a rock to evolve into a person if given enough "time" and enough "chances"? Frankly, the process of a nonliving object transforming into something that has life seems fishy and appears to be unlikely—unless, somewhere in the equation, a profound miracle is incorporated. These are not some peon miracles that chance can explain; the appearance of life itself is a miracle that has defied the very laws of science.

---

90 Lee Strobel, *Case for a Creator* (Grand Rapids, MI: Zondervan, 2004), 277.

This question, and many others like them, stem from the basic presuppositions that Naturalism must assume. This section will look deeper into each of the six presuppositions and examine whether they are logical beliefs in which logical people can confidently place their faith.

1. Nothing Produces Everything. The only way something could come from nothing is through the divine intervention of a higher being. A leap of this magnitude would constitute a miracle within itself. Zero multiplied by any other number—even 1,000,000,000,000,000,000,000—will always, always equal zero. Therefore, it does not matter how many planets, moons, stars, or galaxies there are in the universe because the sum of everything multiplied by *nothing* will always equal zero. In the beginning, there was nothing. Therefore, it is not feasible to attribute creation to chance, because there was nothing with which chance could work; nothing existed.

The question then becomes: "How do we make the giant first leap into having something when there was nothing?" It would be possible to explain how everything developed into the current state if the universe had always existed, but we know that it had a beginning point. Anything that has a beginning point depends upon something else for its cause or creation; otherwise it would not have had a beginning point. Even though scientists now believe that the universe, and everything in existence today, came from an infinitesimally small point before the big bang, the theory still raises the question: where did that infinitesimally small, dense clump of matter come from?

The only feasible conclusion of such a question comes from the principle of contingent and necessary beings, which stems from the cosmological argument (which we will explore in depth when discussing theism in Chapter 7). Dr. Winfried Corduan, in his book *No Doubt About It*, explains that a necessary being is "totally independent of anything else" while a contingent being is "dependent on something else." A necessary being would be God (the Creator), while the contingent being is everything else (that which was created). If you were to logically think about these two properties, you would have to conclude that they are mutually exclusive: any given object is either one or the other but never both, for that would be an impossibility within itself. Just as you are either alive or dead but never both, everything in existence is either the created or the Creator.

In addition to being dependent, a contingent being displays the property that its potential has been actualized. The world had the potential to exist and, since it exists, the potential was actualized. At this point, we must note that a potential is never able to actualize itself regardless of how perfect the scenario may be. An empty coffee cup that sits next to a pot of coffee has the potential to be filled, but it will never be filled unless the potential is actualized by an external force.

Just as a coffee cup can never actualize its own potential, a contingent being could never come into existence of its own accord. The potential of existence must be actualized by a necessary (completely independent) being. Independence of the necessary being is stressed because in order for any potential to be actualized, there has to be an initiator, otherwise potential would always remain a potential. The coffee cup could be filled, but without the independent force (distinct and separate from the cup and the coffee pot), potential could never be actualized.

Furthermore, dependents cannot cause their own existence, just as the coffee cup did not create itself. We know this to be true because the coffee cup did not exist until it was created and thus could not have been a contributing factor to its own existence. This principle is applicable whether we are describing a coffee cup, the conception of a baby, or the creation of the universe. It is only logical to believe that there is nothing which can cause its own existence.

This concept can be explained by the fact that your existence was caused, to a large extent, by your parents. Your parents were caused by their parents (and so forth), and this relation is applicable to all dependent beings. We can examine how this pattern replicates itself, until we come to the very beginning, in which there was only potential. We must also note, however, that infinite regression also does not solve the problem because it ultimately leads back to the beginning (creation), and that is the question we are trying to answer.

Since a potential is never able to actualize itself, there must be an external force to initiate the process of actualization. *Nothing* could exist unless there were an external force to initiate the original creation. As a result of this principle, it would be physically impossible—and absurd—to think that something could come from nothing all by itself. Unless a Creator is included in the equation, any answer is consequently insufficient. As a result, we can confidently conclude that the concept of nothing producing everything is simply not logical, nor is it a belief in which intelligent and thinking people can confidently place their faith.

2. Non-Life Produces Life. In order to describe how non-life could possibly produce life, we need to continue our discussion of contingent and necessary beings.

Since we can conclude that a contingent being is a caused being, we must also conclude that a contingent being could not continue to exist if not for certain sustaining causes (e.g., human beings are dependent upon food and water in order to continue their existence). Contingent beings are also determined in that they not only get their raw existence from an external cause, they also receive the specification of their existence from an external cause. This is explained by the fact that you were not able to determine your race, your sex, or the family in which you were born; you are what you are as a result of external factors.

At this point, we need to elaborate on the concept of a necessary being. A necessary being is one that does not fit into the category of being caused, sustained, or determined. This implies that a necessary being would have to be uncaused and unsustained by anything outside itself and that it is undetermined by external factors. A necessary being's existence is completely *independent* of everything else that exists. This becomes obvious when we note that God exists not because you exist, but that the reverse is true: you exist because God exists.

Based on the characteristics of a necessary being, we can easily conclude that a necessary being has to be one that bears the attributes of God. A necessary being would be independent, unlimited (all-powerful, all-knowing, all-present, all-loving, and so forth), infinite, eternal, unchangeable, and pure actuality (without unfulfilled potential) and would possess all these properties to an infinite degree.[91]

Since creation is the result of a potential that was actualized at some point in the past, everything, by definition, must be the result of an actualized potential that could only have been caused by an entity that was entirely separate from creation—a necessary being (God). Some people claim that the world we live in is a necessary being. This is the idea of pantheism, discussed in Chapter 4. The reason that the world in which we live cannot be a necessary being is that this claim contradicts itself. It has already been established that the world we live in cannot possibly be unlimited, infinite, eternal, or unchangeable, so it cannot be categorized as a necessary being.

91 Winfried Corduan, *No Doubt about It* (Nashville, TN: Broadman and Holdman Publishers, 1997), 113.

In the same argument, one must also concede that only one necessary being can exist. To say that there are multiple necessary beings would also be self-defeating and contradictory, because they must differ from one another in order to be distinguishable. If two necessary beings were not distinguishable, then they would ultimately be the same being; if they differed from one another, then they could not possess all the properties that they need in order to be a necessary being (thus making at least one of them contingent). This implies that, by definition of a necessary being, there can only be *one* God.

The purpose in elaborating on the concept of a necessary being is to emphasize the necessity of that being's existence. An understanding of the concept enables us to conclude: unless there were a necessary being, life could not exist. Life is the product of creation, which can only be explained through the influence of a divine external influence. Even if the Naturalists bypass the real answer to the first presupposition (something came from nothing), they run into another fatal problem: a living organism vastly differs from that which has never been alive. There are insurmountable differences that cannot possibly be linked together unless a miracle is incorporated, but Naturalism rejects any idea of the supernatural.

Even if you were to assume that the earth, sun, stars, and galaxies already existed, until life appeared, all you would have is non-living matter. It makes logical sense to assert that life could only have appeared after the creation of the earth, but the issue is *how* life came into existence when there was nothing alive. It is not possible for something that does not have life to develop into something that is living, unless a miracle occurred. Life is not a result of a chance or a mathematical equation.

Furthermore, the trait of life cannot be passed from an entity that does not have life. You already understand this principle because you know that if you do not have the AIDS virus, you cannot possibly pass it to your children. If you do not have a trait, regardless of what it may be, it is impossible for you to pass it along, regardless of what people may tell you. Even if you have a trait, or gene, that does not directly affect you (such as albinism), you still possess the gene in your DNA and are *able* to pass it along. If you did not have the trait, you could not possibly pass it along, and that is the thrust of the argument.

The understanding of this principle demonstrates how it is impossible for the nonliving to develop into that which is living by natural processes alone *unless* an external force intervened and caused the miracle that occurred. Ironically, the argument of non-life producing life ultimately reverts back to "something from nothing" (an offshoot of "nothing produces everything") because there was a moment, a point in time, where life did not exist, and then, in the next moment, life existed.

These topics are very complex, and we cannot possibly understand everything in regard to how life came into existence, but we can confidently conclude that life cannot be the result of natural processes *alone.* Naturalism distances itself from miracles because the very core of its ideology attempts to explain everything in the absence of God. One of the fundamental flaws with this ideology is that it cannot account for life and how the transition was made from matter that was not living to even the simplest life forms; such as bacteria or single-celled organisms.

The concept is impossible and is not logical unless some type of intelligent designer (necessary being) is added into the equation. As a result, this presupposition is both discredited and negated from being able to constitute truth.

3. Randomness Produces Fine-Tuning. Let's take, for example, the notion that randomness produces fine-tuning and apply it to an everyday scenario that is far less complex than the creation of life. In this example we will discover whether the act of fine-tuning is possible without an intelligent designer in the equation. This example can be explained through the simplistic process of cooking.

Suppose you were to take a rather simple recipe, such as the recipe used to make white bread, and apply to this process the same principles that some Naturalists have applied to the creation of life. Even though we know cooking is certainly not as complex as the creation of life, the simplification of this scenario is used to drive the point home. If this principle does not make sense on a very simplistic level, how much more absurd would it be to use the principles on a level where scientists even struggle to understand basic concepts?

Even though we have brought the level of simplicity down from describing how the universe transitioned from randomness to a fine-tuned entity to an example as simple as cooking, we will simplify even further to quickly demonstrate the thrust and the absurdity of the argument.

We will go ahead and put together all the right ingredients to make white bread, making sure that they are in the exact quantities that the recipe calls for. We will add the flour, active dry yeast, milk, sugar, butter, and salt to the mixing bowl, but we do nothing more. We do not mix, stir, or intervene in any other way except to locate the ingredients in a single bowl.

At this stage in the process, it would be fair to say that all we have thus far is haphazardness because we don't have anything that could possibly resemble food. (I can imagine the critics responding with "That's not random, you put all the ingredients in the bowl!" An excellent observation. Whether anything is actually random is debatable because we do not know whether what we *perceive* to be random is actually part of an overarching goal or a means to an end.) Nevertheless, for the sake of argument, we will assume that the contents are random because we do not have anything that resembles any type of food; everything is currently in a state of disarray.[92]

Up until this point, this collection of ingredients does not resemble anything that is fine-tuned, even though we have all the right ingredients, in their precise quantities, in the right place, at the right time, and in the right conditions so that they might be made into bread.

Now that we have set up the scenario, let's let those ingredients sit in the mixing bowl status quo, and let's ponder the probability of them mixing themselves together on their own accord to produce the dough needed to produce the final product, delicious white bread. Let the ingredients sit overnight. What do you see in the morning? Did the ingredients decide to mix themselves yet? Did the potential actualize itself? Maybe we did not provide enough time for the natural processes to work their magic, so we let them sit an entire week and come back to check if the ingredients have mixed themselves.

After a week we see that the ingredients have not yet been mixed, although they may have changed a little. They are starting to spoil. (But that was inevitable because everything changes. Which is another interesting fact to ponder. If there were once potential for the existence of the universe, did the potential have to actualize within a specific time frame just as the dough needed to be mixed before it spoiled? We know that all contingent beings inevitably change, and if there were a specific time period in which potential had to be actualized, it would further complicate Naturalism's presuppositions.)

Nevertheless, do you think the ingredients would mix themselves on their own accord if we left them alone for two weeks? A month? A year? Ten years? A thousand years? A billion years? Is there any amount of time that must elapse before the ingredients mix themselves on their

92 Disarray: a lack of order or sequence; disorder, confusion.

own precisely as the recipe calls for? These ingredients have the potential to make dough and eventually a delicious batch of bread—a fine-tuned product—but does a potential ever have the ability to actualize itself?

The answer should be obvious; no amount of time will bring these ingredients together without the action of an *intelligent designer*. The intelligent designer (in this case, the chef) must initiate every single step of the process, from beginning to end, until the final product is created. Furthermore, we note that the chef is a separate entity from that which is being creating. Granted, they are both contingent beings, but the point is that the potential was actualized by an intelligent designer and by an external force that was separate from that which was created. Why does that point matter?

Randomness is never able to produce a fine-tuned product because the intelligent designer is required to select very specific ingredients, put them in precise quantities, mix them together to create the dough, and then carry out other steps (such as kneading the dough, shaping the dough, placing it in a pan, and baking it) to realize the intended outcome. The intelligent designer controls when, how fast, and where this process took place. In fact, this scenario perfectly illustrates that nothing can be done without the intelligent designer because no amount of time, or chance, will create the bread (the final product).

How much more complicated are the biological functions of cells, human life, the orbits of our planets and moons, and the entire collection of galaxies that reflect an extraordinarily fine-tuned universe? The intelligent designer was paramount to moving the process along and creating the fine-tuned product. Consider how basic principles still apply to even the most complex functions.

In math, the *basics* are addition, subtraction, multiplication, and division. These basic mathematical operations do not change regardless of whether they are used in algebra, trigonometry, or even calculus. In these subjects, the rudimentary principles are established so the student is able to build and learn far more complex variations and applications. Would it not be logical to apply the exact same principles (randomness is incapable of producing a fine-tuned product apart from an intelligent designer) even to exponentially more complex issues? Would it not be logical to require an intelligent designer to usher in the transition from the random, primitive universe into the fine-tuned entity we see today?

Apart from an external force, randomness has never produced fine-tuning; and it never will. Why should we believe that such a claim, in regard to life and creation, is worthy of trust when it fails at the most basic level? Does the operation of addition change when it is used in calculus?

The question is whether or not "randomness produces fine-tuning" is a valid presupposition in which people can confidently place their faith. Is it logical to believe this presupposition when it refuses to include the most important factor (the intelligent designer)? Would it not be more logical to at least believe in something that makes more sense than pure speculation, attached to an unknown probability, which may have come about due to forces that the Naturalist cannot even *begin* to explain? As a result, this presupposition also fails and cannot be considered Absolute Truth.

4. Chaos Produces Information. Chaos producing information is similar to randomness producing fine-tuning: neither make sense unless an intelligent designer is added to the equation. The difference between the two, in their definitions, is that *randomness* does not have definite aim, reason, or pattern (it is by chance); *chaos* is a state of disorder and a total lack of organization. They are similar, but not the same. Likewise, the end results are different because *fine-tuning* is the making of minor adjustments to produce stability, improvement, or achievement of a precise result, whereas *information* is knowledge, or an understanding, of that which is communicated or received. Through the understanding of these definitions, how could a state of utter confusion possibly transform into something that is intelligible?

First, in order to have chaos, there has to be something that was created. If nothing existed, then it could not possibly be in disarray. As we have already stated, a potential can never actualize itself; therefore, in order to have chaos, some potential must have been actualized. Since the specific chaos we are referencing was presupposed at the beginning of creation, we can automatically negate the possibility of any human being having any influence on the outcome. In fact, the very existence of all dependent beings (humans, animals, plants, etc.) depends on the transformation of this *chaos* into information so that the genetic code of DNA could be written. (As a result, every living organism that needs DNA is also excluded from being able to participate in this process.) Plants, animals, and humans alike need DNA to provide a blueprint of what the cells are instructed to build. Without this essential collection of information, life could not exist.

If all living dependent beings rely on this vital ingredient—DNA—to sustain life, then the only possible entity that could have turned chaos into information is a necessary being entirely separate from the process. This is intuitive because DNA is the basic building block of life, and nothing living could have helped create that which is necessary to be alive! This revelation takes us back to the issues of non-life producing life and randomness producing fine-tuning but ultimately back to nothing producing everything. (For some strange reason, every time we turn a corner to tackle another issue, we run into the Creator......) Nevertheless, a necessary being is the intelligent designer that ultimately guides the transformation of chaos into something that is intelligent and communicable—information.

Through the example of cooking, we have established that randomness, without an intelligent designer, cannot produce a fine-tuned product. Likewise, chaos cannot produce an intelligible product unless intelligence is incorporated into the equation. (Recall that the very definition of information reflects knowledge and the ability to communicate, which demands intelligence.) Intelligence is a trait that is commonly used to describe a living entity. (*Who am I kidding? It is only used to reference the living*!) Something that is not alive cannot have intelligence. Would it not sound silly and outrageous to say to your friend while walking on a nature trail, "Wow, look at that intelligent rock." Likewise, it would be outrageous to suggest that rocks (the non-living) could create information (a product of intelligence) because possibly, through some unknown chance, they might have communicated with one another to create an intelligible product (e.g. life, music, DNA or even the coherent organization of information).

This is the absurdity that Naturalism propagates. It is not coherent to teach that non-living matter could have created a genetic code (as randomness was being fine-tuned) that not only is intelligible, but communicates precise instructions to living cells. We know this is what Naturalists endorse because they have no way to get around the idea that non-life created life; even the simplest life forms, bacteria, depend on DNA for their existence.[93]

Naturalism cannot explain how chaos miraculously transformed into information through natural processes alone. The fine-tuned product of information screams intelligence. Intelligence is a characteristic of the living, but when DNA was being created, nothing could have been alive (except for a necessary being, who was separate from creation). There is a major gap between the original state and the final product, and naturalism

---

93 MSN Encarta, "Genetics," http://encarta.msn.com/text_761574409___42/bacteria.html.

cannot bridge it, refusing to add to its argument the one variable that would make it logical: God.

Therefore, this presupposition is negated from being considered a belief in which logical and thinking people can place their faith. It would take far more faith to believe that the non-living rocks created and organized information than to simply acknowledge the dire need for the existence of God.

5. Unconsciousness Produces Consciousness. If we were to accept this naturalistic presupposition, then consciousness (the mind) must have, at some point, evolved from a simplistic mechanism into the complex one we know and use today. In order to fully grasp the importance of this topic, we need to first define *unconsciousness* and *consciousness.*

Unconsciousness is the state of *not knowing or perceiving.* A rock, for example, does not have consciousness because the rock is not aware of its existence. Since the rock is not aware that it is a rock, it cannot communicate that information to any other rocks. Consciousness, on the other hand, *is* the state of knowing or perceiving. Human beings are conscious because they are aware of their existence. The dictionary goes a step farther and provides some of the characteristics of consciousness, including sensation, emotion, volition, and thought.[94]

Now that the terms have their definitions, we will try to understand whether it is feasible for consciousness to stem from unconsciousness by natural processes alone. Is it logical to suggest that the human mind, our consciousness, could have possibly evolved from lower life forms apart from any intelligent designer?

The thought of unconscious, primitive matter being able to *evolve* into complex, conscious matter is a sharp debate that continues today. On one hand you have Darwinists, such as Thomas Huxley, proclaiming, "Mind is a function of matter, when that matter has attained a certain degree of organization."[95] And on the other side, people like Dr. J. P. Moreland claim that "There will never be a scientific explanation for mind and consciousness."[96]

Before moving forward, I would like to note that Huxley was correct in his observation, but it is the underlying idea and the subtle message he

94 Consciousness. Dictionary.com. *Dictionary.com Unabridged.* Random House, Inc. http://dictionary.reference.com/browse/consciousness (accessed: April 28, 2009).

95 Thomas Huxley, "Mr. Darwin's Critics," *Contemporary Review* (November 1871).

96 Strobel, 268

conveyed to which I object. Mind is a function of matter; that's intuitive, because all contingent beings are made up of matter. In addition to the mind being comprised of matter, I concede that *the mind has also attained a certain degree of organization.* Again, we are stating the obvious; the mind is a highly complex entity that has an astronomical degree of organization. Where the train runs off the track is the fact that Huxley, as a Darwinist, did not allow the *possibility* of an intelligent designer anywhere in the process. We agree on the facts, but in how we arrive at the final product we strongly disagree. Huxley's position is that it is not only possible, but probable, that consciousness was able to develop from unconsciousness apart from any concepts of God.

The second quotation, by J. P. Moreland, does an excellent job explaining our understanding of the transition from unconscious to conscious. Science may never know precisely how, when, and where consciousness first appeared. Even though we may not know all the details, we are able come to a conclusion in regard to the overall concept.

Distinguishing Consciousness from the Body. As we look into the topic of consciousness, some of the supporting evidence will come from an interview between Lee Strobel and J. P. Moreland in *The Case for a Creator.* After examining some parts of the interview, we will take the information and tie it into what we already know to be true.

First, we must establish the fact that consciousness and the body are two completely different entities, yet they work together harmoniously. We can illustrate this point by using an example of a head injury that ultimately resulted in memory loss.

Assume you were to have a bad accident, lose consciousness and, as a result of the accident, lose your entire memory of everything beforehand. When you woke up, it would not be reasonable to conclude that you were a different person even though you might not remember your name, family, or accomplishments. Despite the trauma and the tragedy, you would remain the same person. Even if your personality were to entirely change, you would still have the same body and would utilize the same mind, even though they may have been altered.

The concept of the body and consciousness being separate entities is further illustrated by a hypothetical example of searching for the ego (or self). If we could take a living person and separate all of his or her cells from one another, without hurting or killing the person, and examine each single cell, we would never find the person's soul or consciousness.

We could not look into one cell and conclude, "Within this cell is where thoughts are stored" or "Within this cell is where feelings are stored." The same concept is applicable to a person's memory, morals, and so forth. If we were to pull apart every cell and look into each, we could never find a person's consciousness because it is entirely separate from the physical body.

Conscious Problems. Consciousness is separate from the body, which poses a major problem to the Naturalist because of this simple principle: "If you apply a physical process to physical matter, you will merely get a different arrangement of physical materials."[97]

The examples Dr. Moreland gave in his interview were simple, yet they drive the point home: if you apply heat (a physical process) to water, then you get steam (a physical result). You would never get a *nonphysical* result from a physical process because that is an entirely different type of progression.

The nonphysical is defined as "lacking substance or reality; incapable of being touched or seen; 'that intangible thing—the soul.'"[98] Consciousness, by definition, is nonphysical because it cannot be pinpointed, touched, or seen in itself. This intrinsically means that the method in which consciousness came into existence is not, and will never be, explained through *physical processes* alone (it's impossible).

If you had two dice and rolled them, you could have a number of possible combinations from each roll. You could assign a probability to each number combination, but you would never expect to roll a "13" with only two dice. Likewise, why should people expect the nonphysical to come from the physical or the intangible to come from the tangible? They are not possible, feasible, or analogous progressions.

The Naturalists are aware of this pesky reality, and they cannot stand to confront unexplainable evidence, because it inherently points towards an intelligent designer to explain the unexplainable (and this truth irritates them beyond belief). In fact, Naturalists have become so frustrated with recent discoveries that they are now trying to convince you that you do not have a consciousness and that you are a computer. Dr. Moreland explains:

---

97 Strobel, 264.

98 Nonphysical. Dictionary.com. *Dictionary.com Unabridged.* Random House, Inc. http://dictionary.reference.com/browse/nonphysical (accessed: April 29, 2009).

> However—and this is really important—if you begin with an *infinite* mind, then you can explain how finite minds could come into existence. That makes sense. What doesn't make sense—and which many atheistic evolutionists are conceding—is the idea of getting a mind to squirt into existence by starting with brute, dead, mindless matter. That's why some of them are trying to get rid of consciousness by saying it's not real and that we're just computers. However, that's a pretty difficult position to maintain while you're conscious.[99]

It is truly fascinating how people *create* ways to try and get around an obvious truth. The attempt to convince you that you are not conscious—*while you are aware of your existence*—does not advance objective science. In fact, objective science has seemed to have lost its way among *elite liberal scientists.* The Naturalists have an agenda, and they force scientific discoveries to fit within their specific objectives. If science does not fit within their objectives, then the truth is either distorted, changed, or simply not presented. Nevertheless, the thrust of the argument is that the concept of unconsciousness producing consciousness is not only impossible, but it is absurd. As a result, this is also not a logical belief in which people can confidently place their faith.

6. Non-Reason Produces Reason. Reason is defined as the mental powers concerned with forming conclusions, judgments, or inferences.[100] This presupposition is advanced because it is one that automatically assumes multiple miracles have already occurred.

First, the miracle of "something came from nothing" (creation) had to take place. Second, we must have had the miracle of "randomness producing fine-tuning" and "chaos producing information" so that the stage can be set for any complex organism to exist. Third, we have to have the miracle of "non-life producing life." We need a living organism in order to have reason because we know rocks do not think and cannot reason. Even when we get to a stage where there are living organisms, we cannot assume that life is the only prerequisite to being able to reason; countless plants are living, but they are also unable to think and cannot reason. Thus,

99 Strobel, 264.

100 Reason. Dictionary.com. *Dictionary.com Unabridged.* Random House, Inc. http://dictionary.reference.com/browse/reason (accessed: August 25, 2009).

in order to reason you must also have the miracle of "non-consciousness producing consciousness." As you have most likely noticed, the miracles keep building upon one another. Without the first miracle, none of the subsequent miracles could exist.

(Wow; it is truly amazing that we were not only lucky in just terms of creation; *we have been lucky throughout the entire process!* Every time a miracle was needed or where the impossible had to have occurred, luck was standing by to help us out. Think about it; out of all the potential outcomes and possibilities, our little solar system defied chance with luck each and every single time it was needed! If I won the lottery each week, every time I played, would that be considered chance as well?)

After the Miracle of Consciousness. Once we have a complex organism that has been created and fine-tuned and has come to life and is conscious, we can analyze the ability to reason. The ability to reason is the most advanced stage in creation because no other living organism, in the entire known universe, has the capabilities of the human mind. Of course, there are many intelligent animals, but none have the ability to draw conclusions, create judgment, or process information as do human beings. The human mind is truly unique when compared to even the most sophisticated mind of an animal; there is really no comparison to the difference in advancement.

Just think of everything that we humans have accomplished in our short span of existence on this earth. We have been able to understand mathematics, chemistry, physics, biology, cosmology, psychology, and countless other fields of study. We have constructed breathtaking monuments, cathedrals, temples, skyscrapers, and edifices that no other living organism has been able to build. We have the ability to reason and persuade one another through complex languages and systems of writing. We have been able to build economies and produce some of the finest music, art, drama, and literature. We have created computers and robots and have even established space stations. We also have the ability to annihilate an entire city with a nuclear weapon that can fit within a briefcase.

Human accomplishments are endless, but the Naturalists cannot explain how an organism can make the leap from not even being coherent to having the intelligence and the reasoning that human beings, alone, possess. This is a phenomenon that is unexplainable, but don't take my word; consider what Michael Ruse, a devout Naturalist, concedes on the issue: "No one, certainly not the Darwinian as such, seems to have any answer."[101]

Could it be that natural phenomena, guided by natural processes alone, have finally been stumped? Could it be that there is not a logical way that reason can be explained unless we incorporate an intelligent designer? Even Darwinists acknowledge that they do not have an answer. Once again, *even Darwinists acknowledge that they do not have an answer.* This is a major breakthrough for the Naturalists, because it seems some of them are finally beginning to realize that the answer is not feasible through natural processes alone. Just as it makes no sense to suggest that everything we see today is a result of mere chance or that I can win the lottery each and every time I play, it is not reasonable to assert that consciousness is a fluke.

Space stations, robots, and nuclear weapons did not appear by chance; they were engineered by some of the brightest and most intelligent minds in the world. If something as simple as a robot needs an intelligent designer, how much more do the complexities of the human mind scream that there is, in fact, an intelligent being who created us? The driving point is that it takes intelligence to create something that is intelligible (i.e. information).

The truth is that nobody can explain how or where consciousness came from, because it suddenly appeared. Nobody can replicate the results, because they surpass our understanding. When is the evidence against Naturalism enough? Naturalism certainly cannot give us an answer; if anything, it unnecessarily creates far more confusion when it refuses to recognize the existence of God. The miracle of "non-reason producing reason" is simply unexplainable when you negate the possibility of an intelligent designer.

The reason Naturalists refuse to provide an answer is because they also know that it takes intelligence to create something that is intelligible. Think about that for a moment: when something is created, it looks created. Creation often has personality and can reflect the character, and sometimes the feelings, of the creator. Paintings, sculptures, and other works of art are all different, but they reflect intelligence because they were designed and created. Even more interesting is the underlying reason why Naturalists refuse to address the issue: they simply say that they have no idea! In Chapter 15, we will examine whether science is truly unbiased

---

101 Dinesh D'Souza, *What's So Great about Christianity* (Washington, D.C.: Regnery Publishing, Inc., 2007), 149.

and whether Naturalism would ever withhold pertinent information in an attempt to push an agenda.

Nevertheless, how much more complicated are the biological functions of life, weather systems and the human body? Everywhere you look, you cannot help but see the fingerprints of intelligence and meticulous design. Earth is not some random and thrown-together clump of matter, a product of mere chance. It is quite the opposite and that becomes more and more obvious the more you learn about the earth and how everything within is extraordinarily complex and fine-tuned.

Therefore, we can confidently conclude that Naturalism does not have the answer; indeed, they have already acknowledged that fact. Let's help them take their statement one step farther by making the assertion that these numerous miracles were not—could not have possibly been—a product of mere chance. From logic, as well as Naturalism's self-incriminating evidence, we confidently conclude that this is also not a presupposition in which logical and thinking individuals can confidently place their faith.

The Final Nail in Naturalism's Coffin

Recapping the Major Facts. This has been an extraordinarily long topic, as it has taken two chapters to discredit, but this discussion is offered with the goal of revealing Naturalism's prevalence in our society and the dire need for the religion to not only be confronted, but ultimately removed. These two chapters demonstrate that Naturalism misrepresents the truth in science (Chapter 5), which has led to its illogical presuppositions (Chapter 6). Such a combination confirms that Naturalism is bankrupt as a source of spiritual truth or theological doctrine.

Let's recap the previous chapter. Miller's experiment was flawed because it was an inaccurate representation of the primitive atmosphere. In fact, when the experiment is run with what scientists now believe to be an accurate representation of the atmosphere, the results are lethal to any life that would have been present. Despite this revelation, the actual results are ignored and are not presented in some textbooks. Darwin's Tree of Life has been disproved by the Cambrian explosion (scientists cannot explain how the sudden changes appeared), but Darwinism is taught as if it were a fact. Haeckel's embryos were blatant lies, and his contemporaries accused him of fraud. Even though the embryos never represented the earliest stages of life and the drawings were manipulated, they still appear in science textbooks as support for Naturalism.

In this chapter, we explored whether Naturalism was a logical belief to which rational people could entrust their faith. We began by pointing out that Naturalism is trying to prove a negative—an impossible task. Proving a negative is impossible because human beings would either have to be all-knowing or would have to present the theory of God as an intrinsically impossible idea. The conclusion was that human beings cannot be all-knowing and that it is actually quite possible that God exists. In reality, the likelihood of God becomes more evident the more we examine Naturalism (a fact somehow frequently overlooked).

Next, we examined six basic presuppositions that the Naturalist must assume. We broke them down to discover their true meaning. The result of the examination leads to a confident conclusion that none of Naturalism's presuppositions are meaningful unless they incorporate a necessary being into the equation—and the only possible candidate for an entirely independent and uncaused being is God.

Through our analysis it appears as if Naturalism places a low priority on truth and is pursuing an ulterior motive. It appears as if Naturalism has an agenda to promote a specific theology[102] (or an opinion in regard to God), regardless of whether the information is entirely truthful or accurate. It is clear that Naturalism is not concerned with what the truth has to offer, but the real question deals with how its adherents will react as even more overwhelming evidence disproves their position. Would these scientists actually embrace madness before accepting an obvious truth? The answer to this seemingly outrageous question will soon be answered, but through our analysis, it is easy to see how, and where, Naturalism is fundamentally flawed. It does not take a genius to discover that faulty science leads to inaccurate presuppositions, which in turn lead to a misrepresentation of the truth, whether intentional or not.

It is interesting to note that the nineteenth and early twentieth century's greatest thinkers, according to progressives,[103] were Darwin, Freud, and Marx. Even more interesting, two of these "scientific" thinkers (Freud and Marx) have already fallen. The dwindling followers of Darwin, Freud, and Marx no longer claim that their insights were based on any methodology

---

102 Theology: the study of the nature of God and religious truth; rational inquiry into religious questions.

103 Progressive: One who advocates greater government regulation of just about anything. Progressives claim to want to help out the average Joe but really want everyone to live according to their politically correct, elitist socialist agenda. Progressives are also much nastier people than liberals, and are often hypocrites (urbandictionary.com).

remotely comparable to that of experimental science, and we may very well see the last of these "great thinkers" take a plunge into the history books as purveyors of fatally flawed ideas, but certainly nothing more.[104] Johnson dealt a fatal blow by pointing out the fragility Naturalism, "No one in our day should find it hard to believe that a cultural tower built on a materialist foundation can look extremely powerful one day and yet collapse in ruins the next."[105]

The truth shall set you free, but only when you accept the truth for what it is, refrain from distortion, and withhold nothing. At a minimum, scientists owe an honest and accurate representation of the facts.

Be Optimistic—The Glass Is Half Full

Naturalism Is Inherently Negative. Have you ever noticed that the Naturalist's outlook is inherently negative? When we take a look at the theist (one who believes in a heaven and hell) and compare that person's outlook to a Naturalist's (one who does not believe in a heaven or hell), the differences are astounding. A direct comparison of the two worldviews paints a clear picture that enables us to see why some Naturalists are very cynical; but even more important is understanding the root of Naturalism's pessimism. Understanding the root of a problem, or a negative perspective, opens up the possibility of presenting effective solutions that directly address the problem or the negative perspective.

Many times people try to fix a problem but cannot seem to make it permanently disappear. Days, weeks, or months later the problem returns, and they have to try to solve it again and again. Problems are like weeds: if you do not destroy the root then the weed keeps coming back. The weed will continue to come back until the root system has been destroyed. Likewise, we will search out the roots of Naturalism and how the very nature of the ideology has an inherently negative connotation. In our approach, we will work backward by finding what motivates and encourages people to persevere through the toughest of times. Some motivators are trivial, last a short while, and work only temporarily; others last a lifetime. It is the lifetime motivators that give the greatest meaning and drive to people as they live out their daily lives.

104 Phillip Johnson, *Defeating Darwinism* (Downers Grove, IL: InterVarsity Press, 1997), 113.

105 Ibid.

For most hard-working and ambitious people, it is the reward, the result, or the achievement of an ultimate goal that is often the motivator that drives them. Producing results gives people meaning, satisfaction, and ultimately a purpose to wake up in the morning. Without these crucial motivating factors, the very essence of life is diminished.

The motivation that we have can be compared to running an extraordinarily long marathon. In this example, the marathon is life, the time that we have on Earth. When we first start, we are excited, have lots of energy, and give our all because the possibilities are endless, and the world seems to be in the palm of our hands. We dream about the possibilities, but as we grow older we must make decisions that affect the direction of our life.

The initial burst lasts for a while, and we run hard, but as time marches forward, we can lose some the motivation that we once had because the race becomes monotonous as we run mile, after mile, after mile, after mile. After all, the race does take a lifetime to complete, and we discover that it is not impossible to sprint the entire way. We begin to think about the race, why we're running, and how well we will finish. We compare ourselves to others and dream of the relief we will have when we finally finish. We anticipate crossing the finish line because we know that a celebration of our victory awaits. The only catch is that the celebration cannot commence until victory is at hand and the race is finished. Nevertheless, we keep pressing, pushing harder and harder toward the finish line. We absorb the pain and the struggles that the race brings, and we tolerate that pain because we have faith that the end justifies the means and that the victory is worth living now.

Even though we have never seen the finish line, we believe that it exists because every race has a finish line. Besides, we have heard countless accounts of the immense joy, excitement, and fulfillment awaiting us at this celebration of our victory. It is hard to fathom the relief or the enjoyment of this victory, but the anticipation of greatness gives us hope, encouragement, and peace. When it felt as though we could not go on any longer, we remembered that we were not alone. When we fell down, we somehow found the strength to get back up. When we were tired, we somehow found the motivation to keep running. When we became discouraged, we somehow found the encouragement to press forward because the ultimate goal and the relief would be worth the temporary struggles.

Since the race is analogous to life, everybody will obviously complete the race, but somehow *just completing the race* is not the greatest motivator. Who would keep pressing toward the goal, keep running despite tough times, and persevere, if the ultimate goal was to finish and ultimately perish, never to exist again? The greatest motivator is what takes place after the race (the celebration of victory). So far, we have believed that there was a finish line, that victory was possible, and that there was a celebration waiting for us, so that the end would justify the means.

There Is No Victory. Imagine how easy it would be to become depressed, lonely, or discouraged if you knew that you have to run your entire life and that, upon completion, no real victory is possible. There will be no celebration at the end because once you finish, you cease to exist. The end could not possibly justify the means because there is nothing beyond the race; the only meaning must lie in the means and the temporary enjoyment that they bring. The only encouragement and hope must be found in this transitory life, and the only motivating factors that could compel you to keep going are found only within the very race you were running. Essentially, Naturalism teaches that we run until we drop dead, get chunked in the ground and nothing else happens.

Consider another example. You strive to become a respected CEO in corporate America. Your ambition is to reach the top of the corporate ladder—to enjoy at last the fruits of your labor. You tolerate the struggles and the long hours that come with the job because you have hope and faith that the end justifies the means. That the peak is worth the climb. But what if at the climax, the moment you reach the peak, you automatically die? Would you then have the same motivation?

Morale is defined as a person's "emotional or mental condition with respect to cheerfulness, confidence, zeal; especially in the face of opposition and hardship."[106] People's morale greatly depends on their outlook and expectations; it coincides with motivation. If you believe that there is a better place at the end of the race and that you can enjoy the fruits of your labor, then you naturally have hope (no pun intended). It is that hope that boosts your morale and drives you to finish the race or climb the corporate ladder.

On the other hand, if there is no reason to persevere and there is no hope, then morale naturally begins to deteriorate. Why would this happen?

---

106 Morale. Dictionary.com. *Dictionary.com Unabridged.* Random House, Inc. http://dictionary.reference.com/browse/morale (accessed: September 25, 2009).

You start to realize that you will run your entire life, tolerating the pain and the struggles that come along, and yet there will never be any relief. There will never be a celebration of victory, and there are neither rewards nor any such thing as true justice.

A Brutal Confrontation with Reality. With respect to life, it is the theist who believes that there is a celebration after the race and that victory is obtainable. The celebration is heaven, and it is the ultimate victory that motivates. The Naturalist, on the other hand, is the marathon runner without hope or the CEO who knows that there are no rewards for diligent labor. By the very definition of Naturalists' beliefs, they have absolutely nothing to look forward to because they believe such a celebration could not possibly exist. The only enjoyment that comes from life is the scenery they encounter as they run the race or the temporary enjoyment as they climb the ladder; but it could not be anything more.

Naturalists refuse to believe in theism's hope, and they refuse to have faith, despite having always heard that victory is obtainable, that they can enjoy the fruits of their labor, and that a grand celebration does in fact exist. They reject the invitation of salvation because they are closed-minded and because they cannot see the finish line or fathom the celebration of victory that lies ahead; but you know that they would desperately like to participate in the celebration if it actually existed.

It would be easy to believe if we saw the end before we started, but the very nature of this race does not enable us to see the end. It is by faith that we believe in the prophets, disciples, and apostles who testify to the truth of its existence. Some have testimonies that constitute that of a firsthand witness because they have seen the glory! Let me suggest that Naturalists are not so different from the theist because they also need hope to keep going, and they desperately want to have peace that the end justifies the means. After all, who chooses not to have hope? Who desires to believe that there is nothing beyond the limitations and struggles of a physical life—especially when it is not necessary?

The belief that the physical life is the ultimate reality is a major contributing factor to the inherently negative outlook of Naturalism. Naturalism's pessimistic root is the unbelief that anything greater beyond this life can exist because the supernatural and the spiritual are rejected. Without the anticipation of life after death, the only motivation is found within the physical life alone.

Unfortunately, the physical life and material possessions do not bring ultimate peace, joy, and fulfillment. If this were so, then every millionaire, celebrity, and wealthy person would be the happiest people in all the world. But we know that this cannot be true. It is not true. Material possessions and wealth cannot be the ultimate end because some of the most miserable people in the world have an abundance of wealth, fame, and material possessions yet lack the ability to enjoy their blessings.

There must be something more to life when the poorest of the poor are able to express unsurpassable joy despite their lack of material possessions. There must be something greater that gives these people purpose, peace, and fulfillment. They must have a reason to persevere and must be motivated by something else besides material possessions. Perhaps this revelation is proof that there *is* something greater than material possessions. Perhaps there *is* something beyond the natural world.

The contention of this book is that there is a light at the end of the tunnel. There is life that supersedes the physical, and together we *will* find it. Speculation, theories, and hope alone are not sufficient. We have serious questions, and we need serious answers. Together we will discover the evidence and celebrate the findings, as they are the very essence of motivation and joy in life!

Best Case, Worst Case Scenario. Hopefully, this presentation of best and worst case scenarios will provide an entirely different outlook with respect to religion and the existence of God. The intent is to help people open up to considering a new possibility if they have not yet done so. The mind needs to be open and receptive before Absolute Truth is presented; otherwise, the message may not be as effective. Consider the following proposed best and worst case scenarios with respect to Naturalism and theism as they pertain to life after death.

The Naturalists' *best case scenario* is that when they die, there is no life after death. Their hope is that they essentially "wink out" or enter into an "eternal sleep," never to wake up again. This is their *hope* because they cannot, by definition, prove that their theory constitutes truth beyond a shadow of a doubt. Proving Naturalism's position, as we have concluded, is impossible; thus they can only have hope. When you compare the Naturalist's best case scenario to the theist's, we discover that this is the theist's absolute *worst case scenario.* If the theist is wrong and there is no life after death, then the theist is neither benefited nor punished as a result of inaccurate belief.

On the other hand, if theists are right, then they will be in eternal paradise while the Naturalist will be eternally damned. Following theism's basic doctrine, rejection ultimately has consequences, and there is actually a place where those who reject truth regarding God will be punished; they will go to a place of eternal destruction—described in the Bible as a place of "weeping and gnashing of teeth."[107] This is a place where the damned will never be able to reverse their judgment because they have rejected the free gift of salvation.

The question that we must ask ourselves is: What is there to gain by rejection? If it is still possible to live a happy, prosperous, and fulfilling life while also believing in an afterlife, what benefit is there to gamble with one's soul? If you could have an insurance policy that was not only free of charge but had all-inclusive coverage and entirely prevented you from exposure to any damage, why would you refuse?

Logic would tell us that the temporary gain could never overcome the eternal pain if the theist is, in fact, correct. If we could know for certain whether or not heaven and hell actually exists, would you really reject eternal life in exchange for a "hope" that is, by definition, "unprovable"? If you are not a Christian, would you change your mind if it could demonstrated to you that there is a 100 percent chance of Naturalism being disproved through the positive demonstration that another theology is entirely true? Part Two will address this question and present the arguments in support of Christianity being entirely true.

---

107 Matthew 8:12; 13:42, 50; 22:13; 24:51; 25:30; Luke 13:28.

Part Two

The Discovery of Absolute Truth

Chapter 7

Examining Theism

"You believe that there is one God. Good! Even the demons believe that—and shudder."

—James 2:19(NIV)

"If the whole universe has no meaning, we should never have found out that it has no meaning: just as, if there were no light in the universe and therefore no creatures with eyes, we should never know it was dark. Dark would be without meaning."

—C. S. Lewis

What Have We Done?

Four Minus Three Equals One. Throughout Part One, it has been established that three of the four major categories of religion fail to demonstrate the characteristics needed in order to be considered Absolute Truth. Agnosticism, pantheism, and Naturalism each had their specific reasons as to why they failed, but the recurring theme was that they all contain fundamental flaws. Since these categories of religion, by nature, cannot be entirely true, we, as intelligent and thinking people, could not possibly place faith in them. Since the book began with four categories of religion, and three have been proven to be false, only one unexplored category remains—theism.

Previewing Part Two. In this chapter, we will examine the arguments that demonstrate the necessity of the existence of God. We will then consider three subcategories: polytheism, deism, and monotheism. After the arguments for the existence of God have been made, polytheism and deism will be disproved, because they embrace doctrine that contradicts itself and the attributes that God *must* have. Finally, we arrive at the one and only subcategory of religion that does not contradict itself or descend into illogical beliefs. Monotheism is the only category of religion whose ideology correlates with reality; therefore, it is the only one that is able to *begin* explaining the unexplainable.

However, when we arrive at monotheism, our work has only begun. Monotheism as a subcategory has multiple religions falling within its definition, including Christianity, Judaism, and Islam. Interestingly enough, these monotheistic religions disagree with each other because they all make exclusive but mutually exclusive truth claims. The quest cannot conclude at this point because an incomplete journey might allow a person to choose a fundamentally flawed faith that does not acknowledge or worship the one true God—not something I want on my conscience.

Therefore, one purpose of this book is to demonstrate how *every* religion except one is false so that no questions remain. Closing in on truth does not mean that we know all the answers, but it does provide the confidence that the right decision is being made. While on earth, we will never be all-knowing, so it's not feasible to demand answers to every question before placing *faith* in God. However, it will be demonstrated that there *is* enough convincing proof to confidently place faith in one religion—and that is our objective.

Since the book has taken a Christian stance since the Preface, the outcome can be accurately predicted without much effort. Answering the how and why questions regarding Christianity forms the essence of Part Two. As such, the thrust of Chapters 7 through 10 will be entirely dedicated to establishing Christianity as the one true faith along with supporting evidence and rationale. These chapters will venture into the infallibility of Scripture and the exclusive claims that Christianity makes. We will examine the person and character of Jesus Christ; establish the credibility of the resurrection and why people need Jesus. Finally, it will be demonstrated that there are only four approaches people can take with respect to Jesus Christ (liar, lunatic, legend, or Lord).

As Chapter 10 concludes, Absolute Truth will have been sufficiently established so that the stage is set to quickly rule out all the remaining monotheistic religions, leaving Christianity as the only faith standing. Even though a deductive method was used in Part One, there is no need to beat around the bush and take the time to disprove each and every single monotheistic religion in existence before proving Christianity to be entirely true; that would take entirely too long and is beyond the scope of this book. After Christianity is established, the simple answer is, "If any religion contradicts Christianity, then it is false, since it contradicts the Absolute Truth." Even though this argument could be used disprove Islam and Judaism, we will take the time to demonstrate how and why they are not true, in view of their standing as the two largest monotheistic religions left.

Part Three is short but was needed so that Christians can evangelize with precision. The Apostle Peter made it clear that Christians should "always be prepared to give an answer to everyone who asks you to give the reason for the hope that you have."[108]

Since our "answer" would not be complete without an examination of the major monotheistic religions, the defenses against those religions will be provided so that you, as you begin to evangelize, will have the confidence and the knowledge to make concise and logical arguments on behalf of Jesus Christ. Even though evangelism is not without rejection, the Christian's mission is accomplished when we share the faith. Nobody is guaranteed positive results with evangelism every time, but we are nevertheless called to share the faith, because it is the only way Christianity can possibly grow—and it is the only way America can be restored to her Christian foundation.

It is imperative to remember that in order for something to be considered Absolute Truth, it must not only be proven to be logical and correct, but it must be shown to falsify all contradictory beliefs, by definition. The *truth* is what we seek, and we will not settle for anything less. This book will not present a portion of the truth, nor will it be watered down to appease those who cannot handle truth. We will search until we find the truth—the whole truth and nothing but the truth. When we find truth, we will not be ashamed of our discovery. We will *not* cower in the face of danger. We will not be silenced by opposition.

Nor will we refuse to share. Truly caring for our family and friends implies evangelizing if they are not Christian. Nothing will keep our lips sealed, because we know that this Absolute Truth we seek is humanity's

108 1 Peter 3:15.

only hope. How would it benefit our family and friends if we knew the way to God, yet refused to share it?

Disclaimer—This Ain't Hollywood!

The Term Missing from My Vocabulary: Political Correctness. The conclusions of this book will be regarded, by some people, as narrow-minded or exclusive because they go against the open-minded and pluralistic mantra that is hailed in today's society. As seekers of the truth, we are not concerned with popularity; we are concerned about being right. We concern ourselves with discovering the *truth*, regardless of what that truth may be or where it may lead.

In response to the criticism of being narrow-minded and exclusive, let me remind the critic in advance that "all truth is narrow and all truth is exclusive. Truth cannot reach out and say you're right, you're right and you're right" when multiple contradictory truth claims exist.[109] This becomes evident when we look up the definition of truth. Truth is the true or actual state of a matter (actuality)[110] or the property of being in accord with fact or reality.[111]

The concept that truth is narrow can be further explained by using the Law of Excluded Middle, which states that every proposition is either true or untrue. Consider the following example: *you are alive*. You are either alive or not alive (dead), and there is no in-between. Similarly, the Law of Contradiction states that two antithetical propositions cannot both be true at the same time; *X* cannot be non-*X*.[112] The two propositions *you are alive* and *you are dead*, if made at the same time, are contradictory. Therefore, one must be false. All logic and rational thought depend on these two principles, and all meaningful conversations demand they are operative; to deny them is to deny all truth.

In your understanding of truth, you already knew that. Two plus two always equals four; never will it equal three or five. Water boils at precisely two hundred and twelve degrees Fahrenheit at sea level (never less), and

109 Dr. Richard Lee, "What Should We Believe? Why Is Jesus the Only Way to God?" There's Hope Ministries, 1998.

110 Truth. Dictionary.com. *Dictionary.com Unabridged*. Random House, Inc. http://dictionary.reference.com/browse/truth (accessed: May 1, 2009).

111 "Truth." Merriam-Webster Online Dictionary, 2009. Merriam-Webster Online. 2 May 2009. http://www.merriam-webster.com/dictionary/truth.

112 Antithetical: Directly opposed or contrasted; opposite (http://www.spurgeon.org/~phil/articles/lawofcon.htm).

water freezes at precisely at thirty-two degrees Fahrenheit at sea level (never more). You already knew that gravity pulls matter toward the center of the earth and never pushes objects away. Each of these statements constitutes *truth*, because they are the actual state and are in accordance with reality. We believe them and know that they are true because their properties can be proven and their truth can be known beyond a shadow of a doubt.

Furthermore, truth is not relative: it does not change from person to person. Consider the true statement: Gravity is a force that always pulls an object toward the center and never pushes an object away. That statement is true; it does not change from person to person, nor does the definition of gravity change in different parts of the universe. The *effects* of gravity are relative, since it is a function that takes into account variables such as mass and intervening distance. Even though the effects are relative, the definition of gravity is not.

Truth is also indifferent to opinion. All people are subject to the gravitational pull of the earth, while on earth, regardless of whether they place their faith in gravity. An opinion about that which is true does not affect the truthfulness of truth—although it certainly affects that person. The reality is that truth will continue to be true regardless of how much people dislike, disbelieve, or criticize that which is true. Unlike Hollywood, truth is never coerced by popularity.

To put into perspective the independence of truth from opinion, consider this example: A person who refuses to believe in gravity can jump off the top of a high building, professing disbelief in gravity the entire way down. The end of the matter is that the person will quickly discover that the truth is entirely indifferent to such disbelief. In fact, the person discovers that opinion, though fervently held, does not affect truth, and that they are wrong, at precisely thirty-two feet per second *per second* until they slam into the ground below. Discovering what happens to that person next is the central focus of this book because we will all leave earth in one way or another. It is critical to understand what happens next, and people need to be prepared for death; their eternal well-being teeters on the decision they do, or do not, make in regard to Absolute Truth.

Arguments for the Existence of God

Teleological Argument. The teleological argument is a very simple yet profound way of looking at the existence—and necessity—of a Creator. One reason the argument is convincing is that the answer is so intuitive that people cannot help but agree with the conclusion when they see it through the teleological paradigm. Even as we grow in our understanding of the complexity of our universe and the world that we live in, the teleological argument continues to make sense. In fact, I would suggest that the more complex we discover our universe to be, the more the argument will make sense.

The teleological argument was advanced by William Paley in the nineteenth century. The name is derived from the Greek word *telos* which means "end" or "purpose." The central theme of the argument is that it is more plausible to believe that the universe was created by an intelligent designer, to accomplish a specific purpose, than to believe it resulted from a random series of events that just mysteriously happened. This argument states that logic does not align with a person who believes that chance miraculously stumbled upon life and the immense precision and order visible in the universe. Paley begins his argument by observing that the universe we live in is much like a watch—particularly in displaying the property of having a maker.

We will borrow a scenario from Dr. Winfried Corduan's book, *No Doubt About It*, to drive the point home.[113] Imagine you and a friend decide to take a hike through a forest. Along your hike you see something lying along the path in the distance that is reflecting light as the sun's rays penetrate the canopy of leaves. As you come closer, you discover that the reflection you saw was the face of a watch. You would immediately notice that this watch is a complex machine that could not have come into existence through natural phenomena or random chance; a machine of that caliber and precision must have had an intelligent designer (a watchmaker). No rational person would suggest that the collection of atoms making up the watch are a result of random chance or that the metal was formed through millions of years of wave erosion because the likelihood of that occurrence is vanishingly small. Even if a Naturalist were the one to discover the watch, he would also concede that the watch was the product of intelligence and that chance did not play a part in its creation.

Paley then asks us to observe an even more complex, precise, and well-running machine: the universe we live in. The thrust of the teleological argument is that if a simple watch needs an intelligent designer, how much more does the creation of the universe demand an intelligent designer? The fine-tuned precision of creation is mind-blowing if one considers, for

113 Winfried Corduan, *No Doubt about It* (Nashville, TN: Broadman and Holdman Publishers, 1997), 56.

example, the devastating climate effects of even the slightest shift in the distance between the earth and the sun or the far-reaching effects of having a slightly larger or smaller moon.

It's truly astonishing how easy it is for people to conclude that a watch found in the forest needs an intelligent designer to account for its existence, but how skeptical people can be when they face the much more complex issue of a universe that is so fine-tuned that nothing but intelligence could possibly account for the results. The fingerprints of an intelligent designer have been left all over creation, but people often reject the simple and most logical answer for that which is counterintuitive and demands more faith than accepting the obvious.

Nevertheless, the teleological argument is an extremely simple and logical argument. It takes a simple scenario whose explanation is obvious and applies the same principles to one that is much more complex. The results are the same in the sense that they both require intelligence; the difference is the level of intelligence required and the complexity of the entity created. From the approach we have taken, it would only be rational to accept the proposition that *God exists.*

Cosmological Argument. The cosmological argument deals with the dire need to have an eternal, all-powerful God; otherwise nothing else could possibly exist. The version of the cosmological argument that I am presenting stems from Thomas Aquinas and was refined by Dr. Winfried Corduan.[114] The cosmological argument will prove to be not only intuitive but relevant to every aspect of life. Let's begin with the basic summary of the argument, and then we will defend and explain each step in detail.

The cosmological argument is as follows:

1. Something exists.
2. Each thing that exists is either necessary or contingent.
3. A necessary being would have to be God.
4. The world cannot be a necessary being.
5. There can be only one necessary being.
6. Unless there is a necessary being, there cannot be any contingent beings.
7. A necessary being exists.
8. Therefore, God exists.

114 Ibid., 109–119.

9. There exists, only one God exists.
10. The God of theism exists.

Explanation of Cosmological Argument

1. *Something exists.* We begin with the belief that something exists. You exist because you are reading this book right now, but anything will do—a car, tree, dog, or even your clothes. They all exist, and you know they exist because you have seen and interacted with them at some point in your life. If you doubt this proposition, your doubt exists, and your doubt means that you exist, and that's good enough.
2. *Each thing that exists is either necessary or contingent.* A necessary being is one whose existence is completely independent of any- and everything else; the existence of a contingent being is dependent upon something else. Nothing can be both necessary and contingent at the same time, because they are mutually exclusive propositions. This is where the Law of Contradiction comes in. Just as you cannot be both alive and dead at the same time, you cannot be a necessary and a contingent being at the same time; you must be one or the other, but never both. Furthermore, a contingent being would have to be caused (it could not create itself). You were created (in part, by your parents); sustained (in order to survive you must continually eat, drink water, and take care of your body); and determined (your physical characteristics were something you could not choose—you are who you are through no influence of your own). On the contrary, a necessary being could not fit into any of the above categories.
3. *A necessary being would have to be God.* As we just stated, a necessary being is completely independent of everything else and needs nothing else to contribute to its existence; it is uncaused, unsustained, and undetermined. The characteristics that must be attributed to God are as follows: independent, infinite, unlimited, eternal, omnipresent, immutable (unchangeable), and exhibiting pure actuality (has no potential). A necessary being would have to possess all these characteristics to an infinite degree.
4. *The world cannot be a necessary being.* To claim that the world is a necessary being and that it has the attributes of God is

contradictory; this is pantheism, and we have already proven it to be false. The world is not immutable because it constantly changes. The world is also not infinite, nor is it eternal.

5. *There can only be one necessary being.* The reason that there can only be one necessary being is simply because a necessary being would have to possess every relevant property to an infinite degree. We know that for two things to be different, they must be distinguishable; they must have different properties. There cannot be two necessary beings primarily because the required difference would negate, at a minimum, the properties of being unlimited and infinite. A necessary being must have all the right properties; no more, no less. If two beings were infinite, they would actually constitute one.
6. *Unless there is a necessary being, there cannot be any contingent beings.* By definition, a contingent being is one that is dependent upon external factors, not controlled by that being, for its existence to be possible. You exist, in part, by your parents. However, we cannot trace mankind's existence back infinitely because at some point the universe was also created; it too is dependent. The universe is dependent because it cannot be a necessary being (it changes, is not eternal, etc.). Therefore even the universe needed a cause, because a potential cannot actualize itself. An infinite regress leads nowhere; it only delays coming to the inevitable reality that no contingent being can cause its own existence. Therefore, at some point, everything was created, and the only entity that could have the ability to create is a necessary being.
7. *A necessary being exists.* Through the logical analysis of the cosmological argument, we can conclude that a necessary being can exist and that it *must exist* for anything else to be in existence.
8. *Therefore, God exists.* Since a necessary being is a synonym for God, we can conclude that God does in fact exist.
9. *Therefore, only one God exists.* Since we have established that it would be impossible for multiple necessary beings to exist, there can only be one God.
10. *The God of theism exists.* Since there cannot be multiple gods, polytheism cannot be the answer. It would be contradictory for God to be everything, including the world, so pantheism

> or panentheism cannot be the answer. Since all contingent beings, including the universe, are dependent upon a necessary being, Naturalism cannot be the answer. Since all contingent beings require a necessary being, we have enough information to determine whether such a being exists, therefore agnosticism cannot be the answer. Thus, the God of theism exists.

Ontological Argument. The ontological argument is a very basic and simplified argument that supports the existence of God. It links intuitive ideas with one another, such as *you cannot have a mountain without a valley* or *a square must always have four 90-degree angles and four sides of equal length* or *you cannot have time without distance or speed.* Some ideas always go with one another, not only because they are logical but because they are inseparable.

Just as you cannot have a mountain without a valley, a square without right angles, or time without speed, you cannot possibly have a *creation* without a *creator.* The idea that everything that was created has a creator is profoundly intuitive, which is exactly why you would assume that a watch found in the middle of a forest would have a watchmaker. Nobody in their right mind would blindly assume that all the roads, infrastructure, and high-rise office buildings (a form of creation) are a product of chance and are without the need for the builder (the creator); that would be an extraordinarily naïve assumption.

Nevertheless, the ontological argument that René Descartes formulated is one with only three propositions:

1. God, by definition, has all perfections.
2. Existence is a perfection.
3. Therefore, God exists.

The argument, to some people, will seem too simple. Others will disagree with the first proposition and consequently disregard the entire argument before they ever move to the second and third propositions. Before a decision is made, let's work to understand what Descartes is trying to convey.

In this argument Descartes uses "perfection" in a different context than we would normally use it. Descartes believes that actual existence is perfection in itself and that it is far better to exist than not to exist. Since existence is a perfection, the very idea of a God that did not actually exist would lack perfection. If God were not perfect in every way, then it could no longer be God. The idea of a perfect being without existence is not an intelligible statement; in fact it is quite contradictory. Finally, since existence is a perfection, and since God has all perfections, God must exist. Descartes argues that attempting to conceive of God as not existing would be the same as trying to conceive a mountain without a valley or trying to calculate time without speed or distance; they simply cannot be done. Therefore, God exists.[115]

Moral Law Argument. The moral law argument makes intuitive sense because people have a moral conscience. The fact that humans have the ability to discern right from wrong (to any degree), is a characteristic that distinguishes humans from nonhumans. No animal in the world has the capability of determining right versus wrong or justice from injustice because all animals are devoid of a moral sense. This section will demonstrate how the very existence of a moral conscience proves that God must exist. Let's begin with the following scenario to put into perspective the differences between man and animal.[116]

Imagine a beautiful summer morning with absolutely no clouds in the sky. The birds are chirping, the sunshine is exceptionally bright, and you decide that you want to take a walk to enjoy the marvelous weather. As you walk down the sidewalk, you smile as you watch children playing because they are enjoying their summer vacation.

If, while watching the children playing, you witness a cute little boy (just learning to run) helplessly fall to the ground and scrape his knees, it would evoke an emotion. If, right after the fall, a man walked up and kicked the boy in the face, knocked out his front teeth, and then shot him in the back of the head, this, too, would prompt an emotion. The next question is why. Why should an execution-style murder of an innocent boy produce any degree of emotional response in a human being, while the birds and squirrels (who also witnessed the event) continue with their lives as if nothing immoral had occurred?

The birds and squirrels, after recovering from the startling gunshot, would certainly not shed a single tear or feel any inclination to attend the funeral and pay their respects to the victim. There would be no reason

115 Internet Encyclopedia of Philosophy, "Rene Descartes (1596-1650): God," http://www.iep.utm.edu/d/descarte.htm#SH5b.

116 This section distinguishes man from the "beasts of the earth" because humans have the presence of a moral conscience.

for the animals to cry, mourn, or offer a moment of silence. In fact, any expectations of sorrow on behalf of any animal would be absurd, because animals cannot think or act in a way that requires a moral capacity. On the other hand, human beings would feel pity or sorrow when the boy fell and scraped his knees, but *anger* and *outrage* when an innocent child was murdered in cold blood. The reason this event would be traumatizing is because it would be absolutely horrifying to see such a perversion of justice.

Why should we care at all about some small boy who was murdered when he was not even related to us? Worrying about this boy or his family or what happens to the criminal will never help us get ahead, make money, or be successful. Why should we even care? Even though worrying about the boy or his family will never help us materially, we demand justice because the retribution of evil is the only way we can possibly live in a civil society. The establishment and enforcement of a Moral Law is a prerequisite for peace; this is why, at a minimum, unlike the animals, we care about what happens to the criminal. C. S. Lewis has argued that the moral law is the Law of Nature and that all people are born able to distinguish right from wrong. Essentially, if right and wrong did not exist, nobody could condemn that which we call evil. Lewis explains:

> This law was called the Law of Nature because people thought that every one knew it by nature and did not need to be taught it. They did not mean, of course, that you might not find an odd individual here and there who did not know it, just as you find a few people who are colour-blind or have no ear for a tune. But taking the race as a whole, they thought that the human idea of decent behaviour was obvious to everyone. And I believe they were right. If they were not, then all the things we said about the war were nonsense. What was the sense in saying the enemy were in the wrong unless Right is a real thing which the Nazis at bottom knew as well as we did and ought to have practised? If they had no notion of what we mean by right, then, though we might still have had to fight them, we could no more have blamed them for that than the colour of their hair.[117]

117 C. S. Lewis, *Mere Christianity* (New York: HarperSanFrancisco, 1980), 5.

Ironically, people know that right and wrong exist because if you were to steal a person's wallet in front of them, they would object (even a criminal would object to you walking away with *his* wallet!). Even though we know that right and wrong exist, some people claim that morality does not prove that God exists. They argue that since people have different degrees of morality and since the different civilizations have had different types of laws, morality is relative. They claim that since morality is relative, it cannot be a constant or universal trait that all human beings have. Therefore, it cannot be used to prove God's existence. However, it must be pointed out that this is only half of the truth.

I agree with the statement that morality is relative, but only to a certain degree. We know that morality differs among people and governments because some civilizations have allowed the beating of women, the use of slaves, the feeding of prisoners to wild animals—even the murdering of weak, incompetent, or unborn children. Morality is relative to the degree that a person has developed a moral conscience. Essentially, the level of morality that a person has is dependent upon each person's priority and usage of their moral conscience. Morality is like a muscle: the more attention it gets, the more notable it becomes. Saints have a very high degree of morality because they constantly strive toward moral perfection; at the other extreme, the morally depraved despise morality and neglect their moral conscience.

Interestingly enough, debating the superiority of morals is an entirely different conversation, but our original question is still unanswered: Does the existence of a moral conscience prove the existence of God? The second half of the truth (the half that liberalism is reluctant to discuss) is that all people *have* a moral conscience even though some are more mature than others. The presence of a moral conscience is not relative; its existence is not dependent upon external conditions, nor do people have a choice about whether they have a moral conscience. The moral conscience is not relative, and since people have one even if they don't want it, its forced presence is the constant we need to prove that God must exist.

You Can't Give What You Don't Have. If you have ever bounced a check, you have learned the lesson that you cannot give what you do not have. If there is no money in your checking account, you cannot purchase a good or service because you are unable to exchange value for value—regardless of how great your desire may be! You already knew this to be true because if you do not have a Ferrari, you cannot possibly give one away. If you do not have any change in your pocket, you cannot possibly give any to the Salvation Army as you walk into a store. If you do not have compassion, you cannot offer compassion; if you have a little compassion, then you can offer a little. If you do not have the AIDS virus, then you cannot possibly infect another person because it's physically impossible to give away that which you do not have. This is a simple yet profound principle of life.

This principle is as applicable to plants and animals as it is to the nonliving universe. This principle is precisely why Naturalists struggle so much with the concept of creation: they are forced to account for how life could have possibly come from that which was not living (apart from a divine intervention). These scientists also know that consciousness is another leap that is unexplainable without including God—which is exactly why, as pointed out in Chapter 6, scientists are now trying to convince you that your consciousness is an illusion! The presence of a moral conscience is very similar to the miracle of unconsciousness producing consciousness because morality is also finite. There was a moment when humankind did not have the knowledge of good and evil, but in the next moment, after the fruit was eaten, humans had a moral conscience.[118]

Since the presence of a moral conscience is exclusive to humankind, we know that it cannot be traced to purely natural causes. This truth is problematic to secular scientists because when we look at the material universe, we cannot find *any trace* of morality. Nowhere does it exist! We know this to be true because morality cannot be found in any animal, rock, moon, star, or galaxy. Our conclusion is easily verified by noting that plants, animals, and rocks have no need to create laws to enforce moral standards—they do they need jails, death penalties, or judicial systems with judges to interpret penal codes. The reason that plants, animals, and rocks cannot be convicted of a felony is because they are all morally devoid and unable to do that which is wrong.

A moral conscience is also a nonphysical result; it is like "that intangible thing—the soul." Nobody can explain the presence of a moral conscience because physical processes of evolution can only account for physical results—it's at a loss of what to say about the nonphysical. This is why

118 Interestingly enough, humankind has not always had a moral conscience (as indicated by Genesis 3:5). There was a time when only one sin existed (to eat from the forbidden tree). However, once the fruit from the tree of the knowledge of good and evil was eaten, humankind gained the knowledge of all good and evil; hence the birth of the moral conscience as we know it today.

the Naturalist Michael Ruse conceded that Darwinism does not have the answer.

Since nothing else in creation has a moral conscience (but we know that it exists), this truth poses a slight problem to the secular scientists trying to explain the origin of morality. This complication is evident when we return to our inconvenient principle that states *you can't give what you don't have*. Since the entire universe is morally devoid, it would have been impossible for humans to have evolved into moral beings because *not even evolution can evolve from something it never had*. Therefore, to explain the presence of our moral conscience inadequate answers would include evolution, chance or an accident.

God Gives That Which God Has. Since the principle *you can't give what you don't have* has been applicable to all creation, dare we take it to the next level? Absolutely; not even God can give that which He does not have. Before we move forward, this statement must be put into context! Since we know that God has explicit attributes that define His being (as established in the cosmological argument), if any one of these attributes were compromised, then God could not be God. Since God is holy and just, God could never be evil.[119] Since God could never possess evil, He could never give that which is rooted in evil. As a result, God never gives away lies, despair, or hatred. Therefore, we begin to understand that God is all-powerful, but only within His attributes because we know that God is unable to be or possess evil. The limitations that prevent God from being evil may be touted by evil as making Him somehow incomplete or less than all-powerful. However, this person does not understand that God's greatest strength is His inability to sin. This is extraordinarily important for any Christian because we can know, in absolute confidence, that God will never be able to default on His promise of redemption through Jesus Christ.

Nevertheless, since we believe this principle to be true, we must also believe the inverse of this principle: *You are able to give that which you have.* This intuitively implies that if you have a Ferrari, you are able to give away a Ferrari; and so forth. Since God is holy, God can give that which is good: encouragement, peace, joy, and anything else associated with righteousness. Likewise, since God has knowledge of good and evil (and all other creation has no knowledge of good and evil), God is the *only* entity

119 Isaiah 6:3; Titus 1:2; 1 Peter 1:16.

with the ability to give that knowledge to humankind.[120] Therefore, the miraculous appearance of mankind's moral conscience reveals the presence of God as morality cannot be explained without a divine intervention (which requires the existence of God).[121]

Polytheism

The Partial "I Am" Is Not. Polytheism is the religion that teaches that multiple gods coexist with one another. These coexisting gods each have different powers, but they all collectively rule over the heavens and the earth. The best-known of polytheism would be the mythical Greek gods. Greek gods include figures such as Zeus, Hera, Apollo, Athena, and so forth. However, the polytheism is not limited to ancient mythology; it can be found in modern religions such as Hinduism and Shintoism. The belief in and worship of many gods is not a theology that has been abandoned because Hinduism, one of the most widely held religions in the world, is polytheistic. This means that there are hundreds of millions of people who continue to place their faith in polytheism.

Since millions upon millions of people continue to believe that multiple gods coexist, there is a need to address the issue. There are some fundamental flaws of polytheism that prohibit it from being entirely true, and they must be brought to light. Polytheism cannot be true because it relies on presuppositions that are mutually contradictory. The religion is false not because of a person's opinion but because the doctrine it teaches is, frankly, impossible and does not correlate with truth. Polytheism was actually discredited by the cosmological argument, but since it was only mentioned in passing, I would like to reemphasize some of the major contradictions that disqualify polytheism from being Absolute Truth.

The polytheistic contradiction becomes evident when we test its doctrine against the characteristics that a necessary being *must* possess in order to be considered God. In the cosmological argument, we established that God, by definition, *must* be independent and never has to rely on another

---

120 Angels and demons (fallen angels) are the only potential exception. They are a potential exception because we do not know enough about them to generate an all-inclusive answer. Angels are believed to have knowledge of good and evil because they once had a chance to side with God or Satan. However, angels are unable to give humans the knowledge of good and evil because they are also contingent beings. Only a necessary (all-powerful) being can give a moral conscience to another being. (E.g., we cannot give a dog a moral conscience; only God would have that ability.)

121 In the absence of God, morality could not exist because nothing would exist.

being for His existence. We established that God has to be all-powerful (in order to create something from nothing—a miracle). We established that God has to be all-knowing (because God created everything, even knowledge). We also established that God must possess all His attributes to an infinite degree. Infinity is the key attribute because unless God is infinite, by definition, God could not be God. If God were finite, then the being would fit the definition of a contingent being, and this would mean that God is dependent, which cannot be the case.

Infinite is defined as "endless" or "subject to no limitation," so it would not make sense to give a necessary being partial power; that is contradictory and self-defeating.[122] To teach that multiple gods coexist with one another is teaching this inherently flawed contradiction of a finite God (which cannot be true). It does not make sense to divide God's power in order to teach that one god has power over creation and destruction, another god has power over all good causes, and yet another god has power over war, murder, and bloodshed, because it demonstrates that *none* of these beings is all-powerful or infinite. As a result, none of these "gods" fits the characteristics that must be attributed to a necessary being. When one god relies on another god, they are actually *dependent* on one another to collectively rule the heavens. Since multiple gods would be dependents, we know that they would be finite and unable to cause their own existence. Therefore, it would be *impossible* for multiple gods to exist.

The idea of numerous infinite beings coexisting makes a mockery of simple logic and is as silly as saying "infinity plus one": how can you possibly add to something that has no end? As thinking people, we must refrain from blindly placing our faith in a belief merely because a claim was made and we were *told* polytheism constitutes truth. Anybody can make any claim they want, but we know that simply making a claim does not necessarily mean that it constitutes truth. If I were to claim that Zeus and Apollo are both gods, it would be just as ludicrous as if any President of the United States were to claim deity and assume Messiahship, declaring himself to be the one we have all been waiting for.

Addressing the Christian Trinity. Even though we are not yet into Christianity, we should go ahead and address the accusation of some that Christianity teaches polytheism. Christianity is adamant in proclaiming the existence of only *one God*. Scripture makes it clear that polytheism is

122 Infinite. Merriam-Webster Online Dictionary, 2010. *Merriam-Webster Online.* 12 April 2010. http://www.merriam-webster.com/dictionary/infinite.

not a core belief, even though the one God Christians worship exhibits *three* distinct manifestations: the Father, Son, and Holy Spirit. Some people may claim that since there are three parts to the Christian God, this God cannot exist. However, we must reflect on what the Scriptures teach and couple that with what we know to be true. The triune God that the Bible teaches has never taught that there are actually three separate Gods.[123] Instead Christianity teaches that there is one God, but that this one God has three distinct aspects in a single being.

Consider an example. You, because you were made in the image of God, are a triune being as well. The three elements of your being comprise a mind, body, and soul. The mind is different from the body, which is different from the soul, but they are inseparable from one another. The components are distinct from one another, but they perform different functions. Just because you have three parts to your being does not mean that you are actually three separate persons (that would be silly to suggest).

Likewise, a triune God is still one God. All parts of the Trinity are infinite and have always existed. We know this because John 1:1 references Jesus Christ in the beginning (before creation of the universe). Christianity vastly differs from polytheism because polytheists claim that there are multiple gods who *differ* from one another in power and ability. Therefore, there is no contradiction to the Christian triune God.

Deism

The Hybrid Religion. Deism is an interesting belief system that may appear to be credible at first glance, but it too has fundamental flaws within its self-contradictory doctrine. If I were to briefly describe the religion to a person who had never heard of it before, I would call it a hybrid that pulls ideas from a variety of different religions that include atheism, agnosticism, and theism.

Deism borrows ideas from theism when it affirms the *necessity* of having a Creator. Since this book gives credit where credit is due, deists are commended for at least acknowledging the fact that God's existence is necessary for anything else to exist. Even though deists score some brownie points, these are quickly lost when they deviate from truth by claiming that God *cannot* perform the supernatural. Deists, by definition, must believe

123 John 10:30: "I and the Father *are one*" (emphasis added).

that God is unable to perform a miracle or, to cite the dictionary, they "deny the interference of the Creator with the laws of the universe."[124]

Deism is drastically different from theism: If a deist were to claim that God *could* perform miracles but chooses not to perform miracles, then it would be taking the same position as theism: God would have the power, but may choose not to utilize that power. However, we know that deism deviates because it teaches that God is unable to perform a miracle (even if God had a desire to interfere with the laws of the universe).

Since God is not able to interfere with the laws of nature, a deist must believe that Christians are wrong because Jesus never was born of a virgin, nor did He live a sinless life. Jesus could not have performed miracles, healings, or resurrections. It was also impossible for Jesus to rise from the dead. Deists also reject the divine inspiration of the Bible because it is not possible for God to intervene through inspiration.

Deism would also disagree with other religions. Judaism is wrong because God could not have sent the plagues to Egypt, parted the Red Sea, flooded the Earth, sent fire from heaven to defeat Baal, and so forth. Islam is wrong because Muhammad never had a vision (an alleged divine intervention) from a supernatural source. As a result, deists would believe that the Qur'an could not be divinely inspired. This same concept would apply to all other religions: deists make no exception nor allow for special circumstances, or they would no longer be considered "deist."

Deism crosses over into agnostic and naturalistic territory when the implications of deism are realized. The deist presentation of God can be appealing to both atheists and agnostics, because they would not have to worry about the Ten Commandments or any moral law put forward by a higher being. They do not have to worry about morality because it would be impossible for God to communicate with mankind. Any divine moral code would presuppose this communication, making it a supernatural phenomenon—which they claim is impossible. As a result, deists are able to live their lives without the fear of punishment or repercussions from any wrath God may have. Deists claim that they could not be punished

124 Deist. Merriam-Webster Online Dictionary, 2010. *Merriam-Webster Online.* 12 April 2010. http://www.merriam-webster.com/dictionary/deist.

for doing wrong simply because God could have never established a moral code – a "reverse" catch-22 situation.[125]

The Religion of Contradictions. Deism has created a hybrid religion that clearly pulls ideas and doctrines from many different categories of thought, but is the resulting doctrine free of contradictions? The answer is crucial because a contradiction is defined as "a proposition, statement or phrase that asserts or implies both the truth and falsity of something."[126] If deism teaches a contradiction, then this religion cannot be considered Absolute Truth because the religion, by definition, would not be entirely true.

As predicted, deism is not free of contradictions. The greatest contradiction is that deism teaches that God is unable to perform any type of supernatural miracle. This "inability" is problematic because God must be infinite in *all His attributes* in order to be considered a necessary being, but deism teaches that God cannot even perform good acts in the world that He created.[127] Since God is limited within His attributes, we now have a God of partial power. Since deism's God has partial power, this God cannot be infinite. Since this God is not infinite, this God *must be dependent.* Hence, the deist God cannot exist.

When Contradictions Collide. Even though we know that this God could not exist, we will still take a closer look at precisely why a finite God is illogical and contradictory in order to prove a point.

Deists claim it is absurd to think of God establishing the rational laws for the universe only for Him to turn right back around and break them. Deists make the argument: Since God is a rational being, God will not act in any way that is irrational or contrary to the laws He has established.[128]

However, there is a tremendous problem when we venture back to the concept of creation, an event that even deists claim God initiated. When

125 Catch-22: the phrase was coined by Joseph Heller in his novel, *Catch-22.* It refers to a "paradox in rules, regulations, procedures, or situations in which one has knowledge of becoming a victim but has no control over it occurring" (wikipedia.org). This is a reverse catch-22; perfect impunity; not victimhood, with no possible escape.

126 Contradiction. Merriam-Webster Online Dictionary, 2010. *Merriam-Webster Online.* 12 April 2010, *http://www.merriam-webster.com/dictionary/contradiction.*

127 Since God is holy, God is unable to sin. The inability of God to sin does not infringe on the all-powerful concept because God is only all-powerful within His attributes. (This is a great strength because God could never take away the redemption that is offered through the blood of Jesus Christ.)

128 Corduan, 90.

we reexamine creation, how would it be possible to account for creation from nothing without a miracle? To even have *anything* in existence, we must automatically contradict a deist law that states "God cannot perform miracles."

The deist logic begins to fall apart with creation because it takes a miracle by God to create everything in existence (from nothing). Deism has an inconsistency within its fundamental teaching as indicated by the following two claims:

1. God performed the miracle of creation; and
2. God does not perform miracles.[129]

Even if we concede that before the initial creation there were no laws of nature and that God could not have contradicted any laws when He performed the miracle of initial creation, we still run into tremendous problems. (This is a sneaky way to try and escape the contradiction presented above, but the logic still fails.) Why is it impossible to believe that the only miracle that God could have performed was initial creation since it took place before the laws of nature were created? Because we already know that *not everything* was created on the first day, nor was everything created at the same exact same time in its full form. More contradictions must inevitably follow. (The Bible makes it clear that there is a progression in which the initial creation transforms into its current state, but we will not yet use the Bible as a defense because deism needs to be proven fatally flawed apart from a contradiction with the Bible. After we have seen how the Bible is Absolute Truth, the "biblical contradiction" argument can be used.)

Nevertheless, since all matter was created on the first day, but living creatures do not appear until much a later time, we are developing an entirely different problem. Even if God could have performed a miracle before the laws of nature were created with the universe, subsequent miracles are also necessary for life to exist. The very presence of *life*, which was once derived from nonliving matter, is nothing less than a miracle that only God could have initiated, but the problem is that life came after the laws of nature were already in place! (Contradictions are starting to collide, and this is not turning out well for deism.) As a result of deism's presuppositions, it must assume yet another contradiction:

129 Ibid.

1. Life is a miracle in itself.
2. God cannot perform miracles after the laws of nature were established.
3. The presence of life came *after* the laws of nature were established.
4. But, when life was created, nothing else was alive except God.
5. Therefore, God could not have created life.
6. We now have an irreconcilable contradiction as it must now be assumed that the non-living produced life; which is impossible because life is a nonphysical result that is unable to originate from physical processes alone.

In addition to the miracle of life, there are other troublesome miracles that deism cannot explain, such as the existence of consciousness. How does something that was not previously conscious suddenly become aware of its existence unless a miracle by God is involved? The moral law is yet another contradiction. How does morality miraculously show up when morality was not existent before mankind was granted the knowledge of good and evil? The list could go on and on, but when reality sets in, there are numerous miracles that deism cannot begin to explain. Deists have attempted to explain the miracles without supernatural intervention, but they *cannot* logically explain them in the absence of a supernatural miracle.

The irony is that deists must, by nature of the religion, believe that certain contradictions are true when they cannot, by nature, be true because they do not correlate with actuality. As we will discover in the next few chapters, many miracles demonstrate that God is actively involved with the human world. The mere fact that the Messianic prophecies were written four hundred years in advance *and were fulfilled* demonstrates the necessity of a divine intervention, but this section has established that deism is illogical without recourse to the Bible.

Since deism has multiple contradictions that prevent God from being God, deism should not be a belief in which people can confidently place their faith. Ultimately, because deism self-destructs under a logical examination, it cannot be a candidate for Absolute Truth.

Monotheism

Closing In on Truth. Monotheism is the category of religion that exalts and worships one God and recognizes the need for God to infinitely possess all the attributes of a necessary being. This is the only category of religion that is adamant that there is a *personal* Creator who created everything that we see in existence today—the universe, galaxies, Earth, plants, animals, people, and anything else imaginable.[130]

Monotheism vastly differs from the other types of religions because it also asserts the existence of a divine judge before whom all humanity will one day be held accountable. However, within monotheism, judgment and methods of redemption may differ because there are a variety of different religions within this category. The three major monotheistic religions are Christianity, Judaism, and Islam, and they make mutually contradictory truth claims with respect to God and salvation. We know the claims are contradictory because each religion leads its congregants down different paths of redemption.

Christianity teaches that Jesus Christ was born of a virgin, lived a sinless life, was crucified and resurrected, and was God incarnate. As a result, Christians believe that Jesus paid the ultimate price of sin with His blood and has consequently enabled humans to place their faith upon him to receive the gift of eternal life.

Judaism rejects the deity of Jesus Christ, the New Testament, and the triune Godhead (Father, Son, and Holy Spirit). Since believers in Judaism reject the deity of Jesus Christ, they do not believe that redemption is attainable through Jesus. Judaism observes the Law of the Old Testament, but the idea of salvation is elusive and differs among the different Jewish groups because the concept was not fully developed in the Old Testament.

Islam teaches that Jesus was merely a prophet and that Allah is the one true God. The Islamic prophet is Muhammad ibn Abdallah, and Muslims believe that he was sitting in a cave outside Mecca in AD 610 when he began to receive visions from what he believed to be the archangel Gabriel.[131] The angel declared that there was only one true God; Muhammad spoke of him

130 Everything in existence ultimately reverts back to God because God created all matter. Even though humankind transforms the matter that God created into chairs, clothes, and computers, these items are an original product of God.

131 Thom Rainer, *The Unexpected Journey: Conversations with people who turned from other beliefs to Jesus* (Grand Rapids, MI: Zondervan, 2005), 174.

as *Allah*, a name that simply means "the God."[132] Islam denies the Trinity and also rejects the deity of Jesus Christ. The Islamic religion claims that salvation is possible (without having deeds judged) if a Muslim becomes a martyr for Islam. Otherwise, each person's deeds will be judged, and based on that judgment, people will be sent to either heaven or hell.

Where To from Here? As we can see, each of the monotheistic religions places a different spin on salvation, and each makes an exclusive claim on truth. These multiple, contradictory truth claims mean they cannot all be correct. The remaining chapters in Part Two will be entirely dedicated to discovering the Absolute Truth surrounding the one true God. Thus far, a deductive method has been used: we have been disqualifying one religion after another from being entirely true. At this point, we are able to confidently conclude that monotheism is the only possible category of religion that can contain truth. Instead of disproving other monotheistic religions before establishing the Absolute Truth, we will first establish Christianity as entirely true before moving to disprove other monotheisms.

The first task (Chapter 8) in establishing Christianity as entirely true will be dedicated to defending the Holy Scriptures and demonstrating how they are the product of a divine intervention. Once it has been demonstrated that the Bible is a product of God, everything it contains must be entirely true because God is unable to lie or deceive. Thus, we arrive at the conclusion that the Bible is Absolute Truth.

In Chapter 9, we examine some exclusive claims that Christianity makes with respect to salvation. The plan of salvation that the Bible provides will be examined along with its significance. Finally, we will examine some of the boldest and most audacious claims ever made in human history. The claims that Jesus made undoubtedly turned heads, but since they are presented in the Bible, they are entirely true because the Bible is a product of divine intervention, and God cannot lie. Chapter 10 examines the facts surrounding the life, ministry, death, and resurrection of Jesus Christ and explains how important it is for every person to know Jesus Christ as their personal Savior. Chapter 11 examines the four positions that one can take with respect to the identity of Jesus Christ—Liar, Lunatic, Legend, or Lord. Each of these categories is examined, and three of these identities will be disproved.

---

132 Ibid.

From Chapter 8 onward, this book will exalt the Bible as the *ultimate authority* with respect to all morals, ethics, decisions, and revelations of Truth. Until this point, biblical doctrine was not included in the process of disproving agnosticism, deism, Naturalism, pantheism, panentheism, and polytheism. We did this in order to demonstrate how each fails to be entirely true even without relying on the Bible. Even though it could be established that these religions are entirely false by claiming that they contradict the Bible, it needed to be demonstrated that they all fail, apart from the Bible, in order to create a far more powerful presentation of the Gospel that will undoubtedly reach a different group of people.

Enough of the preview. Let's begin the journey of understanding, strengthening, and defending the Gospel of Jesus Christ.

Chapter 8

Presenting the One Source of Absolute Truth

"For prophecy never had its origin in the will of man, but men spoke from God as they were carried along by the Holy Spirit"

—2 Peter 1:21

"All Scripture is God-breathed and is useful for teaching, rebuking, correcting and training in righteousness, so that the man of God may be thoroughly equipped for every good work."

—2 Timothy 3:16

"Sanctify them by Your truth. Your Word is truth."

—John 17:17 (NKJV)

Not All Sources Are Equal

Distinguishing Good from Great. There are good sources and there are great sources. In this section, good sources are secondary, while great sources are primary. Primary sources are original or firsthand accounts of an event and are written during or close to the actual event; they are factual rather than interpretive[133] Even though secondary sources may contain excellent information and critiques, they are secondary because they are

133 BMCC Library, "Primary vs. Secondary Sources," http://lib1.bmcc.cuny.edu/help/sources.html.

an interpretation, analysis, or secondhand account that draws on one or more primary sources.

A few examples will demonstrate the difference between the two. *The Diary of Anne Frank* would be primary, while the secondary source would be a book that was written about diaries that were kept during the Holocaust.[134] The great source has firsthand experience by a person who lived through the tragedies associated with the Holocaust; the author of the good source cannot possibly understand the fear, pain or grief that somebody like Anne Frank experienced; they can only analyze and try to interpret the meaning or importance of that experience.

A primary source would be a scientist who published the results of a landmark scientific breakthrough, while the secondary source would write about the significance of the breakthrough. A primary source would be an actual movie, while the secondary source would be a review or an opinion of the movie. A primary source would be U.S. Census data, while a secondary source might reference the data in an attempt to offer an explanation.[135] There are vast differences between the two types of source materials. For many reasons, a primary source is preferable to a secondary source.

Even though there are vast differences between primary and secondary sources, they have one feature in common that needs to be addressed. Both are subject to being inaccurate or false. Even a primary source, a scientific study for example, can publish an experiment that was inaccurate.[136] If a secondary source embraces the conclusions of the primary source, then the secondary source also risks being inaccurate. We know sources are constantly wrong and disproved because scientific theories change from year to year. Since both primary and secondary sources are subject to the possibility of being inaccurate, the question now becomes: Is there any source which can be held as entirely true? Is there a source where Absolute Truth exists and everything within can be trusted beyond a shadow of a doubt as entirely true?

---

134 Ibid.

135 Ibid.

136 The most recent phenomenon (as revealed in leaked e-mails) was the "Climate-Gate" scandal. The only problem with global warming is that the model violates the first and second laws of thermodynamics. Another "inconvenient truth" is that the earth has actually been in a *cooling period* for over a decade. Perhaps these facts influenced the dire need to change the name from "Global Warming" to "Climate Change" in order to establish credibility? (http://www.globalresearch.ca/index.php?context=va&aid=10783).

If we look to human accomplishment and human literature, the answer is no; humans are finite beings. Since humans are finite and cannot possibly have an infinite perspective, the possibility for error will always exist. Even though numerous scientific theories and experiments seem to be irrefutable, we cannot label them as Absolute Truth because science continually changes and is rarely constant; changes occur as fast as new technology is invented.

In order for any source to be considered Absolute Truth, it must never change; it must never be proven wrong; in fact, it cannot be disproved. Clearly, it must be written by an infinite being so that no contradictions will ever arise at any point in history. Does a source of this magnitude—meeting this seemingly insurmountable bar of perfection—exist? Is it possible to label even one as entirely true, the ultimate authoritative source by which all decisions must be made? Knowing the answer to this all-important question can radically change your life.

The "Daddy" of All Sources. If you thought secondary sources were "the greatest thing since sliced bread," you may have been disappointed to learn about the superiority of primary sources. If you thought primary sources were the "cutting edge," then prepare yourself to meet the one source whose very words send chills down the spine, the one far superior than any other source known to man.

This "daddy" of all sources has been the most powerful and the most influential motivator in history. It has sanctified billions upon billions through a salvific process that ultimately brings people to their knees. Reading this source often brings tears of joy, because when you were weak, you found strength; when you were sad, you found joy; when you felt you couldn't go on, you somehow found encouragement. When you recognized your true identity, you accepted salvation because its truth pierces to the soul. The message is crystal clear, it cannot be confused with any other, and its truth is easily verified each time we look into the mirror.

This source has drastically transformed countless lives. It has led people out of the oppression of alcohol, drugs, and slavery to discontent and mediocrity. It has brought families back together, healed the brokenhearted, and has even brought a calming peace to those whose inevitable end was in sight. It's sharper than any double-edged sword, and it can even cause a grown man to weep like a little boy.

This one source alone has reformed nations, justified wars, influenced governments, and established codes of right and wrong. It has been the moral and ethical guide for decisions countless people have made throughout history. This source reveals the past, helps us understand the present, and reveals the future that *will* one day come to pass.

This is the book that has predicted specific events hundreds of years before they took place. Each time, they were fulfilled with a precision unknown to mankind. This is the source that is without error, without contradiction and without flaw despite the obstacles that accompany transcription by forty different men over a period that rivals one thousand nine hundred years by men who spoke different languages, had different education levels, had different occupations, were of different ethnicities and lived in different time periods. Even though most were unable to collaborate, they were able to overcome the odds and generate a source whose one central theme consistently flows from beginning to end. It is the Alpha, and it is the Omega.

This source is the number-one best seller of all-time; no other book has sold more copies. And second place barely strikes its heel. Even though it has been despised by countless tyrants, it has never been defeated. It has never been stamped out, and the truth within will continue to be taught until the very end of the age—precisely as foreordained. Those who have tried to eradicate it from history have, themselves, been eradicated.

Who, what, or how could *anything* stand in the way of the most powerful, the most influential, and the most revealing book that the world has ever known? Who can challenge the wisdom, revelation, and truth contained within? Who dares to take on that which cannot be defeated?

It is a pleasure—an indescribable honor—to present the one source of Absolute Truth, even though words themselves cannot offer the justice it deserves. I present none other than the God-breathed, Holy Spirit–inspired, and infallible Word of God—*The Holy Bible.*

Introducing the Holy Bible

The Purpose of Scripture. The Bible is God's written revelation to humankind concerning Himself, eternity and our relationship to (and hopefully with) Him. The Bible helps us understand the world we live in by offering advice, comfort, and helpful guidelines by which to live. The Bible also gives us history about our past and foreshadows the future. It even describes events that we will one day take part in, but the most important purpose of Scripture is to make known to each and every person the decision they make in regard to their salvation.

People either accept the gift of salvation through Jesus Christ, alone, or they ultimately reject it.[137] It must be understood that not accepting salvation has the exact same consequence as hostile rejection of the Gospel or persecution of Christians (eternal destruction). This is a fact that is revealed by the Bible, and this truth is indifferent to the opinions that people may have.

Divinely Inspired. One of the most important facts to know about the Bible is that the text was never authored by men. This text is far superior to any other in the world because the author is none other than God Himself. God, through the inspiration of the Holy Spirit, used at least forty different men to transcribe the books that comprise the Bible. Since God authored and men transcribed, the Bible not only contains the Word of God; it *is* the Word of God. From Genesis to Revelation, God has revealed to us everything we *need* to know in order for us to successfully make it from sin to salvation so that when we die and leave this earth, we have the potential to enjoy eternal life in a capacity that we cannot begin to fathom.

Since every verse is divinely inspired, we must wholeheartedly believe each and every single one. Nobody, regardless of how much power or knowledge they think they have, has the authority of adding to or deleting from the Scriptures. Only the author (the originator of the text) has the authority to edit. Besides, who are we to tell an almighty God what truth is and what it is not? We were never given such a luxury as to pick and choose what we do and do not like about God or His commandments. Adding and removing various parts of Scripture can produce devastating consequences—not only to one's own faith, but possibly to the faith of future believers and their understanding of Christianity. Distortion of God's Word is to be avoided at all costs; 2 Peter 2:1–3 cautions against distorting Scripture and warns of the wrath that is reserved for those who lead others astray.

The Final Authority of the Faith. Since the Bible is a direct revelation from God, the Bible is the final authority of the Christian faith and practice. This is the one and only text that can be elevated as Absolute Truth. The Bible has supreme authority over every other idea, book, or law. All actions of Christian believers should line up in accordance with the truths and the commandments set forth by Christ Jesus. The Bible is the

137 John 14:6.

"instruction manual of life" and should be consulted on a regular basis so that we may seek out and fulfill the moral will of God.[138]

Preparing to Defend the Scriptures

Reasoning the Faith—A Biblical Example. At this point, I will concede that the claims that have been made for the Bible are extraordinarily daring. After all, this book supports the notion that the *Holy Bible* is nothing less than a God-breathed, Holy Spirit–inspired, divine revelation from God—meaning that the text was authored by God and is without error. There is not another person, source, or cause in the entire world where I could be as remotely comfortable, or confident, in making an analogous claim.

The skeptics doubt, or deny, the inerrancy of the Bible because they already know that a claim is meaningless without supporting evidence, logic, and facts. Even I have demonstrated, time and time again, that anybody can make a mere claim without it necessarily having any correspondence to truth. Since we know that a claim alone is not enough to constitute truth, it would only be normal for some people to have doubts with respect to the authority and the inerrancy of the Scriptures. Doubt can arise because people are *taught* their entire lives that the Bible is the final authority, that it is without error, and that you must never question the veracity of the content within. These are all true statements, but to be *even more effective*, we will go one step further by *demonstrating how* the Bible is nothing less than Absolute Truth.

Ironically, the fact that we are "reasoning" the faith resembles a biblical example where Paul reasoned the Gospel time and time again to the Jews and Gentiles alike. The Apostle Paul had a profound understanding of the power that can accompany reason. When the faith is demonstrated to be reasonable, logical, and rational, it can pave the way for the Holy Spirit to begin working within a person's heart. Before the Holy Spirit can begin to work, the heart must be open and receptive to the Gospel, because it is a gift that cannot be forced (as stated in Revelation 3:20).

Luke also understood the power that accompanied reasoning the faith, and he made absolutely sure to document Paul's relentless reasoning on multiple occasions in the book of Acts.[139] Paul defended the Gospel and demonstrated

138 Gary Friesen, *Decision Making and the Will of God* (Colorado Springs, CO: Multnomah Books, 2004), 115.

139 Acts 17:2, 17; 18:4, 19; 26:25.

how the Old Testament prophecies were fulfilled, but he also argued from the perspective of an eyewitness to the resurrected Christ.[140] Saul converted and became Paul because he knew, without a doubt, that Christianity was entirely true. Since Paul knew the faith was entirely true, he was willing to risk being tortured and ultimately executed in order to preach the Gospel.

Paul also reasoned with people because he knew that it was counterintuitive to assume some the basic presuppositions of the Christian faith (such as Christ's virgin birth, sinless life, Messiahship, and resurrection) but that many people would be convinced through a presentation of overwhelming evidence. Unless the faith could be made reasonable to rational people, some would simply not believe. Logic and proof of biblical inerrancy are not too much to ask precisely because everything within the Bible is entirely true; there is nothing within it that can be disproved. When the heart is receptive and the possibility of the existence of God is embraced, people discover that the Bible is far from being void of demonstrable truth. In fact, our explanation provides overwhelming logic, facts, and eyewitness accounts that amount to an overwhelming amount of corroborating evidence of such power that only a fool (Psalms 14:1) could deny God or the Bible as truth.[141]

Reasoning from a Different Vantage Point. Interestingly enough, we should note the fact that the Apostle Paul was unable to use some of the arguments that will be presented in this chapter in favor of the Bible being entirely true because the New Testament had not yet been completed. As a result, Paul had to rely on other methods and arguments when reasoning the faith (such as eyewitness testimony of seeing the resurrected Christ long after the crucifixion). Unfortunately, with the passing of time, we can no longer accept an argument similar to the Apostle Paul's because we no longer have the luxury of listening to testimonies from eyewitnesses who could personally vouch for Jesus Christ to verify the resurrection. Even though we have lost the eyewitnesses, we are still able to prove the Bible to be entirely true through five simple arguments. They are as follows:

---

140 Although Acts 9:3 references a great light, Paul actually saw the resurrected Christ as referenced in his writings (1 Corinthians 9:1; 15:8; Galatians 1:15–16). Paul knew it was Jesus because they had a brief conversation. Perhaps it was the immense glory that radiated from the resurrected body which blinded Paul for three days?

141 Corroborating Evidence: evidence that is independent of and different from but that supplements and strengthens evidence already present as proof of a factual matter (*Merriam-Webster's Dictionary of Law,* 1996).

1. It was miraculously created.
2. It is verified by fulfilled prophecy.
3. It is vindicated by the Resurrection.
4. Its witnesses accepted martyrdom willingly.
5. It has never been proved wrong.

In proving the Bible to be entirely true, we will take a slightly different approach than simply using verses (that reveal divine inspiration) as evidence to claim that the Bible was divinely inspired. In essence, we will refrain from using biblical verses to demonstrate the inerrancy of the remaining verses (which some would consider a circular argument). Instead of using 2 Timothy 3:16 as supporting evidence to prove that the Bible is God-breathed, we will demonstrate *how* the Bible *must* be a product of divine intervention. A divine intervention is absolutely critical because it establishes God's involvement with the creation of the text. Since God was involved by inspiring the content, and since God is holy (unable to sin), we are able to convey the inerrancy of Scripture as God is unable to lie or deceive. Through establishing the need for divine intervention, we are able to prove that the Bible *is* Absolute Truth.

Question with Boldness, Strengthen Your Faith. Before we get into the sections that prove the Bible to be entirely true, we need to point out the fact that it's actually not shameful to ask tough questions about the inerrancy of the Bible. It's not a sin to want to know how or why it was created. In fact, I believe that knowing the answers to these exceedingly difficult questions can be the greatest and most fulfilling challenge that a person could ever take on and it has been done many times in the past.

Countless people have set out to disprove the Bible with vengeance and with malicious intent, but ironically we discover that many have found such overwhelming evidence in support of Christianity that they too became Christians.[142] The men referenced in the footnote are merely one example of a failed attempt to disprove Christianity. These men despised the faith and they wanted to make Christianity look foolish and Christians like crazy people with absurd beliefs with no basis in facts. Even though they set out to make Christianity look stupid, they discovered an undeniable

142 Gilbert West and Lord Nyttleton tried to disprove the Christian faith in early sixteenth century and ended up becoming Christians. Their book was published in 1767; it documents their findings. (http://openlibrary.org/b/OL13460873M/Observations_on_the_history_and_evidences_of_the_resurrection_of_Jesus_Christ).

truth that led to a conclusion that was the exact opposite from their original goal. Little did West and Nyttleton know, an attempt to disprove that which is impossible would be the very reason for their faith.

Since the previous chapter demonstrates the necessity of God and that He must exist for anything else to exist, it would only be logical to think that God has already covered all avenues of doubt in advance. How naïve would it be to suggest that the finite could disprove the infinite? The trail of proof that God has left is daunting, but we must cautiously note that proof and evidence alone are not sufficient to attain salvation.

The Necessity of Faith! There is no question that faith is the most crucial prerequisite to be a Christian; I am not undermining the faith aspect of Christianity.[143] However, if it can be demonstrated that the Bible is entirely true without relying solely on blind faith, then the Christian faith can be reinforced, and we have yet another beginning point to "reason" with family and friends. If logic and factual evidence are used to prove divine inspiration of the Scriptures, some people will accept them as Absolute Truth that much more easily.

Faith in God can be difficult for many people, but when faith is backed with impeccable reason, faith does not seem so "unreasonable." Reason is what the Apostle Paul used time and time again after he discovered that Christianity was entirely true.[144] If the Apostle Paul reasoned with success, you too can have success when armed with the knowledge of the Word of God. Unlike any other religion in the world, Christianity is the only one that can be systematically proven to be entirely true—even in the face of intense and severe opposition.

The time has now come for the evidence to be presented in favor of the Scriptures being Absolute Truth.

1. Method of Creation

The Miracle Book. Christians are able to confidently place their entire faith—everything they live by—in the text that we know today as *The Holy Bible*. The reason that Christians are able to boldly and confidently proclaim the Bible as Absolute Truth is because the weight of proof lies so heavily in its favor. The weight of proof that we will examine relates to how the Bible was written and the people that God used to transcribe

143 Hebrews 11.

144 Acts 17:2, 17; 18:4, 19; 26:25.

each book. As we will see, these men had virtually nothing in common. The fact that these men were able to independently write sixty-six books in perfect harmony with one another, despite their differences, demonstrates the Bible is the product of one author, but was completed through many transcribers.

This section will examine the Bible and the miracle of its creation. Several questions will be answered in the next section: who wrote the Bible, when was it written, where was it written, and how was it written?

One Author, Many Transcribers. The Bible has only one author, but at least forty different transcribers who physically transmitted God's revelation to humanity so that we may have the ability to read, study, and teach the information it reveals. These men physically documented God's message so that, over the generations, the information would not be lost, distorted, or confused.

You may have noticed that I have not used the term *author* to reference to the forty different men wrote the various books of the Bible. The reason that I have not used *author* is simply because according to the dictionary, the word means "the maker of anything; creator; originator."[145] Although these men physically wrote the words, the content was never their original work or ideas; thus, they cannot be considered the authors. The logic behind titling these men with *transcriber* is because the definition aligns more closely to what these men actually did: they transcribed or *made a written copy* of the information they received from God (who was the originator of the content).[146] We know that these men were not the authors because their task was beyond human capabilities. As one example, no human could accurately predict the name and birthplace of a child over four hundred years in advance.

Differing Time Periods. Although the books of the Bible are not placed in chronological order, it is fascinating to note that the first book of the Bible was written (presumably) by Job in about 2000–1800 BC[147], and the final book of the Bible, Revelation, was written in around AD 90–95

145 Author. Dictionary.com. *Dictionary.com Unabridged.* Random House, Inc. http://dictionary.reference.com/browse/author (accessed: July 14, 2009).

146 Transcriber. Dictionary.com. *Dictionary.com Unabridged.* Random House, Inc. http://dictionary.reference.com/browse/transcriber (accessed: July 15, 2009).

147 Ronald A. Beers, ed., *Life Application Study Bible* (Grand Rapids, MI: Zondervan 1986), 838.

by the Apostle John.[148] A conservative calculation of the difference of the two dates would net a period that spans at least 1,890 years from the first book until the last. The span of time between the first and the last books of the Bible argues convincingly that there is no possible way a mortal author could have lived through the two millennia that it would have taken to physically complete the text. Common sense alone negates the possibility of a single author as well as the possibility of a conspiracy theory or the idea of a master plan created in advance by one individual (assuming God was not involved).

Why is a master plan or conspiracy impossible? It would be ridiculous to suggest that a master plan was created by mankind to ensure that the content—each of more than 31,000 verses—would conform to the first book's theme and purpose.[149] Realistically, the time period stretched too long for any author to have micromanaged, because nobody has the ability to bark orders and give instructions from the grave. It's hard enough to get people to do exactly what they are told (even when they agree with you and *are* micromanaged). How much more difficult would it be to give specific instructions if the original author were dead and lived thousands of years earlier? For these reasons alone the idea of a mortal author is preposterous and impossible.

Since most of these men did not know or live in close proximity with one another, they were consequently unable to purposely harmonize their thoughts and writings as each wrote down his particular book.[150] The fact that Job and John lived in different time periods and never knew one another demonstrates there could not have been a link between these two men (apart from God). This "inconvenient truth" alone rules out the possibility of a conspiracy theory simply because these two men were unable to conspire—join in a secret agreement—to create the texts we refer to as the Bible. As a result, God is the only being who could have aligned all thoughts to His.

Differing Backgrounds. The Bible was transcribed by many different men who were very different from one another. Many came from different

---

148 Ibid., 2295.

149 Got Questions Ministries, "What are some interesting facts & stats about the Bible?" http://www.gotquestions.org/Bible-stats.html.

150 The Old and New Testament transcribers could not collaborate. However, in some sections, Matthew and Luke contain very similar content as Mark. Even though these texts slightly overlap, it does not diminish the Truth that they represent.

time periods, cultures, ethnicities, races, economic statuses, social classes, and backgrounds and even spoke different languages. Some held ordinary jobs such as a shepherd, fisherman, herdsman, farmer, or tax collector. Others held much more prestigious positions: king, military general, prophet, physician, or scholar. Some were so close to the powerful rulers of their day that they were considered royalty. Some were experts in the law and doctors, while others had no formal education whatsoever. Despite these vast differences, we see how these seemingly important factors were entirely irrelevant with respect to God's selection. In the end we are left simply with a group of great multiplicity.

Unless God was involved and unless God brought these men together through divine inspiration, they would certainly not have worked together on the same book. Kings do not follow in the footsteps of shepherds. Would a king not rather forge his own path and leave an unequalled legacy of power and prosperity that would astonish future generations? Kings are expected to lead, not follow. What glory could powerful and mighty kings (David and Solomon) receive by *following in the footsteps* of a murderer who became an Egyptian fugitive and finally a shepherd before becoming a prophet (Moses)?[151] Kings are not followers of fugitive shepherds—unless there is a real and powerful God who takes hold of their hearts and molds them so that they choose to leave a legacy not for themselves but for God Almighty. Apart from God, there is no logical explanation for this extraordinarily strange situation.

Written in Unlikely Places. In a dream world, we might think that the Bible was written by the most educated people in the world and in an academic setting that would rival Harvard or Yale. Why would an educational setting with the world's most prominent scholars be appealing? It would give some people comfort because competence is often associated with the number or type of degrees that a person holds. Therefore, it would be more appealing to have the most educated people write in the most prestigious academic arena.

Yet, when we research where the books of the Bible were written, it's soon clear that we have not yet reached the utopia that Thomas More dreamed of because some of the books were written in the most *unlikely*

151 King David and Solomon had the Ten Commandments, and they could read that Moses was a prince (Exodus 2:10), who killed an Egyptian (2:12), who became a fugitive and fled the wrath of Pharaoh (2:15) and who was reduced from royalty to a shepherd (3:1).

places and that God saw fit to use some of the most improbable people. The differences between the backgrounds of these men lead to a variety of dissimilarities on how, when and where the books of the Bible were written. These differences are significant because circumstances influenced each transcriber as to where he began and ultimately finished his book.

Some of the books were written in bizarre places: in the desert, in the wilderness, in exile on an island, in a dungeon, and even in prison. Other books were written in royal palaces where gold, wealth, and the luxuries of life were in abundance. Under normal circumstances, people might not think that it would be an excellent idea to mesh a prison book with the writings of powerful generals and kings; they usually do not accompany one another!

However, when we look at our Bible, we undoubtedly discover that prison books *were* placed side by side with books that were written by royalty. What could place these books together? Nothing but the tug of Jesus. What could create one central theme? Nothing but the tug of Jesus. O precious is the book, that helps me find my God. There is no other cause; nothing but the tug of Jesus. The fact of the matter is that Jesus drew on each of these men's heart to convince them to do the unthinkable—and the results are truly astounding.

Differing Personalities. If we look further into the men that God chose, we discover that they were not all alike in personality. Each had unique traits, and they accomplished their tasks by different methods of leadership and through different styles of writing. To name a few of the most obvious personalities: Paul (a choleric) was extremely bold, decisive, not easily discouraged, and diligent to obey God's commands. Peter (a sanguine) was impulsive, spontaneous and talkative and loved being in the limelight. Moses (a melancholy), was loyal, insecure, self-sacrificing, and reserved.[152]

However differences were not only limited to personality; there are also differences in writing style. Paul wrote very authoritatively and persuasively; in contrast, Luke documented important events, dates, and medical details just as a historian and physician would write. James was extraordinarily blunt in his message, Jude took a negative tone, David wrote poetically, Solomon wrote wisely, while the Apostle John used countless metaphors, symbolic imagery, and prophetic echoes in his writings. Each book is

152 Jay McSwain, *Finding Your PLACE in Ministry* (Alpharetta: MDC Today, 2006), 8.

unique in style, and they differ from one another, but all accomplish one goal as they harmoniously flow together without a single contradiction.

Why am I pointing out differences in personality traits? As we know, it can sometimes be difficult to get along with even our closest family and friends. This is because people are naturally bound to say or do something that we do not like or agree with, because we all have different perspectives, backgrounds, and opinions. People cannot all agree on every issue (*especially religion and politics*), and this is what makes life interesting. Not even all Christians can agree on baptism or whether the earth is thousands or billions of years old—and they worship Jesus Christ!

The point is that people are different, and those who transcribed the Bible were no exception. Still, despite these vast differences, each book is congruent with every other book. Amazingly, the text is without contradiction even though every book contained within the Bible was written on the most controversial subject known to mankind!

Only one explanation can account for how personal bias or opinion was omitted from the books: Each transcriber was inspired by one author who never changes. God is immutable: He is forever the same today as He was yesterday, and He will be just the same tomorrow.[153] God's inspiration on each of the transcribers results in one consistent, perfect, and flawless collection of books. Granted, the personalities of the transcribers are significantly different, but they never clash because God conformed them to His will and for His purposes.

One Central Theme. From Genesis to Revelation, the Bible is a collection of sixty-six individual books, transcribed by at least forty different men, that has 1,189 chapters, more than 31,000 verses, and over 1,200 promises. It is divided into two parts, the Old Testament and the New Testament. The separation of the Old and New Testaments do not represent a division or a change in theology. Instead, the New Testament is the fulfillment of the Old and unfolds the completion of God's perfect plan of salvation. Even though the concept of salvation (as a gift that can be accepted) was introduced in the New Testament, both testaments still harmoniously flow as one single volume without contradiction. They have one central theme that focuses on one overarching message.

We know that there is one theme throughout the Bible by the way each testament positions itself with respect to the other. Both testaments are centered upon redemption, but they present their revelations from different

153 Malachi 3:6.

perspectives. The Old Testament sets forth the messianic prophecies, while the New Testament reveals their fulfillment. The Old Testament centers upon the redemption that the Messiah *will* bring, while the New Testament centers upon the redemption that the Messiah *has* brought. The Old Testament is looking forward to, and anticipating, this arrival, while the New Testament is looking backward and exalting the life, ministry, and salvation that Messiah has established.

It's not a coincidence that the Old Testament is looking forward and the New Testament is looking backward. The fact that both testaments are focused on the same message enables us to conclude that there is one central theme. This common theme is referred to as the *scarlet thread*—the message of redemption through the blood of Jesus Christ. Instead of abolishing the Old Testament, Jesus was fulfilling each and every prophecy so that the Old and New Testaments would be so intricately intertwined that there could be no confusion as to how they have become one.

Furthermore, the New Testament references Old Testament Scripture time and time again. Consider the writings of Matthew, Mark, Luke, John, Paul, Peter, James, Jude—they *all* cite Old Testament Scripture in their work to demonstrate the harmony of the testaments. The most profound reference to Jesus Christ's deity and an account of His existence before creation form the opening of the Apostle John's Gospel:

> In the beginning was the Word, and the Word was with God, and the Word was God. He was with God in the beginning. Through him all things were made; without him nothing was made that has been made. In him was life, and that life was the light of [all people]. The light shines in the darkness, and the darkness has not overcome it.[154]

When John used "the Word," he was referencing Jesus Christ. This becomes evident in John 1:14: "The Word became flesh and made his dwelling among us." Also notice that in your Bible *Word* is always capitalized. John was establishing the deity of Christ and the fact that Jesus existed before the creation of the universe. When we substitute *Jesus* for *the Word* we see how the Apostle John reveals the deity of Jesus Christ. It's fascinating to read the verses with the substitution:

154 John 1:1–5.

> In the beginning was Jesus, and Jesus was with God and Jesus was God. He was with God in the beginning. Through him all things were made; without him nothing was made that has been made. In him was life, and that life was the light of all people. The light shines in the darkness, and the darkness has not overcome it.

Both, the Old and New Testaments exalt, proclaim, and worship one God, whether as the Father, Son, or Holy Spirit.

Differing Methods of Compilation. In 1,900 years a lot can change. Technology, science, and literature undoubtedly progressed from the time that the first books of the Bible were written until Revelation, but somehow each and every book was preserved so that they could later be compiled into a single volume. I marvel at the preservation of the Old and New Testaments because some of the books were engraved in stone and on clay tablets, while others were written on papyrus, leather, parchment, metal, and potsherds (small pieces of pottery).[155] Many of the materials that were used made the text vulnerable, and for many years the Bible was subject to being lost, stolen, damaged, or destroyed.

Today we have the luxury of the printing press and the ability to generate millions of copies a year, but this was not so in the ancient world. They had crude techniques that were not technologically advanced by our standards, yet the books were preserved because God's Word will endure forever.[156] Despite the lack of modern technology and systems of mass reproduction, the materials were preserved until the technology to reproduce them in mass quantities became available. We continue to find the Scriptures in obscure places such as caves (Dead Sea Scrolls), and yet are all congruent with one another.

The One Commonality. As we have ventured through the various sections, we can confidently conclude that the Bible was written over a very long period by many different men who had very little in common. By design, these men couldn't have that much in common! Think about how much we, as a twenty-first-century generation, have in common with the Americans who lived during the Revolutionary War era or even World War Two. Do

---

155 Truthnet, "How was the Bible written?" http://www.truthnet.org/Bible-Origins/4_How_was_Bible_written/index.htm.

156 Mark 13:31.

we dress the same? Have the same technology? Have the same jobs? Now think about how much will change between now and the year AD 3900. Do you think you would even recognize America? Will it still exist? How much could change between now and then? The time span between *today* and AD 3900 is around the length of time between the first and last books of the Bible.

The presence of God is the only commonality that brings all of these men together; without God, they would have had no reason to even speak to one another! Unless God were alive and actively involved with each of the lives, having any harmony between the biblical books would be as difficult as Democrats and Republicans agreeing on every single bill for two thousand years! It's inconceivable to suggest that a group of men who lived in different countries, spoke different languages, had different personalities, occupations, and entirely different cultures could agree on every jot and tittle! But when the presence of God moves people to action, kings and shepherds come together.

Replicate and Demonstrate. By a long shot, I am not the smartest person in the world. But what I am able to discern is that the weight of evidence, with respect to the creation of the Bible, lies so heavily in favor of divine intervention that it would take *more faith* to reject than to simply accept. This section will demonstrate how it does not make logical sense to reject such an explanation, because, without God, the text simply could not have come into existence. The chances that forty different men who spoke different languages, had different occupations, came from different nations, and lived in different times spanning nearly two millennia could create a flawless document, most of which was without collaboration, are so slim that the thought of such an idea actually becomes humorous. Let's discover why.

The Trouble with Harmony. We will create a similar scenario that should put the creation of the Bible into perspective.[157] In this example, we want to replicate a document that is very similar to the Bible. We begin by selecting forty different boys, at birth, and they will become our authors. In the name of simplicity, we will make our group of boys as similar as we possibly can to prove a point. The boys we select will all come from the

157 The scenario is an idea inspired by Dr. Richard Lee, founding pastor of First Redeemer Church in Cumming, Georgia.

same country, speak the same language, live in the same time period, and have similar moral values.

These boys grow up together and attend the same preschool and then the same elementary, middle, and high schools. They all attend the same college, and all will attend the same graduate school. In order to have a diversity of knowledge, each will have a different major so that, all the way through their doctorate degrees, we have a well-rounded group of the best-educated men. After they have earned doctorate degrees in their various fields of study, we separate the men and tell them to begin writing a book that contains a variety of different subjects. The topics that will be divided among them include law, wisdom, morality, history, poems, songs, and parables.

After each scholar receives his respective subject for their book, we let each of them seclude himself so that they can begin writing. Since we only have forty authors, some will have to write multiple books so that a total of sixty-six books are produced. At the end of a specified period (say two years), we bring all the books together. (Keep in mind that, at the end of two years, each of these books has already been finalized; the content cannot be changed.) We collect all the books with the aim of creating one consistent volume that is without a single contradiction or error.

Do you think that it would be possible for each author to individually write different parts of a single book that is without a single error or contradiction? Even though our scholars are very similar, we must keep in mind that not all like-minded people or groups think alike. We know this to be true because Protestants and Catholics (who both worship Jesus Christ) do not render the same interpretations on the exact same biblical verses. Not all conservative lawyers and judges perceive or interpret the law the same. Not all conservative historians have the same analysis or opinion on the exact same historical evidence. Not all financial consultants give the same advice with identical scenarios; the list could go on and on.

The point is that individuals, by nature, differ from one another. Not even identical twins are exactly alike in how they look, think, act, or dress (otherwise nobody could tell them apart, not even their parents). Siblings can also be very different from one another, and they have the exact same parents!

No two people are exactly alike, nor do all people think alike; this is common sense. We must therefore concede that the only way these forty different men could possibly have a congruent collection of books is if they had a mentor who conformed their thoughts to his behind the scenes. If there was one person who guided each author to write with a specific theme in mind and molded their thoughts to his, only then would it be possible to have a document or a collection of books without contradiction.

Pretend Mode—for the Sake of Argument. For the sake of argument, we will let the miracle of creation slip by, and we will pretend that these men were able to create one volume of sixty-six books that are in complete harmony. Whether these men had a mentor or not is immaterial, because the next obstacle that they must hurdle defies any conspiracy because it's impossible to accomplish without a divine intervention. Even though we are pretending that these men were able to create a coherent book that logically flows together and has absolutely no errors, flaws, or contradictions, we must venture into the one topic that we still need to incorporate.

The Trouble with Prophecy. Whoops! In the last section, we did not include prophecy as a topic that these scholars must incorporate into their book. Any similar replica of the Bible would not be complete unless it contained prophecies. Even though we have a document that is without contradiction, we must now figure out how to write hundreds upon hundreds of accurate prophecies.

When we look to the Bible, we note that hundreds of Messianic prophecies were made *at least* four hundred years before Jesus ever set foot on earth. Therefore, in order to make an accurate replica, our authors must also make prophecies about a specific person who will live four hundred years in the future.[158] Writing prophecies of this magnitude would be similar to accurately predicting the President of the United States of America in the year AD 2450 by name (in addition to predicting very specific details surrounding his birth, life, work, and death).

We must temporarily put this scenario on hold in order to examine biblical prophecy. In order to have an accurate replica, we will examine some the prophecies and precisely what the prophets predicted so that we can accurately replicate the process.

---

158 In the name of simplicity, we will omit the other types of prophecies that would venture into topics that concern the final destiny of America (as the prophets predicted the destiny of Israel) and the eschatological prophecies that predict the last days (as they have already been written, are unfulfilled as of today, and could easily be copied).

2. Verified by Prophecy

Prophecy Reveals Divine Inspiration. The previous section examined *how* the Bible was created and the complexity that accompanied transcription by forty different men over a time period of some 1,900 years. There is no doubt that the existence of such a text is phenomenal, but that was merely a preview. It would have been a great tragedy if we could only marvel at how the text was compiled versus the content—the very essence and purpose of its creation! Indeed, the content is of the utmost importance. The mere presence of one fulfilled prophecy is greater evidence of the existence of God than the method by which the Bible was created (due to the complications that arise from predicting an unknown future from a human perspective).

As we begin, we must note that the Bible is filled with hundreds upon hundreds of prophecies that predict(ed) future events. The unusual ability of a mortal man to accurately predict very specific future events, hundreds of years in advance and without error, demonstrates the necessity that each prophet must know the future in advance. This may sound great until we realize that the only problem centers upon the inconvenient fact that knowing the future is an ability that we don't have. Even though common sense tells us that predicting the future is impossible, we nevertheless read time and time again where prophecies were made, and fulfilled, throughout the Bible.

The accurate prediction and fulfillment of prophecy demonstrates a reliance on an external source to provide information that would have otherwise been unknown. This external source of information, as we will demonstrate, must be nothing less than an intervention by God Himself. There is no other explanation as to how future events could have been predicted with the immense precision that we find in the Bible. It is for this reason that prophecy demonstrates that the Bible must be a product of God. As such, the content within must be entirely true as God is unable to lie. The argument that prophecy is Absolute Truth is as follows:

1. The Bible is pervaded with prophecy.
2. Accurate prophecy is an impossible task for humankind to accomplish, as it entails predicting future events with precision.

3. The prediction and fulfillment of prophecy is nothing less than a miracle.[159]
4. A miracle, by definition, is the result of divine intervention.
5. Divine intervention is God's involvement in the human world.
6. God's involvement in the world is limited.
7. Since God is *holy*, God cannot sin.
8. Since God cannot sin, God cannot lie or deceive.
9. Since God cannot lie or deceive, divine inspiration must *always* constitute truth.[160]
10. Prophecy is a product of divine inspiration
11. Therefore, all prophecy is Absolute Truth.

Prophecy will turn out to be a fascinating topic to examine, but due to the vast number and different types of prophecies, it would be beneficial to narrow our scope. In this chapter, we will examine prophecies from the Old Testament that concern the Messiah. Since some scholars estimate that there are over three hundred Messianic prophecies, we must further narrow our scope. Due to the vast number of Messianic prophecies, this section will merely examine eighteen of the Messianic prophecies.

Even though we will only examine eighteen of the prophecies, it needs to be noted that each and every single prophecy was fulfilled precisely as predicted. Even though the scope of this book does not enable an in-depth examination of all the prophecies, Herbert Lockyer has in-depth commentary on them in his book *All the Messianic Prophecies of the Bible.* Lockyer's book is dedicated to proving Christianity to be true through the hundreds of Messianic prophecies.

At Least Four Hundred Years Beforehand. The prophecies that we will examine surround the birth, life, and death of Jesus Christ. Each of these prophecies appears in the Old Testament, and its fulfillment is documented in the New Testament. Malachi was the final book of the Old Testament, and scholars estimate that this book was written approximately

---

159 Miracle: an effect or extraordinary event in the physical world that surpasses all known human or natural powers and is ascribed to a supernatural cause (dictionary.com).

160 Divine inspiration is a form of divine intervention. God's inspiration is what enabled the transcribers to predict future events with a precision unknown to mankind.

430 BC.[161] After the book of Malachi, there was a period of biblical silence that spanned over four hundred years; there were no prophets, prophecies, or extravagant miracles and no new divine inspiration. The Old Testament was sealed shut; no other books would be added.

Since Malachi was the last book of the Old Testament, and we know that it was written well over four hundred years before the birth of Jesus, all prophecies concerning the Messiah were also made well over four hundred years in advance. The period of biblical silence is extremely important because we know that each prophet was long *dead* before his prophecies had any chance of being fulfilled.

Even though the Messianic prophets would never live to see their prophecies fulfilled, they were somehow able to predict the future with extreme accuracy. This accuracy we examine is not human. The only way a prophet could have possibly predicted the future hundreds of years in advance was through a form of divine intervention. All of the transcribers were divinely inspired and guided as they wrote their books; some saw detailed visions and others heard the audible voice of God and were told what to write. Regardless of the *form*, an intervening God that revealed a specific message is the common denominator.

Prophecy is also unique because it can be used to prove the existence of God. Since prophecy is *impossible* unless divine intervention is part of the equation, we know that God must exist; otherwise, the prophecies could not. Since there were hundreds of prophecies surrounding the birth, life and death of Christ and every single one was fulfilled, we *must conclude* that God does in fact exist. Although the fulfillment of prophecy was not included in Chapter 7 when we proved the existence of God, it's an excellent argument that demonstrates how the existence of God is necessary.

Nevertheless, the eighteen prophecies that we will examine make extremely specific predictions. Take a moment to scan through the prophecies; notice what each Old Testament prophecy predicts and where it was fulfilled in the New Testament. [162]

---

161 Ronald A. Beers, ed., *Life Application Study Bible* (Grand Rapids, MI: Zondervan 1986), 1627.

162 Ibid., 1938.

Prophecy	Old Testament Prophecies	New Testament Fulfillment
1. Messiah was to be born in Bethlehem	Micah 5:2	Matthew 2:1-6 Luke 2:1-20
2. Messiah was to be born of a virgin	Isaiah 7:14	Matthew 1:18-25 Luke 1:26-38
3. Messiah was to be a prophet like Moses	Deuteronomy 18:15,18,19	John 7:40
4. Messiah was to enter Jerusalem in triumph	Zechariah 9:9	Matthew 21:1-9 John 12:12-16
5. Messiah was to be rejected by his own people	Isaiah 53:1,3 Psalms 118:22	Matthew 26:3,4 John 12:37-43 Acts 4:1-12
6. Messiah would be betrayed by one of his followers	Psalms 41:9	Matthew 26:14-16, 47-50 Luke 22:19-23
7. Messiah was to be tried and condemned	Isaiah 53:8	Luke 23:1-25 Matthew 27:1,2
8. Messiah was to be silent before his accusers	Isaiah 53:7	Matthew 27:12-14 Mark 15:3-4 Luke 23:8-10
9. Messiah was to be struck and spat on by his enemies	Isaiah 50:6	Matthew 26:67 Matthew 27:30 Mark 14:65
10. Messiah was to be mocked and insulted	Psalms 22:7,8	Matthew 27:39-44 Luke 23:11, 35
11. Messiah was to die by crucifixion	Psalms 22:14, 16, 17	Matthew 27:31 Mark 15:20, 25
12. Messiah was to suffer with criminals and would pray for his enemies	Isaiah 53:12	Matthew 27:38 Mark 15:27,28 Luke 23:32-34
13. Messiah was to be given vinegar and gall	Psalms 69:21	Matthew 27:34 John 19:28-30

14. Others would cast lots for Messiah's garments	Psalms 22:18	Matthew 27:35 John 19:23, 24
15. Messiah's bones would not be broken	Exodus 12:46	John 19:31-36
16. Messiah was to die as a sacrifice for sin	Isaiah 53:5, 6, 8, 10, 11, 12	John 1:29; 11:49-52 Acts 10:43; 13:38-39
17. Messiah was to be raised from the dead	Psalms 16:10	Acts 2:22-32 Matthew 28:1-10
18. Messiah is now at God's right hand	Psalms 110:1	Mark 16:19 Luke 24:50-51

Examining a Few. After taking some time to look at the prophecies and their fulfillment, two need to be highlighted because they are absolutely *shocking* as to what they predict. They are important and are highlighted because they demonstrate that Messiahship was not a choice that just anybody could have made after reading the messianic prophecies. (I contend that the messianic prophecies were not even known or understood until after the resurrection – when it was too late to choose!)

The first prophecy that we will examine predicts the birthplace of the Messiah (#1). The reason this prophecy is in the limelight is because some skeptics are adamant that, since there were four hundred years between the Old and New Testaments, it would have been possible for the Messiah to have fulfilled prophecies because Jesus could have simply read them in the Old Testament. Therefore, they claim, Jesus had the ability to fulfill each of the prophecies surrounding Messiahship.

This argument may sound great up until the point when they discover that there is a prophecy that concerns the Messiah's birthplace. The idea of an unborn infant choosing the location of his birth is absurd (but humorous at the same time). Who do you know that, while in their mother's womb, could determine where they would have been born? (I don't think the umbilical cord works like a telephone line; besides, infants can't talk.) I know this may sound crazy, but for some reason, I have a difficult time believing that an unborn infant could tell his mother where he would like to be born. My bull meter is pegging out because I understand that, by nature, this is not a prophecy that could have been fulfilled by *choice*. (The idea that nobody is able to choose Messiahship will be developed further in Chapter 10.)

The second prophecy that we need to examine (#14) predicts very specific events that would take place during the crucifixion. This prophecy tells us, in advance, what the Roman soldiers would do as Jesus hung from the cross. The shocking part is that this prophecy predicted what others—not Jesus—would do with His garments. Since the prophecies also predict how other people would act, a wrench lands in the skeptic's argument because nobody can control other people's actions. Even if you wave a gun at the bank staff, you cannot force them to give you the code or open the safe without their consent; they must willingly comply. Of course the bank workers are encouraged to comply because you have a gun, but if they are willing to accept death or torture, then your task would become impossible. (Similarly, the Apostles refused to stop preaching the Gospel, and since nobody could force them to be quiet, all but one was executed.)

The point is that not all prophecies surrounded what Jesus would or would not do; they included other people and parts they would play. If the Roman soldiers did not want to cast lots for Jesus' garments, who would be in a position to compel them in order to fulfill the prophecies? Jesus was unable to do anything because he was hanging from the cross. Besides, at this point, Jesus did not have many friends; by now even his own disciples had cursed his name and denied any affiliation with Him—or had simply fled.[163]

It would be absurd to suggest that the Roman soldiers fell in with this scheme, because they were not exactly on friendly terms with Jesus. Remember how much fun they had mocking and beating Him? They thought it was hilarious to dress Jesus up as a king, smash a crown of thorns on his head, put a staff in his right hand (to look like a scepter), and then to bow down before him crying "Hail, king of the Jews!"[164] It is absurd to think of convincing the Roman soldiers to comply with the prophecies; it makes no sense to suggest that they would willingly go along with the prophecies to fulfill them when they were vehemently *against Jesus*! I would suggest that the Roman soldiers did not even know of the prophecies because these soldiers were not Jewish and because the Jewish scholars and disciples did not even know the meaning or significance of the prophecies—the topic to which we now turn.

163 Matthew 26:56, 69–75; Mark 14:50, 66–72; Luke 22:54–62; John 6:66.
164 Matthew 27:31.

The Unknown Prophecies. I would like to consider another interesting point that arises when the messianic prophecies are examined. It's my belief that the significance of the prophecies was *not* fully known until after the resurrection. Until then, nobody really understood who Jesus was or why He came to earth. Jesus' true purpose was not understood, before the resurrection, in the way we understand it today.

There are several reasons for this conclusion. First, to this day the Jews still do not acknowledge the prophecies as fulfilled. The Jews are blind to the messianic prophecies because they are expecting a powerful, military-style leader who would establish an earthly kingdom. Since Jesus did not fit that description, they simply wrote him off as a blasphemer, and the religious leaders ultimately executed the "disruption" to their lives. Was this not the reason that Jesus condemned the religious leaders in Matthew 23:13–39?

Second, the reason that the prophecies were not fully known is simply because of the fact that not even the *disciples* understood why Jesus had to be crucified. The disciples of all people should have known because they were the closest to Jesus; they traveled with Him daily for up to three years before He was executed. We know the disciples did not know the reason for the crucifixion because, when Jesus was predicting His death, Peter vowed to never let such an event take place (which is when Jesus called Peter Satan and told him not to interfere). Also, in the garden of Gethsemane, Peter even tried to step in and prevent Jesus' arrest.[165] If the disciples knew what the prophecies would accomplish, why would they try to interfere? There is no logical reason. The truth is that the disciples did not understand the true meaning of the prophecies; otherwise, they would never have tried to interfere with God's perfect plan.

Third, if the significance of the prophecies had been fully known, then the Jewish religious leaders would not have crucified Jesus. Since the religious leaders were against Jesus (God) for selfish reasons (Matthew 23:13–39), the only way they could have spoiled God's plan—if that were even possible—would be to sentence Jesus to life in prison. Think about the consequences of refusing to execute Jesus! He could have never died for our sins, shed redeeming blood, or been raised from the dead.[166]

Fourth, and even more fascinating, is that even Satan himself did not fully understand the significance of the messianic prophecies! The very fact that Satan entered into Judas, with the sole purpose of betrayal to aid the

165 Matthew 16:23; 26:51; Mark 14:43–52; Luke 22:47–53; John 18:1–11.
166 1 Corinthians 2:6–16.

execution, demonstrates his extreme ignorance of God's sovereign will. Had Satan really understood the significance of the prophecies, don't you think he would have tried to foil God's plan? They are, after all, enemies. Instead, Satan unknowingly fulfilled his role quite nicely as he aided in the execution. If Satan truly had known the significance of the resurrection, he would have never allowed the crucifixion, much less connived to bring it about.

The reason I pointed out that the prophecies were not understood is because the anti-Christian movement parades the idea that anybody could have chosen to be the Messiah by reading the prophecies in advance. If the anti-Christian movement can demonstrate that anybody could have *chosen* to have fulfilled the prophecies (which implies that Jesus was not God and there was no divine inspiration), then the prophecies are reduced to being meaningless. However, if it can be demonstrated that the prophecies were so specific that they prohibited "just anybody" from fulfilling them by choice, then we know that only one candidate had the credentials to be the Messiah. (The inability for a person to choose Messiahship will be discussed at length in Chapter 10; these facts are setting the stage for a later argument.)

In the meantime, we return to proving that the messianic prophecies are a product of divine inspiration. Objective-minded people understand that it is humanly impossible to accurately predict specific future events without error; yet the major and minor prophets predicted distant future events in great detail hundreds of years in advance without error. We also note that the prophecies were not limited to one prophet. In the eighteen messianic prophecies that we examined, there were five different transcribers involved. The fact that there are multiple transcribers involved destroys the idea of fulfilled prophecy being an obscure fluke or isolated success.[167] Indeed, the truth is actually quite the contrary: these abnormal occasions (or miracles) actually took place time and time again in the Old Testament era. A similar recurring miracle that involves multiple people and extends throughout hundreds upon hundreds of centuries demonstrates that prophecy was an intentional revelation that had a specific purpose.

The anti-Christian movement has also has paraded an unusual idea: that multiple sets of prophecies surrounding each event were created and that only the accurate prophecies were saved and incorporated into the Scriptures. For example, the prophets predicted that the Messiah would be born in Bethlehem, Jerusalem, Samaria, and Capernaum. When it was

167 Fluke: (3) a stroke of luck (merriam-webster.com).

discovered that the Messiah was born in Bethlehem, the other prophecies were discarded so that only the correct ones would remain. Although this may sound like a viable option to the skeptic, we should demonstrate the impossibility of this idea because they may not want to rely on my suggestion alone; this we will now proceed to do.

Raining on the Skeptic's Parade. Finally, we are now ready to pick up our previous scenario (when our forty authors discovered that they had to write prophecies). We will continue with that example (from a secular viewpoint) to demonstrate the impossibility of making accurate prophecies apart from divine intervention. As mentioned before, our group's task in replicating prophecy will be to accurately predict the President of the United States of America in the year AD 2450. Since this date takes place before the election year (2452), they do not have to worry about a potential president-elect (assuming America still exists, the Constitution is actually respected, elections still occur, and they do so every four years).

In order to accurately predict the name of our future President, our group of forty men will need to generate thousands upon thousands of guesses because there is an abundance of names currently in circulation.[168] Guessing the first name alone would be difficult enough, so they should stick with only predicting the first name. They put into writing all their predictions before moving to the next category.

Next, they need to try and predict our future President's birthplace. They begin guessing, but keep in mind the many different possibilities because each state has hundreds of cities with thousands upon thousands of collective possibilities. Nevertheless, they put into writing all our predictions before moving to the next challenge: predicting his occupation before his presidency.

Unfortunately, there are so many different jobs in existence that they might as well try to list each and every one (in addition to predicting future jobs that may be available more than four centuries in advance). The fact that societies progress and jobs change may pose a slight problem, but they write them down anyway.

Pressing forward, they now need to try and predict very specific events that will hallmark our future President's life and even his death. They need to predict how other people (the opposing party, other foreign leaders, etc.) will treat the President and their reactions to his policies, the President's

168 Isaiah 7:14 is the prophecy of the Messiah's name; Matthew 1:23 was the fulfillment.

approval rating as well as what members of his White House staff will be fired or will potentially betray the President. They put into writing all our predictions.

Even though they have not created nearly as many prophecies as there are in the Bible, we have enough to convey an idea. The next step has some unintended consequences that will complicate the process further. In order to accurately replicate the process, they must finalize their prophecies in a published format. This means, for each and every single *type* of prophecy, they must narrow down their predictions to only one answer set that predicts the future President's name, birthplace, occupation, events surrounding his life and death, etc. Why must they narrow down their answer set? After all, the skeptic claims the possibility of multiple answer sets!

The reason they must finalize the prophecies four hundred years in advance is because the Old Testament prophecies were sealed, left in writing for the world to see, four hundred years before the Messiah was ever born. To be accurate, they must replicate the process. Furthermore, we know that there was only one "answer set" of prophecies because, out of the countless Old Testament copies that have survived, all prophecies are congruent with one another. There has never been a contradictory version of the Old Testament with different prophecies, which argues against the possibility of multiple testaments being created to hedge the bet.

Nevertheless, after they finalize their combination of prophecies, they need to publish them. After they have chosen one version of prophecies to be published, the only thing left to do is hope and pray that they are right because they, unfortunately, will not be alive to see the outcome.

'When It Rains, It Pours.' I hate to rain on this parade, but has it occurred to the anti-Christian movement that the task of accurately predicting events four hundred years in advance might be slightly difficult? In this scenario, I was quite nice because I did not make the idea look as foolish as it could have been (by splitting up the different prophecies among five or six people, scattered across the centuries, who would have each been responsible for different predictions and unable to collaborate their efforts). Incorporating these variables into the equation would have certainly increased their chance of being incorrect at an exponential rate as there would have been more moving parts that must have all perfectly aligned with one another.

Think about the chances of accurately predicting one of these prophecies, such as the birthplace. That chance, alone, would be unfathomable. Why would predicting the birthplace of a specific person four hundred years in the future be exceeding difficult? As time progresses, population increases. The increase in population leads to the creation of new cities that would be unknown at the time the prophecy was made. After all, a lot can happen in four hundred years. However, in the ancient world, the prophets had a much more difficult task because, in that era, cities and civilizations were always susceptible to being conquered and destroyed (whereas, in the twenty-first century, a super power recognizes the rights of smaller nations). The prophets not only had the obstacle of choosing between which cities would be created in the future, but they also had to avoid choosing a city that would have been destroyed and abandoned.[169]

Think about the chances of accurately predicting a specific person by name. According to the U.S. Census Bureau, the world population at AD 1 was estimated to be between 170 million and 400 million people.[170] If we take the middle road, and use the mean population, we have 285 million people. Thus, the prophets had a 1 in 285,000,000 chance of being correct. At this point it would be beneficial to note that as we add each subsequent prophecy's chance of coming true, the overall chance rises at an exponential rate. As more and more prophecies are made, the chances of being wrong drastically increase while the number of eligible people decreases; this is but common sense as the predictions become more narrow and exclusive.

In his book, *Science Speaks*, Peter Stoner estimates that the probability of even fulfilling eight of the prophecies is unfathomable: "We find that the chance that any man might have lived in the present time and fulfilled all eight prophecies is 1 in 10^{17}." Thus, we move from one in 285,000,000 (accurately predicting a name) to one in 100,000,000,000,000,000 and we are only at eight fulfilled prophecies. I know, I know—these numbers are starting to look like our national debt because they are incomprehensible, but Stoner gives us a visual aid to put the chance of fulfilling eight into perspective:

> Suppose that we take 10^{17} silver dollars and lay them on the face of Texas. They will cover the state two feet deep.

169 Micah 5:2 predicts Messiah would be born in Bethlehem. Peter Stoner, in his book *Science Speaks*, predicted the chance of one man being born in Bethlehem was 2.8 x 10^5 or 1 in 300,000 rounded.

170 U.S. Census Bureau, "Historical Estimates of World Population," http://www.census.gov/ipc/www/worldhis.html.

> Now mark one of these silver dollars and stir the whole mass thoroughly. Blindfold a man and tell him that he must pick up one silver dollar and say that this is the right one. What chance would he have of getting the right one? Just the same chance that the prophets would have had of writing just eight prophecies and having them all come true in any one man, from their day to the present time, providing they wrote in their own wisdom.
>
> Now these prophecies were either given by inspiration of God or the prophets just wrote them as they thought they should be. In such a case the prophets had just one chance in 10^{17} of having them come true in any man, but they all came true in Christ.
>
> This means that the fulfillment of just eight prophecies alone proves that God inspired the writing of those [eight] prophecies to a definiteness which lacks only one chance in 10^{17} of being absolute.[171]

Realistically speaking, the chances of fulfilling only a few prophecies are so mind-boggling that people struggle to put them into perspective. If the probability of fulfilling merely eight prophecies was equivalent to stacking the entire state of Texas with silver dollars two feet high, marking one and then having to choose the right silver dollar on the first attempt, shall we ponder the probability of each and every single prophecy being fulfilled? Josh McDowell, in *Evidence that Demands a Verdict*, estimates that the probability of every prophecy being fulfilled is $1{:}10^{157}$—or one in 10,000,000,000,000,000,000,000,000,000,000,000,000,000,000,000,000,000,000,000,000,000,000,000,000,000,000,000,000,000,000,000,000,000,000,000,000,000,000,000,000,000,000,000,000,000,000,000,000,000,000,000,000 (10 followed by 156 more zeros).[172]

Beating a Dead Horse. It's quite possible that I have run this argument into the ground, and any further discussion of this subject could be considered "beating a dead horse." But why stop the fun? Shall I point out that we, as the intelligent human beings we are, fail at predicting the future today? Even with our sophisticated technology, it's virtually

171 Peter Stoner, *Science Speaks* (Chicago: Moody Press, 1969), 106–107.

172 Josh McDowell, *Evidence that Demands a Verdict* (San Bernardino, CA: Here's Life, 1979), 167.

impossible to *accurately* predict anything in the future in great detail. Think about it: the weather forecasters (with all their satellites, computer programs, algorithms, and radars) are unable to predict the weather in the next twenty-four hours with absolute certainty and yet there were people, without any technology, who accurately forecasted the future hundreds of years in advance!

Nevertheless, the point is that without divine inspiration, it would have been impossible to produce even one of the messianic prophecies. Yet, when we open the Bible, we find hundreds of published messianic prophecies, and *every one of them* was fulfilled. We could not replicate the biblical process even if we tried, and this is why our scenario fails. Even if there was a mentor who conformed all the authors' writings, skeptics cannot account for how the Bible has made accurate prophecies (unless, of course, they embark on a crusade to try and rearrange the dates of prophecy so they become "prophecy after-the-fact" because allowing the possibility of God is unacceptable). Since the fulfillment of prophecy demands a divine intervention, fulfilled prophecy must constitute Absolute Truth, because God is unable to lie or deceive.

3. Vindicated by Resurrection

The Eyewitnessed Miracle. The resurrection of Jesus Christ was nothing less than a miracle—a divine intervention—on the part of God. The resurrection is significant because it vindicates each and every single claim that Jesus made during his ministry. The resurrection by itself proves that the teachings of Jesus Christ are entirely true. We know that the words of Jesus must be entirely true because God is holy and unable to lie. Since the resurrection proved that Jesus was God, Jesus must also be holy and unable to lie. Thus, Jesus could not have lied under any circumstances. Therefore, the teachings of Jesus Christ are Absolute Truth. (To avoid being redundant, this section is brief because of the subject is treated in detail in Chapter 11.)

4. The Willingness to Accept Martyrdom

The Unintended Consequences of Hatred. The first century anti-Christians were brutal people and they were some of the most intolerant bigots the world has ever known. The first-century anti-Christian movement not only hated Christians because of their religious beliefs but also relentlessly persecuted, tortured, and even executed them for being "Christlike." Without a doubt, what it meant to be Christian was entirely different in the first-century world than in a twenty-first-century America. When the Apostles lived, preaching the Gospel was abominable, and the consequences sometimes led to an offense that was punishable by death. We know this because eleven out of the twelve Apostles were executed for professing faith in Christ, and the twelfth was tortured and then exiled.[173]

Yet, for some reason, the more these early Christians were persecuted, the more they shared the Gospel. The more the enemy tried to silence them, the louder they preached. The more intense their beating, the more they "gloried" in the Lord! Each and every time the enemy tried to stamp out Christianity, there was an even greater push back.

The question we must ask ourselves is why. Why would these early Christians *willingly* choose to be persecuted and tortured? What could possibly compel them to accept martyrdom before committing apostasy and turning their backs on Christ? It seems odd that in a time period, when taking a stand for Christ sometimes meant losing everything, these early Christians were willing to sacrifice their own lives. Discovering the answer to this pointed question will be revealing because the desire to accept martyrdom is counterinstinctive. People are engrained with a "flight or fight" reflex because we are programmed to survive. Furthermore, people instinctively try to avoid putting themselves through agonizing pain and discomfort, but all these tendencies were disregarded by the early Christians.

Before we can answer the "why" question, we need to discover one commonality between all martyrs. Regardless of religion, we know that all martyrs have *faith* that they are sacrificing their life for a cause that they believe is entirely true. Essentially, martyrs believe they are exchanging value for value (their life in anticipation for a heavenly reward). If martyrdom were not perceived to be an exchange of value for value, what could possibly motivate an inherently selfish being?

When the September 11th terrorists hijacked four airplanes with the intent to use them as weapons of mass murder, these Muslim jihadists genuinely believed that they would be rewarded by Allah for their act of

173 Apostles.com, "Which of the 12 Apostles were Martyred?" http://www.apostles.com/apostlesdied.html.

war.[174] When the Apostle Paul decided that he would rather be executed than turn from his faith, he genuinely believed that he would be rewarded for his unwillingness to submit in the face of intense persecution. When Cassie Bernall was asked during the Columbine massacre whether or not she believed in God, she genuinely believed that her Christianity was entirely true and that she would be rewarded for being martyred in the Jesus' name.

The common denominator in these examples is that these martyrs genuinely believed that they were dying for a cause that was entirely true. Unless a person truly believes in their faith, martyrdom is simply not considered. Who could convince a person to believe that the earth is flat because the clouds are made of iron, to the point that they would be willing to be whipped until the flesh fell off their back and to the point where they would be willing to sacrifice their own life in defense of that particular belief? I believe that I could not find a person in the entire world who would die for that belief because there is absolutely nothing to gain! Martyrdom for believing in a flat world and iron clouds would be impossible because people know that the proposition is simply not true. I would suggest that there would be few Christians willing to die for their faith, based on the percentage of people who evangelize—and they believe their faith to be true beyond a shadow of a doubt!

Since we know that, at a minimum, people are willing to die only for that which they believe to be entirely true, let's examine who was in the position to make the best decision. If we look to the Muslims, we know that their decision was based upon *pure faith* (no verifiable eyewitness accounts). Muslims, as we will examine in Chapter 12, cannot prove their faith to be entirely true nor can Muhammad's "revelation" be confirmed by anybody except Muhammad. Nevertheless, Muslims believe their religion is entirely true because they have faith. Cassie Bernall believed that Christianity was entirely true, but she also had faith in God. Even though Cassie could have systematically proven the Bible to be entirely true, she was still reduced to what she hoped for and certain of what she did not see (the definition of faith in Hebrews 11:1). All Christians must have faith that Jesus Christ is Lord—except for a select few.

The only people who could have known for a fact that Christianity was entirely true were those who saw the resurrected Christ. People may be willing to die for what they have faith is entirely true, but the eyewitnesses

174 Jihadist. Dictionary.com. *WordNet® 3.0*. Princeton University. http://dictionary.reference.com/browse/jihadist (accessed: April 7, 2010).

to the resurrection are the only people in world who have never needed faith in order to believe that Jesus was God. These eyewitnesses knew for a fact that Jesus was God and it's not a coincidence that each and every single Apostle was *willing* to suffer torture, persecution, and even execution.

The only reason why the Apostles could have been willing to sacrifice their lives was that they were bound by that which was Absolute Truth.

5. Never Been Proved Wrong

You'd Be Surprised at What God Knows! Since one of the basic attributes of God is infinity, God must also have infinite knowledge and wisdom. Since God must know everything, and He inspired the Bible, does it seem likely that a person could prove the Bible wrong? Did it ever occur to you that nothing has ever occurred to God?[175] The Bible cannot be proven wrong. Most of the skeptic's concerns and objections are answerable, but an effort to address their every concern would warrant a book in itself. Instead of correcting misconceptions, we will reverse the approach and affirm the Bible's veracity by pointing out the extreme wisdom that far surpassed all knowledge during its era.[176] Instead of trying to argue, we will merely note *some* of what the Bible taught before science could prove these facts true.

Russell's Rant on Biblical Accuracy. The Bible is not only without error, it's extraordinarily accurate with what we know to be true today. Contrary to what some people claim, many different fields of science conform, and ultimately concur, with the Bible. (Science must agree *with the Bible* because Scripture was written long before science enabled us to verify the following scientific truths.)

Even though scientists teach that creation emerged from a singularity—that is, out of nothing—at some point in the past, the Bible first taught creation (out of nothing) thousands of years earlier.[177]

---

175 Dr. Richard Lee, founding pastor, First Redeemer Church, Cumming, Georgia.

176 *Most* is stressed because the Bible is not all-inclusive and a skeptic can always connive an unanswerable objection.

177 Genesis 1:1. The big bang singularity is, in theory, the moment before creation in which space and time did not exist. It's believed that all matter in the universe originated from one infinitesimally small point.

Even though scientists teach the big bang theory, the Bible referenced this vast explosion of light thousands of years earlier.[178]

Even though scientists teach the sun and the moon had to be created before life could have existed on earth, it was first taught in the Bible.[179]

Even though scientists teach that shrubs, plants and animals did not exist—indeed, could not have existed—on the earth until there was rain (or a source of water), the Bible taught it first.[180]

Even though scientists teach that the sea creatures and the birds existed before the land animals (i.e., the theory of evolution), it was first taught in the Bible.[181]

Even though scientists teach that mankind was last of the living things to appear on the earth, it was first taught in the Bible.[182]

Even though scientists teach that mankind is distinct from every other animal and is superior in many ways, it was first taught in the Bible.[183]

Even though scientists teach that mankind is also distinguished from every other animal on the planet because we have something that is referred to as a "moral conscience," the Bible taught it first.[184]

Even though scientists teach that mankind is basically comprised of the same molecules that constitute dust and that when we die, we return to dust, the Bible taught it first.[185]

Even though scientists teach that the earth is a sphere and was never flat, the Bible taught it first.[186]

Even though scientists disagree with other religions because the earth was never held up by Atlas or by five mythical pillars, the Bible first taught that the earth is suspended over *nothing*.[187]

Even though scientists teach that everything that is seen is made out of that which is not seen (molecules/atoms), the Bible taught it first.[188]

---

178 Genesis 1:3. A reference to the first light is presumed to have been the light caused by the big bang when all matter was created. Atheists are now trying to dispose of the big bang theory because it implies a finite universe and the necessity of God's existence.

179 Genesis 1:14–19.

180 Genesis 2:5.

181 Genesis 1:20–23.

182 Genesis 1:26.

183 Ibid.

184 Genesis 3:5.

185 Genesis 2:6–7; 3:19.

186 Isaiah 40:22.

187 Job 26:7.

188 Hebrews 11:3.

Even though scientists teach that the earth will one day be destroyed by fire in one form or another, the Bible taught it first.[189]

Even though scientists can now see far into the depths of the universe and now teach its incomprehensible magnitude with certainty, the Bible first taught, thousands of years before the telescope was invented, that the nations (on this earth) are but a *drop* in the bucket and are like *dust* on the scales.[190]

Even though scientists cannot give meaning, purpose, peace, or joy to life, the Bible also has that answer.[191] Where science falls short, the Bible picks up. Before science could explain how, the Bible revealed what. Before science was, God had always been. Is it mere coincidence that science just happens to agree with the Bible?

To Believe, or Not to Believe, That is the Question. Was it really possible for the author of Hebrews to understand the molecular structure of the universe without divine inspiration? Was it really possible for the Apostle Peter to know, for a fact, that the earth would one day be destroyed by fire without divine inspiration (a scientific theory that would not develop for another two thousand years)? Was it mere chance that Job knew that the earth was suspended over *nothing* when all other religious doctrines endorsed myths that described pillars or Atlas supporting the world? Was it a fluke that Isaiah somehow knew that the earth was a sphere, and that God sits enthroned upon the circle of the earth, without divine inspiration? (By the way, if you take any sphere and look down on it, amazingly, you see a circle.) Mere chance that all of these verses just happened to reflect truth even though, at the time they were written, there was no possible way to verify or prove them?

At some point, enough is enough! How much more evidence does one need in order to believe? There comes a time—when chance after chance after chance is added up—that the *chance* of all those chances coming true is not even coherent. When obvious logic and truth are disregarded, refusal to accept the obvious is ultimately reduced to selfishness—an

---

189 2 Peter 3:7. If nothing else brings this to pass first, when the sun is about twice its present age, it will slowly expand into a red giant phase, enveloping the orbits of the inner planets—including Earth.

190 Isaiah 40:15. The first telescope was credited to Hans Lippershey, of Holland, and he was the first scientist to apply for a patent for the telescope in 1608 (http://www.astronomy2009.org/static/archives/presentations/pdf/educational_whoinvented.pdf).

191 Colossians 1:16.

unwillingness to acknowledge what is obviously true in order to fulfill personal gain, desires, or satisfactions. What other reason could account for or justify rejection?

The Bible is not evil; it teaches humankind how to live a happy, fulfilling, and prosperous life (in the physical, spiritual, and eternal realms). Everything within is designed to help the reader. Nevertheless, scientists are just now discovering the immense truth that had been documented for thousands of years. They are merely discovering what God has known, and taught, all along. Everything within the Bible is entirely true, and if science disagrees, science has some catching up to do. Science once taught the earth was flat, but eventually concurred with the Bible. If we know one thing to be entirely true, we know that science continually changes, but the Word of God has stood *unchanged*—and it remains as true today as it always was.[192]

In the last section, it seemed as if every time the scientists turn around and make another discovery, it was first explained by the Bible. These "inconvenient truths" are becoming so problematic that many scientists are desperately trying to escape from the singularity of the big bang. After all, a finite universe demands the existence of God because something cannot of itself come from nothing. They are trying to convince you that you are not conscious because consciousness cannot be explained without divine intervention. The Naturalists will suggest *anything* "no matter how mystifying" so that they do not have to include God into their lives.[193] The true motive of Naturalism's science will be examined in Chapter 15; be ready with a stress ball when their true motive is presented in their own words, because you may need it.

Case Closed. Below is the case summary, and it incorporates all the arguments presented in this chapter.

The Final Argument that the Bible is Absolute Truth

1. The method by which the Bible was created constitutes a miracle.
2. The fulfillment of prophecies constitutes a miracle.
3. The resurrection of Jesus Christ constitutes a miracle.

---

192 Malachi 3:6; John 17:17.

193 Marxist Richard Lewontin, *New York Review of Books,* January 7, 1997: 31.

4. The inability to prove the Bible wrong is the result of a miracle.
5. The apostles only accepted martyrdom because they personally verified the veracity of these miracles.
6. A miracle, by definition, is a divine intervention.[194]
7. Divine intervention is God's involvement in the world.
8. God's involvement in the world is limited.
9. Since God is holy, God cannot sin.
10. Since God cannot sin, God cannot lie or deceive.
11. Since God cannot lie or deceive, divine intervention must always constitute truth.
12. Divine inspiration is a form or type of divine intervention.
13. The Bible is a product of divine inspiration.
14. Therefore, the Bible is Absolute Truth.

The Bible Can Even Verify Itself

Can a Source Verify Itself? The question often comes up with respect to proving the Bible true by using the Bible: "How could a source possibly be used to verify *itself*?" More specifically, the question becomes "Can the Bible actually be used to prove itself as entirely true?" There seems to be division about the answer to this question, so we will attempt to answer it once and for all.

No; It's a Circular Argument. In the traditional sense, the same text should never be used to validate itself as credible, much less to prove that the given text is entirely true. Some people advocate that the rationale behind not using the Bible to prove the Bible is essentially a "circular argument."[195] A circular argument is still "begging the question" because it's "an argument that commits the logical fallacy of assuming what it is attempting to prove."[196] The circular argument also "uses its own conclusions as one of its stated or unstated premises. Instead of using proof, it simply asserts the conclusion in another form, thereby inviting the

194 Miracle: an effect or extraordinary event in the physical world that surpasses all known human or natural powers and is ascribed to a supernatural cause (dictionary.com).

195 Positive Atheism, "Introduction to Activistic Atheism," http://www.positiveatheism.org/faq/faq1114.htm.

196 About.com, "Circular Argument," http://grammar.about.com/od/c/g/circargterm.htm.

listener to accept it as settled when, in fact, it has not been settled."[197] As a result of the circular argument, many non-Christians are adamant that Christians must not use the Bible as supporting proof of God's existence or of the entire truthfulness of the text.

Naturalists and agnostics alike love using this argument to try and bypass the authority of the Bible and the fact that the Bible establishes the existence of God. To their credit, the Naturalists and the agnostics are entirely correct, but only to a certain degree. I will demonstrate how using the Bible to prove God's existence and the authority and the credibility of the Scriptures is entirely permissible as well as the reasons why.

Yes; the Bible Is One Volume, with Many Books. This section will demonstrate how the Bible can be used to prove itself true beyond a shadow of a doubt as well as to prove the existence of God. How is this possible? Well, the Bible is a text that is unlike any other in history. As we have demonstrated, the Bible is actually a volume—a collection or library—of sixty-six individual books that constitute *one*. Since the Bible was transcribed by forty different men throughout a period of some 1,900 years, the Bible is certainly unlike any other text in existence today. When we use one biblical book to confirm or verify the content of another, they do not necessarily rely on the same book or transcriber. The diverse nature of the Bible excludes it from being considered a "circular argument."

The circular argument concept is disproved by examining prophecy. Since the prophets made prophecies surrounding the birth, life, ministry and death of the Messiah, the circular argument is not applicable to the Bible because these prophets could not have used "their own conclusions as their stated or unstated premises." How is this possible? Well, when the prophets began prophesying about the Messiah, we know that it was at least four hundred years prior to His birth. Since the Messiah would not be born during these prophets' lifetimes, they could *not* have used *a verifiable conclusion* as a premise, and their texts could not have "assumed what [they were] attempting to prove" because, at the time the prophecies were made, the outcome was unknown; it was only potential that had not yet been confirmed or actualized. Besides, the significance of the prophecies, as demonstrated, was unknown. Since there is an obvious break in time between the original prophecies, the fulfillment of the prophecies, and the documentation of the fulfillment of the prophecies (the Gospel writers did not write until decades after prophetic fulfillment), Christians are able

197 T. Edward Damer, *Attacking Faulty Reasoning* (Wadsworth, 2001).

to confidently use the Bible to prove itself as entirely true without using a circular argument. The very method by which the Bible was created prevents this argument from gaining any traction.

Just because the Bible is a combination of sixty-six different books brought together in one volume does not automatically discredit the Bible, nor does it prevent one book from being used to verify or prove another; this is the beauty of Scripture. The Bible can be used to support itself just as a research paper is deemed to be sufficiently supported when forty different books that were written by different authors are used as references. For many research papers, forty references would be overkill. For some reason, though, when the same logic is used in supporting the Bible, non-Christians have a double standard and deny what they would ordinarily accept or deem permissible. Does this make any sense, or could the non-Christian movement be pushing an agenda? (The answer awaits in Chapter 15).

The Hypothetical If. Perhaps, if the entire collection of canonical books were written *at one time* and were transcribed by *one person*, the circular argument would be credible. If the entire Bible had been written at one time, then the non-Christians could conclude that the Bible "uses its own conclusions as one of its stated or unstated premises." But there is no reason to even venture into this hypothetical example because we know for a fact this example could not possibly represent the Bible.[198]

Pinnacle Point

Nothing but Absolutes. We are now at the pinnacle point of the book. The Bible *is* Absolute Truth, since it is God's written revelation to humankind. We know this to be entirely true because it has been established that the text is nothing less than a miracle that could have only been accomplished through a divine intervention; there is no other way to account for the five arguments that were made in this chapter. Establishing the Bible as Absolute Truth implies that all the facts, principles, accounts, stories, and claims within are without exception *entirely true*.[199]

198 The circular argument would be entirely permissible with the Qur'an because the text was written by one author whose revelation was solely limited to Muhammad.

199 The Bible is still Absolute Truth even though we may not yet know how to accurately interpret all of the prophecies (especially in the book of Revelation).

As a result, each subsequent chapter in this book will be grounded on the foundation of Absolute Truth. Without first building an indestructible foundation, it was not possible to boldly write about Christianity or defend the many spiritual truths conveyed through Scripture. The foundation has been established; the facts have been presented; and now it is time to progress further to the heart and soul of Christianity.

Venturing into Exclusivity. In the next chapter we will dig deeper into what the Bible teaches in regard to salvation, the path by which all must travel, the provision they all must appropriate, in order to attain heaven. Since the Bible, both Old and New Testaments, centers on the figure, teachings, and ministry of Jesus Christ, He will be the next major topic. Our objective will be to discover precisely who He is and the many bold and audacious claims that were made during His ministry on earth.

Chapter 9

The Exclusivity of Absolute Truth

"I am the way, the truth, and the life. No one comes to the Father except through Me."

—*John 14:6* (NKJV)

"Whoever has God's Son has life; whoever does not have his Son does not have life."

—*1 John 5:12* (NLT)

Thus Saith the Lord

A Tough Pill to Swallow. The last chapter established how the Bible is a product of God and therefore must be entirely true. Since we already know why we must wholeheartedly believe the entire Bible, we can now begin digging deeper into what the Bible actually teaches in regard to eternal life and salvation. For some people, the theological implications of the Bible may be a tough pill to swallow because the Bible does not leave much room to vacillate. This chapter presents the extremely exclusive claim on salvation that the Bible makes, followed by an examination of the character and claims that Jesus made while living on earth.

An Exclusive Claim on Truth. The Bible makes it clear to each and every reader that there is only one way that a person may enter into Heaven. In this section, we will briefly cover seven verses that encapsulate the Gospel message.

Romans 3:23. We begin looking at the plan of salvation by establishing a universal need—one that every person has (regardless of race, sex, nationality or background). The one commonality that all people have is sin; we are all children of wrath.[200] This does not mean that we are currently under the wrath of God, but it does mean that all of us are born with a sinful nature and that we are experiencing in life some of the punishment that stemmed from Eden. From Eden, humankind has always had a sinful nature; we can easily verify that nature by observing children.

When was the last time you had to teach a child to do wrong? Do you need to teach them how to fight, throw a rock through a window, or take toys from one another? Of course not; children are taught right because they inherently do wrong. Since all people are, by definition, sinful in nature, we have a common beginning point which we can begin presenting the Gospel. Romans 3:23 reads: "All have sinned and fall short of the glory of God." This scripture teaches that we all have done wrong, and we all fall short of God's perfection.

Romans 6:23. Since we have all sinned, we need to know whether or not there are any consequences. If there are consequences to sin, we may want to know about them before it's too late. (Ignorance of the law is not an excuse for breaking the law.) According to Romans 6:23, "The wages of sin is death, but the gift of God is eternal life in Christ Jesus our Lord." From this passage, there is both good and bad news.

First, the bad news. Each and every time you sin, something dies. If you are married, every time you lust over another person, something dies within your marriage. You may lose a portion of the love you had for your spouse, or you may lose the ability to convey genuine affection. You may not have as much respect for yourself as before, or you may begin to undermine the relationship you have with God—whatever it may be, the fact is that something has died. However, death in Romans 6:23 is not limited to the physical realm; death is threefold.[201] Death can be physical (such as a loss of love with a spouse) or spiritual (impacting your relationship with God), or it can take a lifetime to actualize (eternal death). All people are accountable to God for what they have done wrong. The

200 Ephesians 2:1–3.

201 Death occurs in the physical, spiritual, and eternal planes.

punishment of all sin, regardless of how big or small, is spiritual death. The spiritual death is an eternal separation from God, and the Bible describes it as a place of "weeping and gnashing of teeth."[202] Hell is the punishment God has established for the transgressions committed against Him.

Now for the good news. Even though there has been a pessimistic tone thus far, this is an amazing passage because it also provides an escape. We do not have to choose to bear our punishment (eternal damnation and the wrath of God) if we choose not to shoulder that burden! God offers every single person an escape, a "gift" that will enable us to have eternal life. Scripture makes it clear that the gift can only be received through Jesus Christ; His blood, however, will atone for the sins of those who place their faith upon Him.[203]

John 3:3. How does a person accept this gift of eternal life? How can a person possibly be granted permission to enter the kingdom of God? John 3:3 (TNIV) reads, "Jesus replied, 'Very truly I tell you, no one can see the kingdom of God without being born again.'" For some, this is an unusual passage. People may reply, "What does it mean to be born again?" or "How can I be born again when I have already been born?" However, this passage references the birth of the soul. Like God, each person is a triune being that consists of a mind, body, and soul. When a person is physically born, the mind and body is alive, but the soul is dead. In fact, the soul will remain dead until a person is spiritually born again.[204] Since a spiritual rebirth is a very important part of the plan of salvation, we need to know precisely how a person's spirit comes to life.

John 14:6. The Bible explicitly reveals that there is only one way in which any person—regardless of status or accomplishment—can be born again. In order to be spiritually reborn, we must first understand where to go for the answer. Some people look to other religions, alcohol, sex, drugs, or material possessions for an answer, but the answer cannot be found in a substitute. John 14:6 reads: "Jesus answered, 'I am the way and the truth and the life. No one comes to the Father except through me.'" This is a fascinating verse because Jesus makes an exclusive claim: unless people go through Jesus (the gate), there is no other way to be saved. In other words,

202 Matthew 8:12; 13:42, 50; 22:13; 24:51; 25:30; Luke 13:28.

203 Matthew 26:28; Romans 3:25.

204 Ephesians 2:1–5.

only Jesus is able to give the gift that all people need for eternal life; there is no sufficient alternative or substitute.[205]

Now, the stage is set: we know that we all have a common problem. There are serious consequences, but God has left us an escape that can only be found in Jesus. The next passage explains how to be born again and accept the gift of eternal life and how all people pass through Jesus.

Romans 10:9–11. According to Scripture, *how* is actually quite simple. Romans 10:9–11 reads:

> That if you confess with your mouth, "Jesus is Lord," and believe in your heart that God raised him from the dead, you will be saved. For it is with your heart that you believe and are justified, and it is with your mouth that you confess and are saved As the Scripture says, "Anyone who trusts in him will never be put to shame."

Confession is an acknowledgment that we, on our own efforts, cannot meet the requirements of absolute perfection that God demands for entrance into heaven. Repentance is the actual change that we make as we try and live a godly life. Repentance is key because it's a vital part of the change that Christians should undergo. Confession and repentance go hand in hand because you cannot meaningfully confess without repenting. Apologizing, feeling bad, and promising to do better are nice, but actually changing demonstrates true remorse. Then, believe that Jesus is God and that He was resurrected to atone for your sin. That was it! That's all people have to do in order to be spiritually reborn and bound for heaven!

These verses are the most important in the plan of salvation. Even if every other verse is understood and accepted, a person remains spiritually dead without putting into action the belief that brings confession, repentance, and acceptance. This is where people ultimately make their decision because Scripture forces a choice: either they confess, repent and believe, or they do not. There are many people who completely understand

205 Since today's all-accepting society has a tendency to exalt the open mind, Christians are branded as intolerant, bigoted, and fundamentalist. The problem with that label is that Christians are merely passing on the message given by Jesus Christ. Christians do not speak for God; He speaks for Himself. As a result, Christians must continue to teach this exclusive message regardless of how hip or cool or popular it may or may not be. In addition to the exclusive claim, the inverse truth is serious: a person without faith in Jesus Christ cannot have eternal life.

the plan of salvation, yet they are not saved because they never accepted the gift. Others understand the Gospel but refuse to submit and consequently reject the Gospel message.

To become a Christian, a person must voluntarily choose to join the ranks. Salvation is a gift, and like any gift, it must be received. If a person does nothing, the gift is still there, but it is of no benefit until accepted. Furthermore, we can only accept the gift of salvation while we are living on earth.[206] The next verse will help us understand repentance more clearly.

2 Corinthians 5:15. As mentioned above, repentance is a critical part of truly placing faith in Jesus Christ. Without repentance, there can really be no change in the life and heart of the believer. The message of repentance is clearly found in 2 Corinthians 5:15:

> He died for all, that those who live should no longer live for themselves but for him who died for them and was raised again.

In this verse, Paul makes it clear that Jesus died for all, but also that those who accept salvation "should no longer live for themselves." Denying the self is a redirection of lifestyle, and it refocuses the purpose of life so that the Christian lives for Jesus. Accepting salvation demands a reordering of priorities: God first, family second, and so forth.

Revelation 3:20. The entire plan of salvation has been presented, but there is one verse left. Since Jesus will not force anybody to confess, repent or accept, the only way to receive is to invite Him by opening the door of your heart. Jesus is patiently standing by for acceptance, Revelation 3:20 reads:

> Here I am! I stand at the door and knock. If anyone hears my voice and opens the door, I will come in and eat with them, and he with me.

Jesus Christ is an active God who is actively pursuing all people because He wants them to accept His gift of eternal life. To put into perspective

206 Since salvation is a gift that every person must individually accept; people cannot be born into Christianity. Salvation cannot be bought or sold; it cannot be stolen or lost.

how desperately Jesus Christ desires to know us, consider what He went through to even make salvation possible. Jesus left the comforts and the luxury of heaven, humbled Himself to become a mortal man, and set foot on the face of the earth. Jesus entered into a ministry that would ultimately cause Him be ridiculed, mocked, tortured, and finally executed. The pain and agony Jesus went through, to bridge the gap between humankind and God, is a testimony in itself of the passion that God has for us. Jesus is standing at the door; He is knocking. The question now becomes: Who will answer?

The Character of Christ

Getting to Know Jesus. One of the most controversial topics that a person can mention in today's "all-accepting" society is Christianity. Why is Jesus such a controversial topic? For some reason, it does not seem to be offensive when people talk about other religions such as atheism, agnosticism, Islam, or Hinduism—but as soon as Jesus Christ is brought into the conversation, people become exceptionally quiet. Perhaps it's because people are well informed about Jesus and the claims that He made while on earth.

There is no question that Jesus Christ is *the most* influential being who ever walked the face of the earth. He has had an impact that no other king, warrior, or celebrity has ever had throughout human history. The effects from Jesus' birth, life, death, and resurrection continue to ripple out through the generations. Even today, thousands of years later, we see the effects of His existence. Consider a few examples of the influence Jesus Christ has had in the modern world.

The calendar year centers on the birth of Christ. The largest religion in the world (Christianity) centers on Jesus Christ. The best selling book of all time, the Holy Bible, centers on Jesus Christ. The most celebrated holiday in America (Christmas) centers on Jesus Christ. Lent, Ash Wednesday, Palm Sunday, and Easter all center on Jesus Christ. Thanksgiving is where we, as Americans, give thanks for the blessings that were bestowed on us by Jesus Christ. The Constitution and the Bill of Rights center on the Judeo-Christian ethic (which centers on Jesus Christ).[207] Monuments all over the United States contain etched scriptures that cannot be erased (the Bible centers on Jesus Christ). The courts, until recently, openly displayed the Ten Commandments, and the entire Bible centers on Jesus Christ.

207 Refer to the *American Patriot's Bible* edited by Dr. Richard Lee.

Jesus was not an ordinary man who lived an ordinary life. This will become evident as we examine some of the bold and audacious claims that Jesus Christ made.

Jesus Claimed to Be God. In the New Testament, we see time and time again where Jesus claimed that He was equal with God. Listed below are a few verses where these claims of deity cannot be mistaken:

- John 10:30: "I and the Father are one."
- Matthew 27:43: "for he said, 'I am the Son of God.'"[208]
- John 8:12: "I am the light of the world. Whoever follows me will never walk in darkness, but will have the light of life."
- John 8:58: "'I tell you the truth,' Jesus answered, 'before Abraham was born, I am!'"
- Matthew 4:7: "Jesus answered [Satan], 'It is also written, "Do not put the Lord your God to the test."'"

If we look to the other major religions, we discover that no other prophet or religious leader ever claimed *to be God.* Moses, Muhammad, and Confucius all claimed to know about God, but they never actually claimed to be God. Granted, some interesting characters here and there have claimed to be God, but none of these people are remembered because they could not prove their claim. Jesus is remembered in history because He claimed to be God and then proved to the world that He was God with a resurrection (which will be explored in depth in the next chapter).

Nevertheless, after reading only a few passages about Jesus, we are able to conclude that Jesus Christ not only equated himself with God but also claimed to *be* God

Jesus Claimed to Be the Only Way into Heaven. Jesus not only claimed that He was God but went a step farther when He also claimed that He was *the only way* that any man, woman, boy, or girl could enter into the gates of heaven. This is an extraordinarily daring claim because the reverse implication is that, without knowing Christ, nobody is able to enter into the gates of heaven, regardless of their level of morality, intent,

208 Matthew 27:43 is a taunt from those who accused and mocked Jesus. This verse was added in order to emphasize the fact that Jesus' enemies knew the weight of His claim.

accomplishments, religion, or denomination. We know that Jesus made this claim when we read the following verses:

- John 14:6: "I am the way and the truth and the life. No one comes to the Father except through me."
- Matthew 10:32 (TNIV): "Whoever publicly acknowledges me [Jesus] I will also acknowledge before my Father in Heaven. But whoever publicly disowns me I will disown before my Father in Heaven."
- Acts 4:12: "Salvation is found in no one else, for there is no other name under heaven given to men by which we must be saved."

With respect to salvation and how people receive redemption, Christianity differs from all other religions. Every other religion is humanity's attempt to reach God, whereas in Christianity we see God's attempt to reach humanity. Jesus descended out of the luxuries of heaven and was willing to be executed on a rugged cross so that His blood would suffice as the final atonement for all sin. Accepting salvation enables God to cleanse us from sin. Unless Jesus is the only way to heaven, the redemptive work would have been a waste—it would have been the greatest tragedy conceivable. It's for this reason that Jesus proudly proclaims "I am the way and the truth and the life."

Jesus Claimed to Have All Power. When we read the Gospel accounts, we cannot venture very far into any of them without noticing that there is something special about Jesus: He had supernatural abilities. The power that Jesus possessed astonished people because He continually worked miracles, healed the sick, drove out demons, resurrected the dead, walked on water, accurately foretold future events, and ultimately defeated Satan with His own resurrection.

Although Jesus was never *not* God, He submitted Himself to become human. As a result, He was subject to natural phenomena such as gravity, time, age, pain, sickness, and fatigue and was even obedient to death for a period of three days. We do not have the capacity to fully understand the power that God has or how Jesus could be fully man and fully God at the same time, but we do know that He limited Himself and His power in order to complete the redemptive work on the cross.

Even though Jesus allowed Himself to become mortal and subjected Himself to human limitations, it's comforting to know that the power He gave up was only *temporary*. As soon as His mission was completed, Matthew provides us with an account that confirms the power and authority of Jesus Christ over all heaven and earth. Matthew 28:18 reads "All authority in heaven and on earth has been given to me." Jesus was not granted some authority, not a little authority, not partial authority, but *all authority* over heaven and earth was restored to Jesus Christ before he ascended back into heaven. When Jesus told the disciples that all authority was restored to Him, He undoubtedly claimed to have absolute power.

Jesus Claimed to Completely Forgive Sin. Jesus claimed to be able do something that no human is capable of: to have the authority of completely forgiving the sin of any and everybody who asks, regardless of what they have done.

- Matthew 9:2: "When Jesus saw their faith, he said to the paralytic, 'Take heart, son; your sins are forgiven.'"
- Mark 2:5: "When Jesus saw their faith, he said to the paralytic, 'Son, your sins are forgiven.'"
- Luke 5:20: "When Jesus saw their faith, he said 'Friend, your sins are forgiven.'"
- Luke 7:48: "Jesus said to her, 'Your sins are forgiven.'"
- Acts 10:43: "All the prophets testify about him that everyone who believes in him receives forgiveness of sins through his name."

Even though Acts 10:43 does not contain the words of Christ, it does reflect the message that Jesus conveyed in the first four verses. There is no question that Jesus made it clear that He is not only able but *willing* to completely forgive our sin. God's forgiveness is not limited to who we are or what we have done, and it's quite unlike any other forgiveness we have ever encountered. The forgiveness that God offers is permanent; in the eyes of God, it is as if the sin never happened. When God forgives, He completely erases the event from history. There are metaphors in the Bible illustrating the completeness of God's forgiveness. It is described as the blotting out of our sin (with ink), never to be remembered again; separating the sin from us as far as the east is from the west; and having our sins thrown into the depths of the sea where they will never be found again.[209]

The forgiveness that Jesus offers is truly remarkable—especially when we realize that we are part of the reason Jesus had to sacrifice Himself on the cross. For a moment, let's pause to reflect on divine forgiveness and how it affects us. The consequence of sin is death; we feel guilty, wrong, burdened, and unworthy when we grieve the heart of God. However, complete forgiveness is unlike any other because God does not simply grant a temporary pardon, only to bring it back and remind us later. The forgiveness that God offers is *permanent.* When God forgives, it's as if it never happened! Complete forgiveness positively affects us because it enables us to have an insurmountable feeling of relief because we are freed from the mental and physical captivity that sin can bring into our lives. This type of forgiveness is not human. Some people view confession with a negative connotation, but it's actually one of the better gifts that Jesus offers because it relieves us from having to carry the burden of sin.

If I could put God's forgiveness in the most politically correct statement, I would say: Jesus Christ is an equal opportunity forgiver who encourages everybody—regardless of race, sex, color, religion or background—to experience His forgiving power and to capitalize on the gift of eternal life.

Jesus Claimed He Is Worthy of Worship. Many times throughout the New Testament Jesus indirectly alluded to the fact that He is worthy of worship, but He never made this claim to the public. Perhaps the reason that this claim was never made public was because the Jewish religious leaders would have tried to prematurely execute Jesus. Or perhaps the people were not yet ready to handle the entire truth. Or perhaps Jesus did not come to be worshipped on earth because He had a very specific redemptive mission. Whatever the reason may be, we know that Jesus indirectly implies that He too is worthy of worship because He constantly equates Himself with God (and, of course, God is worthy of worship).

Within the entire New Testament, there is only one verse where Jesus explicitly revealed that *He alone* is worthy of worship.[210] After Jesus had been in the wilderness fasting for forty days and forty nights, Satan showed up with the hopes of taking advantage of Jesus because he was

209 Psalms 51:1–2; Psalms 103:12; Micah7:19.

210 Matthew 4:10.

physically exhausted and weak due to fasting for such a long time.[211] Since Jesus subjected Himself to human limitations (such as physical weakness, fatigue, and hunger), Satan knew that this would be the opportune time for temptation. As a result Satan tempted Jesus three times: to turn stones into bread, to throw Himself off a cliff where angels would break His fall, and to bow down and worship Satan in exchange for his earthly kingdom.

Throughout all these temptations, we know that Satan already knew Jesus' true identity because, in the first temptation, Satan provocatively taunted Jesus with "If *you are* the Son of God, tell these stones to become bread."[212] (Ironically, if Jesus were truly not God, then Satan would have had no motive for tempting Him.) We also know that the other demons that Jesus encountered also knew His true identity, because many called Jesus out by name and title, and they often begged Him not to torture them before the appointed time.[213] Before the resurrection, only demons truly knew Jesus' identity because they are spiritual beings that are not of the physical world.

Since Satan and the demons already knew precisely who Jesus was, it would have been nothing new for Satan to have heard, "Away from me, Satan! For it is written: 'Worship the Lord your God, and serve him only.'"[214] When we combine the many claims of deity that Jesus made with the demons calling Jesus God (and sometimes begging for mercy), it's not hard to conclude that Jesus was referencing Himself. Jesus not only equated Himself with God, but in the desert Satan was reminded that all beings—whether human or angelic—must worship and serve one God.

The Importance of Understanding the Claims

Knowing What to Defend. Christians need to know the many different claims that Jesus made and the exclusive claims that the Bible makes so that we know what we believe and the reasons why. Biblical illiteracy has been a major problem for Christians, and I have read time and time again, in personal evangelism books, where former atheists and agnostics complain that they were better informed about the Bible than the Christians they

---

211 According to the *Guinness Book of World Records*, the longest hunger strike (without being forcibly fed) on record is ninety-four days. This record was set in 1920 during the Irish Civil War.

212 Matthew 4:3 (emphasis added).

213 Matthew 8:28–29; Mark 1:33–34, 5:6–13; Luke 4:33–36, 41; 8:28–33; 10:17.

214 Matthew 4:10.

knew. Biblical illiteracy poses a problem because when Christians do not firmly know what they believe or why, they cannot possibly formulate an effective or convincing argument on behalf of their faith. Are we not instructed to "study to shew thyself approved unto God"?[215]

The only way that the Christian faith can grow is through the propagation of the Gospel. If Jesus is truly a priority in our lives, it should not be a burden to spend some time reading the Bible or praying. These should be natural tendencies because we should have a burning passion to learn about the Lord our God and to tell Him our desires, problems, and requests. We know that our desires shape our priorities, because the Bible says, "Where your treasure is, there your heart will be also."[216] Prayer and the Bible are the two primary means of communication between us and God, and if we never take the time and invest in the most important relationship conceivable, we do not have much of a chance of being faithful with the knowledge, talents and abilities that we have been given.

The first purpose of knowing the claims is to know what we believe. The second purpose is to be able to share, and defend, our faith with family and friends. Equipping believers to present and defend the faith is the primary purpose of this book. The second will be a desperate attempt to revive America from the devastation that accompanies liberalism.

How Can the Claims Be Vindicated? The question is often asked, "How can I know that Jesus' claims were actually true?" The answer to this very important question needs to have an answer that not only makes sense, but proves, beyond any doubt, that the claims are entirely true and worthy of our trust. Christians can be reassured in many ways that Jesus' claims are entirely true because they are presented in the Bible (which is a product of God and must be true), because every Apostle was willing to die for these claims, because they cannot be proven wrong, but most importantly because Jesus Christ was resurrected to physically vindicate each and every single one of them as Absolute Truth.

Without the resurrection, the Apostles would not have been willing to die for Jesus Christ. Without the resurrection, the Bible could not be hailed as Absolute Truth. Without the resurrection, Christianity could be disproved. Without the resurrection, Christianity would be no different than any other religion that has made a truth claim about God, because

---

215 2 Timothy 2:15 (KJV).
216 Matthew 6:21.

it would have absolutely no verifiable physical proof. The resurrection is of utmost importance to the Christian faith.

It's for this reason that the entire next chapter is dedicated to examining Jesus. We need to know precisely who Jesus is and how He proved, beyond a shadow of a doubt, that each and every single claim that He made was entirely true. If Jesus predicted His death and resurrection and then proved it, each and every single claim would be vindicated.[217]

---

217 Matthew 16:21–28, 17:22–23, 20:17–19; Mark 8:31–38, 9:30–32, 10:32–34; Luke 9:21–27, 9:44–45, 18:31–34.

Chapter 10

Who Is Jesus, and Why Do I Need Him?

"Salvation is found in no one else, for there is no other name given under heaven by which we must be saved."

—Acts 4:12

"Father, the time has come. Glorify your Son, that your Son may glorify you. For you granted him authority over all people that he might give eternal life to all those you have given him. Now this is eternal life: that they may know you, the only true God, and Jesus Christ, whom you have sent."

—John 17:1–3

The Crux of Christianity

One is Unlike the Others. Jesus Christ is the absolute focal point of Christianity; without Him the faith could not exist. Since the entire faith revolves around Jesus, we need to know whether or not His claims were true. After all, Jesus made some very bold claims when He claimed to be God, all-powerful, the only way to heaven, able to forgive *our* sin, and worthy of *our* worship. Jesus also predicted His death at least three times and claimed that three days later He would be resurrected.[218]

Since the Bible is a result of divine inspiration, and the resurrection claims are found in the Bible, we know that they are entirely true. But instead of merely claiming that the claims are true because they are found

218 Matthew 16:21–28; 17:22–23; 20:17–19.

within the Bible, we need to know precisely how each and every single claim was vindicated. The only way that Jesus could have vindicated each and every single claim was to be executed and then actually rise from the dead. If Jesus could not even rise from the dead, then it would exceedingly difficult to believe that He was truly all-powerful. On the other hand, if it can be demonstrated that Jesus, in fact, did rise from the dead, then all of His claims *would be* physically verified and proven true; which would also prove that every other claim that Jesus made is also true.

Without a doubt, Christianity is the only religion in the entire history of the world that is able to claim—and also prove—a resurrection. No other religion in the world can compare, because none has nearly as much evidence, logic, or supporting facts. Therefore, the resurrection is the crux—the heart and core—of the Christian faith; *without it, Christianity would be as meaningless as every other religion, and people would still be dead in their sins.*[219]

The Inferiority of a Claim. Claim is defined as "an assertion of something as a fact."[220] A claim alleges that a proposition is true, but whether that proposition *is true* depends on whether it corresponds to reality. A claim may or may not be true, but we are unable to verify veracity unless we have supporting proof or evidence. This intuitively makes sense because anybody can claim to be able to restore sight to the blind, but unless they prove or physically demonstrate their ability, their claim is essentially meaningless.

Every other religion on the face of the earth differs from Christianity because they all lack convincing verifiable proof. Sure, other religions make many truth claims. Sure, they may believe, with their entire soul, that they are correct. Sure, they may be able to offer some logic as to why they believe. Sure, they have a view—an opinion—on truth, but opinions alone cannot verify truth because truth is always indifferent to opinion.

Proof is sufficient evidence that *establishes* the proposition in question (the claim) as a fact; it corresponds with reality or with what actually occurred. A claim without proof is always inferior to a claim with proof, because a claim that is unsupported is certainly an attempt to establish truth, but it fails because there is no way to verify whether or not that claim is true.

---

219 1 Corinthians 15:17.

220 Claim. Dictionary.com. *Dictionary.com Unabridged*. Random House, Inc. http://dictionary.reference.com/browse/claim (accessed: January 12, 2010).

Thus, the difference between Christianity and every other religion is verifiable proof. Muhammad claimed he had a revelation, but that vision cannot be confirmed because it was limited to Muhammad alone. Confucius had some philosophical and religious views, but what evidence does he have? "The sources of Confucius' life [come] later and do not carefully separate fact from fiction. Thus it is wise to regard much of what is known of him as legendary."[221] The Greeks had many gods, but none came to earth to reveal their existence. Hindus believe in many gods, with one supreme god, but none have proved their existence. The Canaanites once thought Baal was an actual god, but when put to the test, not even Baal could not perform.[222]

Before creation, God was. Before the Messiah set foot on the face of the earth, He had a plan. Before the skeptic ever doubted, God supplied ample proof. Before every other religion was established, God knew the difference would lie within the proof. Hence, the distinguishing factor is not a coincidence.

Each time I venture into proof, I am reminded that proof, alone, is not sufficient; only faith can bridge the gap to salvation. This is entirely true, and *faith* is the topic of the entire eleventh chapter of Hebrews. Therefore, I need to put proof into its proper context. Proof invokes reason (the basis or the cause of a belief); reason justifies faith ("being sure of what we hope for and certain of what we do not see"); faith is the faculty by which a person accepts salvation. There is no conflict between faith and reason, and the Apostle Paul demonstrated this truth time and time again.

The Superiority of Proof. Proof is, indeed, far superior than any claim that has no supporting evidence. It is not an accident that no other religion can supply convincing proof that reveals the glory of God.[223] It is not an accident that Christianity has an overwhelming supply of eyewitness accounts, irrefutable facts, and concrete evidence in support of Absolute Truth.

Christians are blessed with having physical proof, eyewitness accounts, and the assurance of an errorless source to back up the claim of a resurrection. We now embark on discovering how the proof of Christianity overwhelms

221 *The Stanford Encyclopedia of Philosophy*, "Confucius," http://plato.stanford.edu/archives/fall2008/entries/confucius/.

222 1 Kings 18:26–40.

223 Judaism is true, but it is partial truth. Judaism rejects Jesus, who is the completion of Absolute Truth. Judaism will be examined in detail in Chapter 13.

all other religions and reduces them to pure conjecture whose claims cannot be verified.

Encapsulating Easter. We begin with a very brief summary of the events before we examine the details.

Jesus was born of a virgin, lived a sinless life, and entered into a ministry where He would fulfill the messianic prophecies. Jesus was accused of blasphemy when claimed to be God. Jesus died upon a Roman cross after being severely beaten and condemned to die. The physical death of Jesus was verified by both the Jewish and Roman people before the body was taken down from the cross. In fact, the death of Jesus was never disputed by any of the major groups of people that lived during that time period. Instead, people accepted the death of Jesus as common knowledge. The death was common knowledge because the event caused an enormous uproar and the trials and execution drew significant attention. Some supported Jesus, but most were against Him.

Even though Jesus died on the cross, He was ultimately resurrected to reveal the powerful plan of salvation. We now examine, in detail, the events that led up to the crucifixion so that we are equipped to defend the resurrection. We begin in the garden of Gethsemane.

Gethsemane to the Cross

The Arrest and Trials. The events that led up to the execution reveal the hatred that the Jewish religious leaders had for Jesus Christ. In this section, we will examine the final hours of Jesus' life until the time that He paid the ultimate price for salvation.

While in the garden of Gethsemane, Jesus prayed the high priestly prayer and was mentally and spiritually preparing Himself for the cup that He was about to drink. Jesus' intense prayer was interrupted when Judas led a large crowd, which included a servant of the high priest, directly to Gethsemane, the garden where Jesus was arrested. Judas Iscariot betrayed Jesus by offering to help the Jewish religious leaders arrest Him in exchange for thirty pieces of silver.

After Jesus was arrested, He had multiple trials before very powerful men.[224] The first division—or series—of trials began with Annas. This trial took place during the night when few people were awake. This pretrial was conducted in secrecy because the Jewish religious leaders had no grounds to charge Jesus, but they hoped to build evidence by formulating accusations through false witnesses.[225] During this first trial, Annas concluded that "it would be good if one man died for the people."[226] Afterward, Jesus stood trial before Caiaphas. During this trial "the chief priests and the whole Sanhedrin were looking for evidence against Jesus so that they could put him to death, but they did not find any."[227] Finally, the high priest asked Jesus "Are you the Christ, the Son of the Blessed One?"[228] Jesus acknowledged himself as the Christ and was consequently condemned to death very early that morning.[229] The Sanhedrin confirmed the decision, and he was taken to Pilate to be tried because Jews were unable to administer capital punishment.

Jesus' second series of trials began before Pilate, but when Pilate discovered that He was a Galilean, Jesus was sent to Herod Antipas. Herod was temporarily in Jerusalem because it was the week of Passover, and he wanted to gain political support by attending the festivities. Herod was eager to meet Jesus because the news of miracles had spread throughout Israel, but the trial ended up in mockery as Herod taunted and mocked Jesus. Jesus was mockingly dressed up as a king before being sent back to Pilate.

Upon His return to Pilate, the third and final trial would begin. The charge against Jesus was blasphemy, and the chief priests and rulers and many of the Jewish people were adamant that He must be sentenced to death. After the charges were made, Pilate began his interrogation. After concluding his interrogation, Pilate found no fault with Jesus. Pilate initially found Jesus "not guilty" of the charges, but because there was an

---

224 The trail had two divisions. The first was the Jewish phase where Jesus appeared before Annas (John 18:12–14, 24), Caiaphas (Mark 14:53–64), and the entire Sanhedrin (Mark 15:1). In the Roman phase, Jesus appeared before Pilate (Mark 15:1–5), Herod Antipas (Luke 23:6–12), and again before Pilate (Mark 15:1–5) (Thomas D. Lea, *The New Testament: Its Background and Message,* 101).

225 Ronald A. Beers, ed., *Life Application Study Bible* (Grand Rapids, MI: Zondervan 1986), 1920.

226 John 18:14.

227 Mark 14:55.

228 Mark 14:61.

229 Mark 15:1.

angry mob demanding execution, Pilate succumbed to the people's wishes and ultimately sentenced Jesus to death.

Pilate issued a death sentence to an innocent man solely to preserve order within the territory that he governed. Pilate was worried that, if he did not execute Jesus, the Jewish people might revolt, which in turn might cause the Roman authorities to remove Pilate as procurator for failing to keep order.[230]

The sentence Pilate issued was scourging followed by crucifixion. Scourging and crucifixion are two of the most brutally inhumane sentences that a prisoner of any generation could have suffered. To fully understand what Jesus went through, we venture into the details of both parts of the death sentence.

Death Sentence, Part I: Scourging. Scourging is one of the most horrific methods of torture. Although scourging was not designed to be a form of capital punishment, many times prisoners could easily be beaten to the point of death from a loss of blood or infection due to the exposure of open wounds. The graphic details that surround Jesus' scourging are presented because many people are not familiar with this portion of the sentence.

The process of a typical scourging would begin with the prisoner's hands being chained to a short wooden post about knee high.[231] The prisoner was then stripped of all clothing—completely naked and in front of an audience.[232] Then the prisoner was forced to kneel on his hands and knees while leaning forward, exposing the back entirely (this is a very vulnerable position). Leaning forward also presented a flat target for the Roman soldiers to strike. After the prisoner was positioned correctly, the beating would commence. There would be two soldiers (one on each side of the prisoner) who would alternately strike the prisoner's back.

The whips that the Roman soldiers used were not like those we see in the movies. The whips that we think of today would make Roman soldiers laugh and shake their heads in disapproval. A Roman whip (a cat-of-nine-tails) was an instrument of destruction designed to literally rip flesh from

230 Luke 22:47–23:25; John 18:19–19:24.

231 An accurate replica of the scourging and crucifixion can be found in the movie *The Passion of the Christ.* Although the scene is gruesome, the depiction was scaled back for the twenty-first-century viewer.

232 The entire sentence was carried out in public. People were able to come and witness the public humiliation, torture, and execution from beginning to end.

the prisoner's back.[233] The whip had nine separate leather straps; each with pieces of broken glass, bone, and nails embedded and a heavy lead weight at each tip. The lead weights increased the velocity of each strike, transferring momentum to the body and allowing the bones, nails, and glass to pierce the skin and lodge themselves deep into the victim's flesh.

Unfortunately, at this point, the stroke was only half over – this soldier needed his whip back so that the other could proceed. The only way to remove the whip from the prisoner's back was to yank it out; which would consequently rip out chunks of skin and muscle, in the process shredding the circulatory system. The prisoner would bleed profusely; this is why it's not hard to see how the Roman soldiers had to be careful in the event that their prisoner *was not* sentenced to death. Even a normal or a light beating could cause premature death from loss of blood, infection (due to the exposure of internal organs), and lack of medical technology. Premature death from scourging could occur before the end of the beating, or it could come days after the sentence had been carried out.

In Jesus' case, the scourging was not intended to kill immediately; the Jewish religious leaders had different plans in mind for the execution. Even though we know that Pilate had Jesus scourged, "it is not known whether the number of lashes given to Jesus was limited to 39, in accordance with Jewish law" or whether the soldiers were given free rein to strike Jesus as many times as they deemed necessary.[234] One thing that we know for sure is that those who wanted Jesus dead also wanted him to *suffer immensely.* Since these men had no compassion whatsoever for an innocent man, it would have been possible for the Jewish religious leaders to ignore their own law (as they had already done) by giving the Roman soldiers full authority to strike Jesus more times than the law allowed.[235]

In any case, whether the lashes were limited to thirty-nine or not, the severity of the scourging was most likely intensified by the presence of many powerful people in the Jewish community. Just as people tend to work harder when a supervisor is present, it's reasonable to suspect that Jesus' sentence was intensified because of the fact that this was a "high

233 Nature's Designs, "Roman Cat-of-Nine-Tails," http://naturesdesignsonline.com/Cat-of-nine-tails.htm.

234 Ibid.

235 The Jewish religious leaders ignored their own law multiple times. An illegal trial was conducted during the middle of the night; there was no justification for the trial (no crime had been committed); and, without evidence, the religious leaders desperately tried to find witnesses to falsely testify of any crime.

profile" trial and it just also happened to be the highest priority of the most powerful people.

Death Sentence, Part II: Crucifixion. After the Roman soldiers completed the first part of Jesus' sentence, they forced Him to carry the horizontal member of His cross. Jesus, even with all his remaining strength, was so badly beaten and so weak that he was physically unable to carry the cross alone. As Jesus struggled to drag the cross outside Jerusalem, the Roman soldiers snatched up a man passing by and ordered him to help carry the cross.[236]

With the help of Simon, they dragged the cross to a place outside the city, where crucifixions took place. This crucifixion site was referred to as Golgotha (which means "the Place of the Skull").[237] Golgotha is where the second part of the sentence would be carried out. This too was a public place where people could witness the events unfold, either as they passed by or as they gathered to watch as if it were a recreational event.

After the group had reached Golgotha, the crosspiece was laid flat on the ground. Jesus was placed on his back on top of the cross. On each side of the horizontal beam, there was a hole where a seven- to nine-inch spike would be driven through each wrist with a sledge hammer.[238] The metal spikes had to be driven through the radius and ulna bones at the wrist because the hands could not support the entire weight of a human body.[239] The Bible references nails being driven into the hands because the meaning of the Greek word for hand includes both hands and wrists.[240]

As the first metal spike was driven into the wrist with a sledge hammer, it would tear through veins, arteries, nerves and would send excruciating pain throughout the entire body. The second nail would be more difficult. In order to drive this nail into the wrist, the Roman soldiers would need to stretch the remaining arm across the horizontal beam far enough so that the second wrist lines up with the second hole. One soldier would hold the wrist in place while other nailed the spike into it. This nail would do similar damage and redouble the victim's pain.

---

236 Matthew 27:32; Mark 15:21; Luke 23:26.

237 Luke 23:33.

238 Dr. Cathleen Shrier, "The Science of the Crucifixion," Azusa Pacific University, http://www.apu.edu/infocus/2002/03/crucifixion/.

239 Ibid.

240 Ibid.

After the upper body had been nailed into place, the Roman soldiers would secure this crosspiece atop the stake and then proceed to nailing the feet. Nailing the feet, on an angled support, required a much larger spike because it had to be hammered through both feet and exit through the back of the cross, where the protruding end was bent perpendicular. The lower spike was a tool that provided support and the Romans used it to prolong the life of the person being crucified. If a person hung on the cross *without* the bottom spike, death would be hastened: the hanging body would create tremendous pressure on the lungs, and death would be very quick because the person would suffocate from not being able to alleviate the pressure from the lungs in order to take a breath of air.

Allowing Jesus to die too quickly was unacceptable to the Jewish religious leaders. As mentioned earlier, the religious leaders were adamant in making Jesus suffer the most torturous death possible. Even though the overall result would be the same (death), the purpose for nailing the feet was to give Jesus just enough support so that he might push up with his feet, take a breath of air, and prolong his suffering until the inevitable—death.

Returning to the lower spike, it had to be driven into the feet with a sledge hammer because it would need to wedge itself in between the bones of the feet. As the spike was driven into the feet, it would break bones and would also tear through veins, arteries, and nerves, adding to the victim's agony. The ends of all three spikes needed to be bent perpendicular so that the body would not fall off the cross, face first, when stood upright. Therefore, each nail was bent perpendicular so that Jesus would hang in place until death. However, bending the nail perpendicular was only the beginning. Death was not yet in sight because crucifixion, as we know, is a tremendously slow and agonizing death. Minutes become an eternity, and hours are simply unfathomable. It is approximated that Jesus hung on the cross from 9 AM until 3 PM.[241]

Cause of Death. By the time Jesus reached Golgotha, he was very weak from the scourging and from being forced to drag the cross. Since Jesus had lost a significant amount of blood, he was most likely in hypovolemic shock.[242] In *The Case for Easter*, Lee Strobel interviewed Dr. Robert J. Stein who describes the symptoms:

---

241 Thomas D. Lea, *The New Testament: Its Background and Message* (Nashville, TN: Broadman & Holman Academic, 2003), 101.

242 Hypovolemic shock means the person is suffering the effects of losing a large amount of blood. (Strobel's Interview with Alexander Metherell in *The Case for Easter*, 16).

> Hypovolemic shock causes the heart to race and try to pump blood that isn't there; second, the blood pressure in the body drops; third, the kidneys stop producing urine to maintain what volume is left; and fourth, the person becomes very thirsty as the body craves fluids to replace the lost blood volume.

Hypovolemic shock is most likely the reason why Jesus was unable to carry his cross to Golgotha, why he thirsted on the cross, and also why he died before the thieves that were crucified on either side. In another interview, conducted by Lee Strobel, more details were presented as they relate to Jesus' cause of death. In the interview Strobel had with Dr. Alexander Metherell, we learn how the victim struggled to even breathe.

We begin by examining the effects crucifixion has on the body. As a person hangs from a cross, the shoulders would quickly if not immediately become dislocated.[243] When the shoulders were dislocated, intense pressure was placed not only on the shoulders but also on the lungs. The pressure on the lungs meant that the crucified person could not take a breath without pushing up with the legs (from the support given by the nail in the feet). Pushing up with the legs would temporarily relieve the pressure on the lungs, enabling the individual to inhale. Each time the victim needed to take a breath of air, the process must be repeated.

Dr. Stein reveals that after time, the body grew physically exhausted, and exhaustion caused breathing to eventually slow. As breathing slowed, the person would enter into what medical experts call respiratory acidosis (when too much carbon dioxide is being dissolved into the blood stream). Respiratory acidosis causes the acidity of the blood to increase. An increase in acid in the bloodstream would increase the heart rate of the individual and thus create an irregular heartbeat. An irregular heartbeat would eventually lead to cardiac arrest, the probable cause of death.

As Jesus hung from the cross, He most likely felt His heart rapidly pounding in His chest. He could sense His life was drawing to an end; which is when He spoke some of His final words: *"Eloi, Eloi, lama sabachthani?"* (My God, my God, why have you forsaken me?).[244]

---

243 Psalms 22:14.
244 Mark 15:34.

Expediting the Process. From the accounts in Scripture, we know that Jesus died before either of the criminals beside Him. The crucifixion took place right before Passover, so the religious leaders (being short on time) needed to expedite the crucifixion process.[245] Since it was the Preparation Day, they needed this crucifixion business settled and out of the way because they had more important business to attend to; besides, they were important men who had important ceremonies to lead. Image was everything, and it would not be good for the "image" to have dead men hanging from crosses on a high day.[246] To keep from having dead men hanging on the cross on a holy day, the Roman soldiers were ordered to break the legs of the three men being crucified (if they were still alive).

Breaking the legs would remove the only form of support that enabled the crucified person to continue breathing. Being unable to breathe would quickly cause death by asphyxiation within a matter of minutes. Asphyxiation occurs when normal breathing is interrupted; it causes a lack of oxygen and a surplus of carbon dioxide to build up in the body. This leads to unconsciousness and eventually death.[247]

After the order was given, the soldiers broke the legs of the men to the right and to the left, but when they came to Jesus, they saw a lifeless body; which led them to believe that He was already dead. The soldiers couldn't afford to make an *assumption* on an execution as "high profile" as this one. In order to verify Jesus' death, the soldiers thrust a spear into His side. It's believed that the thrust punctured the ribs, pierced the right lung and all the way into the heart. This conclusion is drawn because the Gospel of John records both clear fluid and blood that came out of the body when the spear was removed.[248]

Clear fluid followed by blood indicates, and medically supports, the fact that Jesus was in hypovolemic shock as fluid built up around the membrane of his heart and lungs. The final conclusion by Dr. Metherell: "There was absolutely no doubt that Jesus was dead."[249] Since the intended result of crucifixion is always death, there was no need for the Roman soldiers to break Jesus' legs.[250]

245 John 19:31.

246 Jesus accused religious leaders of hypocrisy in Matthew 23:25–28.

247 Asphyxia. Merriam-Webster Online Dictionary, 2010. *Merriam-Webster Online.* 12 April 2010, http://www.merriam-webster.com/dictionary/asphyxia.

248 Lee Strobel, *The Case for Easter*, (Grand Rapids, MI: Zondervan, 2003), 20-22.

249 Ibid., 22.

250 The Roman soldiers unknowingly fulfilled the prophecy that the legs of a sacrifice must not be broken (Exodus 12:46 and Psalms 34:20).

Pronounced Dead by the Enemy. There is great irony in the fact that Jesus was pronounced dead by the enemy. The Jewish religious leaders were so adamant about the death of Jesus that they were the ones to personally verify the completion of the execution. This is a very important fact because we must firmly establish that Jesus was *dead;* there were no signs of life whatsoever. If it can be proven that Jesus was, in fact, dead and that the enemy verified the death (and were satisfied with the outcome), then the testimony of the Apostles and the hundreds who saw Jesus alive, after the burial, is greatly strengthened because some people claim that Jesus never really died.

Another important fact is that, when trying to prove the resurrection, it is actually far more beneficial, for the propagation of the Gospel, to acknowledge that the enemy confirmed the death. Why is the enemy's confirmation so important? Since the enemy confirmed the death of Jesus, it automatically discredits claims made today that Jesus was not really dead. To reject the death of Jesus would contradict the knowledge of both Jesus' allies and His enemies, and these people were not only living in the first century, but they watched the events unfold! Who is more credible—eyewitnesses of the accounts or others speculating about them two thousand years later?

Furthermore, we know that the death was confirmed simply because there is no other way to explain—let alone justify—the actions of the Roman soldiers, Pilate, the Jewish religious leaders, and the family and friends of Jesus. The actions of each group all correlate with what was reasonably expected. How can we know that the religious leaders confirmed the death? In order to demonstrate how the death of Jesus was confirmed, we will examine the actions of all the parties involved with the crucifixion.

The Roman Soldiers. If Jesus was alive on the cross, then the Roman soldiers would have broken Jesus' legs because a specific order was given to hasten the deaths so that dead bodies would not be hanging on a very sacred Jewish holiday. Jesus' legs were not broken because the soldiers already thought Jesus was dead. They confirmed their belief by thrusting a spear so far into the chest cavity that it pierced the heart. Even after this horrific thrust, Jesus' body remained lifeless; there was no reaction; there was no pain; there was no movement whatsoever. The most logical conclusion is death, because the soldiers did not care about Jesus or his feelings or how He felt; they had one mission, and that was to kill Jesus.

We know the soldiers had no respect for Jesus and did not value His life because they had perverse fun in the events that led up to the execution. Think about the disrespect when the soldiers dressed Jesus up as a king, smashed a crown of thorns on his head, and played prophecy games where one would blindfold and then strike Him in the face and then demand to know who the perpetrator was. These men despised Jesus, and they mocked Him on the cross. The offered no care because when Jesus was thirsty, they gave Him gall to drink (very bitter) instead of water, and they even played games and gambled with one another (cast lots) for the clothes he wore (they gambled for them as Jesus hung from the cross entirely naked for the world to see). Based on the way the Roman soldiers treated Jesus, we can confidently conclude that they did not value Jesus' life in the least. Nobody could justify a claim that the soldiers had any amount of compassion because everything they did was designed to inflict physical or emotional pain.

After observing the perverse and prideful actions of the soldiers, are we really to expect them to let Jesus live? No, these men had no motive for allowing Jesus to live. Besides, we also need to note that direct disobedience to a commanding officer's orders was punishable by death. Therefore, when the order was given to break the legs and hasten death, the fact that Jesus' legs were not broken demonstrates that the soldiers knew, for a fact, that Jesus was dead. I can guarantee you, those soldiers would not have died for Jesus or His cause if push came to shove. Jesus was dead, and they had completed their orders.

Pontius Pilate. Pilate also confirms the death of Jesus Christ. After Jesus died, Joseph (one of Jesus' disciples) went to Pilate to request possession of the body in order to provide a proper burial.[251] When Joseph made his request, Pilate was surprised to hear that Jesus was already dead.[252] However, Pilate confirmed the death by summoning the centurion to give an account and to verify that Jesus was, in fact, dead.[253] Since Roman soldiers had an allegiance to Pilate, and there was a penalty of death for direct disobedience, the centurion not only carried out the orders but

---

251 Matthew 27:57–58.

252 Mark 15:44.

253 Ibid.

accurately reported the death to Pilate.[254] Upon verification, Pilate handed over the body to Joseph so that Jesus could have a proper burial.

We need to note that Pilate would not have handed over Jesus if He were still alive. Recounting the facts, we know that Pilate found Jesus innocent of the charges and pleaded with the religious leaders three times not to execute Him. Pilate even sent Jesus to Herod to prevent himself from being forced to make the decision.[255] Why did Pilate not want to execute Jesus? One reason may be that his wife told him, "Don't have anything to do with that innocent man, for I have suffered a great deal today in a dream because of him."[256] Automatically, we see a contradiction between the desire and the actions of Pilate. Therefore, we need to understand his motive to put into perspective the last fact surrounding Pilate's confirmation of Jesus' death.

Pilate's motive is pretty clear; he pleaded with the religious leaders not to execute Jesus, yet he turned right around to order the execution. Why would Pilate contradict his own convictions and succumb to the will of the Jewish religious leaders? The motive is nothing less than self-preservation of status and power. There was a tremendous uproar on the part of the Jewish people, and Pilate was worried about his political status. We know Pilate was frightened after he scourged Jesus because the Jewish crowd was large, and they were acting very irrational (they set free an insurrectionist and a murderer rather than a truly innocent man whom they could not charge with any crime).[257] Pilate complied with the Jewish religious leaders' demand for execution, for fear of the possibility of a revolt by the Jews; which could have jeopardized his own position as governor. In an attempt to salvage his political status and power, Pilate gave in so that the uproar could be resolved quickly.

Now, we fast-forward to after the death. After Jesus' body was handed over to Joseph, we see a new situation develop. Even though Jesus was dead, the religious leaders were still not satisfied. The religious leaders remembered Jesus saying, "After three days I will rise again."[258] They knew that Jesus alluded to some sort of resurrection, although they had no clue of its significance or its purpose. Nevertheless, the religious leaders wanted to try and prevent this alleged resurrection at all costs. In an attempt

254 Mark 15:45.
255 Luke 23:6–8, 22.
256 Matthew 27:19.
257 Luke 23:19; John 19:8.
258 Matthew 27:63.

to prevent the resurrection or to prevent the disciples from stealing the body, the religious leaders demanded that Pilate place guards at the tomb after Jesus was buried.[259] Pilate, following his previous motive of self-preservation, complied to preserve his status and power and responded with "Take a guard … Go, make the tomb as secure as you know how."[260]

The request from the religious leaders is further confirmation that Pilate knew, without a doubt, that Jesus was dead. Pilate's centurion confirmed it; a disciple came to claim the body; and the religious leaders demanded a guard at the tomb. None of these actions would make sense if Jesus were alive.

The Jewish Religious Leaders. As we have established, the Jewish religious leaders were willing to do virtually everything within their power to make sure that Jesus was dead—not almost dead, but a lifeless body that they themselves would want to verify. Reflecting on their enormous hatred, why would the religious leaders ever allow Jesus, if He were still alive, to be buried? Allowing Jesus to be buried alive could have undermined their entire purpose of demanding execution; they were not about to let this happen. The Jewish religious leaders knew Jesus was dead because they *allowed* the burial which they would not have allowed to take place unless they had confirmed the death in person (which they did).

Another method we can confirm death is that the religious leaders would have demanded that Jesus' legs be broken to hasten death if He was not yet already dead. Furthermore, why would the religious leaders demand a guard at the tomb of a dead person? They knew that Jesus had been predicting a resurrection and was teaching that He would come back to life. The religious leaders were fearful of Jesus' words, and though they did not believe it was possible for a dead man to come back to life, they did believe that the disciples would attempt to steal the body—which is why they exclaimed that "this last deception would be worse than the first."[261]

The religious leaders did not demand that Jesus' legs be broken. They allowed Jesus' body to be buried and even went to the trouble to demand that a guard be placed in front of the tomb to prevent theft. We are able to conclude with ease that the Jewish leaders also knew, for a fact, that Jesus was dead.

---

259 Matthew 27:64.
260 Matthew 27:65.
261 Matthew 27:64.

Family and Friends. Although not enemies, it's also beneficial to note that family and friends also confirmed the death of Jesus. Both Joseph (a disciple) and Nicodemus (a Pharisee), prepared Jesus' body for burial.[262] As they laid the body in the tomb, women who had come with Jesus from Galilee also saw the tomb and watched the body as it was laid to rest.[263] Mary Magdalene and Mary, the mother of Jesus, were specifically noted as being present, and they saw where the body was laid.[264]

Jumping ahead (after the tomb was discovered empty), we can confirm that the disciples truly believed Jesus was dead based on their first reaction to the news of the resurrection. When the women came back from the tomb to tell the disciples the good news (that Jesus was alive), most did not believe their account: "They did not believe the women, because their words seemed to them like nonsense. Peter, however, got up and ran to the tomb."[265] The refusal, of some of the closest people to Jesus, to believe in a resurrection (even after Jesus had assured them of it on at least three separate occasions) demonstrates their deepest conviction of what they knew to be true: Jesus had truly died. As a result, they were deeply sad and were mourning.

No Reason to Lie

The Snake Venom Tale. Opponents of Christianity sometimes claim that the death of Jesus was a lie—that Jesus lived through the scourging, crucifixion, and spear thrust and miraculously escaped past the Roman guard.[266] The Snake Venom Tale begins with an eccentric belief: Jesus was poisoned as he hung from the cross. The gall that we read about in the New Testament was really not gall, it was actually snake venom. Now the snake venom that Jesus was fed would not take effect instantly; these opponents claim that it would take hours for the poison to do its work.

While hanging on the cross, Jesus was ultimately knocked out and became unconscious. After Jesus became unconscious, He was thought to be dead and placed in the tomb. After He was placed in the tomb, Jesus' friends came and helped Him escape, and He stayed with friends until

262 John 19:38–39.

263 Luke 23:55.

264 Mark 15:47.

265 Luke 24:11–12.

266 The Ishwar Sharan Acrhive, "Did Jesus Die in Kashmir?" http://hamsa.org/resurrection.htm.

He recovered. Since Jesus did not die, the disciples really did not lie when they said they saw Him, because He was alive and well—just not in the resurrected state portrayed in the New Testament.

Even though this story may seem credible to the skeptic, we need to address at least one serious issue. According to Dr. Steve A. Johnson, at the University of Florida, snake venom is generally not toxic if swallowed. The question was asked on the University of Florida's website: "What is the difference between poison and venom? If you *drink* [not taste] *venom*, will it kill you?"[267] The University of Florida replied to the questions with the following answer: "Poisons are substances that are toxic (cause harm) if swallowed or inhaled. Venoms are generally not toxic if swallowed, and must be injected under the skin (by snakes, spiders, etc.) into the tissues normally protected by skin in order to be toxic." In other words, *if a person actually drinks poisonous venom, generally* (or usually; commonly; ordinarily) *they are not toxic*. This is shocking. Perhaps we need to know the difference between *taste* versus *drink* and specifically whether Jesus drank the gall.

Utilizing the dictionary, we know that *taste* is defined "to eat or drink especially in small quantities," while *drink* is defined "to take liquid into the mouth for swallowing." The meanings are similar, but the terms are entirely different from one another because of the quantity that is consumed. Next, we need to know whether Jesus drank the gall (that is alleged to be venom). In Matthew 27:34, we read an account that specifically addresses our question: "There they offered Jesus wine to drink, mixed with gall; but after tasting it, he refused to drink it." Even if we pretend that venom is toxic if consumed like a beverage, the greatest problem is that Jesus never drank the gall! Once the substance hit His tongue, Jesus refused to drink any more. As a result, the Snake Venom Tale is a fable, and it has been *busted*.

In addition to the Snake Venom Tale not concurring with what Pilate, the Roman soldiers, the Jewish religious leaders, and Jesus' family and friends knew to be true, the proponents of the Lie Theory do not understand how a lie would have been devastating to every party involved. Next, we examine how a lie, before the resurrection, would have been devastating.

---

267 Dr. Steve A. Johnson, "Frequently Asked Questions about Venomous Snakes," University of Florida, http://ufwildlife.ifas.ufl.edu/venomous_snake_faqs.shtml.

Devastation to All. Did Jesus really die? Would anybody have had motive to lie about Jesus' death? The situation contends, no: nobody could have possibly benefited from a lie in the three-day period that precedes the resurrection; afterward, as we know, a lie was desperately needed to cover up the obvious. This is an interesting topic, but it demonstrates what everybody knew to be true. If we can establish that Jesus was dead and that all parties would have no motive to lie, then the resurrection gains further credibility.

Anybody who looks at and reflects upon the details surrounding the death would have to admit that Jesus was pronounced dead by His enemies. Nobody can get around this fact because there were too many people who wanted confirmation and had it. The reason that nobody would have been willing to lie about the death is because it would destroy everything that *all parties* were desperately trying to accomplish and the unintended outcome would have been catastrophic.

Group 1: The Supporters. The people who supported Jesus had no reason to lie; they wanted Him to live! Jesus' supporters thought that the Messiah had come to establish an earthly kingdom (which, by the way, is what the Jewish people hope for today). Jesus' family, friends, and followers loved His teachings and marveled at His miracles, and they desperately wanted Him alive so that He could reestablish David's and Solomon's kingdom. We know the disciples wanted Jesus to live because they tried to interfere with God's perfect plan by trying to prevent Jesus' arrest, and they even tried to rebuke Jesus when He predicted His death.

Furthermore, if the disciples were to lie about Jesus and actually fake a resurrection, it would have destroyed the entire ministry of Jesus Christ. Jesus could no longer have been hailed as having an honest ministry because stealing the body would have reduced the disciples to fraudulent liars and thieves. But stealing the body was also out of the question, even if they wanted to succumb to liars and thieves, because it would have been impossible without being noticed! The Jewish religious leaders had demanded a Roman guard in front of the tomb. Even if the disciples pulled off the heist of the century and accomplished the impossible task of stealing the body without being noticed, what next? Without a living body, who would believe the resurrection allegation? Nobody, because there would be no proof and because the religious leaders prevented any possibility of theft. (We thank the religious leaders for destroying this possibility.)

On top of destroying the ministry, the disciples were not in any state of mind to start lying or to even continue Jesus' ministry. The events leading up to the crucifixion completely devastated the disciples; they were scattered and afraid, and some were actually denying any affiliation with Jesus! Think about what was happening. Some of the disciples (the men whose lives centered upon Jesus and those closest to Him) were denying that they knew even Him, and all of them fled (except John). The disciples were not willing to be scourged or executed at this point because they did not even truly know who Jesus was or why He had to die. (If they knew the outcome or the significance of the crucifixion, then their actions would resemble the boldness they possessed after the resurrection.)

The disciples were in no condition to lie; they were confused, scared, and consumed with deep sorrow. I can't blame them because they watched the man they loved, and absolutely revered, be treated worse than a dog as He was beaten beyond recognition and then mercilessly executed as if this were some sort of recreational game or a joke. Watching the events unfold terrorized the disciples; as a result, they *were not willing* to stand beside Jesus. Since Jesus' supporters had no clue as to why Jesus was executed and deserted Him, they would have had no motive whatsoever to embark on a lie (which would have easily been discredited). As a result, a lie was inconceivable on the part of Jesus' supporters.

Group 2: The Jews. The last thing the Jewish religious leaders would have done was lie about Jesus' death; they were the group that wanted him dead! If they told a lie and claimed that Jesus was alive, it would have destroyed everything they were trying to accomplish, and they would have ultimately defeated themselves. Preserving their power, prestige, and social status was their utmost concern, and they made sure that every ounce of their power and influence destroyed Jesus. Jesus threatened their power because many people were turning away from Judaism, and countless people were following Jesus; this was unacceptable. These men were not incompetent and would have had absolutely no motive for lying about Jesus' death before the resurrection. As far as the religious leaders were concerned, it was mission accomplished.

Group 3: The Romans. The final group involved with the execution that we need to examine are the Romans. In the beginning of the trials, Pilate appeared to be indifferent toward Christ, but he quickly took an opposing position. Even though Pilate originally found no fault with Jesus and continued to press His innocence upon the people, this stance did not sit well with the Jews, so Pilate ultimately made a decision that placed the Romans in direct opposition to Jesus. Since Pilate took an opposing stance, the Roman soldiers naturally followed suit because they were required to follow Pilate's orders or accept a death sentence of their own.

We have already established that the reason Pilate reversed his decision (and murdered an innocent man) was to preserve his political power and position in the Roman Empire, so we can conclude that Pilate's greatest concern was pleasing the religious leaders. Murdering the innocent demonstrates that Pilate would go to *great* lengths to keep the Jewish people satisfied. Since Pilate's ultimate goal was self-preservation, he could not possibly have had a motive to lie about Jesus' death; this would incite the very revolt he desperately hoped to prevent. Pilate was an astute politician, and he diffused the situation as fast as he could and with as little damage as possible.

A lie on the part of the Romans is inconceivable, and it was the last thing on their mind.

Conclusion. The time between the death and the resurrection of Jesus Christ was very delicate for all parties. None of the parties could benefit from forcing a lie, but we have seen the devastation it would work on all parties involved. Since there was no opportunity for any party to benefit from a lie, all motive instantly dissipates. As we have seen, Jesus' family and friends were downcast, frightened, and confused; the other two groups were entirely satisfied with the outcome and did not want to stir the pot any more. Letting things settle was the best course of action for all parties, as they had time to digest the extreme events that had just taken place.

Too Many Witnesses Spoil the Lie. Just as too many cooks spoil the stew, too many witnesses spoil the lie. A lie could never have gained traction, because there were entirely too many witnesses who saw Jesus before, during, and after His death. Since the scourging and execution were *public events,* it would have been impossible to convince people that Jesus was alive without a living, breathing, and talking body! Jesus was a "big deal" because the entire city was consumed with *everything Jesus.* It did not matter whether people loved or hated Him; they took their fill because He was the absolute center of attention the moment He rode into town. Jesus was so popular that people naturally gravitated around Him to try and hear His message, see the miracles, and witness the massive, historic events as they unfolded.

A conspiracy is also out of the question because there were too many witnesses who knew the truth. If a rumor had begun, it would have quickly died. If the lie went against Jesus, the firsthand witnesses who supported Jesus would have squashed it. If a lie found favor with Jesus, the religious leaders would have squashed it. Since we are still within the three days before the resurrection, any rumors could easily have been refuted by reopening the tomb: the body would have been there because the resurrection had not yet occurred. The thrust is that the truth was easily verifiable, since the entire sentence was public, and the truth could have been confirmed by reopening the tomb.

These facts make it impossible for anyone to have created any type of lie or conspiracy. Liar, Legend and Lunatic will be covered in greater detail when we arrive at Chapter 11.

The Resurrection

Glory Be to the King of kings and the Lord of lords! Without question, the single greatest event in the history of mankind *is* the resurrection of Jesus Christ; it was a demonstration of absolute power by none other than God Himself. Who, among humankind, has the power to restore life to a dead body? For three entire days the body lay in a tomb and was lifeless. Then, suddenly, that same exact body was filled with life. Jesus had returned. He had conquered death itself.

The remaining part of the chapter will examine the resurrection accounts and their significance. Returning to His tattered body was the *grand finale*, and for the next forty days He would be revealing to the Apostles the significance and purpose of the resurrection and how every single event fell within the perfect plan of God. The world would never be the same.

The Morning That Changed the World. By evening of the second day, hope itself must have been nonexistent. Jesus was dead; He had been beaten, mocked, treated worse than a dog, and executed like a criminal. Everything was dim, and the mood was solemn. The disciples were utterly confused, trying to put into perspective—to even begin to understand—the events that had just taken place. How could Jesus have performed countless miracles, taught with supreme authority, and claimed to be

God, only to predict His death and leave them without a clue as to *why*? Everything seemed so incomplete—but then again, Sunday had not yet come.

Little did the people of Jerusalem know that, at dawn on the first day of the week, a surprising discovery would be made that would change the world forever. When Mary, and the women with her, came to the tomb that Sunday morning, they had no clue that they would be the first to discover an empty tomb and that they would ultimately begin spreading the news and setting into motion a new era where Jesus Christ *is* the way, the truth, and the life.[268]

When Mary discovered that the stone that sealed the tomb had been rolled back, she also noticed the guards (who were supposedly guarding the tomb with their lives) were stupefied. The Roman soldiers were so frightened that the Bible describes their extreme shock this way: they "became like dead men" and unable to move.[269] The soldiers were scared stiff because there was a violent earthquake, and then they saw an angel of the Lord, whose "appearance was like lightning and his clothes white as snow."[270] The angel had rolled back the stone to the tomb, revealed to the women that Jesus was alive, and gave them specific instructions. They were to go and tell the disciples that Jesus had risen from the dead and that He was already awaiting their arrival in Galilee.[271]

By this point, Jesus was alive and well. The worst was past, and He had almost fulfilled his entire mission of coming to earth. The remaining part of the forty days that He had left on Earth was dedicated to revealing Himself to the disciples so that they would be prepared for the ministry and for the inevitable persecution that they would soon encounter by propagating the Absolute Truth.[272] The resurrection was the one event that fueled the sudden boldness in all of them. However, this is a dramatic shift of events that needs to be addressed. One evening the lifeless body lay in the tomb, and the next morning, it was gone. Was the body stolen? Was Jesus resuscitated? What is the evidence that lies behind the resurrection, and how can we know, beyond a shadow of a doubt, that Jesus was actually alive and not the subject of a crazy myth?

---

268 John 14:6.

269 Matthew 28:4.

270 Matthew 28:3.

271 Matthew 28:1–15; Mark 16:1–20; Luke 24:1–12.

272 Acts 1:3.

Testifying: Alive, Dead, and Alive Again. The resurrection was an event that could not have been faked, distorted, or misconstrued. We can confidently trust in the resurrection because Jesus was seen alive by hundreds of people after He was confirmed dead.

Furthermore, we see a radical shift in the cowardly disciples: they transformed into bold Apostles! Something significant had to have happened to explain such a dramatic change. People are not willing to die for a lie. Even Muslims, who are willing to be martyred, die for what they believe to be true. However, there is a great distinction between the Muslims and the early Christians: the Christians had the advantage of being eyewitnesses to the resurrection while Muslims rely on faith (sure of what they hope for and certain of what they do not see). Therefore, we need to examine the accounts that demonstrate that Jesus was alive and that there was no doubt as to the events that actually unfolded during the forty days Jesus was on earth after the resurrection.

First, note that the resurrection was not meant to be common knowledge until after it had occurred. Why? Because the perfect plan of God was not going to be in jeopardy of being thwarted. Imagine how the events could have drastically been altered if Judas Iscariot, the disciple who betrayed Jesus, knew about the resurrection. Since Judas turned against Jesus, he could have shared that knowledge with the enemy, and the outcome might have been drastically altered.

However, the resurrection was never intended to be a secret forever. In fact, the resurrection was designed by God to be the greatest discovery the world would ever stumble across. Why did humankind stumble across the greatest discovery? Because the discovery was unexpected, and it was shocking to discover that Jesus had been resurrected and was alive for the entire world to see. How do we know that Jesus was actually alive? After the resurrection, Jesus began making appearances to hundreds upon hundreds of people. This *fact* is documented in the first letter Paul wrote to Corinth as indicated by the excerpt:

> What I received I passed on to you as of first importance: that Christ died for our sins according to the Scriptures, that he was buried, that he was raised on the third day according to the Scriptures, and that he appeared to Peter, and then to the Twelve. After that, he appeared to more than five hundred of the brothers [and sisters] at the same time, most of whom are still living, though some have

> fallen asleep. Then he appeared to James, then to all the apostles, and last of all he appeared to me also, as to one abnormally born.[273]

This passage is phenomenal because it reveals the magnitude of the number of people who physically saw Jesus alive and well *after* He was confirmed dead by Pilate, the Roman soldiers, the Jewish religious leaders, and His own family and friends. At one setting, Jesus appeared to over five hundred people. It has been demonstrated that the events that surrounded Jesus were common knowledge, because Jerusalem was entirely consumed with "everything Jesus" regardless of whether people were for or against Him. Jesus was the center of attention, and if there had been newspapers, He would have undoubtedly been on the front page of every single one. This is significant because the people were current with the events as they unfolded. When Jesus appeared to the mass congregation of brothers and sisters, they knew that Jesus had died and been buried, but when they saw Him in person, it was *absolutely shocking.*

Were the Witnesses Crazy or on Drugs? The skeptics have concocted the idea of *mass hallucinations*, where people were so consumed with Jesus that they thought they saw Him after the crucifixion.[274] Well, we should probably know what a hallucination is in order to confirm or disprove the theory. A hallucination is "a sensory experience of something that does not exist outside the mind, caused by various physical and mental disorders, or by reaction to certain toxic substances, and usually manifested as visual or auditory images."[275] Are we really to believe that every single person who confirmed the resurrection, and was an eyewitness, had a "physical [or] mental disorder" or had a "reaction to certain toxic substances," otherwise known as drugs? Are we really to believe that every single Christian was on drugs or mentally deranged?

This idea seems quite odd. It actually reminds me of some of the current events going on in today's world! Let's digress for a second. In America, if you oppose the liberal or the "progressive" ideology (for any reason), the media paints a picture that is a little extreme. The media portrays all who

273 1 Corinthians 15:3–8.

274 Lee Strobel, *The Case for Christ* (Grand Rapids, MI: Zondervan, 1998), 238–240.

275 Hallucination. Dictionary.com. *Dictionary.com Unabridged.* Random House, Inc. http://dictionary.reference.com/browse/hallucination (accessed: November 5, 2009).

are against the liberals as hatemongers, racists, and intolerant bigots (i.e., consider the "love" the liberals have for the Tea Party movement). Such people are portrayed as those who "cling to guns and religion." It would seem, from the outside looking in, that all who oppose liberalism are "un-American" and racist Tea Party extremists, but is this really the case? Are all people against the immorality of liberalism actually hatemongers, racists, or un-American? This seems like a gross overgeneralization that simply is not true. Some people in this nation have morals, and they stick to them, even if it is not popular and they are smacked with the "intolerant" label. So how does this scenario fit in with proving a resurrection? Actually, quite well.

Like morals, a hallucination is limited to the individual. Even Christians have different standards of morality, and that is based on their relationship with Christ and their convictions. So it is highly unlikely that the gross generalizations of all the people who take the "unpopular" side and vouch for Jesus have the same "disability" or "condition" or are all "confused." Likewise, a hallucination is limited to the individual, just like a dream; this is common sense. I cannot have a dream one night and then wake up to ask a friend, "What did you think of my dream last night?" if I had not told them beforehand. Is it really feasible to suggest that hundreds upon hundreds of people miraculously had the exact same hallucination of the exact same event at the exact same time? (What an amazing coincidence!)

On a serious note, what drug actually makes people hallucinate in harmony with one another—you know, that popular idea of the "collective experience." I will venture out on the notion that this is not possible, but we should confirm this answer with an expert on the subject. Meet the words of Gary Collins:

> Hallucinations are individual occurrences. By their very nature only one person can see a given hallucination at a time. They certainly aren't something which can be seen by a group of people. Neither is it possible that one person could somehow induce an hallucination in somebody else. Since an hallucination exists only in this subjective, personal sense, it is obvious that others cannot witness it.[276]

276 Strobel, 238–239.

Intelligent people recognize that this argument is not possible. To believe that these people all had hallucinations far surpasses the faith required to believe in Jesus Christ as Lord and Savior. If reason and faith accompany one another, then there seems to be a slight problem with the hallucination idea. Somehow, it is not reasonable to even reason with the idea that over five hundred people had the same exact hallucination all at once. Even crazier is the fact that other people at different times had the same hallucinations, and they kept occurring for a period of forty days. Then another miracle happens: at the end of those forty days all hallucinations magically cease. But then again, I also remember that there were *absolutely no* hallucinations what-so-ever before resurrection Sunday! They all occurred during a very specific time period, all were congruent, and all radically changed the witnesses' lives and the world as we know it today.

Nothing but Death Itself Will Stand in My Way. Although this may not be too popular to point out, I find it fascinating to observe that the disciples were cowards before the resurrection. How could they be described in any other way? Peter denied even knowing Christ. Better yet, Matthew reveals how strong Peter's denial of even knowing Jesus was: "then began he to *curse* and to *swear*, saying I know not the man. And immediately the cock crew."[277] Peter did not deny knowing Jesus once or twice. Nor did Peter casually dismiss the fact that he knew Jesus. On the contrary, Peter vehemently denied even knowing who Jesus was, and he began to curse and to swear. Peter, who thought he was so brave, found himself denying and cursing the man he had earlier vowed to die for and never to desert (even if all others should fall away).[278]

What about the other disciples? The other disciples did not fare any better. When Jesus was arrested in the garden, they all deserted Him and fled; one even ran so fast that he did not even bother to pick up his clothes and ran away in the nude![279] If the mystery streaker was not acting like a coward, why did he leave behind *his clothes* to run for his life? Recall the prophecy of which Jesus reminded His disciples: "It is written: 'I will strike the shepherd, and the sheep of the flock will be scattered.'"[280] The

---

277 Matthew 26:74 (KJV), emphasis added.
278 Matthew 26:33–35.
279 Mark 14:51–52.
280 Zechariah 13:7; Matthew 26:31.

disciples' desertion of Jesus was already accounted for in the divine plan: it was prophesied over 500 years in advance![281]

Why would God inspire a prophet to prophesy about the disciples and their reactions to the crucifixion? Why would God have a prophet allude to the fact that they would become cowards—that like sheep without a shepherd, they would be scattered? This was not a coincidence; it is a testament to the truth of the resurrection.

The "before and after" shots of the disciples tell the entire story. It reveals that which they knew to be the Absolute Truth. The resurrection was not fake, and it is demonstrated by the fact that Thomas, who was skeptical about the resurrection, touched Jesus' hands and then actually reached into His side where the spear had been thrust.[282] Thomas doubted the resurrection when he said: "Unless I see the nail marks in his hands and put my finger where the nails were, and put my hand into his side, I will not believe."[283] Those are powerful words that demand physical and undeniable proof! Little did Thomas know, a week later he would have the proof, and he, too, would be forever changed.

After Jesus had revealed the plan and answered the "who, what, when, where, why, and how" questions, the former cowards became the boldest and most audacious proclaimers of the Truth that the world would ever known! These men did not need the faith that we have today. They saw and even touched the wounds. They knew, beyond a shadow of a doubt, that Jesus was precisely who he claimed to be: the Son of the living God. The apostles were so adamant of the truth that each and every single one (with the exception of John) would proclaim the Truth until they were forcefully stopped with an execution.

How much more evidence does the skeptic need? When will the truth be enough for the searching soul? Perhaps understanding the significance of the resurrection will help.

---

281 In the book Zechariah, chapters 9–14 were written approximately 480 BC. When added to the approximate age of Jesus at the time of the crucifixion, the prophecy was written over five hundred years in advance (NIV Life Application Study Bible, p. 1608).

282 John 20:27.

283 John 20:25.

The Significance of the Resurrection

Vindicates the Claims of Jesus Christ. The resurrection of Jesus Christ is the single greatest event in all of history. Nothing else can begin to compare to the power and the impact it had on the world; it has had a ripple effect that can be felt even today. The impact of the resurrection is found in every generation and in every nation since that time.

First, the moment that Jesus was resurrected, it instantly validated each and every claim that He made. By coming back to life, Jesus demonstrated that He was in fact all-powerful. Since Jesus is all-powerful, then we know for a fact that Jesus is God. If Jesus is God then he is worthy of our worship, is the only way to heaven, and can completely forgive sin. The resurrection was designed to be the focal point of Christianity and a method that we can use to systematically prove the faith to be entirely true.

The Key to Heaven. Second, the resurrection gives every person the opportunity to receive salvation, regardless of whether they realize it or accept it. Jesus died for the sins of all people, and a person's refusal to accept the gift of salvation does not imply that it was never there. The person has simply refused to take what was already offered. This is an important fact to understand because some people think that heaven is only reserved for a certain number of people or a certain type of people. The truth is that the resurrection has enabled all people to accept salvation, *if they are willing.*

The Living God. Third, the resurrection is significant because of the fact that we know Jesus is not dead and His body is not rotting in the grave, even though the body was temporarily placed in the grave shortly after His death. Jesus is *alive*, and He was seen by hundreds upon hundreds of people. This is significant, because we know for a fact that we serve and worship a *living God* and not some dead statue or gold idol or material possession that cannot help us when in need. There is but one God. He is alive, and it was proven to hundreds of people, and we read their accounts and recognize the drastic shift in their attitudes and actions.

The Difference between a Relationship and Pure Faith. Finally, the resurrection is significant because it separates Christianity from all other religions. All other gods and religious leaders all throughout history—Muhammad, Buddha, Confucius, the Pharaohs of Egypt, and all other prophets—currently lie in their graves *except* for Jesus Christ.[284] If you were to physically dig them up, you would find their remains still in the grave because they have never been resurrected.

Since the resurrection was verified before hundreds upon hundreds of people, who were both for and against Jesus, Christians have something that no other religion can claim: Christians worship a God who is living and actually exists. No other religion has the kind of proof that Christians have, nor will they ever have proof that rivals Christianity because it does not and cannot exist; it would contradict the Absolute Truth.

The significance of the resurrection cannot fully be comprehended, nor can it be explained in a mere book. However, we are able to know enough to confidently place our faith upon Jesus Christ as Lord. This is the greatest significance the resurrection offers.

The Importance of Faith

More than Enough. There is more than enough evidence surrounding the crucifixion and resurrection of Jesus Christ to systematically prove these events to be entirely true. Hebrews 11:1 commends the ancients for being sure of what they hoped for and certain of what they could not see. This verse was commending their faith in God because it was only by faith the ancients could believe (they did not have the luxury of modern technology to verify what we now know today). The reason faith was so important was because the Father revealed himself to only a select few (mostly prophets); thus there was little interaction between God and humankind when you compare the Old and New Testaments.

In the New Testament, God came to earth to live among His people. Jesus was not some obscure mystery that people wondered about; He was physically there every day for approximately thirty-three years, and people had the ability to get to know Him personally as well as watch His ministry grow.

As a result of this daily interaction God had with people, there are countless personal testimonies and eyewitness accounts of the life, ministry, death, and resurrection of Jesus that enable us to confirm the events that took place. The people who saw Him before and after the crucifixion knew for a fact who He was; ironically, these people did not need the faith that we need today because they knew it to be entirely true. Although we were

284 With the exception of Elijah; he is not on earth and never died. See 2 Kings 2:11.

not physically there to verify everything that was documented about Jesus in Scripture, we have the ability to verify them with science, logic and through the inerrant Word of God. As a result, we need less faith than the ancients, but more faith than those who were eyewitnesses and testified to the truth in the first century.

As a twenty-first-century generation, we must understand that faith is still applicable. In order for us to be saved, we must place our entire faith in Jesus Christ, alone. It is wonderful that we are able to physically prove that: God exists; that every religion *not* centered upon Jesus Christ is false; and that Jesus is exactly who He said He was—God. However, proof alone still cannot bridge the gap between us and God. The only mechanism that can bridge the gap is faith and faith alone. By faith we believe that Jesus was born of a virgin, lived a sinless life, died on a cross, rose again on the third day, currently reigns in heaven as God, and will fulfill His promise of eternal life to those that believe.

It is with the mouth that we confess our sin, but it is with the heart that we believe and are justified.[285] Thus, in order to *believe* that Jesus Christ is Lord, you must first have faith. The definition of faith is to have *confidence* or *trust* in a person or thing.[286] If you cannot trust Jesus or the promises He has made to you, then you, by definition, do not have faith. Even though we have never physically seen Jesus, we can be sure of what we hope for because Scripture is entirely true and also because the resurrection of Jesus Christ is a proven and undeniable fact.

Transitioning from Old to New

The Old Covenant. Since the fall of Adam and Eve, there has always been a gap between mankind and God. In the Old Testament, the high priest served both God and God's people in an effort to bridge the communication gap. Prayers, sacrifices, and offerings were given to the high priest, who would then offer them to God. The reason that there had to be a mediator between God and His people is because the Father is so holy that we cannot have direct contact with Him. Sin cannot coexist with the Father; which is why entering into the Father's presence would kill us.

There is a reason why the Old Testament high priest had to spend countless hours washing and preparing himself before he entered into the

285 Romans 10:10.

286 Faith. Dictionary.com. *Dictionary.com Unabridged.* Random House, Inc. http://dictionary.reference.com/browse/faith (accessed: July 27, 2009).

most holy room of the tabernacle. If the high priest were not ceremonially clean, he would be killed the moment that he entered into the most holy room. Since nobody but the high priest could enter into this room, it would have been physically impossible to retrieve his body, which is why a rope was tied around his ankle. In the event that the high priest entered into the presence of God without following God's exact instructions and was killed, he would be pulled out of the room by the rope. This is symbolic of the enormous gap that separates men from God. However, this is not the case in the New Covenant.

A New Covenant. The resurrection of Jesus Christ has transitioned God's people from the Old Covenant into the New Covenant. The Old Covenant established the method in which people, of that time period, could have their sins removed; which was through sacrifices and various types of offerings. The New Covenant is the new promise that God has made with His people, and it greatly differs from the Old Covenant.

The New Covenant is different because it enables all people to have a personal relationship with God, which was previously impossible. The reason that we are able to have a personal relationship with God, pray directly to God (without having to go through a priest), and are released from the strict adherence to the Law is because Jesus provided the final atonement for sin. Recall that in the Old Testament continuous sacrifices were needed in order to cleanse sin, but that they no longer occur. The reason that the old sacrifices are no longer needed is because Jesus Himself was the perfect—and final—sacrifice for all sin. Jesus' blood is able to cleanse all sin, because Jesus is perfect and holy in every way. Therefore, sacrifices are no longer needed because the price for sin was paid in full once and for all.

Another change that occurred is the ability to have a personal and intimate relationship with God. We are able to have that close relationship with God because the resurrection established Jesus as the *one and only* great High Priest.[287] Scripture also teaches that each Christian is a priest, and, since we are priests, we can directly pray to and worship God.[288] As a result of this revelation, Christians no longer are required to confess sins to one another, nor are we required to pray through a priest. Replacing the dominant role of the former high priest with Jesus Christ, and establishing

287 Hebrews 2:11–17; 4:14–16; 7:23–28.

288 Isaiah 61:6; 1 Peter 2:5; Revelation 1:6.

all Christians as priests, has ultimately given us a tremendous amount of freedom. However, freedom does not come without responsibility.

As priests, we are held to the highest standards because we directly represent God as ambassadors.[289] Therefore, we must always conduct ourselves in a way that would never weaken or compromise our testimony. We are a direct representation of the joy and peace that God alone can offer. If Christians never come out to be a separate people, as God has commanded, then we will never be distinguished from society.[290] If we cannot be distinguished from others, appear just as miserable, and regularly participate in sin without impunity, then what attraction would anybody have to Christianity? Finally, though, despite our weakness and failings, Jesus acts as the mediator and advocate between humankind and God the Father.

Your Greatest Ally

More than Just a Priest. Since we have scripturally established that all Christians are priests with Jesus Christ being the only High Priest, we are now able to move forward so that we can fully understand what your faith in Christ will ultimately accomplish.

Decider of Your Eternal Fate. Jesus Christ is much more than a priest to whom we offer our prayer, worship, and praise. He is the one who will ultimately decide whether you will to enter into heaven. Jesus referred to himself as the Gate all people must pass through in order to enter into heaven.[291] In order to pass through the gate, your name must be found within the *book of life.*[292] The book of life, as indicated by Scripture, is the record of people who will receive eternal life; the names of those who die without Christ will not be found within this book upon their judgment.[293] The scriptures indicate that Jesus Christ will personally vouch on behalf the Christian while we stand before the Father and the angels.[294] This means that Jesus will personally confirm that you belong to Him because you are one of His believers.

---

289 2 Corinthians 5:20.

290 2 Corinthians 6:17.

291 John 10:9.

292 Philippians 4:3; Revelation 3:5; 20:12, 15.

293 Revelation 20:15.

294 Revelation 3:5.

Before you enter into your eternal place, everybody will be judged according to what they have or have not done. Both Christians and non-Christians are accountable to God, but many scholars believe that there is a tremendous difference between the two judgments. The Bible gives us a glimpse into how the believers and nonbelievers will be judged. Some scholars assert that believers and nonbelievers will not be judged at the same time. There will be two separate judgments: one for believers (the bema judgment) and another for nonbelievers (Great White Throne judgment).[295] The bema judgment is for believers, and it establishes the rewards that you will receive in Heaven, based upon what you have done for Christ while living on earth. This judgment has nothing to do with your salvation because that was determined, in advance, the moment that you accepted Christ.

On the other hand, some scholars suggest that the Great White Throne judgment will be for all nonbelievers. The nonbelievers will be resurrected and judged after the millennial reign of Christ, and at this judgment they will be chastised for their unbelief and wickedness and ultimately thrown into the lake of fire.[296] You do not want to be a part of the second judgment because nothing good can come from encountering the wrath of an almighty God.

Decider of Your Earthly Fate. Establishing a relationship with Jesus can influence your fate on Earth through various blessings that are given from above. It is always good to have connections with people in high places, and by establishing a relationship with Jesus Christ, you are inevitably linked with the greatest and most powerful ally you could possibly have while living on earth. What could be more beneficial than having an all-powerful God backing you and the decisions you make?

God desires to immensely bless your life just as many parents desire to bless their children. Parents inevitably want the very best for their kids as long as what they give them does not spoil or ruin them. There is great joy in seeing one's children become successful and prosperous. Likewise, God desires to bless each and every single one of His children because He delights in seeing us enjoy the blessings that He has given as they are used for the glory of God. As with anything, too much can be harmful. Too

295 Bema judgment: Matthew 25:31–46; 1 Corinthians 3:13–15; 2 Corinthians 5:10; Psalms 50:3–5; Revelation 20:4–6. White Throne judgment: Revelation 20:11–15.

296 Revelation 20:5, 11–15.

many blessings may distract you from your faith and could ultimately cause you to backslide.

Since too much can be harmful, God will only bless you with as much as you can responsibly manage. The Bible teaches that if we are faithful with little, then we can be trusted to manage greater sums of wealth and greater blessings.[297] From this passage, we can conclude that God desires to bless your life but will only do so to the extent of the blessings you can handle. Therefore, be faithful with the little that God has given you so that you will be prepared when God desires to bless you beyond your wildest imagination. God owns everything, but we are given the responsibility of managing that which is His. As you grow spiritually, you will inevitably be blessed with more and more; this is yet another benefit of placing your faith in Christ.

Do people still have doubts about the identity of Jesus Christ? Unfortunately, there are several misconstrued perceptions about the identity of Jesus Christ. In the next chapter we will examine those ideas to determine whether or not they constitute truth.

297 Matthew 25:14–30.

Chapter 11

Liar, Lunatic, Legend, or Lord?

"You must make your choice. Either this man was, and is, the Son of God: or else a madman or something worse. You can shut Him up for a fool, you can spit at Him and kill Him as a demon; or you can fall at His feet and call Him Lord and God. But let us not come with any patronizing nonsense about His being a great moral teacher. He has not left that open to us. He did not intend to."

—*C. S. Lewis*

Making a Decision about Christ

Exposure Forces a Decision. Once people have been exposed to the Gospel, they must, and will, ultimately make a decision. Even if a person hears the Gospel and shrugs it off as if it were meaningless and as if never having heard the message in the first place (for whatever reason), that person has still rejected the message. Although people may have many different opinions about Jesus, there are really only two sides that one can take on the matter. One either accepts Jesus Christ as personal Lord and Savior or rejects Him; there is no middle ground between those two positions. There is no such thing as a partial believer, nor is it possible for a person to pick and choose the parts of the Christian faith that are most appealing. Granted, it would be easier to pick and choose the best parts about the Bible (pretend there is no hell or consequences for doing wrong and live our lives in any way that we please), but the reality is that the Absolute Truth reveals to us that right and wrong actually exist (common sense) and that there are consequences for our actions. The Bible tells us that there is a heaven and a hell (literal destinations for all people, not some metaphor describing earthly circumstances) and people will be judged and sent to their respective places according to their belief in Jesus. It continually perplexes me how the consequences of rejection are *unfathomable*, yet the solution is so simple. We cannot begin to put into perspective the degree of pain required for a person to literally grind their teeth away due to the immense agony of the flames, but we can put into perspective the solution by demonstrating the impossibility of the Liar, Lunatic, and Legend arguments so that some might change their eternal destination.

Even though people will inevitably accept or reject Jesus, we must address the different reasons on which people base their rejection. As a result, this chapter will be dedicated to examining three of the major reasons that a person might reject Jesus as God incarnate and as personal Lord and Savior. The people who outright reject the Gospel will be found to hold one or more of the following opinions about the person or existence of Jesus Christ: Liar, Lunatic, or Legend. No matter how a person tries to justify unbelief, to do so is to claim that Jesus either lied, was a madman, or was a myth that people came up with long ago.

Liar

The Liar's Argument. Throughout history countless people have rejected the Gospel because they believe that Jesus was a liar and that His claims were simply not true. Since these people believe that Jesus was a liar, they consequently believe that the Bible is flawed and is, in their opinion, not a credible source. Therefore, these people do not place their faith in Jesus and reject their salvation.

It appears we have a dilemma: did Jesus lie about his identity, or was he telling the truth? To some people, it would seem entirely possible that Jesus could have lied or could have been deceptive about His true identity. Since the accusation has been made and some people have bought in hook, line, and sinker, we need to understand whether this claim has merit. Was Jesus a liar? Does this accusation constitute truth? This is an extremely important topic for Christians and non-Christians alike. People must fully understand the facts, the supporting evidence, and the feasibility of a lie so that they can make an accurate decision in regard to the Christian faith and the salvation Jesus offers.

Consequences of a Lie. If Jesus was a liar, then all Christianity is worthless; Jesus was not the perfect sacrifice sent to redeem humankind from sin.[298] If Jesus was not the Redeemer whom God sent, then all people are still lost in their sins, and their faith is futile. Christians are false witnesses to God and Christians are to be pitied above every other person, religion, or people because *everything* they have done for the faith has been in vain.[299] Everything is meaningless, because all of creation, history, and the Christian's purpose for living ultimately rests upon the figure of Jesus Christ as Lord.

If Jesus was not really God, then all Christian churches should close their doors. Christians should become agnostic, atheist, or whatever else they want because it really does not matter.[300] If Christianity was a lie, then this book is also in vain, and we may as well begin a new search for Absolute Truth.

The ripple effect of Jesus being a liar has a far greater effect than we could possibly imagine. Since Jesus, through His Spirit, authored the Bible, it would consequently lose all credibility of being Absolute Truth simply because it would have been authored by a liar. Since the Bible contains all standards (i.e., laws, justice, and morality), there would be *no* standards, because they too would be meaningless. There would be no restraint on evil, no incentive to do good, and no justice; in fact, there would be utter chaos.

Why would all these tragedies occur? The Christian church, since its conception, has been a major restraint on evil. The second largest religion, Islam does not restrain evil. In fact, as we will discover in the chapter on Islam, this religion actually promotes violence against women, the murder of infidels, waging jihad, and martyrdom in exchange for seventy virgins. Later, we will examine Islamic doctrine and consider whether it can coincide with Christianity, but the point of this argument is that the Christian church is the major restraint of evil and that the Bible is desperately needed to establish laws, morality, and justice so that we can live civil lives in society.

Glance at the Middle East, where Christianity is scarce, and note that fear and terrorism run rampant in daily life. Glance back at the United

298 1 Corinthians 15:14.

299 1 Corinthians 15:17–19.

300 Dr. Richard Lee, *What Should We Believe? Jesus—Who Says He Is God?* There's Hope Ministries, 1998.

States where the Christian church has a much greater influence. Look at America's Christian foundation and how Jesus Christ has been interwoven into the very core of our nation. Then note our prosperity, freedom, and civility. Is this mere chance? If Jesus were a liar, I would concede chance. However, if Jesus did not lie, America is *currently* under the blessing of an almighty God.

The Contradiction. Discovering whether or not Jesus was a liar is really quite simple. Verification simply entails reading the accounts of Jesus that are provided by both the Bible and secular history. As you read the accounts of Jesus, you will not find one instance where Jesus lied; nor did He ever contradict Himself in any of His actions or teachings. Nobody could possibly say that Jesus was *not* moral, loving, kind, or just; everything that Jesus did was good. Jesus healed the sick, made the lame walk, resurrected the dead, made the blind see, fed the hungry, and continuously gave to the poor.

Nowhere do we read about Jesus equated with being selfish; it was all about giving, giving, giving to everybody else while withholding nothing for Himself. Jesus was even buried in a borrowed tomb, and this fact demonstrates that He had minimal material possessions to His name. Even those who most despised Jesus recognized that He was a man of great integrity. Even the Jewish religious leaders recognized that Jesus taught the way of God in accordance with truth and that He was not swayed by the opinions of men.[301]

When Jesus was brought before Pilate in trial, Pilate found no fault with Jesus. Pilate found Jesus innocent of the charges and pleaded His innocence to the Jewish people *three times.*[302] Pilate even tried to release Jesus, but the Jewish people's hearts were so hardened that they demanded the release of an insurrectionist and murderer instead.[303]

In fact, the only teaching that the Jewish religious leaders vehemently objected to was when Jesus claimed to be God. The religious leaders accused Jesus of blasphemy and of dishonoring God by claiming deity. The Jewish religious leaders refused to even consider the possibility of Jesus' statement containing truth because they had a personal motive to preserve their social status, their power—and frankly, Jesus was getting in their way. As a result, the Jewish religious leaders did not consider the

301 Matthew 22:15–22; Mark 12:13–17; Luke 20:20–26.

302 Luke 23:22.

303 Luke 23:25.

truth and made a false accusation against Jesus, which was conveniently punishable by death.

Why did they make this false accusation when earlier they hailed Him as a man of great integrity?[304] When the Jewish religious leaders decided that it was no longer beneficial for Jesus to live, they forced Him to acknowledge His identity because it was the only way they could claim blasphemy and ultimately execute Him. The reason that they could not charge Him with anything else is because Jesus had never done anything wrong, and at His trial they could not produce any truthful witnesses to testify against Him on any type of sin.

Ultimately, the charge against Jesus was blasphemy. By making this charge, the Jewish religious leaders were indirectly accusing Jesus of being a liar. Jesus said that he was the Son of God and the Messiah, but the religious leaders disagreed. Since the religious leaders did not believe the claim to be true, they consequently sought out a method by which they could legally execute Jesus.

In this section we have two contradictions that we need to examine. The first contradiction centers upon Jesus' true identity. Jesus claimed that he was God (the Messiah), and the Jewish religious leaders claimed that Jesus was not God. The second contradiction centers on the claims and the actions of the Jewish religious leaders. It is a contradiction in the pattern of thought to acknowledge Jesus as being a great man of integrity one day and then turn around and call Him a blasphemous liar when it was no longer convenient to have Him alive.

Thus, the objective will be to determine whether it is possible that Jesus lied about His identity. We take a step back to look at the surrounding facts, the evidence, and the prophecies that ultimately reveal precisely who the Messiah was and the time period in which He would set foot on earth. First, however, we need to return to a principle that we covered earlier, because it is applicable to this scenario as well. Truth is indifferent to any perspective, accusation, or opinion. Truth will continue to be true whether it aligns with popular opinion or not; never be influenced by the popularity of an idea alone. Either Jesus was God (the Christ, Messiah, Son of God, etc.), or He was not. Either Jesus was a liar, or He was not. By definition, since we have a contradiction surrounding the identity of Jesus, somebody has lied. Thus, our objective is to discover which party has lied.

---

304 Matthew 22:16.

Challenges to the Lie Theory. One way we can prove that Jesus was not a liar is by examining a few of the prophecies surrounding the Messiah's birth. The Messiah, as indicated by Scripture, would be God in the flesh.[305] Therefore, the Messiah and God are interchangeable terms. When Jesus claims to be God, He claims to be the Messiah. When Jesus claims to be the Messiah, he is ultimately making a claim of deity; God in the flesh. Furthermore, God will only live among and die for His people one time; there is no other or future Messiah.

In regard to this one Messiah, there were hundreds of prophecies that were fulfilled, but we only need *three* to demonstrate the impossibility of a lie. The three prophecies that we will examine predict when and where the Messiah would be born and the family from which He would descend. Since these prophecies were made hundreds of years in advance, they automatically negate the possibility of any person fulfilling them by mere chance or even by choice. The nature of these prophecies prohibits a person from falsely proclaiming to be the Messiah, because it is impossible for anyone to decide when, where, and to whom they will be born.

The three prophecies that we will use are found in the Old Testament; which was completed and sealed approximately four hundred years before Jesus lived.[306] Moreover, these prophecies were written by *different* men whose lifespans did not overlap, so there is no possibility of a conspiracy because there was no collaboration. In addition to having multiple predictions by multiple authors, who lived in different periods, we note that the veracity of Messiahship can easily be determined by referencing the Old Testament prophecies. We are able come to a conclusion as to whether or not Jesus' claim constitutes truth. We will now look at some of the challenges to the lie theory to demonstrate Messiahship was not a choice that could have been made.

Challenge #1. We have already established that the prophecies were not fully known or understood during the time Jesus lived.[307] Chapter 10 pointed out that all major parties involved (disciples, religious leaders, Jews today and Satan himself) had no concept of the significance or the reason behind the events that were taking place. This conclusion was based upon

305 Isaiah 9:6–7.

306 Dr. Wendell Jackson, *Between the Testaments* (Cumming: Dr. Wendell Jackson, 2006), 1–2.

307 Ephesians 1:9.

the actions, and reactions, of each group. If the prophecies were explicitly known, then all parties would have acted entirely different.

If the disciples had fully understood the prophecies, they would not have acted so cowardly when Jesus was arrested, while He was on trial, or during His execution. If Satan fully understood the prophecies, he would not have entered into Judas to betray Jesus and expedite the execution (a true enemy would try to foil, not fulfill, God's plan). We also know that if the true meaning and significance of the prophecies had been understood, then the Jewish religious leaders would not have had Jesus executed. Recall that the best way to have destroyed God's perfect plan was to refuse to execute Jesus.[308] The fact is that Jesus' disciples, who knew He was the Messiah, did not fully understand how everything was being pieced together until after the resurrection when they had the chance to study the Scriptures to see how Messiahship and prophecy aligned with one another. (During the forty days Jesus lived on earth after the resurrection, I imagine Jesus filled in many blanks and the will of God became crystal clear; along with Jesus' predictions and the fulfillment of prophecy.)

Since the prophecies were not fully known nor their meaning understood, a person could not have fully known their implications, and this means that it would have been impossible for anybody to have *chosen* to be the Messiah based on the significance we attribute to those prophecies today.

Challenge #2. Prophecy predicted the precise city in which the Messiah had to be born. As Herod's Bible scholars discovered when the Magi came searching for baby Jesus; Micah 5:2 reads: "You, Bethlehem Ephrathah, though you are small among the clans of Judah, out of you will come for me one who will be ruler over Israel, whose origins are from of old, from ancient times."

This is very interesting because it not only predicts the *only city* in which the Messiah must be born, but it also reveals that the Messiah would be God incarnate, in the flesh. The "from of old, from ancient times" phrase is a direct reference to deity. The author is explicitly revealing to the reader that the Messiah existed before all creation and was present with God before anything came into existence. We see this Old Testament revelation confirmed by the New Testament hundreds of years later when John wrote the first chapter of his Gospel (John 1:1). By the time this Gospel was written, John had personally verified Jesus' true identity. However,

308 1 Corinthians 2:8.

for now let us ignore this and also pass over pointing out that everything within the Bible is entirely true, so that we might continue demonstrating the impossibility of a lie for argument's sake.

In addition to being born in Bethlehem, the Messiah had to be born of a virgin (not the typical conception in the ancient world). Nevertheless, Isaiah 7:14 reads: "The Lord Himself will give you a sign: The virgin will be with child and give birth to a son, and will call him Immanuel." Since the Messiah must be born in Bethlehem of a mother who had never had sexual intercourse, it would be impossible for a person to be the Messiah unless they were born in Bethlehem and from a virgin. Since Bethlehem, at the time, was a very small city and it's not every day that virgins give birth, the number of potential candidates for Messiahship is drastically reduced.

Challenge #3. I believe that the most interesting prophecy surrounding the birth of the Messiah predicts the time period in which the Messiah had to be born. God always has a perfect plan because He knows the future. God knows what you will do in the future before you ever decide what to do. Since the Messiah had to be rejected and ultimately executed in order to provide the perfect atonement for sin, God strategically placed the Messiah in a time period when He knew the people would reject Him regardless of whether the Messiah came or not. This is a very important concept to grasp because God does not send anybody to hell; people, by rejecting salvation, send themselves to hell. The reasons that the Jewish religious leaders rejected the Messiah were because they were selfish, corrupt, and more concerned with legalism than truly pleasing or worshipping God. These people valued power, money, social status, public opinion, and the like more than they valued God.

It would not make sense to send a sacrificial savior to die and atone for sin if the people would have openly accepted the Messiah. Therefore, the Messiah had to be sent in a time period in which He would be rejected even if God appeared to them in person (which is what happened). What could have been a better time to send the Messiah than when the high priest and the religious leaders were already more concerned with themselves and their social status and power than they were about pleasing God? This is why Jesus came at the time period we read about, but even more interesting is that this time period was selected beforehand because of a prophecy found in Daniel.

In Daniel, we read a prophecy that predicts the precise period in which the Messiah must be born in order to be rejected by His contemporaries. Daniel 9:25–26 reads:

> Know and understand this: From the issuing of the decree to restore and rebuild Jerusalem until the Anointed One, the ruler, comes, there will be seven "sevens," and sixty-two "sevens." It will be rebuilt with streets and a trench, but in times of trouble. After the sixty-two "sevens," the Anointed One will be cut off [killed] and will have nothing.

To calculate the time period in which the Messiah must be killed, we must first calculate the number of years from the issuing of the decree to restore and rebuild Jerusalem until the Anointed One will be cut off. The "sevens" referred to in Scripture here indicate a period of seven years. If you add seven periods of seven years to sixty-two periods of seven years, you get a total of 483 prophetic years: 7(7) + 62(7) = 483 years. Prophetic years are based on a lunar calendar of twelve months, each consisting of thirty days (the lunar calendar was very common in the ancient civilizations). The ancient Hebrews used a lunar calendar, and the Bible also references the use of a 360-day lunar calendar.[309]

The Bible's use of a lunar calendar does not imply that the measurements of time are incorrect, per se. It would be analogous to measuring an object in kilograms and then converting the weight to pounds. They are both correct measurements, but each system attributes different numerical numbers to the weight, and the numbers can be converted between the two systems. Therefore, we must measure from the lunar calendar and then convert to our 365-day solar calendar in order for the time period to be meaningful for our purpose.[310]

To convert the 483 prophetic years to solar years, we multiply the 483 years by the number of days in that year and come up with the total number of days that period spans. 483 years x 360 days = 173,880 total days. To convert this number to the solar calendar, we divide the number of days by 365.25: 173,880/365.25 = 476 solar years. Now that we have converted lunar time to solar time, we need to know when the decree to

---

309 Genesis 7:11, 24; 8:4, Revelation 12:6, 13–14; Daniel 9:27.

310 Harold W. Hoehner, "Chronological Aspects of the Life of Christ," *Bibliotheca Sacra* (January 1975): 63–65.

restore Jerusalem was issued so we can calculate when the Messiah was expected to arrive.

In the Old Testament, we can find a passage where the exact words of the decree are provided; by examining the surrounding text, we are able to easily determine the time period.[311] In this passage, Nehemiah is grieved when he hears of the desolate condition of Jerusalem. The king asks Nehemiah why he is grieved, and Nehemiah explains how the city where his fathers are buried lies in ruins. The king asks what Nehemiah wants, and he replies, "If it pleases the king and if your servant has found favor in his sight, let him send me to the city in Judah where my fathers are buried so that I can rebuild it."[312] Long story short, the king granted Nehemiah favor and he left to rebuild Jerusalem's walls. Now that we know that the decree was established; we now need to know when.

Based upon secular sources and scripture, we can estimate the date in which the decree was given. We begin with Nehemiah 2:1: "In the month of Nisan in the twentieth year of King Artaxerxes ..." This verse tells us Nehemiah was given the decree twenty years after Artaxerxes became king. Now we need to know when Artaxerxes began his reign. We know that he became king around 465 BC.[313] We then add twenty years to the year Artaxerxes became king, and we come up with 445 BC. Therefore, we can estimate that it was during this period that Nehemiah left to rebuild Jerusalem. (I am not concerned with the specific day and month that the decree was issued because that is an entirely different issue, and it also would not help us since we are looking for approximations; hence the use of the term *period*.)

Now that we have the approximate date of the decree and the number of years prophesied by Daniel, we need to put them together to come up with a time period in which the Messiah would be "cut off" or killed. Recall that Daniel's prophecy was in *periods of seven years*, so the exact date of the Messiah's death cannot be pinpointed, but the period can be approximated. We will now work backwards to find out when the Messiah had to be killed, and from that point we will then estimate the time period in which Messiah had to be born.

If we begin around 445 BC and add the 476 years that Daniel prophesied, we come to around AD 31 (the time when the Messiah would

311 Nehemiah 2:1–8; 2 Chronicles 36:22–23.

312 Nehemiah 2:5.

313 The History Channel, "PERSIA," http://www.history.com/encyclopedia.do?articleId=219001 (accessed July 29, 2009).

be "cut off" or executed). Now that we know when the Messiah would be executed, we are able to determine, by working backwards, an approximate time period of the Messiah's birth. In Jewish culture, the age of maturity was thirty, and this was also the point in which a Jew could begin a ministry and begin teaching publicly.[314] Since we know that the absolute minimum for the Messiah to have entered into ministry was thirty years of age, we will subtract 30 years from AD 31 and come to around AD 1. Since the prophecy in Daniel narrows the time within seven years, we can estimate the time period as far back as 6 BC, but it may extend farther back a few years because we are assuming that Jesus began his ministry at precisely thirty years of age when he could have waited longer; thirty was the minimum.

Since we cannot pinpoint specific events, we cannot confirm exact dates (not even the exact day or month of the Messiah's birth is known; we symbolically celebrate Christmas because it's near the winter solstice). From the information that we have gathered and sifted through, we can approximate the time period of the Messiah's birth to be between 6 BC to AD 1. However, I will be as *liberal* as I possibly can with the dates in order to prove a point. I will double the time period from seven years to fourteen years, in spite of the fact that we have the ability to be more accurate. As a result, we will loosen our approximations to specify the expected time of the Messiah as during a fourteen-year period that extends from AD 1 back to 13 BC (a date so far back that virtually no historian believes it is accurate). We can assume, with confidence, that the time period in which the Messiah had to be born was between 14 BC and AD 1.

The fact that the Bible presents a specific time period in which the Messiah had to appear, it negates all people from their candidacy in Messiahship who were not born between the two dates listed above.

Challenge #4. Prophecy also predicted the precise family in which the Messiah would be born.

Isaiah 11:1–3 reads: "A shoot will come up from the stump of Jesse; from his roots a Branch will bear fruit. The Spirit of the Lord will rest on him—the Spirit of wisdom and of understanding, the Spirit of counsel and of power, the Spirit of knowledge and fear of the Lord—and he will delight in the fear of the Lord."

314 Thomas D. Lea, *The New Testament: Its Background and Message* (Nashville, TN: Broadman & Holman Academic, 2003), 96–97.

We also note that another prophecy (which was written by a separate author in an entirely different time period)[315] reveals the "righteous Branch" will come from King David's lineage. Jeremiah 33:15-16 reads:

> In those days and at that time
> I will make a righteous Branch sprout from David's line;
> he will do what is just and right in the land.
> In those days Judah will be saved
> and Jerusalem will live in safety.
> This is the name by which it will be called:
> "The Lord Our Righteousness."

This Branch (Isaiah 11:1; Jeremiah 33:15), according to the following verse in Jeremiah, will be called: "The Lord Our Righteousness." This verse explicitly reveals that the Messiah will come from David's lineage.

At first glance it could appear that there is a contradiction because two entirely different names were mentioned, but a look at the family tree confirms that Jesse was the father of David and that both prophecies are correct. Therefore, we have confirmation by two different prophets in two different time periods that reveal one lineage. Since the family in which the Messiah had to be born was chosen hundreds of years in advance, this prophecy excludes all people not of Davidic descent.

Now, let's put these prophecies together to see the chances of *just anybody* being able to fulfill them.

Piecing the Puzzle Together. Keep in mind that our objective was never to prove whether Jesus lied about claiming Messiahship; we already know that the claim was made because that was the very reason for His execution. All the interested parties (Jews, Romans, and early Christians) acknowledge this as Jesus' claim and an undeniable fact. Instead, we are concerned with whether the claim of Messiahship made by Jesus Christ constitutes truth.

As we look at the situation and begin to think about the different prophecies and the stringent criteria surrounding Messiahship, we begin to understand how narrow and restrictive the selection processes were and

315 Chapters 1–39 in Isaiah were written approximately 700 BC, while chapters 40–66 may have been written around 681 BC. Jeremiah was written approximately 627–586 BC (*Life Application Study Bible*, pp. 1166; 1283).

how they rule out virtually everybody else from qualifying. In fact, the criteria surrounding the Messiah were so narrow that only one person in all of history could have fulfilled them: none other than Jesus Christ—born in Bethlehem of a virgin, a descendant of Jesse and David, and born during the correct time period.

Joseph and Mary had other children, but they never claimed Messiahship. Furthermore, the early family moved frequently. Before Mary's baby was due, Joseph and Mary made a trip to Bethlehem to register for the census. From Bethlehem, they moved to Egypt in order to escape Herod's baby slaughter. After Herod's death, the family then moved back to Nazareth, their hometown.[316] The family *briefly* stayed in Bethlehem, but that is where the prophecy predicted the birth. Since the family line temporarily lived in Bethlehem, it's impossible to imagine any child other than Jesus fulfilling this prophecy. Consequently, of all Mary's and Joseph's children, only Jesus meets this requirement for Messiahship.

Think about it; how many people were born in Bethlehem between 14 BC and AD 1? Out of that group, how many were born into the direct lineage of King David? Out of that group, how many were born of a virgin? When a person strips away bias, logically examines the criteria, and sees that only one person could fulfill the prophecy, the chances of a random person to qualify for, or choose, Messiahship is not even a coherent option. From prophecy, we learn there was only one chance of fulfillment, and if Jesus did not meet the requirements, then nobody else in history could have assumed the role of the Messiah, regardless of how desperate they were to fulfill that role. Messiahship was not random; it was meticulously planned so that nobody could impersonate or falsely claim to be the Messiah.

Why was it impossible for just anybody to claim Messiahship? Because God did not enable Messiahship to be a choice that a person could have made; the One who would fill that role was chosen in advance so that there could be no confusion in regard to His identity.

Also, consider the prophecies and the likelihood of accurately predicting the future hundreds of years in advance. Can a person accurately predict the city, family line, and time period of a person over four hundred years in advance? Absolutely not; meteorologists (with all their sophisticated technology and knowledge) can hardly predict the weather even twenty-four hours in advance. How much more difficult is it to predict when, where, and to whom a specific person will be born?

---

316 Matthew 2:13–15, 19–23; Luke 2:1–7.

Frankly, it would have been impossible to accurately predict the future unless the information was revealed by an all-knowing source who definitively knew the future. The only entity that can definitively know the future is God. The text predicting the Messiah was the Bible, and as we already know, the author of the Bible was God. This could only mean that the all-knowing entity knew the future and selected the best time for the Messiah to be born, and it was therefore determined in advance. Since God knew precisely how and when the plan would be executed, He began revealing it to the Old Testament prophets so that there would be no mistake about the identity of the Messiah, either in the ancient world as the events were unfolding or today. These prophecies were written for you—right here, right now—as you are reading this book to aid in your decision or to aid in sharing the Gospel message. Prophecy is powerful, and it helps bolster the faith against the illogical and absurd accusations against Jesus Christ.

Addressing the Lie Theory. Now that we have properly put the facts into perspective, we need to address the Lie Theory. Since prophecy predetermined who would be the Messiah, and since we know fulfillment was not a matter of choice, we begin to understand that the only lie that Jesus could have told was any statement that *denied* Messiahship. If Jesus were to claim that he was the Messiah, he would only be telling the truth and accurately reflecting fulfillment of the prophecies. The only way a person could claim that Jesus lied was if he actually fulfilled the prophecies (was born at the foreordained time, place, and family) and then turned around to deny his own identity. But we already know, from secular and biblical sources, that Jesus did not deny Messiahship because the Romans and Jewish religious leaders executed Him for claiming to be equal with God—the Messiah.

The Liars Insist. Recently, there has been another attempt to claim that Jesus was a liar. This claim suggests that Jesus was the Messiah but not the Son of God because he was not deity. This implies that Jesus fulfilled the prophecies but that he was not part of the Godhead. This does not make sense because it contradicts the Bible, which we have proven to be entirely true and without error. This claim also contradicts the resurrection (witnessed by over 500 people)[317] that vindicates each and every single claim that Jesus made.

317 1 Corinthians 15:6.

Jesus' ministry was not a secret; it was not done in private or behind closed doors. His birthplace, family lineage, and time period of birth are easily verified just like His miracles, death, and resurrection. This theory also fails to establish credibility and a belief in which any logical and thinking individual could place their faith.

From the stringent requirements of prophecy, we have learned that only one person could have been the Messiah and that the only way the Messiah could have lied was to deny His identity. Since Messiahship is not something that could have been chosen, and Jesus did not deny His identity, we can confidently conclude that Jesus did not lie about His true identity. The liar's argument has failed to establish itself and, as a result, is not considered *truth.*

Lunatic

The Lunatic's Argument. Throughout history, people have also made the claim that Jesus was a lunatic—that He was deranged and was mistaken about His identity. Ironically, this theory *does not* question whether Jesus existed, whether He lived a moral and upright life, or whether He made all the claims that historians have recorded. Instead, this theory maintains that Jesus was confused and mistook Himself to be God's chosen Messiah when He was not. The advocates of this theory believe that Jesus' claims of divinity were false. Second, this theory tries to dismiss the entire ministry and doctrine of Jesus based on the belief that Jesus was mentally unstable and that He did not fully understand the consequences of His actions.

The claims of divinity are explained away by this theory through the belief that Jesus, in His heart, was so convinced (and was so adamant) about being the Messiah that He actually began to believe that He was God when in reality He was merely a carpenter's son from the small town of Nazareth. This theory claims that as Jesus grew older, the obsession with and belief in Himself as God's chosen Messiah eventually led Him into a downward spiral at the end of His life, when His claims became bolder and more controversial. The downward spiral finally ended as the madman was crucified for His outrageous claims.

Reasons for Claiming Lunacy. The proponents of this argument claim that Jesus' obsession not only drove Him to become mentally unstable and unaware of His original identity, but it also distorted His perception of reality as He eventually quit work in an attempt to begin a ministry. The sole intention of His ministry was to try and convince the world He was the Messiah. The proponents of this argument also claim that the attempt of Jesus to fulfill the prophecies of His mistaken identity explains Mary's extreme distress and grief for her son. Mary, in her own heart, knew her son was going crazy and would soon be executed, if He continued on His daring crusade to convince the world that He was God.

In short, the overall theme of this theory is to try and discredit the entire ministry and doctrine of Jesus Christ. The proponents of this argument claim that people should not believe in Jesus as the Messiah—or any of His doctrines—on the grounds that Jesus was not mentally stable at the time that He was actively engaged in His ministry. This argument concludes that one must be insane to be willing to die for *all people*. It is natural to be reluctant to sacrifice oneself for a loved one because people are inherently selfish; how demented must He have been to die for the entire world (even for people who cursed, tortured and executed Him)?

Jesus must have been crazy, mentally unstable, and delusional to have sacrificed Himself in one of the most inhumane deaths imaginable, say adherents of the Lunatic Theory. If Jesus had understood the implications of the claims that He was making, then He would have never entered into His ministry, taught His doctrine, or died on the cross for humanity. The actions of this man, they claim, were so weird that He could not have been normal.

The Importance of Jesus' Mental State. Without a doubt, portraying Christianity as a faith that closely follows the direction and leadership of a mentally incapacitated lunatic (who had no concept of reality and wasted away His own life for nothing) is calculated to push people away from the faith. After all, who wants to be associated with a raging lunatic who claimed to *be God*? No wonder people who have this distorted mind-set scrutinize Christians; they are under the impression that Christians are also loony because they believe Jesus!

Apart from personal opinion or claims, the issue at hand is whether or not Jesus was *actually* mentally unstable. Was Jesus a lunatic? Did He have the mental capacity to fully understand and take responsibility for His actions? How can we definitively know that Jesus was mentally stable? The bottom line is that we need to know for a fact whether or not Jesus was mentally stable during His ministry, trial, and execution. If Jesus was a lunatic then His claims are bogus and Christianity is false, fundamentally flawed, and Christians should outgrow it. But if it can be proven that Jesus was not a lunatic, then the faith has been further strengthened by yet another example of how faith in Jesus Christ is *entirely true.*

We begin to answer the above questions by taking a closer look at Jesus.

A Closer Look at Jesus. Before we get started, we need to redefine a few basic terms so they will be fresh in our minds as we examine the mental state of Jesus.

Sanity is a legal term describing people who are of "sound mind" and able to bear full responsibility for their actions.[318] Insanity, on the other hand, is a legal term that is defined as a "mental illness of such a severe nature that a person cannot distinguish fantasy from reality, cannot conduct her/his affairs due to psychosis, or is subject to uncontrollable impulsive behavior. Insanity is distinguished from low intelligence or mental deficiency due to age or injury."[319]

Our objective will be to examine Jesus' actions and determine whether there is sufficient evidence to draw a conclusion about His mental state.

Extreme Knowledge/Wisdom. The knowledge and wisdom that Jesus displayed during His ministry greatly surpassed that of any religious leader, Pharisee, or teacher of the law (the Bible experts) in Judea. Many times throughout the Gospels, we come across a situation where an *expert* in the Jewish Law would present Jesus with an extremely difficult question or scenario. These inquiries, purposely done in public, were attempts to trap Jesus in His own words with the hopes that His inability to answer would destroy His credibility.

The intent of the religious leaders, by asking extraordinarily difficult questions, was to show the people of Israel that Jesus was a fool. If they could trap Jesus, then they could claim that he was really not God because he was not all-knowing; he could not even come up with answers to their questions. Unfortunately for the Jewish religious leaders, the plan backfired. Each and every time Jesus was challenged with the impossible, He always answered in a way that baffled and amazed all who heard it.

Let's examine a few examples of the knowledge and wisdom that Jesus displayed when directly challenged by His enemies.

---

318 Wikipedia, The Free Encyclopedia, "Sanity," http://en.wikipedia.org/w/index.php?title=Sanity&oldid=229747382 (accessed August 4, 2008).

319 Law.com Dictionary, "Insanity," http://dictionary.law.com/default2.asp?selected=979&bold=|||| (accessed August 26, 2008).

Challenge #1. After Jesus entered into Jerusalem, He told a parable that was very critical of the religious leaders and their actions. Out of their anger, they went out and devised a plan to try and trap Jesus in his own words. The religious leaders sent their disciples with some Herodians to Jesus. These disciples challenged Jesus, trying to provoke an expected response that they hoped would anger the Herodians.[320]

The disciples said to Jesus, "Teacher, we know you are a man of integrity and that you teach the way of God in accordance with the truth. You are not swayed by men, because you pay no attention to who they are. Tell us then, what is your opinion? Is it right to pay taxes to Caesar or not?"[321]

Now Jesus already knew their evil intentions, so he responded with "You hypocrites, why are you trying to trap me? Show me the coin used for paying the tax." His questioners brought a coin to Jesus, and He asked, "Whose portrait is this? And whose inscription?"

"Caesar's," they replied.

Then Jesus said to them "Give unto Caesar what is Caesar's, and unto God what is God's." When the disciples of the religious leaders heard His response, "they were amazed, so they left Him and went away."[322]

The Bible does not specifically tell us what the disciples of the religious leaders did when they left Jesus, but one could only imagine that they went back puzzled by this man's wisdom and were ashamed because they had to report defeat to their superiors, who were none other than the angry and vengeful religious leaders. These religious leaders were most likely furious by this point because Jesus was strongly denouncing them in public and was warning people to stay away because their path led to spiritual ruin and separation from God. In retaliation, the religious leaders came up with another plan to try and trap Jesus.

Challenge #2. "That same day the Sadducees, who say there is no resurrection, came to him with a question. 'Teacher,' they said, 'Moses told us that if a man dies without having children, his brother must marry the widow and have children for him. Now there were seven brothers among us. The first one married and died, and since he had no children, he left

320 A Herodian was a member of the political party that supported Herod Antipas and the policies instituted by Rome.

321 Matthew 22:16–17.

322 Matthew 22:15–22; compare Mark 12:13–17 and Luke 20:20–26.

his wife to his brother. The same thing happened to the second and third brother, right on down to the seventh. Finally, the woman died. Now then, at the resurrection, whose wife will she be of the seven, since all of them were married to her?"[323]

This may have seemed like an impossible question to those who were watching because the answer was perceived by the religious leaders to be unclear and unavailable; no matter what his response they thought had Him trapped! It would take unprecedented knowledge and wisdom to counter a question of this magnitude because the answer cannot be found in the Old Testament (and the New Testament had not yet been written).

A mental illness would have prohibited Jesus from being able to distinguish fantasy from reality and from conducting His affairs due to psychosis,[324] but Jesus quickly and authoritatively replied with "You are in error because you do not know the Scriptures or the power of God. At the resurrection people will neither marry nor be given in marriage; they will be like the angels in Heaven. But about the resurrection of the dead—have you not read what God said to you, 'I am the God of Abraham, the God of Isaac, and the God of Jacob'? He is not the God of the dead but of the living." This response again astonished the onlookers.[325]

Challenge #3. After the Pharisees had gotten news that Jesus had silenced the Sadducees and had embarrassed them in front of a multitude of people, they got together to devise another question to try and trap Jesus. Among them was an expert in the law who tested Jesus with the following question: "Teacher, which is the greatest commandment in the Law?" This is significant because Judaism, at this point, was immersed in legalism and there were countless laws on the books. The thought of choosing just one to an elevated status would certainly contradict another law, but Jesus' reply astonished the religious leaders yet again because they could not even challenge this new and profound wisdom.

In response to the question, Jesus replied: "'Love the Lord your God with all your heart and with all your soul and with all your mind.' This is the first and greatest commandment. And the second is like it: 'Love your

---

323 Matthew 22:23–28.

324 Psychosis: A mental disorder characterized by symptoms, such as delusions or hallucinations that indicate impaired contact with reality (dictionary.com).

325 Matthew 22:29–33; compare Mark 12:18–27 and Luke 20:27–40.

neighbor as yourself.' All the Law and the Prophets hang on these two commandments."[326]

Challenge #4. The final challenge that we will examine does not come from the Pharisees, but rather from Jesus Himself as he would pose a question that would leave the religious leaders unable to answer.

> While the religious leaders were gathered together, Jesus asked them, "What do you think about the Christ? Whose son is he?"
>
> "The son of David," they replied.
>
> He said to them, 'How is it then that David, speaking by the Spirit, calls him 'Lord'? For he says,
>
> 'The Lord said to my Lord:
> "Sit at my right hand
> until I put your enemies
> under your feet."'
>
> "If then David calls him 'Lord,' how can he be his son?' No one could say a word in reply, and from that day on no one dared to ask him any more questions."[327]

Further Proof of Mental Stability. As we continue to review the record of Jesus, from both secular and religious history, we cannot find a single instance where Jesus acted as if He were mentally ill or insane. In fact, as we review the records, we learn that Jesus actually restored the mentally ill to a normal and healthy state. Jesus healed those who were demon possessed, blind, unable to walk, or suffering from disease and even brought back people from the dead.

In addition to healing the mentally insane, Jesus also went through the most gruesome and torturous execution conceivable. We cannot begin to comprehend the pain and suffering that Jesus went through on the cross. As Americans, we have never experienced, nor have we ever seen, cruelty in that degree. Despite the torturous and gruesome execution, we never read an account where Jesus lost control of His emotions or His composure or acted in a way that would lead us to believe that He was mentally ill. We never read an account of Jesus retracting His statements, denying His doctrine, reversing His claim of divinity, pleading with the officials to let

326 Matthew 22:34–40; compare Mark 12:28-34.
327 Matthew 22:41–46; compare Mark 12:35–37 and Luke 20:41-44.

Him go, or apologizing for what He had done. Since human beings are inherently selfish and we have an instinct to survive, this would have been understandable—but nowhere did this happen! Jesus never retracted any of His claims or expressed remorse for his ministry.

The records actually reveal to us that, even as Jesus suffered and was dying on the cross, He carried out a *conversation* with the two thieves that were crucified on either side. This is mind-blowing: Jesus had a *coherent and intelligent* conversation at the climax of His execution! Even as Jesus hung from the cross, He led one of the thieves to salvation. Jesus told the thief that he would reign with Him in glory after his death and that he would be able to enter into the gates of heaven. This is truly a testament to the extreme mental *stability* that Jesus had. It is amazing that even as Jesus stared death in the face, He maintained His composure, continued to teach the truth, and even led a person to salvation while on the cross.

The Lunatic Theory portrays Jesus as a madman who was perhaps also mentally incompetent. We must ask whether it stands up in light of the portrait laid out in Scripture.

A Contradiction in the Pattern of Thought. There is a severe contradiction between what the Lunatic Theory claims and what the records reveal.

Again we note the definition of insanity: a "mental illness of such a severe nature that a person cannot distinguish fantasy from reality, cannot conduct her/his affairs due to psychosis [mental disorder that impairs contact with reality], or is subject to uncontrollable impulsive behavior. Insanity is distinguished from low intelligence or mental deficiency due to age or injury."[328] This is what the proponents of this argument claim: Jesus was mentally ill in such a way that He could not conduct His affairs due to psychosis and was subject to uncontrollable impulsive behavior. As a result, Jesus could not understand His true identity and mistook Himself to be God.

As we reflect on how Jesus went about His business, nowhere do we find any instance where Jesus acted in any way that would fit the above description. In fact, Jesus demonstrated an extraordinary amount of knowledge, because He was able to defeat the religious leaders in their own schemes by presenting far superior knowledge, wisdom, and understanding of the Scriptures. Jesus also maintained His composure during His

328 Law.com Dictionary, "Insanity," http://dictionary.law.com/default2.asp?selected=979&bold=|||| (accessed August 28, 2008).

torture and crucifixion. Even at the climax, Jesus never demonstrated any characteristics of a madman.

We need to understand that people were not astonished at the answers that Jesus gave simply because His words made sense (although His answers were impressive). Instead, Jesus' answers demonstrated that He knew far more than Scripture could ever teach at that moment in time. Second, Jesus could not have known the answers to questions of that magnitude without first being mentally stable, with the ability to formulate and present complex answers. Jesus' answers were a revelation of God's glory that no other person understood. Make no mistake, the religious leaders posing the questions were educated individuals whose lives were devoted to studying, teaching, and enforcing the Law. The answers that Jesus gave could not have been found within the entire Old Testament.

As we conclude this section, we must not only note what we can conclude from the historical accounts but also what Jesus' contemporaries did not claim. It is ironic to note that the Jewish religious leaders did not view Jesus as a lunatic; nor did they ever make that claim. (Granted, it was claimed Jesus was demon possessed.[329] However, it needs to be noted that lunacy differs from demon possession because lunacy is many times a permanent state from birth until death, while demon possession is not.)

Instead, the religious leaders were astonished and ultimately silenced by the mental capacity that Jesus had, because He far surpassed their own understanding. After Jesus answered their questions and silenced them with a question of His own, they dared not challenge Him again in public.

However, we are not concerned with the beliefs of the religious leaders or what the people of Jerusalem believed, because their time to decide on the issue is over. The time is *now*, and you must decide on the issue. You have been presented the Lunatic Theory and the evidence against the accusation, but you are the one who must make a decision that will determine your spiritual fate. Do you really believe that Jesus was a lunatic—a mentally impaired madman who had no idea what he was doing?

Lunatic Theory Is Disproved. This section concludes that there is sufficient evidence to determine that Jesus was not a lunatic. Contrary to the claim, Jesus had an extraordinary amount of knowledge and wisdom that trumped even the most educated scholars in the Old Testament Law. Furthermore, the fact that Jesus had an intelligent and coherent conversation with the

329 John 7:20; 8:48–56.

thieves on the cross leads to the conclusion that Jesus understood the events that were unfolding. As a result, it is not feasible to depict Jesus Christ as a lunatic. The Lunatic Theory is consequently discarded as a belief in which logical and thinking individuals can confidently place their faith.

Legend

The Argument for a Legend. The final major argument against Jesus is that He was a legend. Since it is an undeniable historical fact that Jesus was an actual person who was born in Bethlehem, grew up as a carpenter, began a ministry, and was sentenced to death because of His radical views, the opposition cannot deny that he existed. As a result of the impossibility of disproving Jesus' existence, some people who oppose Christianity have created a theory that claims the apostles and disciples of Jesus Christ concocted a legend to glorify their slain leader.

The purpose of the legend is simple: it was created because Jesus' apostles wanted all of mankind to revere him as a great martyr who died for a good cause. These people claim that Jesus was really not God and never rose from the dead and that the story of this supernatural phenomenon was nothing but a legend. This legend was needed to cover up Jesus' mortality because people needed to believe He was deity for their legend to be credible and in accordance with the Scriptures. This theory also claims that the miracles, healings, and resurrections that Jesus performed were fake, created in an attempt to enhance the appeal of the apostles' story to appease the weak minds of those who "cling to religion" (guns did not yet exist, otherwise they might have "clung" to those as well).[330]

The idea of a legend, at first glance, may sound promising and seems to be a possibility because it could fit the historical evidence. When you begin to dig deeper and review the facts, however, the idea of a legend can be quickly ruled out. Those against Christianity, who claim that Jesus was a legend, must not understand that this legend of which they speak is entirely impossible. The impracticality of such a claim will become evident when it is compared against historical records.

The Flaws of the Argument. A major flaw in the argument for the Legend Theory is that many of Jesus' contemporaries were transformed through

330 Fox News, "Obama Draws Fire for Comments on Small Town America," http://www.foxnews.com/politics/elections/2008/04/11/obama-draws-fire-for-comments-on-small-town-america/.

His ministry. Countless people were healed, witnessed His miracles, and knew Him personally. Also, many of these people were still alive when the Gospel accounts of Jesus' life were written. If any inaccurate or distorted information or blatant lies were found within the Gospel accounts, Christians would have vehemently disagreed and objected.

Nowhere in the immediate history of the Gospels do we see such objections to the accounts offered in the New Testament. This is important because three of the four Gospels in the New Testament (Matthew, Mark, and Luke) were written anywhere from as little as twenty-two years, to as many as thirty-two years after the resurrection. The fourth Gospel (John) was written between fifty and sixty years after the resurrection of Jesus Christ.[331]

If the Scriptures lied about Jesus, which the Legend Theory claims, then those who loved and admired Jesus would have created a tremendous uproar. Family, friends, followers, and those whose lives were changed by the ministry of Christ would have fought back against any false accusations because these people knew, without a doubt, that Jesus was God. In fact, many early Christians were so adamant in their faith that they were willing to be publicly executed in Jesus' name. Since they were prepared to die for Jesus and proclaimed their faith regardless, we are able to conclude that what they believed was entirely true.

As we know, people will not die for a lie. Even if they are wrong in their beliefs, people who die for a cause genuinely believe they are correct. Consider Islam: Muslims, who are willing to be martyred, strongly believe they are correct in their theological doctrine and are therefore willing to sacrifice their lives. A belief in itself does not constitute truth, but martyrs demonstrate that they genuinely believe their faith is true. They must believe that they are entirely right because only such faith enables them to sacrifice their lives. If the radical Muslims did not genuinely believe in their cause, do you think that they would willingly sacrifice themselves for a lie? Of course not; life is precious, and these martyrs genuinely believe that they are exchanging value for value. In this case, Muslims believe that they are exchanging value for value by sacrificing their life for a reward given by Allah.

Unless one is suicidal, one typically does not want to die in exchange for nothing. This is important because the apostles of Jesus Christ were very motivated individuals; they were specifically called to evangelize the

331 Ronald A. Beers, ed., *Life Application Study Bible* (Grand Rapids, MI: Zondervan 1986), 1636, 1722, 1782, 1866.

world on behalf of Jesus Christ. These men were not suicidal and did not desire death, but were willing to stay committed—even if it came down to choosing death over apostasy.[332] This is critical to note because the early apostles were also *firsthand witnesses* to the truth surrounding Jesus Christ. These men knew beyond a shadow of a doubt that Jesus Christ was Lord because they saw Jesus after He was dead and buried for three days. The apostles knew that their belief was entirely true, and this explains their willingness to be martyred.

Frankly, the apostles of Jesus Christ were not about to let the greatest revelation in human history slip through their fingers and ultimately die for a ridiculous and inaccurate myth if they did not believe that it was entirely true.

An Example to Consider. Nowhere in history can we find discontent among the early Christians with the written accounts of the life, ministry, claims and actions of Jesus Christ. Although this may seem like a small and insignificant argument, it would carry the same effect as an author today writing a book that made the accusation that John Lennon was a horrible role model who murdered, raped and tortured little children—a despicable human being.

Since John Lennon was murdered not even thirty-one years ago (1980), if a completely unrealistic and false book were to be published, stating that he murdered, raped and tortured children, people would fight back. Many people alive today were and remain fans of John Lennon. There are many people who admired and followed him closely. We would have certainly heard John's fan base fight back as they would try to restore his reputation by telling the truth and revealing once again who John Lennon really was.

On the other hand, if another book were to be published today about John Lennon, and it told the complete truth and the book hailed him as a great hero to music, then we would not think anything of it. We would already know that the information in that book was true because many people alive today lived through that era and have firsthand knowledge of the real John Lennon. If the book were true, there would be no need to refute anything. Silence on the issue is of great importance.

This is analogous to the scenario with Jesus Christ and the Gospels, which were essentially biographical texts. Within a few decades of the

---

332 Apostasy: a total desertion of or departure from one's religion, principles, party, cause, etc. (dictionary.com).

resurrection, written accounts of Jesus Christ began to appear. These accounts provide the entire world with an insight into the life and ministry of Jesus Christ. The Gospels tell us who Jesus was, reveal His doctrine, describe events that occurred during His life, and convey the positions He took on major issues. The Gospels also give us very accurate and detailed accounts of His life, the people he dealt with, the places He went, and ultimately how He was crucified, defeated death, and rose from the grave.

If the biography of Jesus Christ (the most influential person that has ever walked the face of the earth) were distorted or inaccurate, don't you think that we would have heard about it by now? Wouldn't the early Christians have published volumes of literature to try and refute the false accusations that were made against the Savior they knew personally? The fact that no such literature was written speaks volumes in regard to the issue.

Myth Busted! Realistically, the accusation that Jesus was a nice legend, myth, or fairy tale is preposterous. The very idea of a legend goes against logic and common sense. Substantial opposition would have arisen if the Gospels did not contain Absolute Truth. As a result, the Legend Theory is not a viable option in which logical and thinking individuals can confidently place their faith. The idea that Jesus Christ was a legend cannot be true.

Process of Elimination Reveals 'Lord'

Recapping the Claims. At the beginning of the chapter, I stated that four beliefs exhausted the possible opinions that a person could have in regard to the person of Jesus Christ and the stories and events surrounding His life. You either view Jesus as Lord, or you reject His deity. If you reject the divinity of Jesus Christ, then you inevitably fall into one of the three rejection categories: Liar, Lunatic, or Legend.

In this chapter, we have systematically disproved each of the three categories of rejection, and we have seen how they are illogical, impossible, and simply unreasonable options for the faith of any objective person. There is no evidence to support any of these preposterous ideas. Ironically, the evidence against these ideas is so great that we begin to see how desperate some people are to reject the truth. It's as if they will believe anything, regardless of how absurd it may be, as long as they can reject Jesus Christ as Lord. It would take far less faith and effort to simply accept rather than to deny the obvious.

Through the process of elimination, we can pinpoint the identity of Jesus Christ without much effort. If Jesus was not a compulsive liar, a mentally impaired madman, or the subject of a mythical fairy tale, then the real identity of Jesus Christ must be as the Bible claims—a holy, almighty, and all-powerful God who loves you and me so much that He sent His Son to reveal Himself and atone for our sin. The three previous chapters have been dedicated to establishing the Word, presenting Jesus' identity, and revealing why people need Him for any hope of eternal life. This chapter, through the use of logic and deductive reasoning, concludes that the accounts of Jesus Christ reflect His actual life and sayings. Jesus Christ is *The King of Kings and the Lord of Lords.*

Reverse Reasoning. If Jesus was God incarnate in the flesh, then everything He said was Absolute Truth because one of God's attributes is holiness (He is unable to lie). Since the identity of Jesus Christ is once again confirmed, we have yet further proof that the Bible is entirely true. Since God cannot lie, we can trust God when He revealed that all Scripture is God-breathed and that *all Scripture* comes from Him and Him alone.[333] If all Scripture comes from God, and God cannot lie, then everything within the Bible must also be true; otherwise, God would not have allowed it to be incorporated within the text.

By establishing the identity of Jesus Christ, we can use reverse reasoning to prove that there is, in fact, a God, that the Bible is entirely true and that you will one day stand before Him to give an account of your belief or unbelief. The resurrection vindicated each and every single claim Jesus made, and this is why people need to understand the claims, so that they are prepared to give their account.

This, That, or the Other. As mentioned earlier, once people have been exposed to the Gospel message, they choose either "this, that, or the other." There is no middle ground, and the question cannot be left unanswered. Refusing to make a decision for Jesus Christ ultimately has the same consequence as blatant rejection because acceptance, by definition, requires action: you must *accept* the gift of eternal life (which is accompanied with

333 2 Timothy 3:16.

confession and repentance).[334] Unfortunately, for many people this may be a hard pill to swallow because it requires change and forces them to shed their sinful lifestyle. However, removing sin with true repentance does not make one's life "dull" or devoid of happiness! On the contrary, this new life is accompanied with abundance, just as Jesus promised.[335]

When defined, abundance is "overflowing fullness" or "extreme plenty."[336] When Jesus promises an abundant life, He is referring not only to eternal life but also to *your* life right here and right now. The abundance of life that accompanies salvation far surpasses anything that this life has to offer. Christians have the *fruit of the Spirit* which far surpasses money, possessions, or fame.[337] Those are powerful influences that drive countless people in our society, but few realize that *things* have never produced lasting peace or joy. Material possessions are temporary, and if you have them long enough, the "newness" and the "excitement" will eventually wear away. Sooner or later, rich, famous people find themselves still searching for what the Christian has freely received. The only difference between a wealthy person searching for salvation and a poor person searching for salvation is their possessions—and they are of least importance when it comes to eternal life.

Where To from Here?

Recapping Part Two. Theism has been examined, the arguments for the necessity of God have revealed His existence as necessary, and polytheism and deism have been ruled out due to their apparent contradictions. The Bible has been presented as Absolute Truth through five powerful arguments. It has been demonstrated that the weight of evidence lies so heavily in favor of the Bible being entirely true that only those who truly despise truth are able to reject it.

Truth, by definition, is narrow; it cannot be all-inclusive. As we have discovered, Jesus has made a very specific claim on truth. Jesus claimed to be the only way by which we are able to enter heaven. We have examined

---

334 Accept: verb (used with object [salvation]) to respond or answer affirmatively to. Accept. Dictionary.com. *Dictionary.com Unabridged.* Random House, Inc. http://dictionary.reference.com/browse/accept (accessed: September 22, 2009).

335 John 10:10.

336 abundance. Dictionary.com. *Dictionary.com Unabridged.* Random House, Inc. http://dictionary.reference.com/browse/abundance (accessed: September 21, 2009).

337 Galatians 5:22–23. Fruit of the Spirit: love, joy, peace, longsuffering, kindness, goodness, faithfulness, gentleness and self-control.

the character and the claims of Jesus Christ. Each and every claim has been vindicated through the resurrection, and we can confidently place our faith upon that Absolute Truth.

Lastly, we examined the four possible stances a person may take concerning Jesus. We have systematically demonstrated how Liar, Lunatic, and Legend simply do not match up with the evidence. Furthermore, these assertions are illogical and a gross misrepresentation of the truth. We have also discovered that a person cannot take a neutral position in regard to Jesus because refusing to accept the gift of salvation has the same consequence as blatant rejection. This revelation emphasizes the dire need for each and every person to understand the Gospel message and the consequences that accompany acceptance or rejection.

What About the Other Monotheistic Religions? Thus far, we have covered in detail only Christianity, polytheism, and deism. The other monotheistic religions have not been discussed as to whether they constitute truth. By definition, if two entirely different religions have contradictory truth claims, they cannot both be correct. Even though Christianity has been presented as entirely true, the remaining monotheistic religions need to be examined.

The next part will disprove Islam and Judaism. Both religions contain doctrine that contradicts Christianity and the Absolute Truth. This poses a problem because the Law of Contradiction does not allow for both to be true. Just as you cannot be both alive and dead at the same time, Christianity and another religion cannot both be true if they make entirely different and contradictory truth claims. Thus, the purpose of the next part of the book is to demonstrate the contradiction. Arguments will only be made for the two largest monotheistic religions (Islam and Judaism), but the same process can be used to disprove any religion that contradicts Christianity.

Is It Naïve or Wrong to Prove Other Religions False? Contrary to the dictates of political correctness, it is not wrong to know what you believe and support it with undeniable facts and evidence, nor is it a demonstration of ignorance. The act of establishing Christianity as entirely true and disproving misguided religions is both biblical and obedient. The Apostle Peter reveals that we, as Christians, must always be prepared to defend and to give an answer as to why we have accepted Jesus Christ as Lord and Savior.[338] This is a profound verse because it not only tells us to be prepared to give a defense of the faith that we have, but also that the act of defending your faith is not wrong.

Defending the faith is essential because it enables the believer to grow spiritually. Understanding what you believe, why you believe it, and how other religions are both contradictory and false bolsters your faith and gives you the necessary confidence to spread the Gospel—obeying another command that came directly from the mouth of none other than Jesus Christ.[339] As we examine Islam and Judaism, we must remember that any apologist is merely presenting the truth that God has revealed.

Even though prophets in the Old Testament were fired up and exceedingly blunt, preaching death, destruction, and exile to Israel, this book will merely present how Islam and Judaism are false because (among other reasons) they contradict the Absolute Truth. Conflict is not the most desired avenue of approach, but sometimes it's the only way to catch the attention of people who need to hear the message. Is this not why Jesus directly confronted the religious leaders in not two or three but seven consecutive woes?[340] Even though we were not there to witness this event, we can imagine that it was pretty intense when Jesus called the religious leaders "snakes" and "brood of vipers"! Our approach will not be as intense, but we will certainly prove a point …

Finally, when another religion is proved to be fatally flawed (wrong), it is not personal attack against any individual. The intent of disproving all other religions is to give Christians the necessary knowledge to defend and strengthen their faith so that they may in turn evangelize the world for Christ. Confronting and pointing out fatal flaws is not wrong or naïve; it's required.

338 1 Peter 3:15.

339 Matthew 28:18–20.

340 Matthew 23:13–39.

Part Three

Refining Theism

Chapter 12

Islam

O people of earlier Scripture! Do not exaggerate in your religion. Nor say of GOD anything but the Truth, most ***surely the Messiah Jesus the son of Mary was no more than a Messenger of GOD****, and a word from Him which was pronounced upon Mary and a spirit from Him. So believe in GOD and His messengers and* ***do not say 'Trinity' deist!*** *It is better for you. Most surely GOD is One God, Glory be to Him!* ***High exalted is He above having a son...***

—Surah 4:171

Indeed they are blasphemers who say, 'GOD is the Messiah son of Mary.' *Say, 'If GOD chose to destroy the Messiah, Mary's son, and his mother and all the dwellers of the earth, who has the power to prevent GOD from this?'*

—Surah 5:17

Introducing Islam

Quick Facts. Islam is the second largest religion in the world—and it is rapidly growing. Current estimates indicate that the number of Muslims in the world range from 1.3 billion to 1.8 billion people or between 20 and 25 percent of the *world* population.[341] Islam is the fastest growing religion in the world, and if it continues to sustain its current growth rate,

341 Foreign Policy, "The List: The World's Fastest-Growing Religions," http://www.foreignpolicy.com/story/cms.php?story_id=3835.

it will overtake Christianity as the largest religion in the world by the mid twenty-first century.[342]

Islam is an Abrahamic religion that was created in the seventh century by Abu al-Qasim Muhammad ibn 'Abd Allah ibn 'Abd al-Muttalib ibn Hashim.[343] According to the Islamic faith, Muhammad, at forty years of age, had a revelation from Allah (the Islamic God) in the form of a vision. This vision inspired Muhammad; afterward he claimed that he was one of God's chosen prophets and, as a result of the vision, began preaching his revelation publicly. The Islamic religious doctrine is centered upon *The Glorious Qur'an*, and Muhammad is credited as being the sole transcriber who was chosen to reveal Allah's will in written form. Islam teaches that the Qur'an is the verbatim word of Allah and that it was God's *final* revelation to mankind. Islam teaches that the Qur'an surpasses all other religious texts and is the ultimate reality of God's revelation.

Islam: The Advancement of Monotheism? Some people claim that Islam is an advancement of the earlier monotheistic religions (more specifically Judaism and Christianity). As we examine the credibility of Islam, we need to note the progression and the relationship of all three of the monotheistic religions in order to better understand the birth of Islam and how it relates to the other Monotheisms. Understanding the details surrounding the birth of Islam and how it interacts with the other two monotheistic religions will prove important for deciding for or against its inerrancy.

Judaism was the first of the Abrahamic religions (its writings essentially consisting of the Old Testament). Christianity was the fulfillment of Judaism and is the advancement of the Old Testament; Christianity outdated humanity's attempt to reach God through sacrifices and offerings (required for atonement) in order to establish God's attempt to reach humankind through the redeeming blood of Christ (the gift we refer to as salvation). Christianity has never contradicted the earlier Scriptures; instead, it fulfilled each and every single messianic prophecy so that the two religions would be so interconnected that *nothing* could separate the two Testaments.

Before Islam, everything appears to have been in perfect harmony in regard to the advancement of monotheism. Christianity completely advances

342 Religious Tolerance, "Islam: The Second Largest World Religion … and Growing," http://www.religioustolerance.org/islam.htm.

343 An Abrahamic religion is one that recognizes Abraham as an important person. The largest Abrahamic religions are Christianity, Islam, and Judaism.

Judaism because it creates a perfect transition, without contradiction, between the two religions. After all, salvation was accomplished through the resurrection, and the Bible actually takes the time to emphasize the perfect completion of Christ's work. The Gospel of Mark makes it clear that Jesus' mission was accomplished when he writes that Jesus has *sat down* at the right hand of God.[344] If salvation was insufficient and there was still work to be done, why would Jesus have sat down? The act of sitting is symbolic and conveys that God's redemptive work is *complete* and in its final form. Therefore, we conclude that the work of Jesus Christ (God Almighty) was sufficient and lacks nothing.

Despite the fact that Jesus' redemptive work was complete, another religion appeared centuries after Jesus had already *sat down* at the right hand of God. Since this new religion tries to advance God's salvific work, some serious questions need to be asked because Islam inherently contradicts Christianity and the perfect plan of salvation already established. We know that Islam contradicts Christianity because the Qur'an does not recognize that Jesus Christ is Lord and that His redemptive work was sufficient.[345] These beliefs become evident when Muhammad advances a new and contradictory revelation that is allegedly from God. If God never changes, why would He send Jesus to die on the cross, only to remove that plan of salvation a few hundred years later?

Some people claim that Islam is the advancement of Christianity, but when the facts are examined, we know that this claim is preposterous because Islam denies all Christian doctrine through the rejection of the New Testament. We know that Islam has virtually nothing in common with Christianity because Islam does not teach the same morals, values, or theology as Christianity. Ironically, if we compare religions to see which one Islam resembles the most, we discover that Islam actually has far more in common with Judaism than Christianity! Both are Abrahamic religions that reject the deity of Jesus Christ; His virgin birth, sinless life, and resurrection; and the Trinity. Furthermore, Islam and Judaism, alike, strongly denounce the notion that Jesus Christ is the Messiah and that through Him, alone, can salvation can be received. In order for Islam to *advance* Christianity, it must first assume the Christian doctrine; this is common sense. Therefore, since Islam rejects the New Testament, we can confidently conclude that Islam is unable to advance Christianity.

344 Mark 16:19.

345 As indicated by bold font in quotes at beginning of chapter.

Since it would be impossible for Islam to advance Christianity, we now need to know whether or not Islam is *able* to advance Judaism. Even though Islam and Judaism have much in common, Islam also contradicts Judaism when Muhammad, Islam's only prophet, fails to meet the Old Testament eligibility standards for being considered a prophet from God. The deviation becomes evident when Muhammad claims that he has had a vision that gives him the charge to write a *new authoritative* text that *contradicts* the Old Testament Scriptures. Instead of fulfilling Judaism, Islam actually circumvents the religion because it deviates from and rejects much of the Old Testament doctrine. Circumvention of the Old Testament will become obvious later in the chapter when we systematically demonstrate how Muhammad fails the Old Testament eligibility test in order to be considered a true prophet from God. Since Islam does not accept the Old Testament standards and doctrine, Islam is unable to advance Judaism because it rejects Judaism's basic doctrine!

In order for Islam to *advance* anything, it must first assume the previous religion's fundamental presuppositions; this is common sense because Islam came last. However, in both cases, we know that this cannot be true because Islam contradicts established doctrine versus advancing earlier Scripture (Judaism and Christianity). Since Islam creates an entirely independent religion, it would be impossible for Islam to advance *any* of the monotheistic religions. Instead of advancing any religion, Islam blatantly rejects all established Scriptures and has established a new and independent religion.

The Provocative Religion. Instead of furthering any religion, Islam is the religion that has gone to great lengths to deviate from the establishment of Judaism and Christianity.[346] Islam is a very provocative religion because it actually steps toe-to-toe with the two religions as if to square off for battle.[347] As indicated by the previous footnote, Islam battles the establishment of religion when it tries to reestablish truth by contradicting the Old and New Testaments—and then *taunts* "people of earlier Scripture" in a

346 Judaism teaches the Old Testament (which is entirely true), but the next chapter will demonstrate that the Old Testament alone cannot be Absolute Truth because it does not acknowledge the *entire truth* (by refusing to acknowledge Jesus Christ as Lord and the New Testament).

347 Christianity cannot choose to battle with (or contradict or assault) Islam because Christianity was established centuries before Islam. Christianity also cannot choose to battle Judaism because it does not contradict a single Old Testament Scripture. (The difference is the interpretation of the *same* messianic prophecies.)

perverted arrogance.[348] (Since Judaism has advanced to Christianity, we will only refer to Christianity from this point forward.) Nevertheless, the provocative words in the Qur'an demonstrate that Islam is actually the religion that has picked a fight with Christianity … and a self-defense argument they will get! Christians must STAND UP! for Truth and defend it if we have any aspirations of fulfilling the Great Commission and doing our part to help grow Christianity through evangelism.

In the defense of Christianity, I will systematically demonstrate the mockery that Islam has made of religion. Islam makes a mockery of religion not only because it contradicts the one source of Absolute Truth (the Holy Bible), but also because the Qur'an has numerous internal contradictions: the text doesn't even agree with itself. Furthermore, it will be demonstrated that Muhammad is a self-proclaimed prophet whose vision, teachings, and writings are unable to be verified because they are solely confined to one person.

When Islam is compared with Christianity, Christians have 1,900 years, sixty-six books, hundreds of verifiable prophecies, and forty different transcribers who created an errorless collection of books that vindicate the text as Absolute Truth. How does Islam compare to Christianity? Islam has one book, one prophet, and one revelation that cannot be confirmed by a singe outside source. Think about it: how easy would it be for one author to write one book and make sure all chapters align? One would think the task would be fairly easy, but Muhammad's inability to create a text without error and internal contradictions demonstrates the difficulties of even one person being able successfully to write an authoritative text without divine inspiration.

Addressing the Coward.[349] If you are easily offended by Truth, you may struggle with this chapter because it was not written for the fainthearted. My goal is not to encourage "closet" behavior or to encourage weakness by telling Christians that everything will be all-right if they just keep

348 Arrogance is demonstrated by the fact that Islam is unable to verify its revelation because it was solely limited to Muhammad, yet the religion has the audacity to contradict eyewitness accounts of the Apostles who knew Truth to a degree that they were all willing to be martyred in the name of Jesus Christ, the King of kings and Lord of lords.

349 Coward: A person who lacks courage in the face of danger, difficulty, opposition, pain; a timid or easily intimidated person (dictionary.com). Synonyms include: baby, chicken, deserter, gutless, invertebrate, quitter, scaredy cat, and wimp (thesaurus.com).

quiet, stay in their bubble, and ignore the defamation of Truth. On the contrary, the objective of this chapter is to encourage all Christians to STAND UP! for their faith *with confidence* by arming themselves with an unapologetic defense of Christianity against Islam. As I pointed out in a previous footnote, Christianity is unable to provoke a battle with Islam. Instead, Christians merely defend the faith from the battle that Islam provoked—but we do so with confidence because *even though we walk through the valley of the shadow of death, we will fear no evil … because He who is in us is greater than he who is in the world.*[350]

It would truly be a travesty if Christians became so spineless that they were unable stand up for truth, whimpering and cowering at the slightest opposition, begging for mercy and understanding. This was not the attitude that the first-century Christians had, but I can promise you that some of the people who have read the previous section will be nervous and afraid because *I* have had the *audacity* to challenge the *great institution of Islam*. Perhaps I have had extreme boldness and have been exceedingly daring to even oppose the religion because of the way Islam treats their opposition, but at this point the Christian coward needs to be reminded of what the Bible promises.

If you are a Christian and you are afraid of Islam, shame on you! Do you not know that you possess the Absolute Truth that is sharper than any double-edged sword? Do you not have faith that God will protect you if it's His will? Even if you were to be killed by a jihadist—do you not know that a martyr's death has far more rewards than death from natural causes? Surely, if you are a Christian, you believe in heaven! If you have faith in Christianity, what are you afraid of—death?! Let me remind the Christian what death will one day bring:

> Then the angel showed me the river of the water of life, as clear as crystal, flowing from the throne of God and of the Lamb down the middle of the great street of the city. On each side of the river stood the tree of life, bearing twelve crops of fruit, yielding its fruit every month. And the leaves of the tree are for the healing of the nations. No longer will there be any curse. The throne of God and the Lamb will be in the city, and his servants will serve him. They will see his face, and his name will be on their foreheads. There will be no more night. They will

350 Psalms 23:4; 1 John 4:4.

> not need the light of a lamp or the light of the sun, for the Lord God will give them light. And they will reign for ever and ever.[351]

I may be radical and this may sound crazy, but I think I would prefer to defend Jesus and take the restored version of Eden (that place called heaven) rather than committing apostasy and clinging to the fading material world, if push came to shove. What greater joy could one have than diligently working to try and earn a crown (a symbol of the approval of an almighty God) so that we might have the *opportunity* to lay that incomprehensible symbol of approval at His feet? I do not know whether cowards have the ability to earn a crown, but the point of this section is to demonstrate that Christians have absolutely no reason to fear death. Remember Paul's words in 1 Corinthians 15:54–58:

> When the perishable has been clothed with the imperishable, and the mortal with immortality, then the saying that is written will come true: "Death has been swallowed up in victory."
>
> "O Death, where is your sting?
> O Hades, where is your victory?"
>
> The sting of death is sin, and the strength of sin is the law. But thanks be to God, who gives us the victory though our Lord Jesus Christ.
>
> Therefore, my dear brothers, *stand firm*. Let *nothing move you*. Always give yourselves fully to the work of the Lord, because you know that your labor in the Lord is not in vain.[352]

Reflecting on the previous verses leads us to realize that death merely ushers in the eternal paradise that Christians were promised. Since it has been established that there is absolutely no reason for Christians to fear death, we are ready to begin living a faith-based life by standing up and defending Christianity against every false religion—even in the face of opposition or hatred.

---

351 Revelation 22:1–5.

352 1 Corinthians 15:54–58 (verses 54 and 58 NIV; verses 55–57 NKJV, emphasis added).

We begin our defense of Christianity from Islam by examining the flaws with the Islamic prophet. After we have established that the Bible (Absolute Truth) does not allow for *any* additions and that Muhammad was *never* eligible to be a prophet (on behalf of the one true God), we will examine the flaws within the Qur'an. Within the text, there are both internal and external contradictions, but we only need one flaw in order to destroy its potential for being considered Absolute Truth.

Since we have two texts (the Bible and the Qur'an) that make conflicting truth claims with respect to God and the way to Heaven, we intuitively know that one must be wrong. Contradictions cannot be reconciled when two entirely different claims are made on the same exact matter.[353] It's not coherent to believe that the Bible (which teaches that Jesus is the only way heaven) and the Qur'an (which rejects Jesus as the only way to heaven) are both true because they blatantly contradict one another. As we will see in this chapter, these two religions are simply not compatible; they make entirely different truth claims and in fact do not worship the same God.[354] We must know whether or not Islam constitutes Absolute Truth because the answer inevitably spells the eternal fate of countless souls.

We are certainly entering into controversial territory, but this information must be offered so that the truth—the whole truth and nothing but the truth—is presented (and defended). We must know how and why Islam deviates from the Absolute Truth so that we can reach out and evangelize the Muslim population.

Flaws with the Islamic Prophet and a New Text

Does Scripture Allow for Additions? The Qur'an was written more than five and a half centuries after the final book in the Bible was completed. Even if we were to use a conservative calculation and calculate from the century that the New Testament canon was completed (in a process that ended by AD 367), Muhammad did not begin his work until more than two hundred years later (AD 610).[355] Unfortunately for the Qur'an,

353 Recall the Law of Contradiction in chapter 6 (that two antithetical propositions cannot both be true at the same time in the same sense).

354 This is an extremely odd sentence because there is only one God and it is only possible to worship Jesus if a person knows Jesus. Despite the obvious contradiction, this sentence was inserted because some may claim that Allah is equivalent to God the Father because Islam is a "universal religion" revealed by all the prophets and divinely revealed Books throughout history (http://www.islam.com/qans2.htm).

355 Encarta Encyclopedia.

canonization sealed the Bible so that there could be no more additions, or subtractions, from God's written revelation. In this section, we will examine a few verses that reveal precisely *why* God's written revelation is sealed and not open for revision.

Since it has been established that the Bible must have been authored by God, we must also conclude that the Bible is a product of God. The Bible is not simply from God, it *is* God's written revelation to mankind. Describing the Bible as a product from God is extremely important because we need to know whether it is feasible to suggest that God—a being who *cannot lie*—could have allowed for additions that would later contradict what He had already established as Absolute Truth. To begin answering this question, we turn to five teachings from the apostles of Jesus Christ.

First, the Apostle Peter wrote:

> His divine power has given us everything we need for life and godliness through our knowledge of him who called us by his own glory and goodness.[356]

This verse explicitly reveals that *everything* we need, in order to enter into heaven, has already been revealed. The inverse implication of this verse is that *nothing* else is needed in order to enter into heaven because Jesus Christ came and completely fulfilled the messianic prophecies. As a result, the redeeming blood and method of salvation that God established was sufficient. Since salvation is sufficient, all people transitioned to a New Covenant with God (which is revealed throughout the New Testament). The transition from the Old to the New Covenant was planned far in advance, but God also reveals to us that this New Covenant would be the final transition that God would make because "everything we need for [eternal] life" would have been provided.

If everything we need, in order to successfully venture from this life into heaven, has already been provided, why would anybody *need* the Qur'an? This serious question that cannot be answered without asserting that God is a liar and that Jesus' redemption is insufficient. However, there is a slight problem with this accusation. Refusing to attribute authorship of the Bible to God is not an option and would be impossible because it's a miracle book (Chapter 8). Therefore, since we know that God authored the Bible and God cannot lie, we must conclude that Absolute Truth was revealed throughout the entire Bible.

---

356 2 Peter 1:3.

If the Bible is not open to revision, do you think that it would take some time to address this very important issue? Absolutely; the Bible not only addresses this problem, but also goes a step farther to reveal that people secretly slip in and try to change the faith from its original form. Since we know that people have made attempts to manipulate God's revelation (and will continue to do so), we need to know what the Bible says in regard to *an additional* authoritative text that is alleged to be the Word of God (especially when this new "authoritative text" contradicts God's already established Truth). Jude reveals that even though the faith was fully delivered, some people "slip in" to change the written revelation of God in order to transform it into a license for immorality. Second, Jude 3 reads:

> Dear friends, although I was very eager to write to you about the salvation we share, I felt I had to write and urge you to *contend* for the faith that was *once for all* entrusted to the saints.[357]

Make no mistake, Jude is revealing to Christians that they should earnestly maintain (or contend for) the faith that was finalized (or once for all entrusted) to every man, woman, boy, and girl. Why should God's people earnestly maintain and defend the truth of the salvation that God has established? Because Christianity has been finalized once and for all; there is no other doctrine. We can confidently believe that there is no other doctrine because God is unable to lie and because the presence of the Bible is a miracle that demands a divine intervention; therefore, all content that the Bible reveals must be entirely true. In other words, Jesus Christ's redeeming blood (the plan of salvation that God established) is a sufficient method of redemption.

Third, the book of Jude continues in verse 4:

> Certain men whose condemnation was written about long ago have secretly slipped in among you. They are godless men, who change the grace of our God into a license for immorality and deny Jesus Christ our only Sovereign and Lord.

357 Jude 3, emphasis added.

Jude 4 is an interesting verse because it reveals how the *changing* of God's grace enables people to manipulate power to their purposes when they can convince others that they were given a *new* revelation from God. In other words, if a "prophet" could convince a group of people that he had been inspired to write an additional *authoritative* text, then those people who were convinced must also believe that this new document was a product of divine inspiration (regardless of content)! Since the people convinced would believe that the text was divinely inspired, it now has the ability to provide the "license for immorality" referred to in the verse above, under the claim that it was *inspired* by God. Since this new text is believed to be mandated by God, what was formerly considered to be immoral would no longer be perceived as sinful.[358]

This is precisely what Islam has done...Muhammad convinced a group of people that he was given a divine revelation; some people believed; a new standard of morality was established; and the people deny Jesus Christ as Sovereign and Lord. This new license for immorality is not as abrupt as abortion or murder, but follow the progression of definitions to see how denying Jesus Christ is actually a license for immorality in itself.

Morality is defined as "a doctrine or system of moral conduct." *Moral* is defined as "of or relating to principles of right and wrong in behavior." *Right* is defined as "conforming to facts or truth."[359] Therefore, when Islam creates a new doctrine that denies Jesus Christ as Sovereign and Lord, the religion is no longer conforming to established facts and truth; thus, its principles of moral behavior (with respect to receiving redemption) are incorrect, and incorrect moral principles are immoral by definition.

In addition to demonstrating how the act of denying Jesus is immoral, we also run back into that inconvenient trait that God is *immutable* (God cannot change). Even though we cannot fully grasp the concept of immutability, we *are* able to conclude: Since God established morality, that which is sinful is not able to transform into that which is righteous. Adultery is wrong, as established in the Ten Commandments, and since

358 The "license for immorality" could be much more subtle and sleek than I have portrayed. An example of the subtleness might resemble the following example: Instead of naming the immoral act of killing an innocent baby "murder," it could be called "pro-choice" because, after all, it's the mother's body, and she can do what she pleases—it's her choice. (Doesn't "pro-choice" sound much better than "murder"?) There are many different ways to rename and repackage sin, but this footnote conveys the general idea.

359 All definitions from merriam-webster.com.

the act of sexually betraying a spouse has been established as immoral by an unchanging God, it can never transform into that which is right.

The same principles apply when examining Islam. When an unchangeable God established Jesus as "the way and the truth and the life," God cannot turn around and deny "the way and the truth and the life," because a contradiction of this magnitude must assume an impossible presupposition (that God is able to change morality into immorality). Not even Allah could change that which is moral into that which is immoral, because the very act defies the nature of a necessary being—regardless of the *name* that people attach to the one and only God.

Since we know that God is unable to change morality, God is unable to change that which is true.[360] The next question is whether or not the Islamic doctrine has altered any of the Old or New Testament truths. The answer is pretty obvious because Islamic doctrine goes against the Bible the instant it denies the deity Jesus Christ. The Qur'an has also altered biblical teachings that include the method of salvation, concept of the Trinity, and rejection of the Old Testament messianic prophecies. Applying logic to these observations—a necessary being is unable to change, the Bible must be the result of a divine intervention (a product of God), the Bible established Jesus as Lord, but the Qur'an (created after the Bible) contradicts the Absolute Truth—we must conclude that the Qur'an was not divinely inspired.

Fourth, we learn from the Apostle Paul that God's revelation would come to an end. First Corinthians 13:8 reads:

> Love never fails. But where there are prophecies, they will cease; where there are tongues, they will be stilled; where there is knowledge, it will pass away.

This scripture explicitly reveals that prophecy will eventually cease. Why would prophecy cease? Refer back to 2 Peter 1:3, which reveals that everything necessary for life and godliness has been already revealed and that it was *adequate*. There is no longer a need for prophets, nor is there a need for any more prophecies or authoritative texts because everything, until the second coming of Jesus Christ, has been already been established and Jesus sat down. The point is that there are no longer prophets who

360 Refer back to the progression of definitions in the above paragraph to link morality to truth.

directly converse with God and reveal His sovereign will because the need no longer exists.

Fifth, is it mere coincidence that the final book of the Bible, Revelation, concludes with an *incredibly strong* warning to those people who attempt to manipulate, add to, or subtract from the Word of God? Reflect on the implications of the following excerpt from Revelation:

> I warn everyone who hears the words of the prophecy of this book: If anyone adds anything to them, God will add to him the plagues described in this book. And if anyone takes words away from this book of prophecy, God will take away from him his share in the tree of life and in the holy city, which are described in this book.
>
> He [Jesus] who testifies to these things says, "Yes, I am coming soon."[361]

Do you recall the verses from the Qur'an that I placed at the beginning of this chapter? As we reflect on those verses and the message they convey, we need to ask ourselves whether Islam has added to or subtracted anything from what was revealed in the Revelation. By reading those two verses (which come directly from the Qur'an), the answer to this question is obviously: "Yes; the Qur'an contradicts the book of Revelation." We know that the Qur'an contradicts the Revelation because the theme of the entire book of Revelation is the deity, second coming, and glory of Jesus Christ as Lord—precisely what the Qur'an has subtracted through denial and rejection.

Five Strikes and You're Definitely Out. In the last section, we actually presented five strikes against Islam instead of the usual three, accompanied with elimination. Since *everything* we need for (eternal) life has been provided in the redemptive work of Jesus Christ, there is no need for the Qur'an—or any other authoritative religious text for that matter; Steee-rike One! Since Islam is not contending for the salvation that God established once for all, it feels a need to change morality (which goes against God); Steee-rike Two! Since Islam changes morality by claiming divine inspiration, Muslims claim that God was able to do that which is impossible for God to accomplish due to the trait of immutability; Strike Three! Since the once source of Absolute Truth explicitly teaches that

361 Revelation 22:18–20.

prophecy *will cease* (because there is no longer a need—Jesus has actually sat down because His work is complete), Islam's foundational claim that Muhammad is a prophet is defiance of Truth; Strike Four! Since Islam rejects the deity of Jesus, it's subtracting from the book of Revelation by denying the second coming of Jesus Christ; Strike Five! (Strike Six has not been presented yet, but we will soon demonstrate that Muhammad was not even eligible to be a prophet during a time when prophets did not exist.)

'For the Sake of Argument.' For the sake of argument, let's pretend that the Bible did allow new prophets and new authoritative texts, that the blood of Jesus Christ was not sufficient, and that more redemptive work and even more of God's revelation were necessary. For the sake of argument, we will disregard the obvious and enter into the mind-set that the redemptive blood could not atone—precisely as Islam has proclaimed. In that case, we would need *more* insight into God's perfect plan. The eyewitness Apostles were martyred in vain, even though it has been demonstrated that the liar, lunatic, and legend arguments are ludicrous and are simply impossible. Nevertheless, for the sake of argument, we will enter into this scenario to demonstrate the impossibility of Islam, and the Qur'an, to even qualify as an authoritative text from the true living God.

Even though we are in "pretend mode," we still need to be biblical in our scenario. This means that we must use Old Testament verses to establish whether Muhammad could qualify as one of God's prophets. We must use the Bible because it's the only text that qualifies as Absolute Truth. The focus now becomes: "Does Muhammad meet the standards, set forth by the Old Testament, for becoming one of God's prophets?"

Muhammad Fails Biblical Test for Prophets. We begin with a simple question: Why would one of God's prophets contradict that which God had already established (the Bible), if the prophet was truly from God? The most logical answer would be that a prophet from God would not contradict the God that he is serving. Therefore, if we can demonstrate that Muhammad fails the biblical test to become a prophet, then we can conclude that this prophet has not represented the one true God.

Any prophet on behalf of the one true God must fulfill the requirements that the Bible has established for eligibility. Since the Bible is a product of God, we also know that the biblical requirements are the result of a divine inspiration and convey the truth that God desired to reveal. In other words, the Bible has clearly laid out criteria and tests for God's people to be able to discern whether or not a person claiming to be a prophet is actually a prophet. In Deuteronomy, we learn that a prophet cannot contradict previous revelation and will never lead God's people astray. Deuteronomy 13:1–4 reads:

> If a prophet, or one who foretells by dreams, appears among you and announces to you a miraculous sign or wonder, and if the sign or wonder of which he has spoken takes place, and he says, "Let us follow other gods" (gods you have not known) "and let us worship them," you must not listen to the words of that prophet or dreamer. The LORD your God is testing you to find out whether you love him with all your heart and with all your soul. It is the LORD your God you must follow, and him you must revere. Keep his commands and obey him; serve him and hold fast to him.

This is a fascinating scripture! Even though Deuteronomy was written almost two thousand years before the Qur'an, it seems to directly speak about Islam! Consider the following:

- Muhammad claimed to have a dream—a revelation—from God.
- Muhammad announced his revelation.
- Muhammad pulled his congregation away from the Gospel of Jesus Christ by utilizing the claim of divine inspiration.
- Muhammad advocated the worship of "other gods" (gods you have not known) by refusing to worship Jesus Christ.
- Muhammad is pulling people away from the one true God.
- A true prophet on behalf of God, by definition, cannot lead congregants away from God.
- Muhammad led, and continues to lead, people away from Jesus.
- Muhammad fails the test.
- Consequently, Muhammad is unable to be considered a prophet on behalf of the one true God.

Through our examination, we are confidently able to conclude that Muhammad is not even eligible to speak *about* God (because he did not know Jesus); much less an authoritative prophet who speaks on *behalf* of God. Since this section has demonstrated that Muhammad cannot be considered a prophet who represents God, it naturally implies that the Qur'an (Muhammad's creation) is also unable to be considered a text that represents God. Even though we would be able to play "Connect the Dots" to draw this conclusion, it would be far more beneficial to demonstrate *how* the Qur'an is tattered with flaws. Revealing fundamental flaws (internal and external contradictions) demonstrate that the text is the work of a man void of divine inspiration.

Flaws with the Qur'an

The Unprovable Religion. Before we move into the internal and external contradictions of the Qur'an, we should go ahead and note the fact that Islam is simply unable to be proven as Absolute Truth. There is no way to systematically prove Islam as entirely true because there is no corroborating evidence (or logic) that points toward an inerrant truth. One reason there is no corroborating evidence is that the entire Islamic faith centers upon one vision that was revealed to one person, and the entire faith is limited to one book that was inspired by the same person who received the vision; in other words, there is absolutely *no possible way to verify anything that was allegedly envisioned!*[362]

In addition to the faith being unverifiable, there is still more evidence that leads us to believe that Islam cannot be a product of divine inspiration. The fact that the text has some serious internal and external contradictions negates the possibility of the Qur'an being considered a product of divine inspiration because God cannot contradict Himself with respect to morality or revealed truth. The assertion that Islam is entirely true is pure conjecture. Even more troubling is that the religion can actually be systematically disproved by analyzing the book's content. The Qur'an blatantly contradicts the only book that could have been a product of divine inspiration. To this task we now turn.

362 This is a very important fact to note when contrasting the Qur'an with the Bible. For the Bible, the method of compilation and the presence of prophecies constitute enough proof to demonstrate that the text is of divine inspiration because neither could have been accomplished on human effort alone. On the other hand, the Qur'an has contradicted the Bible and has tried to establish truth, yet it has no verifiable proof.

Qur'an Contradicts the Bible. Chapter 8 went to great lengths to demonstrate how the Bible is entirely true because it's a product of a divine intervention. As a result, a true prophet (on behalf of the one true God) could not possibly contradict that which God has already established. The Old and New Testaments center upon Jesus Christ (the scarlet thread), and if any person, prophet, or text contradicts the Bible, then that entity *cannot be in allegiance with the one true God*. Therefore, the next question would intuitively be: Has Muhammad contradicted the Absolute Truth revealed in the Bible? More so than I could have imagined before researching the topic. Muhammad contradicts the Bible when he teaches that Muslims must not believe in Jesus Christ because He was not the Son of God, nor was He ever crucified.[363] The rejection of Jesus Christ is a major contradiction of what we know to be entirely true. In spite of Truth, the Qur'an reads:

> And for their saying, "We killed the Messiah Jesus the son of Mary, the *Messenger of GOD*." Yet they *did not kill* him *nor crucify him*, but it was only made to *appear* to them so. And surely those who disagree about it are doubtful and have no knowledge of it, but only follow *conjecture*, and certainly they did not kill him—But GOD lifted him up to Him, and GOD is Almighty, All Wise.[364]

How do we know that this is a direct contradiction of the New Testament? The divinely inspired text reveals (in a few verses):

- Matthew 27:35: "When they had crucified him, they divided up his clothes by casting lots.."
- Mark 15:24: "And they crucified him."
- Luke 23:33: "there they crucified him, along with the criminals—one on his right, the other on his left."
- John 19:23: "When the soldiers crucified Jesus, they took his clothes ..."
- Acts 2:36: "God has made this Jesus, whom you crucified, both Lord and Christ [Messiah]."
- 1 Corinthians 1:23: "We preach Christ crucified: a stumbling block to Jews and foolishness to Gentiles."

363 Surah 4:157.

364 Surah 4:157–158, emphasis added.

- Galatians 2:20: "I have been crucified with Christ ..."

Once again, we note that the entire basis for Christianity rests on the resurrection—and that was demonstrated to be true beyond a shadow of a doubt in Chapter 10. Jesus Christ did not merely claim that He was resurrected; *it was proven before hundreds upon hundreds of people.*

Furthermore, shall we note another obvious flaw with the above surah? I cannot help but notice that the Qur'an actually has the audacity to depict God as a *deceiver*. Of all depictions of God, why would anybody want to portray their God as a deceiver? It does not make sense when we mesh the text with the definitions that the Qur'an *proudly* attributes to God: a holy and righteous being! Deception is defined in the dictionary as "fraud," and fraud is "trickery, sharp practice, or breach of confidence, perpetrated for profit or to gain some unfair or dishonest advantage."[365]

The God that I revere does not breach confidence for profit through some unfair or dishonest advantage. My Bible tells me that God is love (1 John 4:8) and that love is patient and kind; it is not envious or boastful or proud; it does not dishonor others, it is not self-seeking (1 Corinthians 13:4–5). If I recall correctly, deceit is not one of God's attributes, but *it is* one of Satan's (which was clearly revealed in Genesis 3:1–6). If the resurrection was really not part of God's perfect plan, it makes no sense for a holy and righteous God to reveal, though divine inspiration, that He deceived the entire world with the following surah: "They did not kill him nor crucify him, but it was only made to appear to them so."

There is a major contradiction between the Bible and the Qur'an with respect to the attributes of God. Unfortunately, "Contradictions do not exist. Whenever you think that you are facing a contradiction, check your premises. You will find that one of them is wrong."[366] If we go back to our premises, we find that the Qur'an violates God's nature when it attributes deception to God, that He made it appear that the resurrection occurred.[367]

---

365 Both definitions are from dictionary.com.

366 Ayn Rand, *Atlas Shrugged* (New York: Penguin Group (USA) Inc., 1957), 188.

367 Ironically, the Qur'an states that Allah "loveth not mischief" in Surah 2:205. Since mischief is defined as "a cause or source of harm, evil or annoyance" (dictionary.com), would Allah not love himself? We know that deception is evil because it is the antithesis of what Proverbs 14:5 reveals: "A truthful witness does not *deceive*, but a false witness pours out lies." (Yes, I digress, but these are thoughts to ponder.)

Should We Love or Hate the Enemy? Another contradiction between the Qur'an and the Bible centers upon the teaching with respect to how God's people should treat their enemies. The Bible reads in Matthew 5:44: "I tell you, love your enemies and pray for those who persecute you ..." The Bible tells us to have compassion and love and to actually pray for those who hate us and wish to do evil against us because we are *all* God's creation. Since Christians are held to exceptionally high standards, we not only love the lovable, we are also expected to love the *unlovable*.

Why does the Bible tell Christians to love others? First, the Bible says that God is love.[368] Second, the Bible says that God loves everybody – God loved the entire world so much that he sent his Son to die so that all may have a chance to accept salvation.[369] God even loves those who are not yet saved and even curse his name.[370]

Not so with the Qur'an. The Qur'an teaches that Allah *does not* love everybody. Surah 2:190 reads:

> And fight in GOD's cause those who fight you, and do not transgress, surely GOD does not love the transgressors.

Indeed, this is truly a different God than the New Testament portrays! Surely they cannot be the same. Not only does Muhammad teach that God does not love all people, he teaches that Muslims must *kill* the transgressors and *persecute* those who oppose the faith (thus, the justification for jihad). We know this to be true because Surah 2:191 reads (Abdullah Yusuf Ali Qur'an):

> And slay them [transgressors] wherever ye catch them, and turn them out from where they have turned you out; for tumult or oppression are worse than slaughter; but fight them not at the Sacred Mosque, unless they (first) fight you there; but if they fight you, slay them. Such is the reward of those who suppress faith.

This is another glimpse into Allah's seemingly hateful stance toward those who are not yet Muslim, which vastly differs from the attitude the

368 1 John 4:8.
369 John 3:16.
370 Romans 5:8.

Bible ascribes to God. (When you think that you are facing a contradiction, check your premises.)

Granted, the Old Testament is not without war. However, the Old Testament does not teach hatred or persecution of the enemy. Christians are not taught to kill those who disagree with or reject the truthfulness of the Christian faith. Indeed, there are times when war is justified; as presented by Holman's *The Apologetics Study Bible.*[371] First the war must be declared by the government.[372] Second, it must be in defense of the innocent or against an evil aggressor.[373] Third, the war must be fought by just means.[374]

Furthermore, Jesus is not against self-defense because Jesus encouraged his disciples to have a weapon (for self-defense) when they were transporting money.[375] The Bible also does not prohibit all taking of life; such as killing in self-defense (Exodus 22:2) and in capital punishment (Genesis 9:6). God is love, and we know that love is not possible without justice. Justice demands retribution for sin, and a justified war can certainly be one method by which justice can be executed.

Nevertheless, from the surahs we read in the Qur'an, we can conclude that Allah is not an all-loving entity. The lack of the "all-loving" attribute poses a problem because it's one of the basic attributes of God. The difference between Jesus and Allah is that Jesus died so that all may have the opportunity to accept salvation. Jesus teaches Christians to love and pray for the enemy, but we note that a justified war is permissible if unavoidable. The Qur'an contradicts the Bible because it counsels (offensive) aggression against those who are not Muslim.

Beat the Wife? Another major contradiction that we will examine deals with the treatment of women. The United States of America, a Christian nation, is widely known for its advancement in the treatment of women. As we look back through history, women had a very low status in virtually every ancient culture. We note the low status of women in ancient Greece, Rome, and Middle East. Even today, there are many cultures where women are degraded and treated as inferior pawns.

---

371 Ted Cabal, ed., *The Apologetics Study Bible*, (Nashville, TN: Holman Bible Publishers, 2007), 995.

372 Romans 13:4.

373 As demonstrated in Genesis 14.

374 Deuteronomy 20:19.

375 Luke 22:36–38.

However, we must note that it was Christianity that elevated the status of women. Jesus Christ set the example in his ministry when he defended the woman caught in adultery (John 8:1–11) and offered hope to the Samaritan woman (John 4:1–26), and it was the New Testament that taught men are to treat women much differently than in the past. The Bible does not permit husbands to beat their wives at any time—even if it is a *light* beating (as the Qur'an teaches). Instead, the Bible teaches that a man should love his wife and treat her as he would his own body. Ephesians 5:25–28 reads:

> Husbands, love your wives, just as Christ loved the church and gave himself up for her to make her holy, cleansing her by the washing with water through the word, and to present her to himself as a radiant church, without stain or wrinkle or any other blemish, but holy and blameless. In this same way, husbands ought to love their wives as their own bodies. He who loves his wife loves himself.

Christianity was the first to recognize women as one with their husbands. Women owe that advancement to none other than Jesus Christ. Other religions and cultures have followed suit and have followed the lead of Christianity, but the fact of the matter is that Christianity began paving the path for the world that we know today. Furthermore, there are religions and cultures in the twenty-first century that still treat women in the traditional way. In the Qur'an, we learn that Allah deems it permissible for a husband to beat his wife. Surah 4:34 reads:

> Men are the protectors and maintainers of women, because GOD has given the one more (strength) than the other, and because they support them from their means. Therefore the righteous women are devoutly obedient, and guard in (the husband's) absence what GOD would have them guard. As to the women on whose part ye fear disloyalty and ill-conduct, admonish them (first), (next), refuse to share their beds, (and last) beat them (lightly); But if they return to obedience, seek not against them

> means (of annoyance): For GOD is Most High, great (above you all).[376]

Even a light beating is a beating, just like perjury and lying are still a misrepresentation of the truth; one form just happens to be more severe than the other. Nevertheless, we see degrading treatment prescribed toward women in the Qur'an, and that view is prevalent even today in the Middle East.

Qur'an Contradicts Itself. In addition to contradicting the Bible, there are multiple occurrences where the Qur'an contradicts itself through the presentation of conflicting doctrine. In this section, we will demonstrate how the Qur'an contradicts itself, which demonstrates that the text cannot be errorless or the product of divine inspiration because an all-knowing God would not make these contradictory statements. Even more appalling, the Qur'an acknowledges the contradictions within itself and has even provided a disclaimer in the Introduction to try and trivialize the errors (presented in the next section).

The Creation Account: This, That, or the Other? One notable contradiction in the Qur'an deals with the origin of humankind. We will examine the different claims with respect to the origin of humankind and then compare the claims to one another and ultimately to the Bible.

Surah 6:2 claims that humankind was created from clay: "God fashioned you *from* clay ..."[377] Surah 11:61 claims that mankind was created from the earth: "He has created you *from* the earth ..." Surah 19:67 claims humankind was created out of nothing: "But does not man call to mind that We created him before *out of nothing*?" Surah 25:54 claims that humankind was created from water: "And God is the one who fashioned mankind *from* water, and established relationship of lineage (by men) kinship by women ..." Then Surah 96:1 claims that human was created *from* a clot of blood: "Proclaim: In the Name of thy Lord and Cherisher, Who created—Created man *out of* a (mere) clot of congealed blood ..."

There are obviously many differing creation accounts, but when we compare that with the biblical creation account, we learn that the Bible teaches that "from [the ground] you were taken; for dust you are and to

376 Abdullah Yusuf Ali, trans., "The Holy Qur'an," http://www.thecampusministry.org/factsheets/islam.htm.

377 Also refer to Surah 11:61; 15:26.

dust you will return."[378] The Bible never claims that mankind's origin is from any other source. Furthermore, the Bible never teaches that mankind was created out of "nothing." Instead, the Bible indicates a creation out of dust—matter that was already in existence and was a product of the original creation (the big bang, as indicated by the light on the first day).

Why are these facts important? The Bible is flawless, and it only contains that which is entirely true, although it may not be all-inclusive (as established in Chapter 5). Furthermore, the Bible cannot be wrong because it was authored by an all-knowing God. Since God is all-knowing, He will not and cannot contradict Himself; the Qur'an, on the other hand, has obvious internal contradictions that even undermine the big bang theory with the claim that mankind was created from nothing after everything was created (matter, after the big bang, can only be rearranged).

Simple question: Why would a book of divine inspiration have contradictions and errors if it came from an all-knowing source? It would not make sense for God to stumble and exhibit confusion about the origin of humankind.

"From" and "out of" are italicized because that will be the focal point of this discussion. It would be one thing to claim that humankind came from clay and then in another verse claim they were made from the dust of the earth because these substances may be analogous or interchangeable. The Qur'an claims that mankind came *from* water, from clay, and out of nothing. Clay, water, and nothing are not even interchangeable substances. Was humanity created out of nothing or out of that which was already created? If humankind was created out of that which was already created, was that origin from dust, water or blood?

From clearly indicates origin, that from which something is derived. It would have been entirely different to claim that humans are *composed* of blood clots, clay, and water, but this is not the case; the structure of the sentences found in the Qur'an clearly reveals that Muhammad was referring to the substance from which humankind originated (versus *made of*). If the Qur'an had stated the different substances mankind was collectively composed of, then it would have been an entirely different account because we know our composition is of dust (possibly interchangeable with clay), water, and blood clots—but the Qur'an never makes that distinction. Words have meaning; especially when they are compiled into sentences, and the structure of the sentences found in the Qur'an clearly contradicts that which we know to be true of mankind's origin.

378 Genesis 3:19.

It is interesting to note that the Qur'an acknowledges this shortfall because the Qur'an's Introduction adds the following disclaimer:

> Every description given in the Qur'an of the material world correlates to established scientific fact, *in view of the state of knowledge in the Prophet Muhammad's day,* it is inconceivable that many of the statements in the Qur'an which are connected with science could have been the work of any man.[379]

This is certainly a revealing comment relating to the "inerrancy" of the Qur'an. Why is this statement so revealing? This statement covers up the very flaw in the creation account by making it known that the text only reflects the knowledge of Muhammad *during the era in which he lived.* Does the Bible ever make such a disclaimer? Certainly not; the Bible does not need a disclaimer because everything within the Bible is entirely true. Why is everything within the Bible entirely true? The Bible was actually authored by an all-knowing God. Therefore, we can easily conclude that the Qur'an is fatally flawed with respect to the creation account, and a cover-up was deployed to forewarn the reader that the text may appear to be wrong, but it really was a reflection of the knowledge in that era.

Yea, Yea—Not Yea, Nay.[380] A second notable contradiction arises with the topic of alcohol. Muhammad takes a stand of "yea" before he takes a stand of "nay" with respect to the consumption of alcoholic beverages. The radical change of position, in a way, reminds me of John Kerry with his "Flip Flop Olympics" during his presidential bid in 2004 when he said "I actually did vote for the $87 billion before I voted against it" (along with various other issues).[381] Likewise, Muhammad "flip-flopped" his position on alcohol to suit specific circumstances and to appease public opinion before he was firmly grounded upon his beliefs. We know this because, at the beginning of Muhammad's ministry, he taught that it was okay to drink alcohol. Surah 2:219 reads:

379 Dr. Ahmad Zidan, trans., *The Glorious Qur'an* (Cairo: Islamic Inc. Publishing & Distribution , 1996), X, emphasis added.

380 2 Corinthians 1:17–20.

381 NPR, "Are Candidates' Policy Changes Flip Flops?" http://www.npr.org/templates/transcript/transcript.php?storyId=92254310.

> They ask you about intoxicants and gambling, say: "In both of them there is grievous sin, and *some profit* for people; but the sin is more grievous than the profit." They ask you how much they are able to spend, say: "Whatever you can spare." So GOD expounds His Commands to you, in order that you may reflect-

In the text above, "some profit" was italicized because Muhammad made it clear that there was "some profit" in gambling and with consuming alcohol. Although the sin was more grievous, it was noted that some profit could accompany the people. As Muhammad became more popular, he changed to a less tolerant position on alcohol and taught that you should not drink before prayer. Surah 4:43 reads:

> O you who believe! Do not approach prayers while you are intoxicated, until you can understand all that you say, nor in a state of impurity, except when passing through, until you have washed yourselves, but if you are sick, or on a journey, or one of you comes from the call of nature, or if you have approached women, and you cannot find water, then clean yourselves pure by wiping it over your face and hands, surely GOD is All-pardoning, All-forgiving.

This is an interesting shift; we see the position of "some profit" change to "do not approach prayers while you are intoxicated." Muhammad updates his position to one that is against praying to Allah while you are so drunk that people cannot understand what you are saying. Maybe this was a problem that needed to be addressed. I do not know, but we do know that the stance was changed and that it was published in the Qur'an. As a result, we then see Muhammad's position on alcohol change, but this certainly was not the last. There is one last "flip-flop" with respect to the consumption of alcohol.

The final position on the consumption of alcohol is extreme and to the point where Muhammad calls intoxicants "Satan's handiwork." Surah 5:90 reads:

> O you who believe! Most certainly intoxicants and gambling and idol worship and fortune telling are an

> abomination of Satan's handiwork, so shun it, that you may prosper.

Indeed; the final vote has been cast in this verse. Now the position that Muhammad takes is finalized – do not participate in intoxicants or gambling or idol worship or fortune telling because they are "an abomination of Satan's handiwork." This is a rather extreme position when contrasted to the position that Muhammad originally took when he taught that there was "some profit" with the consumption of drinking alcohol.

The "flip-flopping" is clear as it can be and the fact is that Muhammad *was for alcohol before he was against it* (just like John Kerry voted for the $87 billion to fund the Iraq War before he voted against it). Positions and times change—why not keep up with "the latest and greatest"? Because we need to know how Jesus Christ—God Himself—perceives changing positions when dealing with sin.

In God's text, the Holy Bible, God does not vacillate, nor does He change His mind on that which He has defined as sin. Sin, by definition, is a transgression against God, and it's just as wrong two thousand years ago as it is today; neither sin nor God changes. However, we see a very different picture when we examine the Qur'an. The position on the topic of alcohol sways back and forth, and that was evident from the surahs that were cited.[382]

From the contradiction that has been pointed out, I have just one question: "To Allah, what is alcohol? Is drinking profitable, is it a bad idea before prayer, or is it truly an *abomination*?" I direct the question to Allah because the preface of my Qur'an reads: "The Qur'an is the concrete tangible Word of GOD. The Qur'an identifies itself to us and tells us that GOD is its author, as GOD tells us in Surah 55 verses 1 and 2." In addition to the Preface, the Introduction of the Qur'an also makes it known that: "The Qur'an is the heart and soul of Islam, it is the Wisdom of GOD revealed for all mankind through His Prophet Muhammad (Peace be upon him)."

These citations clearly indicate a strong belief that Muhammad wrote a revelation of God that was inspired by God and accurately represents

382 Some of the surahs I cite are actually from my copy of the Qur'an that I purchased while serving in Iraq. My Qur'an, purchased in the Middle East, was published in Egypt and includes a translation to English (with the original Arabic writing on the same page).

God, but why are there contradictions if Allah is truly all-knowing? Do perspective shifts run rampant throughout the Bible with respect to sin?

The Bible clearly teaches, in Malachi 3:6, that "I the Lord do not change." If Allah's opinion on alcohol changes, as Muhammad has presented, then Allah must not be God because God has revealed that *He never changes* (an intrinsic characteristic of God: immutability). Thus, we arrive on another serious internal contradiction with respect to Islamic theology that leads us to believe that the Qur'an cannot be considered Absolute Truth because it does not reflect the inspiration of an all-knowing and immutable being. The reason that the Qur'an is not flawless, contains contradictions, and is theologically inaccurate is simply that it was not inspired by God. The Qur'an is not the word of God because it takes a position that is in direct opposition to that which God had previously established. The Qur'an was created by the mind of a man (Muhammad), and therefore it will never be elevated to the same plane as *the Holy Bible* (a true product of God).

Drawing the Conclusion

'If It Doesn't Fit, You Must Acquit.' The charge that Islam is Absolute Truth simply does not align with reality. Just as Cinderella's slipper could only fit on one foot, the "glove" of Absolute Truth can only fit on one hand—and it fits on the hand of none other than Jesus Christ. This conclusion makes sense because we have already established that all truth is narrow and all truth is exclusive. Truth cannot be all-accepting; when contradictory truth claims are presented; one must be wrong.

It has been demonstrated that Islam cannot be hailed as Absolute Truth because Muhammad was not qualified to be a prophet, his revelation cannot be verified, the Qur'an contradicts the Bible, and the Qur'an even contradicts itself. We can prove this fact through self-incriminating evidence and the Qur'an even has a disclaimer, in the Introduction, which tries to justify its multiple contradictions with respect to the topics of creation and the consumption of alcohol.

Even though we have barely scratched the surface of this topic, we can already see that there are some major contradictions with Islamic doctrine. As we reflect upon the shocking verses highlighted in the very beginning of the chapter, Christians need to take a strong stand for the Truth. The closing argument will now be made to urge the severity of this chapter and the extreme differences between Christianity and Islam.

Closing Argument. Islam rejects the deity of Jesus Christ, the crucifixion, and the resurrection. Muslims do not believe that Jesus is Lord or that He is able to save people from their sin. To the Muslims, Jesus Christ was a mere prophet who was used as a conspirator on behalf of Allah so it would appear that there was a resurrection.[383] I do not know how it would benefit Muslims to claim that one of their Prophets (Jesus) and Allah were involved in deception and a conspiracy, but it is nevertheless what they teach.

Either you believe Muhammad, who lived six hundred years after the crucifixion with an unverifiable vision, *or* you believe the accounts given by apostles who actually lived and were present during the crucifixion. Either you believe an entirely flawless Bible, *or* you can believe the Qur'an (which we have shown contradicts not only the Bible but also itself). Either you believe in an all-loving God, *or* you believe in Allah who approves of murdering transgressors and beating wives into submission. Either you believe in the Bible, which endorses peace, love, and Jesus Christ as Lord, *or* you believe in Allah, a self-proclaimed prophet who failed the Old Testament test, and a manmade book where flaws, contradictions, and errors abound.

There is no middle ground. We do not worship the same God; you must believe in either one or the other. You cannot believe in both the Qur'an and the Bible. You cannot worship both Jesus Christ and Allah. But most importantly, you cannot get to heaven if you place your faith in Allah and reject the redeeming blood of Jesus Christ.

As a result of this examination, we are confidently able to rule out Islam as a candidate for Absolute Truth.

383 Surah 4:157.

Chapter 13

Judaism

These people come near to me with their mouth
and honor me with their lips,
but their hearts are far from me.
Their worship of me
is made up only of rules taught by men.

—Isaiah 29:13, speaking of Israel

"The time is coming," declares the Lord,
"when I will make a ***new covenant***
with the house of Israel
and with the house of Judah.
It will not be like the covenant
I made with their forefathers
when I took them by the hand
to lead them out of Egypt,
because they broke my covenant,
though I was husband to them,"
declares the Lord.

—Jeremiah 31:31–32

Introducing Judaism

The Pioneer of Religion. Judaism was one of the first monotheistic religions in the world. It is the eldest among the Abrahamic religions and is the progenitor of Christianity. It may be weird to think of Judaism being the parent religion of Christianity because they vastly differ in today's world, but the two are virtually identical when comparing morals, values, or even first-century Christians with first-century Jews. We know that the two religions are very similar because Christianity is the extension, and ultimately the fulfillment, of the Jewish Scriptures (the Old Testament).

However, as we know, there is one major disagreement between the Christians and the Jews—and it's undoubtedly an issue that prevents a person from pledging allegiance to both, the Christian and Jewish faiths. The possibility of being completely faithful to both is impossible because they teach entirely different, and contradictory, doctrines in regard to the identity of Jesus Christ. Judaism differs from Christianity because it refuses to recognize the facts surrounding the birth, life, ministry, death, and resurrection of Jesus Christ as they pertain to the fulfillment of Yahweh's messianic prophecies in the Old Testament.

When one group teaches that Jesus was the Messiah and is God, while the other claims that He was merely a prophet, an ordinary man, or even a blasphemous sinner, we know that both cannot be right because of the Law of Contradiction. Just as I cannot be dead and alive at the same time, Jesus cannot be God and a blasphemous sinner (or even an ordinary man or prophet) at the same time.

Why Must We Discuss Judaism? The objective of this chapter will be to determine whether or not placing faith in Judaism is sufficient to usher one successfully from this life into the next. In the twenty-first century, is it possible to enter into the gates of heaven through Old Testament sacrifices and through Old Testament theology alone?[384] Does it really matter if the New Testament is rejected? In a post-resurrection era, can anybody enter into heaven without accepting Jesus as their personal Lord and Savior? Answering these questions is of utmost importance as the answer will inevitably determine life or death in the spiritual realm of reality. Discovering the answer to each of these questions is precisely the reason why we must discuss Judaism.

This subject hits closer to home than Islam because we, as Christians, have much more in common with the Jewish culture, history, and traditions than with any other religion. Even though this chapter puts us on more

384 Before Jesus was resurrected, God's people were under the Old Covenant. After the resurrection, the New Covenant had been fully established. When presented with the New Covenant, the choice a person made in regard to the gift of salvation became the determining factor in regard to spiritual fate.

familiar ground, we must not refrain from presenting the Absolute Truth. We cannot refuse to evangelize the Jewish congregation because they are *almost* Christian. Why must we do everything we can to reach out and evangelize the Jewish congregation as well? Because to be almost saved is to be entirely lost; there is no intermediate state, and there is no such thing as partial salvation.

Before we proceed to answer the questions that were highlighted in the section above, we need to take some time to refresh our memory about Judaism and the Old Testament. Understanding Judaism's demographics, how its believers deviate from Christianity, and how they have historically rejected God will help Christians formulate a more effective presentation of the Gospel so that we are able to hone in on the objections that the Jewish people have with Christianity. The facts, undeniable evidence, and firsthand accounts of the eyewitnesses need to be presented because the largest objection centers upon the identity of Christ and the resurrection. When Christians are prepared and become focused on the Jewish people's concerns, we are able to formulate the best presentation of the Gospel that not only addresses their concerns but also presents clear evidence of how Christianity is entirely true. This need demonstrates how apologetics and evangelism are intricately intertwined.

Demographics. There are approximately 13.3 million Jews throughout the world with the highest concentration being in Israel (5.55 million) and the next largest concentration in the United States (5.3 million).[385] Within Judaism there are three major divisions: Orthodox Judaism, Reform Judaism, and Conservative Judaism.[386] Orthodox is the oldest and most conservative branch because these Jews strictly adhere to the original customs and practices of the Old Testament. Reform Judaism is the most liberal and permissive version; they do not follow the traditional customs such as diet and apparel, but they still follow the moral and ethical laws as well as the teachings in the Tanakh.[387] Conservative Judaism is a compromise between the Orthodox and Reform positions. Even though

---

385 European Jewish Congress, "World Jewish Population Grows by 70,000," http://www.eurojewcong.org/ejc/news.php?id_article=2835.

386 Thom Rainer, *The Unexpected Journey: Conversations with people who turned from other beliefs to Jesus* (Grand Rapids, MI: Zondervan, 2005), 33.

387 Tanakh: the sacred book of Judaism, consisting of the Torah, the Prophets, and the Writings; the Hebrew Scriptures (dictionary.com).

there are distinctions between these divisions of the Jewish religion, they all deviate from Christianity; this is the topic we turn to next.

Judaism Contradicts Christianity

Theological Differences. As previously mentioned, Judaism is virtually identical to Christianity from many theological standpoints. We know that Judaism and Christianity are similar because they both accept the Old Testament as God's written revelation to man. Judaism's primary source of teaching and authority comes from the Tanakh, and its contents are almost identical to the Old Testament (a Christian term). The major difference, in appearance, is that the Tanakh and Old Testament are arranged in different order. The Tanakh places the first five books (Torah or The Law) first, but the remaining thirty-four books are arranged differently and are divided into sections titled "the Prophets" and "the Writings." Since the Jewish people worship the God portrayed in the Old Testament, they intuitively accept the moral and ethical principles of Christianity. From a moral standpoint, Judaism acknowledges and puts into practice the exact same Ten Commandments, laws, and ethical standards as Christians. Ironically, Judaism even uses and studies the exact same prophecies regarding the Messiah (although their interpretations and views on fulfillment drastically differ).

Furthermore, there are even more similarities when we note the fact that Jesus was Jewish, the disciples were Jewish, the apostles were Jewish, and many of the early Christians were Jewish. Christianity has a Jewish origin, but it's an entirely different faith. The Jewish people reject the idea that Jesus Christ was the Messiah because they envisioned a Messiah who would be a powerful political and military leader, not the humble servant depicted in the Gospel accounts. (Perhaps the Jews are awaiting the Messiah's second coming.)

Indeed, the second coming will be a much more convincing display of power and will truly settle the issue of deity. The Apostle John reveals that many Jews will accept salvation during this final revelation of the power and glory of Jesus Christ.[388] However, the only problem with Judaism is that nobody knows when Jesus Christ will return. Why is this problematic for Judaism? The unknown second coming is problematic because millions upon millions of Jewish people have passed away since the first century, and

388 Revelation 7:4.

if they have not accepted their salvation; they have not met the minimum requirements for entrance into heaven set forth by the New Testament (we all know the unintended consequence).

We have established that the identity of Jesus Christ is in dispute between Judaism and Christianity, but the issue has still not been settled of whether these differences are meaningful. Does it really matter if a person worships the same God but refuses to accept salvation through Jesus Christ? Is it possible to enter into heaven after the resurrection of Jesus Christ without the redeeming blood? The answers to these questions will now be explored.

Implications of Theological Differences. The theological differences between Judaism and Christianity are severe because of the consequences that are established in the New Testament (the teachings of Jesus Christ while he was actively engaged in his earthly ministry). When Judaism rejects the notion that Jesus Christ is God, it naturally refuses to accept the teachings of the New Testament. As a result, Judaism rejects each and every single Gospel account of Jesus Christ; as well Paul's eyewitness testimonies in the Pauline letters and the personal accounts by Peter, James, John, and Jude.

Even though Judaism rejects the authenticity of the New Testament, Judaism does not deny Jesus' existence or His ministry or that He was crucified because of His radical claims. The Jews cannot deny Jesus' existence because they were the people who had Him executed. Therefore, Jews are forced to acknowledge that Jesus was a real person and actually existed in order to be credible, but they reject the notion that Jesus was resurrected and was seen alive after the third day.

Instead of believing in a resurrection, the Jewish religion claims that the body was stolen by Jesus' disciples.[389] Theft of the body has already been ruled out because it has been demonstrated that a lie on the part of any group (Romans, Jews, and family and friends) would have had equally devastating effects for any of them. The result of rejecting the resurrection leads Judaism to the belief that Jesus is neither the Messiah nor the Redeemer through which all people have access to the Father.

Since Judaism rejects the deity of Christ, it also does not acknowledge His virgin birth, sinless life, or resurrection and denies that the Old Testament prophecies were entirely fulfilled by Jesus Christ. Since the

389 Matthew 28:13.

Jews do not believe Jesus Christ was God, they also reject the idea of a Holy Trinity (which would need Jesus for completion of a triune being).

Unfortunately, Judaism actually has a very condescending and negative view of Jesus. Judaism teaches that He was not perfect. In fact, Judaism now claims that He was actually a sinner (blasphemy). Judaism also claims that He lied to his disciples (by promising them one hundred times as much material wealth as what they gave up to serve in ministry)[390] and engaged in violence (sending demons into and drowning swine, overturning the money changers' tables in the temple, and cursing the fig tree)[391] and that he deceived his followers and the world (by wanting to conceal his identity).[392]

Misguided without the Spirit. I'm perplexed as to how Judaism is able to make such radical denunciations against Jesus Christ while maintaining their confidence. The Jewish religious leaders knew that Jesus was dead and that after the third day He was no longer in the tomb; they were eventually forced to account for how the stone was rolled back and why the body was missing. After the resurrection, Jesus lived on earth for forty days and appeared to hundreds upon hundreds of people on numerous occasions. These religious leaders were not ignorant; they knew what was going on, and they heard time and time again that Jesus was alive. Jesus, at the time, was the highlight of the news, and His final days were the greatest story the world had ever reported! The center of Jerusalem was "everything Jesus" and it extended from His triumphal entry, trials, torture, execution, and, yes, all the way to a resurrection from the dead. (These were massive events, and people were talking about them as they were unfolding; this is confirmed by Luke 24:13–24.)

Furthermore, the Jewish people knew many radical changes were also taking place within a variety of different people. People who loved Jesus as well as those who had formerly despised Him were both accepting their salvation and placing full faith in Jesus. The disciples were emboldened and were radically changed as no group of people has ever been. These men were entirely different; before the resurrection they were cowards, but

390 Wealth (or any material blessing) was not found in Mark 10:28–31, but some Jewish scholars teach that Jesus promised material blessings.

391 Matthew 8:28–32; Mark 5:1–20; Luke 8:26–39; and Matthew 21:12–13, 18–19; Mark 11:13–17.

392 Silencing the demons: Mark 3:11–12; Luke 4:41. Silencing His disciples: Matthew 16:20; Mark 8:30; Luke 9:21. Charging those He healed to keep the secret: Matthew 8:3-4; 12:15-16; Mark 1:44; 5:43; 7:36; Luke 5:14; 8:56.

now they were mighty warriors who feared nothing, not even death. At the other end of the spectrum, Saul (a man who persecuted, imprisoned, and approved the murder of Christians), suddenly converted to the faith he hated while en route to persecute even more Christians![393] We know that the Jewish people knew this was taking place because they tried to execute Saul on multiple occasions when he preached an eyewitness account of the resurrected Christ in Damascus, Jerusalem, Caesarea, Tarsus, Antioch, and many other places during his missionary journeys.[394]

The reason that the Jewish people could not understand Jesus (and claimed He was a sinner, liar, and deceiver) is simple: The Jewish people cannot understand or discern the importance of the teachings of Jesus Christ because they have inaccurate presuppositions that prevent them from discerning what the Holy Spirit reveals. Judaism makes its first mistake by denying the truth that is evident, but the tragedy is that it leads to a second critical mistake—trying to understand the significance of Jesus' teachings when they are unable to discern their importance. We know this fact to be true when we read 1 Corinthians 2:14:

> The man without the Spirit does not accept the things that come from the Spirit of God, for they are foolishness to him, and he cannot understand them, because they are spiritually discerned [discerned only through the Spirit].

From the above verse, we understand that Judaism has clearly been separated from the Spirit because they do not accept what came from the Spirit. Closed-minded rejection is distinguished from open-minded searching. The difference is that the closed-minded person will not even consider the possibility of the New Testament being true, whereas all Christians were once lost, but at some point were open to the message. (Hence the reason the Christians accepted their salvation.) As a result, the closed-minded Jewish people are unable to accurately interpret the meaning and implications of Jesus' message and actions. We now need to address the accusations that Judaism has made against Jesus (that he lied to his disciples, engaged in violence, and deceived his followers).

First, we note that since believers in Judaism reject the Holy Spirit, they cannot understand that Jesus was not necessarily talking about rewarding the disciples with *material wealth* a hundred times over, because most of

393 Acts 9:1–2, 13–16, 19–22.

394 Acts 9:23–25, 28–30; 11:25; 13:1–14:20.

the disciples never became wealthy. Judaism references this verse where Jesus said that:

> No one who has left home or brothers or sisters or mother or father or children or fields for me and the gospel will fail to receive a hundred times as much in this present age: homes, brothers, sisters, mothers, children and fields—along with persecutions—and in the age to come, eternal life.[395]

Granted, Jesus specifically promised hundred-fold blessings, but He did not promise the accumulation of money, riches, or any type of material possessions. Instead, this passage seems to be referencing the disciple's manner of life (with a literal fulfillment).[396] The disciples who left all for the sake of Christ were provided with everything that they needed as they traveled. Therefore, the literal promise is that the disciples would receive a hundredfold homes, brothers, sisters, mothers, children and fields for their use and benefit while propagating the gospel. The doubter errs when they substitute "material possessions" in the place of "homes" or "fields" as that which the disciple owns or possesses (ownership was not promised). As a result, we are able to confidently conclude that Jesus did not lie to His disciples because they were, in fact, blessed a hundred fold in use, not possession. (Who has ever owned over one hundred homes at the same time? This idea seems *slightly* unreasonable even for the wealthiest men alive today. The disciples did not expect to own over one hundred homes and neither should we; that would be silly and illogical.)

Second, not only is it outrageous for Judaism to claim that violence was sinful on Jesus' behalf, but it is tantamount to claiming that God the Father was sinful because he sent the plagues on Egypt, flooded the earth, destroyed Jericho, and so forth. Does Judaism really want to make this claim? God the Father killed *people* when he ushered in the flood and the plagues and in his conquests with the Jews to establish Israel in the land of Canaan, but Jesus merely cursed a tree, overturned a table of money changers in the temple, and ordered (upon request, mind you) that *demons* enter into the bodies of swine (not a human) to drown themselves. Jesus never hurt another person because He came to save, to heal, and to love.

395 Mark 10:29–30.

396 Study Light, "The Adam Clarke Commentary," http://www.studylight.org/com/acc/view.cgi?book=mr&chapter=010.

Along with this point, we must always remember that God is just, and justice always demands punishment. Since the wages of sin is always death, God has not committed any sin—and neither did Jesus Christ. The claim that Jesus was sinful demonstrates a severe contradiction with respect to the Jewish position. If Jesus sinned through violence, it could not even compare to the violence on the part of God the Father, and they defeat themselves with this claim. (For clarification, neither Jesus nor the Father is, by nature, capable of committing a sin. Death is the just punishment for sin, and our lives are a gift that can be rightfully taken at any time by God; nobody has an inherent right to life.)

Third, Jesus did not deceive His disciples and followers or the demons by telling them not to reveal his identity. People can speculate why He did not openly flaunt His identity, but the obvious answer seems to be to enable Him to fulfill all the prophecies and to be crucified at the climax of His ministry. Jesus taught for three years, built up a base of believers, and created an enormous stir in the midst of Jerusalem and all Judea. People knew who Jesus was, and they saw miracle after miracle performed. An excellent reason for why Jesus had to prolong His life (by not flaunting His identity) was to enable Him to have an extraordinarily large following so that nobody could explain away or deny the events surrounding His ministry and resurrection. Judaism has obviously tried to distort the accounts of Jesus' ministry, but consider the effects Jesus' followers have had on the entire world since His resurrection. Judaism has a little over 13 million believers; more than two billion people call themselves Christians.

As we look back though history, we understand why Jesus did not flaunt His identity because it was imperative to the propagation of the Gospel. Think how easy it would have been for the Jewish religious leaders to destroy Jesus' influence if they had managed to execute Jesus at the beginning of His ministry? If the Jews only had to cover up one miracle and one claim and prevent a few people from evangelizing, then the outcome would have been entirely different and with minimal results. If Jesus had been executed within the first week (or month) of His ministry, it would have been as if He had never existed because it took years to build His platform. Jesus was not executed in the beginning because He did not flaunt His true identity; however, when Jesus was asked to reveal His identity, He immediately revealed the truth. As planned, Jesus was executed at the climax of His ministry because God always has a perfect plan, and God's plan comes to pass exactly as He determines.

A Weak Argument and a Bad Track Record

Petty Arguments Reveal Weakness. It's amazing to read some of the arguments that Judaism has created in order to justify denying the obvious truth. Judaism refuses to even consider the resurrection even though there is a gargantuan amount of overwhelming evidence, eyewitness accounts, logical deductions from prophecy, and personal testimonies. What more could a person possibly need to demonstrate that the Bible is entirely true? Why is exalting Jesus Christ as the King of kings and the Lord of lords so offensive to the Jewish congregation? God made a promise to the Jewish people regarding a New Covenant, and then they were outraged when He fulfilled what He promised![397]

The point of this section is to demonstrate that petty arguments against overwhelming facts, eyewitness accounts, logic, and prophecy actually reveal their weakness. Creating an argument that portrays Jesus as a sinner because He cursed a tree, sent demons into a herd of pigs to drown, or demonstrated "violence" by confronting corruption in the temple is a weak argument as an attempt to discredit Jesus. Let's be honest, it looks silly for Judaism to try and build a case by calling Jesus a sinner simply because he was mean to a tree and some pigs and stopped corruption (where God's holy temple was being desecrated), when the Jewish people turn right around to call God the Father *Holy*. Do they even think about the unintended consequences of this accusation?

I would suggest not, because if Jewish believers claim that Jesus was, in fact, a sinner, then it does not seem possible for them to turn right back around and claim God the Father is holy when the Father killed everybody on earth with the flood (except those on Noah's ark). The Jewish argument is, by nature, contradictory, and it implies a double standard that fits an agenda (a standard that does not correlate with truth and an argument that defies logic). Since God the Father killed people in the flood and Jesus never harmed a human soul, there are only two arguments that can be made, and the irony is that both discredit Judaism.

The only options are that Jesus and the Father are both without sin *or* that they *both* sinned. If stopping corruption (evil) by overturning the tables is sinful, then somehow right has morphed into wrong, and the reasoning makes about as much sense as me claiming to be a married bachelor. If adherents of Judaism remain consistent with their definition of sin, then either way they turn, they disprove their own religion. The only way that

397 Jeremiah 31:31.

Judaism can prop itself up with the tree, pig, and corruption scheme is to maintain an inherent contradiction in regard to what constitutes sin. Judaism needs to establish what constitutes sin, stick with that decision, and then make the applicable changes with respect to their faith because their claim is unsustainable and, frankly, impossible.

A False Witness is Deceitful. We also need to note that the tree, pig, and corruption scheme is a fairly recent product because, at the time of Jesus' trials, the only accusation against Jesus was blasphemy (which was really not, because His claim was later proven true). The fact that Judaism feels a need to venture out on a fragile limb to reinforce the case exposes further weakness in the argument. If this argument was solid, there would be no reason to try and desperately scrape for more arguments. We know that frantic searching for additional arguments reveals weakness because this task was already attempted by the Jewish people who lived during the time when Jesus walked the earth, and they failed.

During the trial before Caiaphas, the Jewish people desperately tried to pin just one sin on Jesus, but nobody was able to do so. In fact, Jesus ultimately provided their ammunition by revealing what He would accomplish (destroy the temple, but raise it again in three days).[398] Since it took forty-six years to build the temple, they knew that only God could completely destroy it and rebuild it in that short a time (a miracle). Jesus' previous claim (when brought up at His trial) of destroying the temple ultimately led to the next question where Jesus finally revealed His true identity.[399] Ironically, Jesus sowed the seeds for His execution much earlier because He intentionally planted a statement that would later be used against Him and it initiated the final question that led to revealing His true identity.

When Jesus revealed His true identity, we see a drastic shift in the Jewish religious leaders. They never liked Jesus, but until this point, they were never publicly against Him. In other words, the Jewish religious leaders were actually deceitful because they were thinking about plotting to kill Jesus while making "public relations" statements of support. In fact, as we have pointed out, the Jewish religious leaders hailed Jesus as a "man of great integrity" before they turned against Him and demanded execution. Jesus remained constant, but the religious leaders "flip-flopped" their public position.

398 John 2:19; Matthew 26:61.
399 Matthew 26:64.

It's important to note that the religious leaders only changed their public façade, but their inner feelings and attitudes remained constant. They openly supported Jesus, before they openly opposed Him. We know this to be true because they once referred to Jesus as a man of great integrity, before they accused Him of blasphemy. They refused to condemn Jesus (because of Jesus' popularity amongst the people), before they condemned Him. They would not speak against Him, before they spoke against Him.

As you read the Gospel accounts, you notice that the "flip-flop" is very sudden but drastic. Why do we see such a drastic shift with respect to the urgency to execute Jesus? The shift was almost instantaneous because tensions had been mounting. The Jewish religious leaders were doing and saying one thing, while they actually believed another, and then suddenly they exploded with of the demand for a death sentence. It was to the point where there was almost a mob in front of Pilate and they were so extreme that the Jewish people released a murdering insurrectionist so that they could execute Jesus.

The sudden flip-flop reveals deceit and a severe conflict between what the religious leaders truly believed versus the "front" they created. If we go by the Jewish wisdom in the Old Testament (a text that Judaism recognizes as the inerrant Word of God when referenced in the Tanakh), we discover shocking verses that address the root of deceit.

- Jeremiah 6:13: "From the least to the greatest, all are greedy for gain; prophets and priests alike, all practice deceit."
- Psalms 52:2: "Your tongue plots destruction; it is like a sharpened razor, you who practice deceit."
- Proverbs 12:20: "There is deceit in the hearts of those who plot evil, but joy for those who promote peace."
- Proverbs 14:25: A truthful witness saves lives, but a false witness is deceitful."

Even the Tanakh would confirm the veracity of the claims that were made in this section. Deceit created the necessary cover to plot the secret arrest and an unlawful trial before dawn. As King Solomon reveals, a false witness is deceitful. We also discover in Jeremiah's verse that there were false prophets and priests practicing deceit and preaching rebellion against God hundreds of years earlier. The events that unfolded were nothing new because Israel had persecuted the prophets who preached repentance or punishment time and time again when Israel was going in and out of exile. In light of Israel's track record of rejecting their own God, as well as the prophets sent by God, the Jewish people's rejection of the Messiah is not surprising.

The Track Record of Rejection. The Jewish people are the center of the Old Testament and were God's chosen people. Even though Israel is the center of the Old Testament (or Tanakh), they were not exactly a prodigy that other nations should mimic. Israel discovered that rejecting morality—and ultimately God—brings severe consequences. Time and time again, we read the strong denunciation against Israel's actions by the major and minor prophets. The track record of Israel's rejection of God is certainly long, but we will summarize briefly in order to provide a segue to the rejection of the Messiah.

When Israel was freed from Egypt, they were led out of captivity under the leadership of Moses. The exodus began a new and exciting future for God's people—or so it seemed. While in the Desert of Sin (the Sinai Wilderness), the Israelites were most unhappy with their new circumstances. Despite being free, they were ungrateful and bitterly complained about food, water, and the fact that they were in a desert. In fact, the bitterness was so great the people even told Moses that they should have remained in Egypt as slaves, where at least they were provided with food, and some even wished they had died while in Egypt. They complained as if God were not meeting their needs.

However, God was meeting their needs (although not with luxury) by providing food (manna) every single morning. God continually provided the food, but there were a few rules. The Israelites were told that they were to only collect enough food for each person, for each day. In other words, God forbade the people from trying to horde manna or store it overnight in order to test the people's trust in God.[400] Nevertheless, some of the Israelites broke God's first rule by attempting to horde manna and in the process violated the second rule because hording required them to store it overnight. (Only through disobedience could they discover that, by morning, the manna was filled with maggots and began to rot.)[401]

God also commanded the Israelites to refrain from searching for or gathering manna on the Sabbath. God made it clear that He would provide enough food for the Israelites on the day before the Sabbath and

400 Exodus 16:4, 16, 20.
401 Exodus 16:20.

made it clear that this would be the only night that the manna could be preserved until the next morning. The evening before the Sabbath was special because it was the only night that the Israelites could prepare for the next day. Despite clear instructions, some were defiant and went out in search for food on the holy day, intentionally disobeying God's command.[402] In response, God asks His people, "How long will you refuse to keep my commands and my instructions?"[403]

Even though the Israelites were defiant, complaining and refusing to obey God's commands, they were still eligible to enter into the Promised Land. Before embarking into the Promised Land, they were commanded to send spies ahead to report on the condition of the land and to gather information about the people they would have to defeat in battle. After the spies came back, the testimony that Joshua and Caleb gave described the land as "flowing with milk and honey." The land was breathtaking, and it was perfect in every way, but there was one *giant* problem. Israel had to conquer the current inhabitants in order to take full possession. (They were not going to give it up, saying, "Oh sure, you Israelites can have this land. We apologize, we had no idea it actually belonged to you!")

Even though God had *promised* the land (which directly implies victory on their necessary military conquests), the Israelites were furious and were actually prepared to execute God's messengers. The Israelites rejected the report from Joshua and Caleb and were ready to stone them so that they could elect new leadership to march themselves back into Egypt where they would hold out their arms and beg to be enslaved once again![404] Would it even be possible to imagine the frustration associated with trying to provide for a group of people, only to receive in return snarling hatred through bitter complaints, rejection, and defiance? Israel's actions infuriated God, and it was only in response to Moses' pleas that God did not kill all of Israel for their sin.[405] Moses convinced God to spare their lives despite their rebellion, but they would not go unpunished.

> Not one of the men who saw my glory and the miraculous signs I performed in Egypt and in the wilderness but who disobeyed me and tested me ten times—not one of them will ever see the land I promised on oath to their forefathers.

402 Exodus 16:27.

403 Exodus 16:28.

404 Numbers 14:3–4.

405 Numbers 14:13–19.

> No one who has treated me with contempt will ever see it. But because my servant Caleb has a different spirit and follows me wholeheartedly, I will bring him into the land he went to, and his descendants will inherit it.[406]

As we know, the Israelites were punished and forced to wander in the desert for forty years (until the last person who rebelled had passed away). After the death of the last Israelite who had lived in Egypt, the people were then permitted to enter into the land that God had promised. One might think that, after God addressed their disobedience, spared their lives, and continued to provide manna day after day *for forty years*, the people just might begin to place trust in God once again.[407] It would only seem logical that forty years of constant fulfillment would begin to reassure Israel that God keeps every promise.

After the forty-year wandering, the Israelites finally reached the Promised Land. One would expect to read about an abundance of satisfaction, joy, and obedience because, after all, this was the land "flowing with milk and honey"! Not quite; despite the abundance of blessings, the Israelites still had a habit of rejecting God and His commandments. From the time Israel entered the Promised Land until the last book of the Old Testament, the Israelites were warned time and time again by all the prophets to repent and return to God, but the Israelites "mocked God's messengers, despised his words and scoffed at his prophets until the wrath of the LORD was aroused against his people and there was no remedy."[408]

Even though Israel was exiled on numerous occasions and held in bondage by multiple rulers, they never fully accepted God or His message. The entire book of Malachi (the final, and most recent, book of the Old Testament) was written to confront Israel's persistent sin after they had been restored from exile. Malachi condemned the people for their wickedness, urging them to repent. Since Israel had desecrated the Old Covenant, God promised a New Covenant.

The Track Record of Rejection Continues. After the book of Malachi was written, there was a period of four hundred years of prophetic silence. The Bible provides little information as to how Israelites behaved during this period. From the time Malachi condemned the Israelites' behavior

406 Numbers 14:22–24.

407 Exodus 16:35.

408 2 Chronicles 36:16.

until Jesus was born, we know the Jews continued to backslide. We know this because the high priests and religious leaders, at the climax of Jesus' ministry, were so corrupt, self-centered, and blind to the Truth that they proceeded to execute their own Messiah.

Even though this section sounds awful, it does demonstrate a track record of habitual defiance and rejection of God by the Jewish people. This track record enables us, as a twenty-first-century generation, to put into perspective why the Israelites rejected and executed their own Messiah. The rejection of Jesus Christ is similar to how the Israelites rejected Moses, Caleb, Joshua, and the numerous prophets who condemned their wickedness. The Jews have a history of rejection, insubordination, being led astray, complaining, and worshipping false gods. The Jewish people cannot deny this because their story is a major theme of the Old Testament, but it also demonstrates the mercy God has provided if one accepts and loves Jesus.

Judaism's rejection of the Messiah is not based on empirical facts or logic because both have been proven to support Christianity. Instead, the rejection of the Messiah was based on selfish motives, as shown by Jesus in Matthew 23:13–39. Since it was known that the Jewish people would continue in their rejection, Jesus taught that the Kingdom of God would be taken from them and given to those who would "produce its fruit," fulfilling the terms of the New Covenant prophesied in Jeremiah 31:31.

The Fulfillment of Prophecy

Given to Those Who Will Produce Fruit. The Bible is very clear in that the Jews were God's chosen people, but that they no longer are "the chosen" because of their habitual rejection, disobedience and contempt against God. Consider a few verses where Jesus and the New Testament writers reveal that the status of *God's Chosen People* was stripped from the Jews and given to those who will produce fruit:

- Matthew 21:43: "I tell you that the kingdom of God will be taken away from you and given to a people [Gentiles] who will produce its fruit."

- Matthew 23:37–38: "O Jerusalem, Jerusalem, you who kill the prophets and stone those sent to you, how often I have longed to gather your children together, as a hen gathers her chicks under her wings, but you were not willing. Look, your house is left to you desolate."

- John 1:11: "He [Jesus] came to that which was his own, but his own [Jews] did not receive him."

- Acts 28:26–29: "Go to this people and say, 'You will be ever hearing but never understanding; you will be ever seeing but never perceiving.' For this people's heart has become calloused; they hardly hear with their ears, and they have closed their eyes. Otherwise they might see with their eyes, hear with their ears, understand with their hearts and turn, and I would heal them.' Therefore I want you to know that God's salvation has been sent to the Gentiles, and they will listen!"

- Romans 9:27–28: "Isaiah cries out concerning Israel: 'Though the number of the Israelites be like the sand by the sea, only the remnant will be saved. For the Lord will carry out his sentence on earth with speed and finality."

- Romans 2:23–24: "You who brag about the law, do you dishonor God by breaking the law? As it is written: 'God's name is blasphemed among the Gentiles because of you.'"

- Romans 10:21: "Concerning Israel he [Isaiah] says, 'All day long I have held out my hands to a disobedient and obstinate people.'"

- 2 Corinthians 3:14–16: "Their minds were made dull, for to this day the same veil remains when the old covenant is read. It has not been removed, because only in Christ is it taken away. Even to this day when Moses is read, a veil covers their hearts. But whenever anyone turns to the Lord, the veil is taken away."

- Also see the Parable of the Tenants (Luke 20:9–18).

From these passages, we can begin to piece the puzzle together. We understand the background of the Jewish people, their rejection, and how they ultimately turned against their own Messiah, just as they had turned against their prophets and leaders in previous eras. Unfortunately, this is nothing new to the Jewish people, but the good news is that despite continual rejection, God still offers salvation to *all* who seek forgiveness through Jesus Christ.

Call to Action. Even though many will have a tendency to reject, consider the hundreds of prophecies that perfectly align in the New and Old Testaments as they point to Jesus as the Messiah. There are countless eyewitness accounts and testimonies that Jesus Christ was, in fact, resurrected (you already know that He was crucified), and I have pointed out that it's not possible Jesus could have lied, that He was not a lunatic, and that a legend was impossible because those that knew Him were still alive when the Gospels were written!

Now is the time to decide. Now is the time to act, because the presence of the Holy Spirit will descend upon and convict you when you are confronted with the Absolute Truth. Refusing to accept salvation causes the heart to be callused. Continual rejection of the Gospel message over and over hardens the heart, and over time that rejection will cause a person to lose sensitivity to the Gospel. You do not know your time of death, but you do know that you are alive and you have the ability to settle your eternal fate right now.

Everything about Christianity is good, fulfilling, and joyous. The Jewish people make their biggest mistake because they think they have to be *converted* or *changed* to Christianity and give up their Jewish culture, but this could not be farther from the truth! Jewish people who have accepted Jesus Christ as their Savior have not forsaken their Jewish roots, and they have not taken anything away from their culture. On the contrary, Jews who accept Jesus Christ as their Lord and Savior are more Jewish than those who reject, because Jesus was Jewish, and He revealed the new direction Judaism would take through Israel's desecration of the Old Covenant. The following is perhaps the most revealing passage dealing with the prophesied changes in Judaism.

> "The time is coming," declares the LORD,
> "when I will make a new covenant
> with the house of Israel
> and with the house of Judah.
> It will not be like the covenant

I made with their forefathers
when I took them by the hand
to lead them out of Egypt,
because they broke my covenant,
though I was a husband to them,"
declares the LORD.
"This is the covenant I will make with the house of Israel
after that time," declares the LORD.
"I will put my law in their minds
and write it on their hearts.
I will be their God,
and they will be my people."[409]

The promise of a New Covenant was made in the Old Testament. The fulfillment was through Jesus Christ in the New Testament. The eighth chapter of Hebrews is entirely dedicated to revealing this New Covenant, and it even cites the above verses in Jeremiah. The third chapter of Second Corinthians also reveals the New Covenant and its glory. The New Testament was never disconnected from the Old, and it has been demonstrated, though prophecy, as its completion. This is the message Christians need to convey to Judaism.

Conclusion. From our examination of Judaism, we are able to confidently conclude that the Jewish faith is very similar to the Christian faith, but the two drastically differ from one another because of the identity each attributes to Jesus Christ. The rejection of Jesus Christ as Lord and Savior, alone, is enough to disqualify Judaism from being considered Absolute Truth.[410] The Old Testament *contains* Absolute Truth, but we must note that the Old Testament alone is not Absolute Truth because it's not complete without the New Testament; it's only one part.

Consider the oath people must take if they testify in a court of law. Before they are allowed to testify, they promise "to tell the truth, the whole truth, and nothing but the truth, so help me God." Telling the truth consists of telling the *whole truth*. Judaism loses its qualification to be considered Absolute Truth because it does not present the entire truth: it rejects the most critical part of the Absolute Truth. The truth that Judaism refuses to acknowledge is that Jesus Christ is Lord. Therefore, by not telling

409 Jeremiah 31:31–33.
410 John 14:6.

the entire truth, Judaism cannot be considered to hold Absolute Truth because the message is incomplete. It will not help a person successfully venture from this life on earth into heaven, and that is the core of the Gospel of Jesus Christ.

Part Four

Linking Liberalism to Moral Depravity

Chapter 14

The Invasion of Modernism—A Segue to Immorality

"Statesmen … may plan and speculate for liberty, but it is religion and morality alone which can establish the principles upon which freedom can securely stand."

—President John Adams

"Every thinking man, when he thinks, realizes that the teachings of the Bible are so interwoven and entwined with our whole civic and social life that it would be literally impossible for us to figure ourselves what that life would be if these standards were removed."

—President Theodore Roosevelt

"Every Sunday school should be a place where this great book is not only opened, is not only studied, is not only revered, but is drunk of as if it were a fountain of life, is used as if it were the only source of inspiration and of guidance. No great nation can ever survive its own temptations and its own follies that does not indoctrinate its children in the Word of God …"

—President Woodrow Wilson

What Are We Doing?

Piecing the Puzzle Together. In Chapter 1, it was established that America's explorers were Christians seeking to expand the Kingdom of God. These explorers established Christian colonies (their charters reflect their convictions), and America was born a Christian nation. The quotations at the beginning of this chapter reflect convictions expressed by many of our Presidents: they not only acknowledged the Bible, but they also strongly advocated the necessity of incorporating it into American life because *morality* is the only glue that can hold this nation together! Freedom will not survive in the hands of a corrupt and godless society.[411] Immorality is an unsustainable path because it undermines the Constitution (the *only* document that protects you from the government). If freedom is important to anybody in this nation, we must purge ourselves of the immorality that is running rampant. Unfortunately, as I pointed out in Chapter 1, there is a serious problem because Christians are refusing to evangelize. I pray this will no longer be a problem because America needs a revival and she needs to come home and embrace her Christian origin.

Part Four no longer examines theology; instead we will apply our Christianity to our everyday lives because we must focus on the moral and political crisis that our nation is facing. America is at a crossroads: we either choose to restore America to her Christian foundation (where there are immense blessings),[412] or we will turn our back on God and embrace liberalism whether it be in the form of modernism, socialism, or progressivism (and the loss of freedom and depravity associated with ungodly ideologies).[413] It is a myth to think that politics is entirely separate from religion because Christians must elect moral politicians who will preserve the nation—your vote is the only voice you have with respect to policy!

Nevertheless, this chapter will examine the consequences that have inevitably followed from a decline in the church's influence. In this chapter,

---

411 Hosea 5:3-7.

412 Psalms 33:12.

413 As we will establish later, socialism is immoral, and the people lose freedom. One way the people lose freedom is through a redistribution of wealth. In capitalism, giving to the less fortunate is by choice and is known as charity; which is moral. In socialism, the producers in society are *forced* to give to the less fortunate (against their will) through government-sanctioned theft (progressive taxes), and the money is then redistributed through curbed rebates, tax credits, and other government programs that benefit a select group of people; theft is immoral.

we will examine how the invasion of modernism has led to a "blindness to immorality" in the Christian population and how modernism has tried to distort Christianity into a consumer-based faith that seriously lacks fundamental doctrines. Chapter 15 presents how this blindness has enabled our government (through public schools, universities, courts and the legislative branch) to almost entirely transform America from a Christian nation into an Atheist nation. In the next chapter, we will examine *one* example of how the government has radically altered from the former Christ-seeking and Christ-propagating America into one that not only rejects Christ but essentially propagates a curriculum that encourages the rejection of God altogether. Our government's disdain for and rejection of God synergizes the problem through massive government indoctrination of naturalistic ideologies, and we must know whether the Constitution is being violated with respect to the separation of church and state.

The decline of the church's influence, the refusal of Christians to evangelize, and the indoctrination of naturalism by the government has ultimately led to a wave of immorality that threatens our freedom and the Republic. We must recognize that we are at a climax—we are teetering on the peak—and there are two only directions we can fall. We will either fall back to God, or we will turn our back on the God who made this nation great and plummet into the immorality of liberalism. These are the only choices! It's a big deal if you would like to keep the inalienable rights that were endowed by your Creator!

Finally, Chapter 16 is the "equipper": it is designed to encourage Christians to Stand Up! and ultimately guide America back to safety (back into the moral will of God). Chapter 16 will present the three priorities, one of which each person ultimately chooses. Will you prioritize yourself and say nothing? Will you prioritize others and remain politically correct? Or will you prioritize God and Stand Up! for the Absolute Truth before the opportunity is lost? After these priorities are examined, seven crucial steps will be presented that Christians must take in order to *Restore America*. Finally, a call to action will be extended with the encouragement that tomorrow has the potential to be better than today.

Why Does It Matter? Parts One through Three have systematically demonstrated how the Gospel of Jesus Christ to be entirely true. We started in Part One by eliminating the most obvious misrepresentations of Truth, and we negated them without relying on the Bible—even though they could have been instantly discredited by pointing out obvious contradictions with the Absolute Truth. They were negated without relying on the Bible to demonstrate how they are illogical concepts even when separated from the Scriptures. Part Two went to great lengths establishing the necessity for the existence of God and then establishing the Bible as Absolute Truth. Since the Bible is entirely true, everything within must also be entirely true. As a result, the exclusivity of Truth was presented, followed by the examination of Jesus Christ and His claims. The crucifixion and resurrection were proved entirely true, and then it was demonstrated how the liar, lunatic, and legend arguments cannot be true. Part Three examined the two largest monotheistic religions and demonstrated how they contradict the one true God and the reasons why they also cannot be considered Absolute Truth.

Now, we have arrived at Part Four, "Linking Liberalism to Moral Depravity." This is an alarming title for a section because America seems to be enamored with liberalism. Why does the presence of liberalism in our nation matter? Why does the state of our nation matter? These very important questions need to be answered for us to grasp the severity of the times and events we currently face. Since it is undeniable that Christianity is entirely true, we can conclude that it is not a mere coincidence that America's extreme blessings are a direct result of the establishment of a Christian nation that was once centered entirely upon the one true God. No other nation has ever come close to enjoying the blessings, freedom, and prosperity of Americans; we have already examined many other nations and have demonstrated this to be an indisputable fact. I ask again: "Why does this matter?" Does it really matter that there is a correlation between our freedom and blessings and our reliance on the Christian faith?

With confidence, I strongly believe that it matters more than you and I could ever imagine. If we believe that America was blessed because of her reliance on God, we must also believe the inverse truth of this principle. If America, and Americans alike, continue to reject the Absolute Truth and entirely reprioritize God out of our lives, then it is not only possible to see the nation's blessings cease, but it is possible for God to punish America for her idolatry (the prioritization of *anything* above God). Does anybody remember the Old Testament prophets who warned Israel time and time again to return to God or suffer the consequences that would accompany their refusal to return to God? (These consequences are to be avoided, and the consequences will be far worse than the risks of simply taking a stand and telling a friend about the love of Jesus Christ!) Without question, this is a simple concept to understand, but when it sinks in that restoration only comes through action (and that Christians actually must step up, stand up, and speak up), we begin to see resistance. This is, as I will demonstrate in Chapter 16, a result of priorities that do not entirely reflect the priorities that the Scriptures have established.

Why do I focus so much on the Christians when they, for the most part, are not the heaviest contributors to America's moral decline? (Are Christians not held to an extremely high moral and ethical standard?) One simple answer: Since the non-Christians reject the Word of God, they cannot be expected to follow the Word of God; they do not hear or recognize the Shepherd's voice.[414] Why do they not recognize His voice? Because they are rejecting the Shepherd who is trying to help them and, as a result, are unable to discern the importance of His message.

Since Christians recognize the Shepherd's voice and understand His commands, it's the Christian that is the hope of America's future. If Christians ignore Christian principles and refuse to make a difference, can we really expect a restoration? It's because of our faith that Christians need to understand modernism and how this liberal theology ultimately compromises the Christian church's ability to make a difference. Essentially, modernism neutralizes Christianity's effectiveness through the propagation of a watered-down and politically correct theology that strips the faith of any true substance. We must examine the invasion of modernism so it can be purged from the church—and from the nation. To shift metaphors, it's an *anchor* that will keep America from moving toward the restoration she desperately needs.

The Deception of Modernism

A Slow Boil. Ever since World War Two, there has been a gradual shift in American morals, values, and thought (at least the change was gradual until November 4, 2008). The day after election day in 2008, there was a new sense of boldness—a new arrogance—with respect to the flaunting of immorality under the guise of *change*, but immorality has actually been brewing for decades (even in the church). Before we can begin to effectively restore America, we need to take a look at modernism to understand how it has gradually been eroding the church and Christians, alike.

What is modernism, and what does it mean? In order to understand modernism, we must first understand the definition. I began searching for

414 John 10:25–28.

the definition by opening up my *Evangelical Dictionary of Theology*, but, to my surprise, there was no definition. Instead of providing a definition, my theological dictionary referred me to an analogous term where the same exact definition would have been provided, but the author saw no reason to be redundant. Would you be surprised to learn that the term *modernism*, in the dictionary of theology, refers the reader to "theological liberalism"? That's precisely what modernism is all about: liberal ideologies that contradict the Bible.

From a Christian perspective, modernism is defined as "the major shift in the theological thinking that occurred in the late nineteenth century. It is an extremely elusive concept. A variety of shades of liberal thinking exist; it has changed character during the passage of time; and the distinctions between liberalism in Europe and North America are considerable."[415] In this book, we are only concerned with the influence it has had on America and the Christian church in America. From the definition, we understand that there has been a "major shift" in theological thinking. What was this major shift, and how has it affected the church?

Transforming the Evangelical Church. Modernism (liberal theology) is an attempt to transform the Christian church into an entity that is politically correct and "consumer sensitive." In this section, we will analyze some of the major fundamental changes that modernism tries to inflict on the evangelical church. In the next section, we examine how fundamentally transforming the Christian faith is devastating; liberalism butchers the faith to the point where first-century Christians would barely recognize it!

Before we begin, we need to define two very important terms as they relate to the teaching of Scripture. The Bible can either be *translated* or *transformed*. These two positions are explained in the following excerpt from *Christian Theology*, written by Millard Erickson:

> The translators are theologians who feel a need for reexpressing the message in a more intelligible form, but intend to retain the content, as one does when translating one language to another. The transformers, however, as the name would indicate, are prepared to make rather

415 Walter A. Elwell, ed., *Evangelical Dictionary of Theology* (Grand Rapids, MI: Baker Academic, 1984), 682.

> serious changes in the *content of the message* in order to relate it to [and appease] the modern world.[416]

Once again, translating the Bible is where the theologian attempts to convey what the Bible would say if written to us in our present situation; it does not alter principles or morals. Instead, it repackages the text so the content can relate in today's society.[417] Even though the purest form of the Bible is found within the original translation and in its original context, it's sometimes necessary to convey the *same principles* in an updated version or scenario in order to reach different people with different backgrounds.

However, liberals "insist that the world has changed since the time Christianity was founded so that biblical terminology and creeds are incomprehensible to people today."[418] In other words, liberal theologians believe that they actually have the authority to alter God's written revelation to man. This is significant because the original text was inspired by God and was without error. When humankind, an inherently sinful being who is not without flaw, begins to alter doctrine and principles, the text's integrity is severely compromised. (Not a good idea.)

Modernism begins a "fundamental transformation" of Scripture by first making the claim that there is a connection between religious ideas, modern culture, and modes of thinking and that they need to be adapted to conform to people living in today's world.[419] Instantly, you should be shocked! When we read the account of Jesus Christ, we remember that Jesus did not conform His religious teachings to the first-century modern culture or modes of thinking. In fact, they were entirely contradictory to the "modern culture and modes of thinking." We need to ask ourselves, "When has God ever conformed—ultimately submitted—His sovereign will to the desires of the temporary entity of humanity? Does God actually exist to please us, or is it vice versa?" Surprisingly, I cannot find one instance in the Bible where Jesus asked the disciples what their "messianic wishes" were so He could meet their needs. Instead, I read where Jesus rebuked Peter the instant he tried to get in the way of God's sovereign will (by attempting to interfere with or prevent the crucifixion).[420]

---

416 Millard Erickson, *Christian Theology*, (Grand Rapids, MI: Baker Academic, 1998), 123, italics added.

417 Ibid, 126.

418 Elwell, 682.

419 Ibid, 683.

420 Matthew 16:21–23.

The second element of liberalism is a "rejection of religious belief based on authority alone."[421] Liberal theology proclaims that all beliefs must pass the test of reason and experience, and one's mind must be open to new facts. This theology also holds that the Bible is the work of writers who were limited by their times and that the Scriptures are neither supernatural nor an infallible record of divine revelation.[422] As a result, liberal theologians claim that the Bible *does not* have "final authority" with respect to laws, morality, and doctrine.

As we dig deeper into liberal theology, we discover a central idea of "divine immanence": God is seen as present and is dwelling in the world (which is, to an extent, true). However, liberal theology neglects to properly convey the principle of transcendence, which teaches that God is also superior to and separate from the world He created. Transcendence was heavily emphasized in the cosmological argument because God must be separate from that which He created.

Problems arise when immanence is skewed out of proportion. When immanence is overemphasized, God essentially becomes "one of us," and people lose reverence for God because, over time, they do not perceive or realize the vast difference between God and man. When God is trivialized, people eventually lose a fear—an awe or respect—of God and his commands. King Solomon revealed to us that "The fear of the Lord is the beginning of wisdom, and knowledge of the Holy One is understanding."[423] The inverse of this principle is scary because in the absence of a proper fear of God, people become defiant.

When God is trivialized to the point where liberal theologians lose their healthy fear of Him, *only then* can a group of theologians begin to confidently alter Scripture in an attempt to try and make the Word of God conform to mankind and cater to what "feels good" or what is politically correct or to what people want to hear. In the real world, God does not cater to the wishes of mankind. This becomes evident when we use simple math: Unaltered New Testament Doctrine + Malachi 3:6 ≠ Fundamentally Transformed Liberal Theology. Furthermore, Chapter 8 has already demonstrated how Scripture *is* without error and is the final authority in its final form. (In other words, God's word is perfect, even without liberal revision.)

421 Elwell, 683.

422 Ibid.

423 Proverbs 9:10.

Now that we know the method in which modernism has tried to gain credibility, we need to know how modernism is affecting the Christian church. Next, we will break down modernism and examine how it neutralizes the church's ability to initiate a revitalization of the Christian nation.

The Effects of Modernism. Before I wrote this section, I had heard a lot of talk about modernism and how it was compromising the church, but the consequences of modernism really did not hit home until I read *God in the Wasteland: The Reality of Truth in a World of Fading Dreams* by David Wells. The title of this book does not sound too promising, but don't get too excited, because the content is not exactly comforting either: the author paints an accurate picture of the state of the church in the Christian nation (that is, morally deteriorating from the inside out). I can promise you that Wells and I do not enjoy writing about the moral depravity of America, but somebody has to point it out; somebody has STAND UP! for Truth and (yes) even risk our *beloved popularity*! My greatest desire is to write about how America has reversed her course and refocused her priority and how so many people are coming to Christ that Christians are actually running out of people to evangelize!

Nevertheless, we are not at that point (yet). In the meantime, we need to examine some of the content within Wells's book. Wells points out some very inconvenient truths about modernism as a significant contributor to America's obvious collapse in morality. We note our depraved state when we look back at the schools and how chewing gum used to be a serious offense, but today some schools force their students to walk through metal detectors to protect the faculty from being attacked or even murdered; most high schools have campus police. Exotic dancing used to be what Elvis did; now exotic dancers are nude. Television programming used to reflect family values, but now reality TV destroys family values because it gravitates toward some of the most dysfunctional families imaginable. Somehow, the dysfunction is entertaining (otherwise it would not be on television). Murder used to be an abomination, but in today's society, liberals advocate that the murder of innocent children is not only legal, but the *right* of a mother. The list goes on, but we can already see the downward trend. How we got to this point is our next focus.

In his book, Wells pointed out that "modernity" is distinguished from "modernism." Modernity produces changes in the outer fabric of life; modernism alters the values and meanings that emerge from within the context of the modern world. Modernism constitutes the values and meanings that, in the contemporary context, seem altogether normal and natural.[424]

Modernity consists of beneficial technology that enables us to produce products with less cost, time, and effort. Modernity has enabled the discovery of new medicines that cure disease and led to the eradication of smallpox. Modernity, with all its advancements, has drastically changed our lives for the better, but we must be mindful that while humans continually advance and change, God is already perfect. Since God is perfect in every way, God will never change (Malachi 3:6), and this is the inherent problem with modernism—and why it fails to be credible.

Modernism is trying to change the Gospel message (which God already perfected) in order to cater to humanity, but in this attempt it diminishes the soul, creates "hollow people," and ultimately compromises the evangelical church.[425] These are pretty sharp accusations, but they are easily verified. Modernism has slowly crept into our society—like a slow boil—but it is a profound revolution, and its consequences are far reaching. Modernism is considered liberal theology because it has altered the Gospel of Jesus Christ into a religion of "consumer satisfaction," elevating the fulfillment of the self over the service and the worship of an almighty God.[426] Hence the name "liberal theology": the doctrine literally liberates the liberal from the authority of God—which would appear to be normal because that person was taught that Scripture was never intended to be the final authority. However, there is one problem: Truth is always indifferent to opinion. Therefore, feelings, in regard to truth, are irrelevant and meaningless. In short, liberals can certainly believe in whatever makes them feel better, but their *feelings* will never alter truth.

To many, feelings are of utmost importance, and this is precisely how modernism has flourished in America. Modernism has infected the evangelical church because many churches in America feel the need to conform to a consumer-driven market. As consumers, we sometimes find ourselves focused on our needs and what we can get out of a church versus how we can serve the church. In looking for a church, we look for the benefits the church can offer our family versus how we can get involved and invest our lives into that church. Instead of looking for a church with the most theologically correct doctrine, we look for a user-friendly church

424 David F. Wells, *God in the Wasteland.* (Grand Rapids, MI: Eerdmans, 1994), 7.

425 Ibid., 13–16.

426 Ibid, 45.

that has good music and ends services promptly. Instead of "asking God to bless our food" when we eat, we ask "who is going to say the blessing," as if we bless our own food. These are generalizations, but they accurately depict a consumer mentality with respect to Christianity and how liberalism prioritizes *the self* over God and the Bible.

Since Americans are consumer oriented, it's not a shock to discover that modernism has enticed many churches into meshing the Christian faith with modern culture. As a result, some churches are replacing Truth with a noncontroversial message that omits foundational principles of the Christian faith (such as sin, confession, and repentance).[427] The flaw with the church having a consumer mentality is that "neither Christ nor his truth can be marketed by appealing to consumer interest, because the premise of all marketing is that the consumer's need is sovereign, that the customer is always right, and this is precisely what the gospel insists cannot be the case."[428] Essentially, liberalism teaches a Gospel that consists of "a God without wrath bringing people without sin into a kingdom without judgment through a Christ without a cross."[429] Could liberalism be any farther than the truth?

Nevertheless, modernism has sought to mesh the Christian faith with modern culture by ultimately substituting a noncontroversial message in place of the truth. When sin, confession, and repentance are left out, God becomes "weightless." The problem of sin and the need for confession and repentance generate reliance upon God, but liberal theologians tear down this concept, teaching that sin is "imperfection, ignorance, maladjustment and immaturity, not the fundamental flaw in the universe."[430]

Since most people do not like the idea of a Final Judgment, liberalism omits this teaching. Since most people do not like the idea of a very explicit moral standard that all people must comply with, liberalism omits this teaching. Since most people do not like the idea that they are sinful (much less that they must confess to God and ask for forgiveness), liberalism omits this teaching. The wages of sin is death, but since it's not politically correct or popular to teach that refusing to accept salvation leads to death, liberalism omits this teaching.

---

427 Ibid., 82–84.

428 Ibid., 82.

429 Niebuhr, *The Kingdom of God in America* (New York: Harper Torchbooks, 1953), 191–192.

430 Elwell, 683.

The consequences are unavoidable: when the foundational doctrine is removed, God becomes "weightless." The only reason people may not fear God is because they really have no clue who God is or the power that He has. Truly understanding God will bring a reverence—a fear of God Almighty—that most people do not have.

Furthermore (and I find this astonishing), the weightlessness of God that modernism creates can actually distort Christianity so badly that it has enabled some *Christians* to justify voting liberal politicians into office who support political policies that *contradict the Bible*! This is absurdity and madness: the Bible, by definition, is conservative because it makes an exclusive claim on Truth and explicitly establishes right and wrong. Yet somehow Christians are voting for politicians who reject Christian values.

Let me be frank: Modernism is analogous to liberalism. Liberalism *is* immoral. If a Christian votes for a liberal politician, that person was either ignorant or immoral at the time they voted; there are no other categories in which to place that person! Allow me to explain this controversial position in the next section.

The Immorality of Liberalism

More than 'Just a Feeling.' Liberalism, in either its political or theological form, by definition, contradicts the Bible, which is far more than a *liberating* feeling. I contend that it is impossible to embrace liberal theological or political views (such as the ones covered in this section) and be considered an obedient Christian. People who cannot handle an accurate portrayal of the Truth may be offended—but truth is indifferent to opinion. Also, let it be known that I am not passing any judgment on anybody; I am merely presenting to you what the Absolute Truth (your God) has revealed in regard to these topics. It would not be possible for me to judge because I'm also a wretched sinner saved by the grace and mercy of Jesus Christ. The fact that I'm not perfect does not inhibit my presentation of the moral and ethical standards by which God will one day judge humanity. I am merely the messenger; the Perfect One wrote it.

In this section, we will show that many of the positions that liberalism endorses explicitly contradict Christianity and the teachings of Bible. I will also demonstrate how a person who votes liberal is either ignorant or immoral. (I'm pretty sure that this liberal rant will ruin my chance at a Nobel Peace Prize, but I'll risk it anyway.) Nevertheless, liberalism is defined in the dictionary as "a movement in modern Protestantism that emphasizes *freedom from tradition and authority*, the adjustment of religious beliefs to scientific conceptions, and the development of spiritual capacities."[431] In essence, the movement is separating itself from the original teachings of Christianity, but when it comes to *doctrine*, Christians cannot be liberal because we do not have the authority to transform the Gospel. We are not the author; we merely teach what has already been established for thousands of years.

Before we get too far into the topic, it must be said that not all "liberalism" is bad. Even though I cringe at this concept (due to its usual meaning and implication), I know it contains truth because some aspects of Christianity challenge Christians to be *very liberal.* Pastors also need their congregations to have a limited sense of liberality. With respect to the church's tithe and offering, give liberally. With respect to loving and praying for others, liberally offer yourself and your services to fellow believers and nonbelievers alike. When it comes to having compassion and caring for the poor, aid those in need liberally. When it comes to evangelism, share the Gospel liberally and with as many people as possible.

However, when it comes to doctrine, it's impossible to take a liberal position because truth, by nature, is conservative. Remember: "All truth is narrow and all truth is exclusive—truth cannot reach out and say you're right, you're right and you're right" when multiple contradictory truth claims exist.[432] Since Jesus makes an exclusive truth claim with respect to salvation, and since He does not change, God is by definition conservative because God "maintains existing views, conditions or instructions" and is traditional.[433] We now venture into some of the controversial topics that liberalism embraces.

Murdering Innocent Children. The fact that this issue even needs to be covered disturbs me. Nevertheless, some Christians have voted for politicians who endorse the murder of innocent children. Before we proceed, we need to set some definitions so that we never call this process "moral" or "acceptable" again. Abortion is the murder of an innocent

431 Liberalism. Dictionary.com. *Dictionary.com Unabridged.* Random House, Inc. http://dictionary.reference.com/browse/liberalism (accessed: November 17, 2009). (emphasis added).

432 Dr. Richard Lee, *What Should We Believe? Why is Jesus the Only Way to God?* There's Hope Ministries, 1998.

433 Even though Christianity is an extension of Judaism, God never changed. His sovereign will was fulfilled as prophesied in the Old Testament.

child. First, Webster's primary definition for *child* is "an unborn or recently born person."[434] Second, *abortion* is defined as "the termination of pregnancy after, accompanied by, resulting in, or closely followed by the death of the embryo or fetus: as **a:** spontaneous expulsion of a human fetus during the first twelve weeks of gestation."[435] Lastly, the definition of *murder* is "the crime of unlawfully killing a person especially with malice aforethought."[436]

After we reflect on the definitions, we must conclude that a child, by definition, is considered a person, and that definition even extends to the unborn. We know that all people have rights such as life, liberty, and the pursuit of happiness; among others endowed by our Creator. Those rights are precious and are not to be violated; this is why we have the Constitution and a penal code that is designed to protect our rights. In a moral society, we must respect those God-given rights. However, abortion is a direct infringement of those rights against a person incapable of self-defense. Abortion is murder because the cause of death is directly attributed to a premeditated action with malice aforethought that resulted in the loss of life. Essentially, the mother deprived a defenseless child (her own flesh and blood) of his or her life.

The only part of the definition that is missing is the "unlawful killing" part of the murder definition; this is where the controversy lies. Under our law, it's illegal to murder a child, youth, adult, or senior, but somehow the murder of an unborn infant—under America's law—is permissible. Is the murder of an innocent child lawful in the eyes of God? Does the Bible address the topic? If you are looking for a commandment that states, "Thou shalt not commit abortion," it does not exist. However, this does not in any way imply that the Bible is silent on the issue. In fact, the Bible is far from silent on the issue, and we will now discover what the Bible teaches in regard to abortion.

First, we begin with the Ten Commandments. Exodus 20:13 reads: "You shall not murder." Murder is an act that results in a loss of life in cold blood (a state of mind marked by premeditation and deliberateness).[437]

---

434 Child. In Merriam-Webster Online Dictionary. Retrieved November 18, 2009, from http://www.merriam-webster.com/dictionary/child.

435 Abortion. In Merriam-Webster Online Dictionary. Retrieved November 18, 2009, from http://www.merriam-webster.com/dictionary/abortion.

436 Murder. In Merriam-Webster Online Dictionary. Retrieved November 18, 2009, from http://www.merriam-webster.com/dictionary/murder.

437 Cold blood. Merriam-Webster's Dictionary of Law. Retrieved November 18, 2009, from Dictionary.com website: http://dictionary.reference.com/browse/cold blood.

Since an unborn child is a human being, and that child was murdered in premeditated and deliberate cold blood, the act contradicts the moral will of God. It's amazing how simple this concept is, yet some are in denial. Thankfully, the Ten Commandments is not the only place where the murder of children is addressed. Supporting verses in Scripture clarify that abortion is immoral, as presented in the *Evangelical Dictionary of Theology*:[438]

- The sovereignty of God and the recognition that issues of life and death are His domain (Job 12:10; 33:4; Psalms 104:29; Acts 17:25)
- Creation theology, affirming the dignity, the value, and the sanctity of human life created in God's image (Genesis 1:26–27)
- The forthright biblical injunctions against other forms of infanticide practiced in the ancient world (e.g., Leviticus 18:21; 20:2–5; Deuteronomy 12:31)
- The personhood of the embryo or human fetus based upon Old Testament legal precedent (i.e., the principle of *lex talionis*; cf. Exodus 21:22–25. Note the divergences in the English renditions of the passage at two key points: the trauma of the assault resulting in premature birth [NIV] or "miscarriage" [NSRV]; and the application of talion law to the battered woman only [NJB] or to the battered woman and the prematurely born child(ren) [cf. U. Cassuto, *Commentary on the Book of Exodus*, 275–277]; for a detailed discussion on this crucial Old Testament text, see H. W. House, "Miscarriage or Premature Birth; Additional Thoughts on Exodus 21:22–25," WmTJ: 108–23.)
- The personhood of the embryo or human fetus based upon the continuity principle (i.e., one's humanness and personal identity begins at conception, Luke 1:41, 44; 2:12, 16 [where same Greek word *brēphos*, "child," is used for both the fetus in the womb and a newborn infant]; cf. Psalms 139:11–16; Jeremiah 1:5; Isaiah 49:1, 5; Galatians 1:15)
- The priesthood of the embryo or human fetus on the basis of imputed sin as a result of the fall of humanity (cf. Psalms 51:5; 58:3; Romans 5:12–14)

438 Elwell, 16–17.

- The biblical limitations restricting the freedom of choice or the right of self-determination that a (Christian) woman has over her own body (cf. 1 Corinthians 6:18–7:5)
- The biblical ethic of love for all and nonviolence against all persons (including the human embryo or fetus since the Bible grants personhood to the unborn entity; cf. Leviticus 19:18; Matthew 5:38–43; 22:34–40; Romans 13:8–10; etc.)

The people who claim that the Bible is silent on the issue of abortion are truly unaware of the numerous verses that address the issue from multiple perspectives, but the universal message is that the Bible condemns the murder of children. Since it has been demonstrated that the Bible is the one source of Absolute Truth, it's an undeniable fact that a human embryo is a person simply because the Bible recognizes the unborn child as a human being. Since the embryo is a person, the deliberate and premeditated murder of that person (who has *rights*) is immoral because it violates one of the Ten Commandments, which explicitly states that murder is wrong. The conclusion of this topic is that abortion is immoral and that a Christian cannot be in agreement with the Scriptures and at the same time endorse abortion or support a candidate who endorses the murder of innocent children.

Homosexuality. Homosexuality is the "sexual desire directed toward members of one's own sex."[439] Without question, homosexuality has been an issue for thousands of years; this sin is nothing new. However, as Christians, we must be careful to target our disagreement to the act and *never toward the person*. Jesus Christ died for all people, and we must love all people in the name of Jesus.[440] However, God severely condemns the act of homosexuality; it's referred to in the Bible as an "abomination." Since God strongly condemns the act, frankly the opinions of Christians do not matter with respect to the issue because God settled it. Christians must endorse the position that God takes in order to be within the moral will of God.

Homosexuality is often the object of unjustified ridicule, hate, and sometimes violence. Christians must not resort to treating homosexuals unfairly. Christians need to love them and encourage them to turn from their sin through a presentation of the Gospel. Since homosexuality is

439 Ibid., 574.

440 Romans 5:6, 8.

a sin, it is just like adultery, theft, or murder. Even if you claim that homosexuality is nature over nurture in an attempt to justify it, your excuse is still not good enough. This becomes obvious when we note that if a person was born with a natural tendency to be more violent than ninety percent of the population (and yes, violent tendencies can be genetic in origin[441]), would the courts permit the rape, torture, and murder of innocent people on the "nature" claim? Would we really allow those actions to go unpunished because the offender was more "at risk" than the rest of the population?

The above example is extreme, but the principle is just as applicable to homosexuality as it is to murder because virtually every sin imaginable can ultimately be reduced to a choice. Nobody is righteous; therefore nobody can judge except God. However, we are able to convey biblical principles, which need to be taught *and upheld* by the nation, in order to be in compliance with God's moral will. Since God does not recognize marriage between one man and another man or one woman and another woman, Christians are not able to support gay marriage (Genesis 2:24). Since God recognizes marriage as a covenant between only a man and a woman, the issue is not up for interpretation, nor can it be justified upon any excuse. The biblical verses that denounce homosexuality and gay marriage are as follows:[442]

- Leviticus 18:22: "You shall not lie with a male as with a woman. It is an abomination."
- Leviticus 20:13: "If a man lies with a male as he lies with a woman, both of them have committed an abomination. They shall surely be put to death. Their blood shall be upon them."
- Deuteronomy 23:18: "You shall not bring the wages of a harlot or the price of a dog [homosexual] to the house of the LORD your God for any vowed offering, for both of these *are* an abomination to the LORD."
- 1 Corinthians 6:9-11: "Do you not know that the unrighteous will not inherit the kingdom of God? Do not be deceived. Neither fornicators, nor idolaters, nor adulterers, nor homosexuals, nor sodomites, nor thieves, nor covetous, nor

441 *Discover* magazine, "Violence, Genes, and Prejudice," http://discovermagazine.com/1994/nov/violencegenesand446

442 All verses are from NKJV.

drunkards, nor revilers, nor extortioners will inherit the kingdom of God. And such were some of you. But you were washed, but you were sanctified, but you were justified in the name of the Lord Jesus and by the Spirit of our God."

- Romans 1:27: "Likewise also the men, leaving the natural use of the woman, burned in their lust for one another, men with men committing what is shameful, and receiving in themselves the penalty of their error which was due."
- Jude 7: "... Sodom and Gomorrah, and the cities around them in a similar manner to these, having given themselves over to sexual immorality and gone after strange flesh [or the same sex], are set forth as an example, suffering the vengeance of eternal fire."
- 2 Peter 2:6-7: "and turning the cities of Sodom and Gomorrah into ashes, [God] condemned them to destruction, making them an example to those who afterward would live ungodly; and delivered righteous Lot, who was oppressed by the filthy conduct of the wicked."[443]
- Genesis 2:24 "Therefore a man shall leave his father and mother and be joined to his wife, and they shall become one flesh."

The Scriptures, in both the Old and New Testaments, are certainly not silent on the issue of homosexuality. Once again, this particular sin is actually regarded *by God* as an abomination—which is defined as "vile, shameful, or detestable action, condition, habit." Homosexuality is one of a few sins that are severely condemned as it is exceedingly vile, shameful, and detestable unto a *holy* God. Why is this sin such an abomination to God? Romans 1:27 provides part of the answer when this verse states "leaving the natural use of the woman." Homosexuality is simply not natural, it's a perversion of that which God originally created. If it were natural, then the human race would cease to exist; this is not hard to figure out. Gay marriage makes a mockery out of the institution of marriage that God designed. Genesis 2:24 specifically states that a man and woman will be united together to create "one flesh," and this is symbolic of marriage. The

443 Traditionally, Sodom and Gomorrah were destroyed through divine judgment. The cause of their judgment was their habitual sin of engaging in perverted activities such as homosexuality. Hence, the term "sodomy" comes from the destruction of Sodom.

institution of marriage between a male and female is natural, and that was how God designed the joining of two lives. The varying opinions of Christians carry no weight because it was settled by God.

Unfortunately, Christians catch a tremendous amount of flak for merely enforcing or teaching God's moral law, but the Christian must stand for righteousness in order to be in compliance with God's law. We recall that the law is the lowest standard to which people are allowed to stoop without punishment. Laws are the minimum standard, but the goal is not to live as leniently as possible. On the contrary, people should strive to live as righteously as possible in order to truly enjoy the fruit of the Spirit.[444] Nevertheless, it is not possible for a Christian both to willingly support, defend, endorse, or vote for a candidate who supports gay marriage and to be in compliance with God's moral law.

Socialism. Socialism is not change you can believe in, because it is government-sanctioned theft, against your will, at the point of a gun, period.[445] In any socialistic society, the government takes money from one group of people (the producers) in order to give it to another, who did not earn nor do they deserve that money (the moochers), but this process can only be achieved through the sanction of government (the looters); otherwise it would be illegal.[446]

The legality of socialism is an elusive topic, and it seems to be the central issue. Some people claim that socialism is theft; others claim that redistributing the wealth is beneficial because it helps the *collective* well-being of society. However, we must distinguish between what is legal and what is moral. This is a critical point because what's legal in America may not actually be moral (or permitted by God's moral law, which has already been proven to be Absolute Truth). We intuitively know that this principle is true because the government can make anything *legal.* As we have seen in Massachusetts (with respect to Senate seats), if one party is in power, the government can manipulate and change laws to suit very specific goals

444 Galatians 5:22–23.

445 All tax revenue is reduced to being collected at the point of a gun. If you refuse to pay the government the amount that they claim you owe, the police will come knocking on your door to take you into custody (because refusing to pay your taxes is a crime). If you refuse to be voluntarily taken into custody, the process is further reduced to being arrested at the point of a gun.

446 The concept of producers, looters, and moochers is taken from *Atlas Shrugged,* by Ayn Rand. Since Rand was an atheist, Christians should only espouse the economic principles and disregard the theological principles set forth in the book.

by utilizing a double standard. The government can also make abhorrent acts (such as murdering innocent children) legal and permissible by *our laws* even though they defy the moral law. Therefore, the "legality" of socialism is not of any concern in this section; instead, we must examine the *morality* of socialism.

There is a very specific reason as to why we, as Americans, must examine the morality of socialism versus the legality. First, as a free nation, we deeply depend on morality in order to sustain our freedom. Second, but most importantly, the legality of anything is subject to continual change (dependent upon those elected to office), but the moral law is constant. God's moral law never changes because God is forever the same—yesterday, today, and tomorrow. We *must* have a constant to test the legality of anything; otherwise nothing would be concrete, and we would wander aimlessly from one popular idea to the next.

To demonstrate the immorality of socialism, we must venture into an example that does not include the government (because governments make their own rules, which may or may not be moral). If *anybody* were to amass a group of people with the intent to steal money from a billionaire in order to achieve social justice and give to the needy, it would be punishable under our penal code as the crime of theft. The dictionary defines theft as "the act of stealing; the wrongful taking and carrying away of the personal goods or property of another." It's against the moral law to take what is not yours, and your intent does not matter: regardless of whether you intend to keep the plunder for yourself or give it away, theft is always immoral. (And yes, Robin Hood was a thief who violated God's moral law. If Robin Hood were the government, would the action somehow become moral or *social justice*?)

Most people would agree with me that armed robbery of a bank by an individual who intends to give away the plunder is still immoral. Since the immorality in this example is so obvious, socialism must be enacted through another medium. There must be another entity that has the power and the authority to collect money and then disburse it as they see fit. This is precisely where the government comes into the equation. Since the government is also collecting taxes to pay for national defense, schools, roads, and other necessities, what better organization to help bring about the socialist utopia? This is precisely why governments are so enticing to socialists. (The government has power and more guns to induce change.)

The common objection to the argument against socialism is that taxes are "legal" and that they are *required* to sustain the nation. This is true, to an extent. Taxes are necessary for funding the military, providing education, maintaining roads and infrastructure—but where the line is drawn is when the government takes money from one group only to turn around and give it to another group (which coincidentally buys someone's vote)! The government's job description has never included handing out money or financially supporting its citizens. Taking money from the government creates a dependent, and dependency destroys freedom. The Constitution establishes our freedom, but socialism is destroying freedom for both producers and moochers. The only entity that benefits and becomes more powerful from socialism is the government (the looters). Nevertheless, producers find their freedom destroyed because they can no longer *willingly* give to the less fortunate (through charity), while the moocher's freedom is destroyed because the receiver is always slave to the provider.[447] (You already know this because when you were dependent upon your parents for money, you had to comply with their rules.)

We must recognize that the government is engaging in an identical activity as the individual committing armed robbery to give to the poor. The only difference is that the process is justified as "legal" because the government establishes legality. As I promised, we will examine whether socialism is moral when contrasted with a constant, God's moral law.

In the Ten Commandments, the Bible reads: "You shall not steal."[448] To steal, by definition, is "to take away by force or by unjustified means." The government certainly takes the money by force, but is the government justified in taking that money in the form of taxes? Once again, we turn to the Bible for the answer. Paul addressed this issue in his second letter to the Thessalonians: "Even when we were with you, we gave you this rule: 'If a man will not work, he shall not eat.' We hear that some among you are idle. They are not busy; they are busybodies. Such people we command and urge in the Lord Jesus Christ to settle down *and earn the bread they eat*."[449] This is a mighty inconvenient verse for socialism because the principle in these verses is that people must earn—they must work—for their keep. The Apostle Paul is chastising the very notion of one group being forced to support another.

However, socialists are not entirely biblically illiterate. Some socialists have tried to use the Bible as support for socialism because the book of Acts reveals that many people sold their possessions to *give* to anyone who

447 Proverbs 22:7.

448 Exodus 20:15.

449 2 Thessalonians 3:10–12 (emphasis added).

had need. This is a very exciting passage because of its immense love and charity, but this practice is distinct from socialism because the people *gave*, of their own accord, whereas the government *forces* people to financially support others by giving dependents what they have not earned. Many times I have heard that the concept of socialism is taught in the book of Acts, but this is not true. Acts 2:44–47 reads (emphasis added):

> All the believers were together and had everything in common. Selling their possessions and goods, they *gave* to anyone as he had need. Every day they continued to meet together in the temple courts. They broke bread in their homes and ate together with glad and sincere hearts, praising God and enjoying the favor of all the people. And the Lord added to their number daily those who were being saved.

This is a marvelous example of the unity, community, and collective desire of the early Christians to help their fellow Christians out, but notice the word that was italicized: *gave*. The early Christians were selling their property and possessions of their own accord and were *giving* the proceeds to those in need. This, by definition, cannot be socialism because the action was voluntary and not forced through the law. The notion that the Bible advocates socialism is a fundamentally flawed myth because socialism forces the producer to give, while the Bible reveals *charity* (which is a choice). When people freely give, it is done of their own accord. When the government forces a person to give against their will, it is theft; many seem to overlook this profound difference.

The fact is that God loves a *cheerful* giver[450]—not one who is forced by a government to meet social justice or political gain (purchasing votes in the process). *Cheerful* is defined by the dictionary as "in good spirits." I don't know about you, but when I'm forced to give to another person, I lose my cheer. Just as a slave, who is forced to work, is devoid of cheer, so a taxpayer, who has no choice but to support others, also loses his cheer.

The Unsustainable, but Intentional 'Pit-Stop.' There is absolutely no question that socialism is immoral and that the system deprives all people (both producers and moochers) of their freedom. The Constitution of the United States is a one-of-a-kind document that establishes freedom that

450 2 Corinthians 9:7.

is *unprecedented*; freedom of this magnitude had never been seen before! It would seem reasonable to suggest that the freedom we possess is the greatest part of America and that we, as Americans, would never want to surrender our freedom to the government. Was freedom not the very reason that the early explorers created the colonies, so that they could leave their oppressive governments in order to pursue life, liberty, and happiness?

If freedom is our most cherished possession, the next question we must ask is "If socialism destroys our freedom, why do so many people endorse the ideology?" Why are people so enamored with the concept and the fundamental change it *will* bring to every aspect of American life? Perhaps there is a great socialistic movement in America because people do not know the founders or socialism's purpose. If people really knew what socialism was or the direction that it forces a nation to travel, would they really embrace the destruction of their own freedom?

"[Karl] Marx defined socialism as a pit-stop between capitalism and communism. It isn't an end point. While sometimes this change happens slowly, it always ends badly ..."[451] It's sobering to point out that the euphoria that socialism creates is *temporary*; by design the ideology will mash the accelerator, thrusting any nation that embraces it into a form of government where the people are subject to tyranny. The people are subject to tyranny because as a nation moves away from capitalism, freedom is inherently lost. Socialism destroys economic freedom because it mandates the redistribution of wealth against your will, but when the unsustainable system collapses, the end result, as Marx gloats, is communism, where all freedom is lost to the will of an all-powerful government. An all-powerful government is to be avoided at all costs because if a government safeguards your rights, the government can also take them away.[452] It's not a coincidence that communism has great potential to lead to oppression. Not all dictators are tyrants, but all tyrants are dictators. (Hitler, Mao, Stalin, and Hussein were all dictators, and they all committed heinous crimes against humanity. This, in Marx's own words, is socialism's *final destination.*)

The Empty Reservoir. How could Marx so confidently gloat that socialism is a mere pit-stop to his beloved communism? Marx understood that socialism is unsustainable by the very economic atmosphere that it

451 Glenn Beck, "The Revolutionary Holocaust: Live Free or Die," aired January 22, 2010.

452 The government's role is never to provide rights; they are endowed by our Creator.

creates. Eventually, the money that the government steals will dissipate because the minority is unable to support the majority—but, also because the producers will gradually withdraw their compliance and *refuse* to support the group of government-dependent moochers.

When socialism is implemented, productivity is curbed because there is no longer an incentive to produce beyond the optimal tax bracket. Socialism is not free; the money that the government gives away has to come from somewhere! Since the government only consumes money, it must raise taxes to fund the new social programs (no surprise as to why universal health care will force you to pay more taxes). However, there is a point when honest, hardworking people will refuse to work and financially support the system that is destroying their freedom. Whether the loss of productivity stems from a moral or an economic root, people are encouraged to reduce production when over half of their income is taken away by Uncle Sam. This is problematic because most of the taxes are paid by only a few people (the *progressive* tax system). When the highest producers withdraw their support, they create a vacuum that must be filled. Naturally, the tax burden must move downward, and this affects the middle class. The middle class fill the void with their tax contributions because the government still has bills to pay and they have a social obligation—they have made promises—to continue to redistribute wealth.

The equalization process is inherently flawed because not all people are equal. This becomes obvious when we look at bank accounts, test scores, intelligence, and physical fitness. Not all people are equal, but all people must be given the same rights and opportunities to maximize their potential and ability to pursue the American dream. Success is not promised, but the opportunity to freely pursue that dream must exist without government interference.

The equalization process is also flawed because the reservoir that the government depends upon lies within the highest producers. Eventually, that reservoir of money that the government depends upon will dry up because the producers will have quit or because the government has taken all their money, leaving nothing more to steal. (It's impossible to steal from somebody who has nothing.) When the reservoir is barren, the system will implode. By design, the overall result, as Marx gloats, is a restructuring of government that leads to communism because, at that point, there will be a national emergency, and in desperation, the people will even sacrifice their own freedom for what they perceive to be security. (God have mercy upon those people ...)

There is no question that communism is abhorrently immoral and has led to some of the greatest tragedies and mass murders of the twentieth century (approximately 100 million murders among all the tyrants), but what about socialism? Does socialism become abhorrently immoral because it was designed as a pit-stop or segue to communism? Let's rephrase the question: If you push a person out of an airplane with no parachute, is it a crime only after the person hits the ground and dies? Are we really to believe that the actions causing inevitable death are purely innocent? If socialism is moral, then pushing somebody out of a plane must also be moral. (It must have been mere coincidence that both led to a horrific ending …)

We know that socialism is unsustainable and that it was designed to implode, to lead to communism. We know that socialism deprives all people of freedom. We know that socialism creates an atmosphere where production is punished. We know that socialism encourages laziness through dependency on the government. We know that socialism is ultimately reduced to theft because the entire process is a *crime* once the government entity is removed from the equation. Why would anybody willingly vote for a candidate whose *highest goal* is to destroy the American dream, the Christian nation, our freedom and all the blessings that accompany reliance upon Jesus Christ? Socialism is madness, and it must be stopped!

The conclusion is that socialism is legalized theft on the part of the government; otherwise, the process of redistributing wealth would be illegal. Since theft is immoral, it contradicts the moral principles set forth in the Bible. Therefore, socialism is immoral, and a Christian is unable to support or endorse a socialistic candidate and still be within the moral law set forth by God.

The Harsh Reality. Let us apply common sense to the issue of voting for politicians and being obedient to the moral will of God. We know that these three controversial issues are positions that, more often than not, liberals espouse. This is a major problem because each issue blatantly contradicts the moral law set forth by God, and this creates a conflict for any Christian seeking to vote for a liberal politician. The contradictory nature of these positions has been supported by ample verses from the Bible, and it's impossible to deny these facts—unless the Bible is *transformed* into some diluted man-made book of stories and ideas that need to be altered in order to force the Bible to fit an overarching liberal agenda. Thus, we see how transforming the Word caters to liberalism.

The only way liberals can convince Christians to support their immoral agenda is to exploit the Christian base of voters by convincing them that *transforming* the Bible is not only permissible but necessary for twenty-first-century people. If Christians can somehow be convinced that abortion, homosexuality, and socialism (among many other issues) are moral, then liberalism has established an enormous voter base in the Christian nation. Recall that Chapter 4 disproved pantheism because the house was divided and it could not stand. The exact same principle is applicable with respect to our Christian heritage. If the Christian nation is divided against itself, we will cease to be a Christian nation, and we will turn against our own Judeo-Christian ethic.

Granted, these topics are controversial, and to name them as immoral is not politically correct, but then again we must also remember that God did not consult us for our opinion. God created His moral law without our input. The law *is* the law, regardless of opinion. Since right and wrong actually exist, and the Bible explicitly denounces each of these stances, we see how it would be immoral, and against God's moral law, to support a candidate who endorses the murder of innocent children, homosexuality, gay marriage, or socialism. (This is but common sense when Christian morals are applied to the act of voting.)

Now, we return to the original issue where I stated that voting for a liberal candidate is either immoral or was done out of ignorance. The dictionary defines *immorality* as "a violation of moral principles [or laws]." Since God created the moral law, and each of the three positions directly contradicts the moral principles set forth by the Bible, they are, by definition, immoral. Following this rationale, it's easy to see how supporting or endorsing these positions (through voting) must also be immoral.

However, some people may have cast an immoral vote without fully understanding the biblical standard of morality, or they may have cast a vote without fully understanding the position of each candidate on these issues. Either way, these people fall into the category where their vote was cast in ignorance (the state of not knowing). The next question concerns accountability. Even though the vote was cast in ignorance, is their vote still to be considered to be an immoral act? If a person chooses to support a candidate whose stances violate God's moral law, is that person in violation of God's moral law? To try and answer this question, we turn to the application of our laws in our judicial system.

Since we do not know God's *entire* judgment process, we cannot explicitly give a definitive answer per the Bible. Instead of venturing into speculation as to the entire judgment process, we can examine *our* law and its application (which is far inferior to God's) in search of an answer. In our judicial system, ignorance of the law does not excuse a violation. If a person intentionally or unintentionally breaks the law, that person is still held accountable for the violation. If the violation was of a criminal nature, charges will be brought, a trial will commence, and a judge (if the defendant is found guilty) will ultimately judge the convicted criminal. Even if the criminal was unaware of the law, ignorance of the law is not an excuse, nor would it be an acceptable defense in court. Ignorance of the law is a principle that conveys the importance of being aware of the law.

When the Word of God is examined and the moral standards that God established are presented, it becomes obvious how any voter who votes for a candidate (who supports any one of the three previous positions) is either immoral or ignorant—but we must also note that *both* threaten the existence of our Christian nation. Immoral and ignorant voting threaten our Christian nation because freedom entails responsibility. Irresponsible voting and the support of immoral candidates compromise our nation's relationship with the one true God. Since all blessings come from God, we see how depravity ultimately leads to disfavor (the recurring theme of the Old Testament prophets).

The Lesser of Two Evils. In elections, there are sometimes situations where the two opposing candidates *appear* to be equally immoral and virtually indistinguishable. Even though this is not an ideal situation, this dilemma will sometimes present itself and can be problematic when trying to decide which candidate to support through voting. When this situation arises, we must decide which candidate will ultimately win our vote, even though neither candidate fully represents the Christian values. Even in this situation, Christians can discern the best candidate by examining each politician's voting record and the values they endorse.

Since we know that no two people can be exactly alike, there will always be some differences between the two candidates with respect to the issues that each of the candidates endorse. In most cases, one will better align with Christianity's standard of morality than the other. Therefore, it is expedient to vote for the lesser of two evils by voting for the candidate that aligns the *most* with the Judeo-Christian ethic. But what if that candidate goes back on promises made during the campaign?

Even after we vote for the candidate who is best aligned with the Christian ethic, we may still vote in a way that contradicts biblical values, or that candidate may turn from positions advocated earlier. This dilemma underscores the importance, and ultimately the necessity, of selecting good candidates. An entirely different issue is the lack of Christians getting involved with politics and reforming the government by taking a stand for Christianity. The main point of this argument is that Christians need to vote for the candidate that is the most Christian, regardless of the political party (as they now appear to be meaningless).

Nevertheless, all the Christian can do in this situation is to try to elect the best politician because it fulfills our attempt to elect the best candidate. The decisions that the politicians make, after being elected, are out of the voters' hands, and the politicians are accountable to God for their decisions. If the Christians have done their best to vote for the *most* moral candidate, then they have done everything within their power to make the best of the situation given "the hand they were dealt." (Chapter 16 will use Scripture in support of electing moral officials.) The thrust of this argument is that intentionally voting for the more immoral candidate is where the moral conflict lies.

The Lost Donkey and the Elephant Who Forgot. This book does not endorse a party because it's apparent that both parties are confused. Neither fully aligns with the Judeo-Christian ethic, and both have strayed from their Christian morals and principles. Since this book does not seek to be partisan, either party is *eligible* for support. However, this book will always endorse the candidate *most* aligned to the Christian ethic. Since the Republican and Democratic parties are the two dominant parties in our government and they are the only two that make legislation, we need to venture into how both parties have "lost their way" and have distanced themselves from the Judeo-Christian ethic. (Even though the Tea Party movement is not a political party, it is encouraging to know that people are aware of the issues and that people are standing up to both parties and demanding reform!)[453]

Once upon a time, the Republican and Democratic parties were both conservative, but as time has progressed, they have slid away from

453 The Tea Party must not create a separate party of conservatives, because it would be political suicide! Instead, the Tea Party movement needs to reform one of the existing parties so that the conservative Christian vote is not split up while the liberal vote is amassed into one.

the Christian ethic. The establishment of parties—the donkeys and the elephants—now seems to be meaningless in today's world because both parties are confused about the issues they support, and, in some cases, candidates can be interchangeable from one party to the next as their voting records are very similar. From a Christian perspective, when the candidates from both parties appear identical, the problem lies within the more conservative party (whether Democrat or Republican). The reason both parties are included in the last statement is because their roles were once reversed. The Democratic Party used to be more conservative than the Republican Party, whereas today the Republican Party is generally more conservative. Since parties continually change their positions over time, it is not possible to solely back one party with blind support.

The Forgetful Elephant. The elephant (who supposedly never forgets) has forgotten its own history and the conservative values it once stood for! True conservatives are a rare breed and are hard to find these days because the morality of the nation has drastically declined. Furthermore, it is not popular to be conservative when it seems as if the majority of the people are liberal; being "unelectable" goes against a politician's nature. Still, when a *Republican* candidate, in the 23rd Congressional district of New York, supports abortion, is endorsed by ACORN (an organization that is filled with corruption), and then the *Republican* candidate endorses the Democratic candidate, after withdrawing from the race, we know the elephants are dazed and confused—they have no idea what is going on!

The very fact that the elephants let this candidate into the party demonstrates one of two problems: either Republicans have truly lost their sense of morality and are virtually identical to Democrats, or the Republicans are simply not paying attention and are complacent (to the point where they are incompetent in selecting candidates). Indeed, the Republican Party needs restoration; they need direction and a leader who "says what they mean and means what they say."[454] The conservative party needs a candidate who has concrete principles, morals, and ethics, not one with a voting record virtually identical to Hillary Clinton's. A progressive, by definition, is of liberal stance, and that person cannot be considered conservative! Republican Party: Clean up your act, or you will soon find conservatives running in the Independent party (just as we saw in the election in New York's 23rd Congressional District in 2009).

454 One of Glenn Beck's favorite sayings of what the American people desperately desire of a politician.

The Lost Donkey. Now, we turn to the Democratic Party. The donkeys are plain lost, frantically kicking and begging for direction. Donkeys, as we are discovering, have no clue how to lead because donkeys are so accustomed to complaining about George Bush and blaming hurricanes on him that they have also become incompetent. Even more appalling is their method of governing! Not only do the liberals endorse immoral values, they are cramming one socialistic policy after another down the throat of the *majority* (political suicide)! The donkeys have an agenda, and that agenda does not concern the best interest of America or Americans; instead, it is reserved for their own political power and their "pets" (their special interest groups).

America is not a socialist country. If you are a liberal and you want socialism, I invite you to leave. Move to a socialist nation where you can be happy. Wait a second! I vividly recall one liberal who boldly proclaimed, "If George Bush is elected President, I'm leaving for France." Did this happen? Of course not; Robert Altman would rather live in the Christian nation versus a socialist nation![455] This is amazing! Why does this, for some crazy reason, seem like hypocrisy? Maybe it is because of the fact that Mr. Altman does not truly believe in socialism—at least not enough that he would actually follow through with his promise or threat.

An Apology on Behalf of My Generation. I truly believe that most Americans had no idea the devastating effects the 2008 election would have. Little did we know that the *change* would be so fast, radical, and immoral that it would literally "fundamentally transform" America. However, conservatives are not blind today. The Tea Party movement demonstrates that Americans are waking up and that they are *outraged* with the direction our government is heading. Who am I kidding? They are outraged at the direction that the government is forcing us to take against our will! Kudos to the Tea Party movement; patriotic Americans need to keep pushing conservative values because Washington needs to know *who* Americans really are, *what* we believe, and *how* we think. Our founding fathers (even the non-Christian founding fathers) would either die of shock or have a heart attack if they were to come back and take a peek at the depraved state of America and the corruption in Washington.

455 NY Daily News, "Altman's in Gnashville Over Bush," http://www.nydailynews.com/archives/gossip/2000/09/07/2000-09-07_altman_s_in_gnashville_over_.html.

Is the fact that the *non-Christian* founding fathers would be appalled at America's depravity bothersome to anybody?

I will digress for a moment, but I want to sincerely apologize to the true *American Patriots* on behalf of my "young, ignorant, hip, and cool" generation. This is a gross generalization because not all young people are liberal, I understand that, but let's not be fooled either: the 2008 election was won because *young* people voted in droves (66 percent under the age of thirty supported the liberal candidate).[456] Young people tend to be more liberal, but they may reverse their mentality as they discover what it means to work and then have the government take away the fruits of their labor to give their money to somebody else through "social programs."

Nevertheless, I remember watching the election results come in on the evening of November 4, 2008, and I was not a happy camper. When it seemed as if countless people were partying in Washington DC (and throughout the nation), I was solemn because I understood what was happening and how the "American Dream" had literally been stolen from the future generation(s). The dissipation of my generation's American Dream is not unfathomable when the liberal agenda is interpreted with common sense because the very nature of socialism destroys productivity and innovation. Indeed, my generation's American Dream will begin to vanish in the face of unprecedented deficits, which inevitably lead to higher taxes (because *both parties* refuse to stop spending). My ignorant generation put the vast number of liberal politicians into power, and I apologize, on their behalf, because most of the people my age hadn't a clue as to what the issues were or how they would forever alter our future. The young generation only saw "rock stars," and it was "cool" to have "hip" politicians.

Liberalism's Prevalence in School. Nevertheless, as we return to the original issue, it's easy to see how liberal theology is an abomination and it's the antithesis of the Christian nation and American values. We now need to look at how the embracement of liberalism has already transformed the American public education system. Even though we know that liberalism is prevalent throughout the nation, we will focus solely on the education system because it may be the most powerful force that is churning out liberalism at an unprecedented rate; the indoctrination of children is an operation of enormous power.

456 CNN Politics, "Election Center 2008," http://www.cnn.com/ELECTION/2008/results/president/.

When students are indoctrinated, they become loyal to the entity that indoctrinates. Since people naturally resist change, the foundation is being set for a final transformation into socialism (a product of Naturalism) because it will be demonstrated how the public schools not only propagate one religion, but how the propagation of religion is a violation of our Constitution. This travesty is being accomplished through creating dependency on the government and through the loyalty that indoctrination creates to the (almost) all-powerful Federal Government.

Do you truly want an all-powerful government? Do you want the government to have the authority to tell you that you cannot eat *fast food* because the consumption is *unhealthy*?[457] Do we really want a government that involved with our health care? Or a government that has access to our private lives and the ability to examine all of our personal and medical records?

The purpose of the Constitution is to protect *the people* from the *government*, but the Constitution is being ignored by our politicians and by our own government! The politicians are getting away with flippantly disregarding the Constitution, and this is an awful tragedy. So far, the American public has allowed the "hijacking" of the Christian nation and a government that is stripping our Constitutional rights away before our very eyes. Think about the loss of freedom that accompanies the Health Care Bill, the Fairness Doctrine, Patriot Act, and Net Neutrality. Ben Franklin once said, "Those who sacrifice *liberty* for *security* deserve *neither*." Thomas Jefferson once said, "The government is best which governs least." Ben Franklin was also quoted as saying, "When the people find they can vote themselves money, that will herald the end of the republic."

These were our founding fathers! These were the people who created this great nation, but many disregard these words of wisdom, and some find them offensive! How has America cultivated a society that does not even implement the values of our own founding fathers? We need to know what has happened to America. In search of this answer, we will now press forward and examine *one* method by which the "fundamental transformation" has been accomplished.

457 NPR, "Fast-Food Ban Proposed in South Los Angeles," http://www.npr.org/templates/story/story.php?storyId=14459040.

America's 'Fundamental Transformation'

Schools and Indoctrination. Since America's conception, there has undoubtedly been change. The landscape, mentality, and values of Americans have drastically shifted. Some change is good; such as moving closer to God or reversing an unsustainable path. However, when our nation changes in a way that moves America away from her Christian origin, the change is immoral. The act of moving away from our Christian foundation is regression; we are moving backwards with respect to morality and the Judeo-Christian ethic. Change can be induced in many different ways, but this section will analyze only one medium through which fundamental change can accomplished. This section, and the entire next chapter, has been dedicated to the education system—the public schools that our children attend.

We need not fool ourselves: all schools indoctrinate. To indoctrinate is defined as "to instruct a doctrine, principle, ideology, etc.; to imbue with a partisan or biased belief or point of view."[458] Indoctrination itself is not immoral or evil; it's the doctrines, principles, and ideologies that are being ingrained in our children that bring morality into the equation. The question is not whether the schools indoctrinate; rather, the question is *what* the schools indoctrinate.

If biblical principles are being taught, then the indoctrination—the instilment of Christian principles—is in alignment with what the Bible teaches. The Bible teaches indoctrination in Proverbs 22:6 (NKJV): "Train up a child in the way that he should go, and when he is old he will not depart from it."[459] Ingraining biblical principles is beneficial because it instills morality. Immoral indoctrination is the instilment of immoral principles that, by nature, contradict God's moral law.

The question now becomes, "Are our public school systems indoctrinating our children with doctrines, principles, or ideologies that contradict the Absolute Truth?" Are our schools teaching that safe sex before marriage is permissible? That homosexuality is acceptable? That science proves that God cannot exist? That morality is relative and that no morals actually exist?

---

458 Indoctrinate. Dictionary.com. *Dictionary.com Unabridged.* Random House, Inc. http://dictionary.reference.com/browse/indoctrinate (accessed: April 9, 2010).

459 Training up "a child" is distinguished from training up "your child." The training of "a child" conveys the necessity of teaching morality to all children. After all, a free nation depends on morality in order to sustain its existence. Freedom demands moral responsibility.

The answer to that question is of utmost importance; thus, it warrants its own chapter. A note of explanation needs to be made because I endorse the separation of church and state (explained in detail later). Although I strongly advocate that religion should not be imposed on the students in our schools, that does not imply that it's unconstitutional to instill morality that concurs with the Judeo-Christian ethic. Morality can be taught *without* forcing students to accept Christianity—or, for that matter, any religion.

The Power of Indoctrination. Indoctrination is a powerful tool because it establishes *loyalty*. When children are taught from an early age what constitutes truth, they are ingrained with that knowledge. It becomes extraordinarily difficult to remove the bias that has been instilled because a reversal of original indoctrination goes against everything that person has been taught since childhood (on top of the resistance people naturally have toward change). This is why, statistically speaking, it is more difficult for an adult to accept salvation than a child.

Understanding this fact presents a profound principle that we must reverse in order to effectively restore America. The children being indoctrinated in our schools are tomorrow's adults—they are the *key to the future*. If our children are being indoctrinated with a curriculum teaching that God does not exist, that curriculum is not only unconstitutional and immoral, but it presents a future problem in America. When indoctrination removes Christian values and teaches that God does not exist, we are cultivating a society that will eventually turn against its own Christian foundation, and this will be accomplished through the process of voting. Once again, if our children are being taught that it is foolish to believe in God by their teachers and professors, then we are essentially paving the way for massive resistance to anything that relates to Christianity.

Our schools are erasing our Christian heritage because the liberal revisionists do not want your children to learn about America's Christian origin—even though it is the truth! The motive of liberal professors will become evident with the quotations at the beginning of the next chapter (and a section is dedicated to their "Horrifying Motive"). The first quotation begins with the motive of the liberal professor. The second demonstrates the power and the influence that these professors (and teachers) have over their students. The perception of the student is not only that the professors are knowledgeable, but the student also places *trust* in the professors by believing that what they are teaching is right (or accurate). Trust is placed in the professor, but our students are being betrayed. The final quotation conveys the corrupt and vile motive of anybody that tries to teach that God does not exist. This is not only unacceptable in a free nation that depends on morality, it's unconstitutional and this bias must be removed.

As we enter into the next chapter, we will be asking the question, "Has America transformed into an atheist nation?" This is not a topic that should be trivialized, because the education system is a key battleground. The answer to this question may be frightening, but if you are concerned with *what* our schools are indoctrinating, then prepare yourself as we now confirm that Naturalism is truly a religion and whether the propagation of Naturalism is constitutional.

Chapter 15

Does the Christian Nation Breed Atheism?

"So [professors] are going to go right on and discredit you in the eyes of your children, trying to strip you of your fundamentalist religious community of dignity, trying to make your view seem silly rather than discussable … I think those students are lucky to find themselves under the benevolent Herrschaft [domination] of people like me, and to have escaped the grip of their frightening, vicious, dangerous parents …

—Richard Rorty, Professor of Philosophy

"That's when, on this pivotal day in biology class in 1966, I began to learn about scientific discoveries that … 'made it possible to be an intellectually fulfilled atheist.'"

—Lee Strobel

"Fools say in their hearts, 'There is no God.' They are corrupt, their deeds are vile …"

—Psalms 14:1

The Separation of Church and State

What is Separation of Church and State? The idea of "separation of church and state" is a unique concept that was birthed in America—even though the actual words cannot be found in the Constitution. The concept stems from the First Amendment, within the Bill of Rights, per the U.S. Constitution. The First Amendment reads: "Congress shall make no law respecting an establishment of religion, or prohibiting the free exercise thereof; or abridging the freedom of speech, or of the press; or the right of the people peaceably to assemble, and to petition the government for a redress of grievances."

What Is the Purpose of Separation of Church and State? The purpose of the First Amendment (with respect to separation of church and state) is twofold: (1) It prevents the government from establishing, privileging, or forcing any type of religion on American citizens; and (2) It prevents the government from restricting citizens' freedom to exercise the religion of their choice. These are commonly referred to as the Establishment and Free Exercise Clauses, respectively. Since the government cannot establish a religion or prohibit the free exercise of religion, the concept of "separation of church and state" was birthed as the Amendment explicitly implies that government and religion are two entities that must never be mixed.

The separation of church and state undoubtedly plays a *critical* role in preserving American freedoms and the American way of life. Without the First Amendment, the practice of religion would be under the control of the government, which is controlled by the will of the majority. The First Amendment is one characteristic that distinguishes America from communism (where religion, or the lack thereof, is forced on the people by the government). To complete our perspective, we turn to the founding fathers to explain the issue; after all, these men wrote the Constitution.

> *"The purpose of the separation of church and state is to keep forever from these shores the ceaseless strife that has soaked the soil of Europe in blood for centuries."*
>
> *—James Madison, 1803* [460]

460 Letter objecting to the use of government land for churches.

> *"Believing with you that religion is a matter which lies solely between man and his God; that he owes account to none other for his faith or his worship; that the legislative powers of the government reach actions only, and not opinions, I contemplate with sovereign reverence that act of the whole American people which declared that their legislature should 'make no law respecting an establishment of religion, or prohibiting the free exercise thereof,' thus building a wall of separation between church and State."*
>
> —*Thomas Jefferson, Danbury Letter, 1802*

The founding fathers were brilliant because they understood simple principles that have made the difference between an oppressive government and one that must respect the freedom of its citizens. The founding fathers understood that power is like a pendulum: it has a tendency to swing back and forth between conservatism and liberalism. The purpose of the separation of religion from the state was designed to *protect you from the government*!

It's sickening to listen to people complain about their religious preferences not being endorsed, or forced, on students by the public school system. Yes, I understand that America is a Christian nation. Yes, I understand that America was founded upon the Judeo-Christian ethic. Yes, I understand that Christianity is the only way to heaven. Yes, I understand that we are to propagate the Gospel. But do you really want to force it upon the citizens of America by relying on the *government*?

Christianity is a choice—a gift—and you cannot force people to the cross; nor should you ever *try* to force them.[461] Was religious freedom not the very reason America was founded? If you read the charters of the thirteen original colonies, you will see that a major goal was to be able to propagate the Gospel freely but never to force it on the people through the government. The charter states the intent, but the Constitution clearly draws a boundary that separates the two entities.

Consider this scenario: If your preferred party had been elected to power, and the Constitution were changed so that it enabled the United States government to have the authority to impose *your* religion in the public school systems, then you *must also* be prepared to follow the lead of the majority when the pendulum swings in the opposite direction.

---

461 Joshua 24:15; Romans 6:23.

In other words, if you are a Christian and you force Christianity to be taught in the schools, and you force children to pray to Jesus, you need to be okay with the possibility of Naturalism, Judaism, or Islam being forced upon your children if that religious preference becomes the majority. You need to be okay if the school makes your child pray to Allah multiple times at school; and you need to be okay with Sharia Law being enforced—where your daughters could be made to cover their faces or even whipped for wearing bras.[462] You need to be okay if Naturalist teachers impose atheism and strongly advocate the idea that there is no such thing as God or that only fools would embrace the possibility of the supernatural. Forcing religion—any type of religion—is madness! Religion is a free choice that should never be infringed upon. But is this really what is happening today?

We know that the public schools are not forcing children to pray to Jesus. We know that neither scientific Christianity (creationism) nor biblical doctrine is being taught. We know Judaism is not endorsed because the schools do not force the reading of the Tanakh, nor do public schools force boys to wear yarmulkes. We know that *most* public schools do not endorse Islam because students are not forced to pray to Allah, your little girl is not forced to cover her face, and Islamic doctrine is not taught.[463] The point is that the government of the United States of America should not endorse any type of religion (or any opinion, with respect to God) in the public school system, period!

Since we recognize the danger of any majority imposing a religious belief through the school system, we must now ask: Is there truly a separation between *church* and state? Church is religion; and religion propagates a biased position concerning the existence or the establishment of God.[464] State is the government; and the government does not have the authority, per the Constitution, to endorse or promote *any* religion. Therefore, we must now ask: Has the government been faithful to the Constitution?

462 Fox News, "Somali Women Whipped for Wearing Bras," http://www.foxnews.com/story/0,2933,568524,00.html?test=latestnews.

463 Fox News, "New York City to Open Arabic Public School," http://www.foxnews.com/story/0,2933,251883,00.html.

464 All religions have a bias; a religion cannot *not* have bias. Christians, Jews, and Muslims alike all advocate that God exists, while atheism advocates that God does not exist. The only potential exception is benign agnosticism, where the person claims not to have enough information to make a decision, but truly being unbiased is also highly questionable because everybody has bias; even the apathetic position has bias.

Has the government endorsed a biased position that advocates either the existence or nonexistence of any type of God (or religion)?

The answer to this question is of utmost importance, but it's ultimately one that you will have to answer as it relates to you and your public school. I will raise awareness by proving that Naturalism is, in fact, a religion and that, per the Constitution and Supreme Court, the propagation of religion in the public school is unlawful. However, since public school curriculums are all not identical, it's not possible to present a *blanket conclusion* for all public schools in America as the issue may be applicable to some schools and irrelevant to others. This is where the people must get involved as yet another check and balance to ensure that the government is upholding the Constitution. After all, you have the power to vote; and voting will be one of our solutions in the next chapter.

Is Naturalism (Atheism) a Religion?

Shifting a Paradigm. As time marches forward, everything changes. Clothes, cars, and architecture all look different today than they did forty or fifty years ago. Scientific theories change with advancements in technology, and the dictionary is even updated as new words are birthed and old words are given new meanings and different interpretations. The usage and definitions of words change, and the current usage must be respected in its proper context.

In Webster's New Collegiate Dictionary (1973), religion was defined as:

> **Religion 1 a (1):** the service and worship of God or the supernatural (2): commitment or devotion to a religious faith or observance **b:** the state of a religious **2:** a personal set or institutionalized system of religious attitudes, beliefs, and practices **3:** *archaic*: scrupulous conformity: CONSCIENTIOUSNESS **4:** a cause, principle, or system of beliefs held to with ardor and faith

In 1973, the definition of religion was, for the most part, limited to the service and worship of a supernatural being (God), a commitment or devotion to God, and the principles and the system of beliefs of that religious institution. Most people, when asked, "What is religion?" would most likely respond with something like "The worship of God" or "The institution that pertains to the church." These are correct, but as time has progressed, the definition needs to be expanded as the word covers more territory.

When I look up *religion* on dictionary.com, I find nine definitions versus the four provided by Webster in 1973. Why are there more definitions provided today than there were forty years ago? Because the use of the word has expanded to take on new meanings, and the emphasis of the word changes from generation to generation.

Some people claim that their "religion" is football (which falls into the sixth definition, "something one believes in and follows devotedly").[465] Football is not the worship of God; it is the strong devotion—the devout following—of something that is prioritized (such as a sport). In the 1960s it may not have been socially acceptable in society to claim football as a religion, but today many may not object. Other words have also shifted with respect to their definition. One example stands out in my mind of how a word was perceived in the 1960s has shifted.

Gay used to imply "happily excited" or "brightly, lively" and that was obvious because the 1960s cartoon show *The Flintstones* (in the theme song) made the appeal to the viewer of having a great time. "When you're with the Flintstones, you'll have a yabba dabba doo time … a dabba doo time … you'll have a *gay* old time."[466] In that era, *gay* meant something entirely different than it does in today's world. If I were having a lot of fun with a group of friends and then suddenly shouted out, "This is so much fun, I'm so *gay!*" it would kill the moment, and I would most likely get some awkward looks. Why in the world would I be turning heads with that statement? Because the emphasis of the word, in today's society, is predominantly associated with being a homosexual. Since that is the common usage of the word, my friends, after their initial shock, would be thinking, "Did he really just say that?" and I would probably never hear the end of that exclamation as it would be repeated for years, with relentless teasing. (For the politically correct, let me point out that the teasing is a result of an improper use of the word that portrayed me as something I am not—nothing more.)

The point of this section is to prove that words have a specific meaning, but the utilization and the emphasis of a particular word can change over

465 Religion. Dictionary.com. *Dictionary.com Unabridged.* Random House, Inc. http://dictionary.reference.com/browse/religion (accessed: October 24, 2009).

466 Lyrics on Demand, "The Flintstones Theme Lyrics," http://www.lyricsondemand.com/tvthemes/theflintstoneslyrics.html.

time, along with the definition.[467] New words are created and old words are given new definitions. From my experience, *religion* was once a word that referred to the service and worship of an almighty God, but now religion has been expanded to include "something one believes in and follows devotedly." Both these definitions are applicable and both are correct per the dictionary.

Since we know that a definition cannot be erased (as history cannot be erased), we will now utilize one definition of *religion* in an attempt to demonstrate how Naturalism is, in fact, a religion. Naturalism must be considered a religion, because the entity perfectly aligns with the definition set forth by the dictionary; Naturalism has attempted to accomplish what every other traditional religion has attempted to accomplish—teach, or endorse, a specific perspective with respect to the existence of a supernatural being (God).

Religion Defined. According to the dictionary, *religion* is defined as "a set of beliefs concerning the cause, nature, and purpose of the universe, especially when considered as the creation of a superhuman agency or agencies, usually involving devotional and ritual observances, and often containing a moral code governing the conduct of human affairs."[468]

The key phrases in this definition are "concerning the cause, nature, and purpose of the universe" and "often containing a moral code governing the conduct of human affairs." These phrases are key because they provide the motive of any religion.

The Religion of Naturalism. The definition that we examined in the above section is very specific because it reveals the very essence—the purpose, intent, motive, function, etc.—of *all* religions. In the definition, we must also note that the essence of any religion is the ideology and never the building or worship center. Worship centers are excellent, but a church, synagogue, or mosque was never included in the definition because it's impossible for a building (of any type) to hold a belief or to espouse a position in regard to the existence of God. In fact, in the absence of a

467 Words never lose their definition; they can only gain new definitions. It would be impossible to claim that "gay" never conveyed the state of being "happily excited," but it is possible for a term can gain an additional use or definition. Therefore, when the definition of *religion* expands, every definition becomes applicable because the Constitution is applicable to *all religion*—regardless of form, substance, or purpose.

468 Religion. Dictionary.com. *Dictionary.com Unabridged.* Random House, Inc. http://dictionary.reference.com/browse/religion (accessed: April 11, 2009).

building, a religion is able to continue its existence if the ideology is held by at least one person. This is possible because religion is an intangible entity; it's a product of the mind. We know this to be true because religion is incapable of being touched or pinpointed outside the hearts and minds of religious people. (This fact will prove to be crucial later in the chapter.) Nevertheless, the remaining part of this section will demonstrate how Naturalism is a religion because it has accomplished what every other religion has accomplished; there is no distinction (except, of course, for the position it endorses in regard to the existence of God).

A Set of Beliefs Concerning God. Monotheism is a form of religion that advocates Creationism, and it provides an explanation "concerning the cause, nature, and purpose of the universe." Monotheism advocates that the universe and everything in it is the product of an Intelligent Designer (God). On the other hand, Naturalism advocates nontheistic evolution, Darwinism, and other various theories, but it also has a very specific "set of beliefs concerning the cause, nature, and purpose of the universe." Naturalism is exceedingly devout in advocating that the universe and all it contains is a product of chance or natural phenomena without recourse to miracles or the supernatural. Instead of advocating the existence of God, Naturalism rejects the existence of a supernatural and all-powerful God.

Since Naturalism rejects the existence of God, some may claim that it is not considered a "religion." However, this position is false because the dictionary does not state that a religion must endorse, or advocate, the existence of God in the affirmative (e.g., Buddhism). Instead, the dictionary requires a set of beliefs *concerning the existence* of God, and it makes no distinction between endorsing or rejecting a belief in a supernatural being. This point is critical, because Naturalism consequently falls within the definition of "religion."

Furthermore, religion attempts to provide an answer in regard to the existence of "a superhuman agency or agencies." The answer of whether or not a superhuman agency exists consequently affects the meaning and purpose of human life. (For example: If God exists, we should serve Him. If God does not exist, then we should prioritize the self. Either conclusion affects the purpose of life.) Naturalism also falls within the definition of religion because it has accomplished what every other religion has accomplished. Naturalism has established meaning and purpose for human life by creating a set of beliefs that addresses the existence of "a superhuman agency or agencies" (although their purpose and meaning differs from that provided by monotheism).

Granted, Naturalism is not the common religion because it does not advocate a supernatural God per se, but it does advocate a type of *ultimate reality*. Instead of God, Naturalism has established the ego (self) as the ultimately reality because its adherents claim that the supernatural does not exist. (As a result, everything you do should be a matter of your own purpose and benefit.) Instead of advocating a holy text as their final authority, Naturalism has established science as its final authority. (Science is elevated to a status that is equivalent with the Holy Bible. The popular mantra is "If science does not agree, then it must not be true.") Instead of "engaging in devotional or ritual observances," Naturalism refrains from any activity (as it's unnecessary unless the Naturalist desires to worship either the self or science).

The engagement in devotional or ritual observances is often accompanied with religion as people naturally desire to tithe or pay some type of alms to the God or church they revere. However, since Naturalism does not advocate any type of supernatural God, it would not make sense to give money to themselves. In fact, it would be quite humorous to witness a Naturalist paying alms (or tithe) to their self by offering money with their left hand only to accept and bless it with their right. Nevertheless, if we return to the definition of religion, we discover that the definition states: "usually involving devotional and ritual observances." Since *usually* is not all-inclusive, *it is not a requirement.*

The only permissible conclusion, from the facts that were presented in this section, is that Naturalism is a religion; to determine otherwise would deny all truth, logic, and rational thought. (If truth sets a person free, the inverse of the principle [a denial of truth] must lead to enslavement.) Who desires to be a slave to deception and the father of all lies?[469]

A Code of Morality. The second key phrase in the definition of religion was "often containing a moral code governing the conduct of human affairs." Again, the key word is "often." Although a moral code is not a requirement for a set of beliefs to be considered a religion, we can strengthen our argument by presenting the vast similarities between Naturalism and every other religion. (The argument that Naturalism is a religion has already been settled, and the case was closed in the last section. This section merely reinforces and builds upon that conclusion.)

469 John 8:32, 44; 17:17.

Traditional religions advocate that moral codes were brought into existence through a higher being. Christianity, Judaism, and Islam all advocate that the moral law was created by God and given to humanity to implement (for our protection and well-being). Since Naturalism rejects the supernatural, it's unable to advocate a moral code that originates from a higher being. Instead of teaching that morality is a product of God, Naturalists must teach that morality is an entity of human origin. From this foundation, they are able venture into many different beliefs (e.g., individuals each create morality for themselves, or governments collectively decide what is right versus wrong). Regardless of the method by which morality is reached, we must note that Naturalism advocates a type of morality.

Furthermore, the naturalistic standard of morality is subject to the ultimate reality (just like every other religion). Whereas morality in monotheism is subject to God, morality in Naturalism is subject to the ego (self). In monotheism God establishes morality, but in Naturalism the individual establishes that which is right and wrong, based purely on personal preference. We know that this is true because people who do not revere a supernatural God (for the most part) are permissive of sexual promiscuity, homosexuality, abortion, and socialism because a desire will always trump a mandate by a being that they do not believe exists.

Because Naturalism exalts the ego as the ultimate reality (and any morality is relative to each person), we begin to see how the belief system actually "governs the conduct of human affairs" just as the definition of religion states. In this context we must note that *govern* does not imply a "rule by right of authority" because an atheist equivalent of a Pope does not exist. Even if such an atheist authority did exist, a religious entity in America cannot establish an entirely separate penal code (which is required to rule by a right of authority). Instead, the context of *govern* in the definition of *religion* best fits the definition where morality "exercise[s] a directing or restraining influence."[470] In this respect Naturalism, Christianity, Judaism, and Islam alike "govern the conduct of human affairs."

Even if Naturalism were to advocate that morality is nonexistent, it would still govern (or influence) people's decisions, since any opinion on the matter is influential with respect to right and wrong. Ironically, people know that morality exists because they would feel violated if their mother, father, brother, sister, or child were murdered in cold blood. Therefore, there

470 Govern. Dictionary.com. Dictionary.com Unabridged. Random House, Inc. http://dictionary.reference.com/browse/govern (accessed: February 2, 2010).

are only varying degrees of morality, but the problem is that advocating any degree of morality still influences (or governs) the conduct of human affairs. (A low standard of morality permits a liberal lifestyle, whereas a high standard requires a conservative lifestyle.)

The conclusion is that Naturalism constitutes a religion because it's no different that any other religion: Naturalists have conveyed a moral code that intentionally or unintentionally governs. Even though Naturalism has a lower degree of morality than the other religions, any degree of morality is still influential. In the event that people are still not convinced that Naturalism is a religion, we should ask a Naturalist. (He would certainly know the answer ...)

Let's Ask a Naturalist. The idea that Naturalism is a religion is not merely my suggestion. This is not some bizarre idea that I have created to support the topic of this book; this is *real*, and Darwinists acknowledge Naturalism as a religion. In fact, this religion is firmly advocated by proponents such as Julian Huxley (a zoologist who was one of the scientific founders of the neo-Darwinian synthesis or the modern version of Darwin's theory). Julian Huxley gallantly proclaimed in 1959:

> In the evolutionary pattern of thought there is no longer either need or room for the supernatural. The earth was not created; it evolved. So did all the animals and plants that inhabit it, including our human selves, mind and soul as well as brain and body. So did religion.
>
> Evolutionary man can no longer take refuge from his loneliness in the arms of a divinized father figure whom he has himself created, nor escape from the responsibility of making decisions by sheltering under the umbrella of Divine Authority, nor absolve himself from the hard task of meeting his present problems and planning his future by relying on the will of an omniscient, but unfortunately inscrutable, Providence.
>
> Finally the evolutionary vision is enabling us to discern, however incompletely, the lineaments of *the new religion* that we can be sure will arise to serve the needs of the coming era.[471]

471 Phillip Johnson, *Defeating Darwinism* (Downers Grove, IL: InterVarsity Press, 1997), 99, emphasis added.

There is no greater or more convincing argument than one that came from the very mouth of a Naturalist! It not only appears as if I'm not alone in thinking that Naturalism is a religion, but Huxley is predicting the rise of a new and powerful religion. The above passage is an excerpt from a speech that Huxley made in 1959 (which was prewritten with care). Therefore, we can conclude with certainty that his words did not slip, and his acknowledgement is crystal clear. Does the fact that Naturalism falls within the definition of religion become alarming? It should become very alarming because the failure of the Supreme Court to recognize Naturalism as a religion enables the ideology to be indoctrinated into the school systems without violating the separation of church and state.

The effects of Naturalism are far-reaching and are explained very well by Phillip Johnson, in *Defeating Darwinism*, when he explains: "In short, the triumph of Darwinism implied the death of God and set the stage for replacing biblical religion with a new faith based on evolutionary naturalism. That new faith would become the basis not just of science but also of government, law and morality. It would be the established religious philosophy of modernity."[472]

Let's Ask the Supreme Court. Secular humanism is defined as "a way of life and thought that is pursued without reference to God or religion … [I]t is a worldview and lifestyle oriented to the profane rather than the sacred, the natural rather than the supernatural. Secularism is a nonreligious approach to individual and social life."[473] This religion obviously falls into the category of Naturalism because it teaches that "the 'natural' universe, the universe of matter and energy, is all there really is."[474] (Secular humanism is to Naturalism as monotheism is to theism.) By demonstrating that the Supreme Court of the United States protects secular humanism as a religion, we have further proof that Naturalism is, in fact, a religion *and is protected under the Constitution.*

In 1961, the *Torcaso v. Watkins* case was brought all the way to the Supreme Court for a violation of the First and Fourteenth Amendments.[475] Torcaso was appointed to the office of notary public by the governor of

472 Ibid.

473 Walter A. Elwell, ed., *Evangelical Dictionary of Theology* (Grand Rapids, MI: Baker Academic, 1984), 1085.

474 Ibid., 814.

475 *Torcaso v. Watkins,* Supreme Court of the United States, 367 U.S. 488 (1961).

Maryland, but was refused a commission to serve because he would not declare his belief in God.[476] (Maryland, at the time, required persons who qualified for any office for profit or trust in the state to declare their belief in the existence of God.)[477] Since Torcaso would not declare a belief in God, he brought suit in a Maryland circuit court to compel issuance of his commission; which would enable him to serve in full capacity.[478] The Supreme Court reversed the Maryland court's decision and decided:

> We repeat and again reaffirm that neither a State nor the Federal Government can constitutionally force a person to "profess a belief or disbelief in any religion." Neither can constitutionally pass laws or impose requirements which aid all religions against non-believers, [footnote 10] and neither can aid those religions based on a belief in the existence of God as those against those religions founded on different beliefs [footnote 11].

Within the opinion section rendered in support of the decision, footnotes were cited in the text (as indicated by the brackets in the above block quote). Within the eleventh footnote, we read this: "Among religions in this country which do not teach what would generally be considered a belief in the existence of God are Buddhism, Taoism, Ethical Culture, Secular Humanism and others. See *Washington Ethical Society v. District of Columbia* ..." Even though footnotes in Supreme Court cases are merely comments and do not have the weight of a ruling, we begin to see a pattern whereby religion consists of a set of beliefs *concerning* the existence of God versus *affirming* the existence of God.

Clearly, the Supreme Court of the United States of America recognizes Naturalism (secular humanism) as a religion. Both belief and disbelief in God fall within the definition of religion set forth by the dictionary, and both are protected by the Constitution.

Let's Ask a Federal Court. Just in case the definition of religion, self-admission on the part of a Naturalist, and the ruling of a Supreme Court case were not enough proof, perhaps we should examine a federal court's decision on whether or not atheism (ultimately reduced to Naturalism) is,

476 Ibid.
477 Ibid.
478 Ibid.

in fact, a religion. In *Kaufman v. McCaughtry*, an inmate in Wisconsin (James Kaufman) claimed that his First Amendment rights were violated because the prison where he resided refused to allow him to create a study group for atheists.[479] Since the First Amendment cannot prohibit the free exercise of religion, Kaufman brought suit. The case eventually went to the Seventh Circuit Court of Appeals in Wisconsin; where it was decided:

> Prisons must afford prisoners reasonable opportunities to exercise the religious freedom guaranteed by the First Amendment without fear of penalty. The parties dispute whether the free exercise clause applies to plaintiff's case because it is unclear whether atheism qualifies as a religion in need of protection under the free exercise clause. Although this case does not require an answer to that question, I note that the Court of Appeals for the Seventh Circuit has stated that atheism is a form of religion for Title VII purposes. ("If we think of religion as taking a position on divinity, then atheism [Naturalism] is indeed a form of religion.") [480]

As I was researching this case, I read article after article where people were extremely upset when they discovered that atheism was considered a religion by the court. I'm confused as to why a Christian would be upset in regard to atheists having the right to practice or exercise their form of religion. Are not all religions protected under the First Amendment? Refusing to recognize atheism (or Naturalism) as a religion is actually more devastating for the Christian movement and the Christian nation than most realize (despite their outrage against the court ruling). The rationale behind the last statement is of grave importance to the well-being of America!

If, for some reason, Naturalism were deemed not to be a religion, then it would be *lawful* to propagate this ideology in the public schools as there would be no Constitutional violation. The effects would be disastrous because Naturalism would ultimately have free reign in the schools, advocating any position conceivable with respect to God—as long as the school does not affirm the existence of God. It is for this reason that I have

479 World Net Daily, "Court rules atheism a religion," http://www.wnd.com/news/article.asp?ARTICLE_ID=45874.

480 *Kaufman v. McCaughtry,* 192 Fed. Appx. 556.

gone to great lengths to demonstrate how and why Naturalism is a religion according to the dictionary, followed by self-admission on the part of a Naturalist as well as multiple court rulings on the Supreme and Federal levels. (This is by no means an exhaustive list; I merely cite two rulings.)

It would be wonderful to think that all science is objective and free of bias to philosophical motive (that scientists are only in search of the truth, regardless of where the truth may lead). Unfortunately, this is not the case as we have not yet reached the wonderful and much anticipated progressive, socialist utopia. If only the government could domineer *all science*, perhaps there could be universal consent and harmony within the scientific community. If the government was involved and they backed one theory, then it could become so powerful that no other view could gain credibility regardless of truth. But wait … this is what is already happening!

A Horrifying Motive

The Peon Outlook. Science is supposed to be objective and unbiased because *all* scientists are entrusted with a duty to discover truth. However, as I was conducting my research for this topic, I began watching Ben Stein's documentary *Expelled: No Intelligence Allowed* to try and gain a different perspective on how Naturalists perceived those who even *consider the possibility* of an intelligent designer. To my surprise (at least before I discovered their motive), many scientists were not open to the truth. In fact, many scientists in the scientific community discredited, scoffed at, and even "expelled" those scientists who even *considered* the possibility of intelligent design (I.D.), and it did not matter how many degrees, achievements, or awards they had won. (This is appalling because dumb and incompetent scientists would be accepted over intelligent and productive scientists as long as they reject I.D.)

It was truly a solemn day when I discovered that many scientists rejected certain philosophies and would never consider the supporting evidence or research in favor of I.D. As I watched Stein's documentary, it became obvious that these were the elite liberals who know better than you and they expect people like yourself to shut up and sit down (never mind that they cannot *prove* Darwinism). Who are you (the public) to know, much less decide, anything? How dare you even think about such things! Do you not know your place in society? The elites decide, and you *will* follow their lead. (This was the impression they gave as I watched the critics respond to intelligent design.) In this section, I would like to highlight a few responses that make scientists who even consider I.D. look like peons and ignorant fools who are not worthy of their job, to say nothing of tenure, grants for research, or even kudos for at least being open-minded. The critics of intelligent design conclude:[481]

- Intelligent design people are not genuine scientists.
- Intelligent design is a racket [a dishonest scheme].
- Intelligent design is *just* propaganda.
- The only intelligent thing about it is that they've got people to call it that.
- It's really very stupid [to believe] as well.
- To present intelligent design stunts [a student's] educational growth; it stunts their intellectual growth.
- Intelligent design is a set of excuses to squeeze Creationism into the classrooms.
- You get intelligent design in the schools today and we can have school prayers tomorrow.
- Can you imagine anything more boring? The boredom attached to I.D. is supreme! It is so boring that I can't even bother to think about it much anymore. It's just utterly boring.

Everybody is entitled to their opinion because we have a First Amendment right to free speech, but where the line is crossed is when the scientific community expels, or rejects, certain theories from being presented—especially when they are supported by facts, research, logic, and evidence. There is a lengthy list of intelligent design scientists who are not only mocked and severely criticized, but punitive action was taken against these people because of their intelligent beliefs. Once again, we return to *Expelled: No Intelligence Allowed* to highlight a few examples.[482]

- Dr. Richard Sternberg was terminated from the Smithsonian Museum of Natural History for giving intelligent design a hint of credibility. Sternberg was labeled an "intellectual terrorist" by the chair of his department.
- Dr. Caroline Crocker's career at George Mason University came to an abrupt end when she *mentioned* (not taught) the

481 Ben Stein, *Expelled: No Intelligence Allowed*, documentary film.
482 Ibid.

idea of intelligent design. She was immediately disciplined, and at the end of the semester, she was terminated.

- Dr. Michael Egnor, a neurosurgeon and professor, was viciously attacked by the scientific community upon writing an essay to high school students. In the essay, Egnor stated that doctors don't need to study evolution in order to practice medicine. Critics resorted to abusive name-calling and absolutely demanded his termination; all because Egnor diminished Darwin's credibility and importance.
- Professor Robert J. Marks II, a few months after interviewing with Ben Stein, was in the crosshairs of persecution when it was discovered there was a link between his work and intelligent design. His research website was shut down, and he was forced to return grant money (while, at the same time, Naturalists were immune). Professor Marks taught at Baylor University.
- Dr. Guillermo Gonzalez, astronomer and assistant professor at Iowa State University, wrote a book titled *The Privileged Planet*, which argued the universe was intelligently designed. Despite a superior research record (discovering several new planets), his many achievements were meaningless when he applied for tenure. Fierce resistance, in the form of a petition, poisoned the university atmosphere against intelligent design.
- Other professionals appeared on the documentary to elaborate further on the persecution, but they would not dare show their faces to the camera for fear of retaliation. There is certainly an incentive for any intelligent professional not to commit apostasy (to Naturalism) if they have any desire *whatsoever* to excel. Hence the name, "No Intelligence Allowed."

These professionals that were highlighted are only the tip of the iceberg; they were the ones singled out and persecuted in public. How many more examples are unknown? How many more of these professionals desperately want to tell their story but refrain for fear of retaliation? We will never be able to calculate the true number of intelligent scientists and teachers discriminated against behind closed doors (passed up for promotions, raises, tenure, grants, etc.).

The refusal to even allow the presentation of an opposing argument is hypocrisy and violates their liberal creed of being open-minded and tolerant of all views. Refusing objectivity and keeping opponents from presenting their case is hypocrisy and utterly abhorrent. These scientists should not only be ashamed at their bigoted position but also because they (opponents to intelligent design) espouse an ideology that cannot *ever* be proven true!

The rationale behind this argument is that people can take one of two positions: they can either accept or reject the possibility of an intelligent designer. However, the scientists who reject the possibility of I.D. intuitively assume the position that God does not exist. The Naturalists have tried to discredit the idea of God, but the greatest irony is that their own position is one that can *never* be proven true. Recall that in Chapter 5 we established that the Naturalists' position is not provable because they would have to affirm one of the following arguments: (1) Prove a negative (the claim that God does not exist; which requires one to be all-knowing) or (2) Prove God to be an intrinsically impossible idea. It does not matter how much evidence Naturalists discover, they will never be able to prove their position because scientists will never be all-knowing, and God will always be plausible in the creation account.

As if trying to discredit intelligent design for a lack of evidence were not enough hypocrisy to make your blood boil, just wait until you discover their motive. The scientists who despise I.D. want you to believe that they are objective and truly open to all the facts, but when you're not looking, they strictly adhere to an unethical motive that should make you want to STAND UP! and restore America all the more.

Philosophy First, Science Second?! The very idea that scientists would discredit their equally qualified peers for merely considering an opposing view should raise a red flag. (This is not a communist country, so why are different theories expelled and persecuted?) This communist-like red flag propelled me to dig deeper and to discover the root of their disdain towards any person who would have the *audacity* to disagree with Naturalism. The hypocrisy was too great and too obvious for them not to have an underlying motive. Fortunately, this search was not in vain, and I am able to present the motive in their words! Block quotes rule out a conspiracy theory (no conspiracy is possible when they openly flaunt their motive; that's known as public knowledge). In light of this public knowledge, this section will reveal that the true motive of Naturalistic science is a strict religious adherence to a philosophy before ever looking at a single fact, figure, pattern, or sliver of data. They will even adhere to their philosophy before siding with the truth. (Truth is now irrelevant in a twenty-first-century science institution; philosophies and political agendas trump truth and your best interest.)

In order to best demonstrate the insanity of their motive, we need to put all the main ideas back into context; so let's recap what we already know about Naturalism. We know that Naturalism is a belief that excludes God or an intelligent designer of any type. We know that Naturalism has utterly failed in its attempt to prove itself as entirely true; in fact, we discovered that it's impossible for anybody to prove Naturalism true. Even Darwin deserves a brownie point for honesty when he admitted that future discoveries could entirely discredit his theory. (Which we know was disproved by the Cambrian explosion. No branching tree there!) In Darwin's era, honesty and objective science were important, but today many scientists scoff at these old-fashioned and "ancient" principles of morality with contempt. It's as if most scientists would like to ignore the truth in order to manipulate science to fit an agenda. Wait a second! We know that happened because some of the Naturalistic icons represent intentional fraud (Haeckel's embryos), while other icons, even though they were honest attempts, have been completely disproved by subsequent discoveries and by more accurate experiments, yet they are taught as if empirical facts (Darwinism and the Miller experiment, respectively).

It has also been established that it's not even logical to believe in Naturalism when we examined the religion from a free insurance policy or a cost/benefit perspective (Chapter 5). Naturalists have faith (and must desperately hope) that there is no God, but even they know that they cannot prove or scientifically back the conclusion that there is no God.[483] We have also discovered that nothing significant can possibly stem from Naturalism because it strips humanity of true meaning and limits it to a short-lived existence on earth; nothing is cherished except for material possessions, which can offer fun, but certainly not happiness. We know that Naturalists have contempt for the intelligent design theory before any evidence is examined and they severely ridicule or ostracize the I.D. scientists. Now, we want to know why. (I'm not as concerned with why they accept Naturalism as I am with why Naturalists think they have a *right* to silence the opposition or to become a stumbling block and ultimately prevent an honest discussion from ever taking place.)

---

483 This is evident because Darwin began his theory after the first signs of life, but he never attempted to explain how life suddenly appeared. Naturalists despise the presupposition that life came from non-life because they cannot generate a logical explanation.

The answer to that very important question is found within the following excerpt, from geneticist and Marxist Richard Lewontin:

> It is not that the methods and institutions of science somehow compel us to accept a material explanation of the phenomenal world, but, on the contrary, that we are *forced by our* a priori *adherence to material causes* to create an apparatus of investigation and a set of concepts that produce material explanations, no matter how counter-intuitive, no matter how mystifying to the uninitiated. Moreover, that materialism is absolute, for we cannot allow a Divine Foot in the door. The eminent Kant scholar Lewis Beck used to say that anyone who could believe in an omnipotent deity is to allow that at any moment the regularities of nature may be ruptured, that miracles may happen.[484]

This amounts to an admission that the entire institution of science is in jeopardy because Naturalists feel that they must force the institution to conform to a philosophical agenda, regardless of where the facts lead! This is one of the *most revealing* statements about Naturalism because it clearly reveals their true motive behind the rejection of such obvious facts. Naturalists are simply not open to the facts; they do not care what constitutes *truth* and openly claim to ignore "the truth" if it contradicts their philosophy. These naturalists are not objective in their thinking nor have they ever set out to be objective. Let's just be honest about the meaning of the above quotation. It is obvious that the Naturalist will take *any* position, "no matter how counter-intuitive" or "mystifying," and they will reject all evidence because they are "forced by ... adherence to material causes." In other words, as long as your science never points towards an intelligent designer, you'll be accepted in the community. (Does the institution of science in America breed atheism?)

Since it would be a tragedy if Lewontin, alone, was singled out and his "partners in crime" did not get any attention, we should examine a few more examples to "spread the love." Since we will not focus on merely one Naturalist, we shall build a track record that establishes true motive; while simultaneously building credibility. If we can demonstrate that

484 Richard Lewontin, *New York Review of Books* (New York: New York Review of Books, 1997), 31, emphasis added.

numerous Naturalists reveal, on record, a motive of philosophy first, then it will become difficult to twist the truth to make it seem as if this were a position that only a few (radical) Naturalists espouse.

Nobel laureate Steven Weinberg once wrote: "*Anything* that we scientists can do to weaken the hold of religion should be done and may in the end be our greatest contribution to civilization."[485]

"Christopher Hitchens writes, 'All religions and all churches are equally demented in their belief in the divine intervention, divine intercession, or even the existence of the divine in the first place.' [Richard] Dawkins adds, 'The great unmentionable evil at the center of our culture is monotheism. From a barbaric Bronze Age text known as the Old Testament, three anti-human religions have evolved: Judaism, Christianity and Islam.'"[486]

Philosopher Richard Rorty has strongly believed that religious beliefs are "politically dangerous" and declared atheism the only practical basis for a "pluralistic, democratic society."[487]

Psychologist Nicholas Humphrey states, "Parents, correspondingly, have no god-given license to enculturate their children in whatever ways they personally choose: no right to limit the horizons of their children's knowledge, to bring them up in an atmosphere of dogma and superstition, or to insist they follow the straight and narrow path of their own faith."[488]

These proponents of Naturalism are not objective, truth-seeking scientists, anymore than I am Tinker Bell. In fact, these "scientists" are far worse because they are deliberately preventing their students from making a decision based on facts. Instead, they skew the presentation to cater to their philosophy and then use the science (whether outdated, disproved, or fraudulent) to force Naturalism's agenda. The statement from Marxist Richard Lewontin not only reveals to us that the naturalists will go to any lengths to dismiss truth (if it reveals God) but that their philosophy is for them far superior to science! In other words, accepting faulty science is more acceptable to the scientific community than accepting the reality of an intelligent designer; regardless of how foolish their theories appear. Perhaps these Naturalists are afraid the truth would free their students from the chains of Naturalism's propaganda?

---

485 Vaclav Havel, "Paradise Lost," *New York Review of Books*, April 9, 1992. (Emphasis added).

486 Dinesh D'Souza, *What's So Great about Christianity* (Washington, D.C.: Regnery Publishing, Inc., 2007), 23.

487 Ibid., 28.

488 Nicholas Humphrey, "What Shall We Tell the Children?" Oxford Amnesty Lecture, 1997.

The motive is truly horrifying, but is this their only motive? Unfortunately, I must bring the news that Naturalists have actually devised a plan to "miseducate the young."[489]

'I Will Undo What Parents Have Established.' Dinesh D'Souza opens his fourth chapter in *What's So Great about Christianity* with "It seems that atheists are not content with committing cultural suicide—they want to take your children with them. The atheist strategy can be described in this way: let the religious people breed them, and we will educate them to despise their parents' beliefs." This may come as a shock to Naturalists, but it's not in their job description to exploit a position of influence in order to manipulate a student's view of God (which is certainly a violation of the Constitution). Parents entrust teachers and professors to educate their children, not to discredit parents or make them look like unintelligent and utter fools in the classroom. (Naturalism's audacity and arrogance, by forcing an ideology that can never be based upon proven facts, is abhorrent!)

As if hiding the truth, distorting the facts, sometimes committing fraud, and admitting to a philosophy whose sole motive is to disregard facts and continually try and destroy religion were not enough, Naturalists have also contrived a way to destroy what moral and ethical parents have spent *years* trying to instill in their children. Professor Richard Rorty proves this point exceedingly well.

> These parents have a point. Their point is that we liberal teachers no more feel in a symmetrical communication situation when we talk with bigots than do kindergarten teachers talking with their students … When we American college teachers encounter religious fundamentalists, we do not consider the possibility of reformulating our own practices of justification so as to give more weight to the authority of the Christian scriptures. Instead, we do our best to convince these students of the benefits of secularization …
>
> So [professors] are going to go right on and discredit you in the eyes of your children, trying to strip your

489 D'Souza, 31.

> fundamentalist religious community of dignity, trying to make your view seem silly rather than discussable …
>
> I have no trouble offering this reply, since I do not claim to make the distinction between education and conversation on the basis of anything except my loyalty to a particular community, a community whose interests required re-educating the Hitler Youth in 1945 and required re-educating the bigoted students of Virginia in 1993. I don't see anything herrschaftsfrei [domination free] about my handling of my fundamentalist students.
>
> Rather, I think those students are lucky to find themselves under the benevolent Herrschaft [domination] of people like me, and to have escaped the grip of their frightening, vicious, dangerous parents. It seems to me that I am just as provincial and contextualist as the Nazi teachers who made their students read Der Stürmer; the only difference is that I serve a better cause. I come from a better province.[490]

The arrogance is too much! It's nauseating to read the words of elite liberals because they think they are right and that they actually know better than you. These professors try to put the religious students in their place by patronizing young adults as if they were children. How humiliating would it be if your professor talked to you as if you were an ignorant child (in the same manner that an elementary school teacher would talk to kindergarteners)? Rorty is actually under the impression that his students are "lucky" to find themselves under his domination.

In regard to the Nazis, we will not attempt to comment on any view that Rorty may have possessed on the persecution of "stupid religious" people, but we will make the link that the Nazis were also extreme-left socialists, whom were also elitists. Not that this fact is surprising, or anything, but Nazi is actually short for National Socialist German Workers' Party; whose leadership Hitler proudly assumed in 1921.[491] Earlier, it was pointed out that socialism, by design, was unsustainable; there is no better example than Germany. In this great socialist nation, socialism was the guinea pig,

490 Richard Rorty, from "Universality and Truth," in Robert B. Brandon, ed., *Rorty and His Critics* (Oxford: Blackwell, 2000), 21–22.

491 A Teacher's Guide to the Holocaust, "The Rise of the Nazi Party," http://fcit.usf.edu/HOLOCAUST/TIMELINE/nazirise.HTM.

or the "pit-stop" to communism (or, in Germany's case, tyranny). Socialism will always lead to tyranny in whatever form of government (communism, dictatorship, etc.). It would also be fair to conclude that while not all socialists are Nazis, all Nazis were socialists.

How does all this socialism, liberalism, and religious contempt relate to the education system or America breeding atheism? (The short answer: Perfectly!) America is breeding Naturalism because *most teachers and professors are liberal, and most are Naturalists.* This puzzle is not hard to figure out because when Naturalists dominate the education system, they have the platform to implement their horrifying motive. Even though Naturalism is a religion espoused by a minority, *most* of the scientists are Naturalists (yet they force their ideology). In order to prove this point, we should examine some daunting statistics about America and her education system. In *What's So Great about Christianity*, Dinesh D'Souza presents the following statistics in regard to scientists and their belief in God.

> And it seems that a majority of scientists in the United States are atheists. Only 40 percent—a sizable minority, but a minority nevertheless—believe in a personal God. And among members of the elite National Academy of Sciences, only 7 percent of scientists can be counted among the ranks of believers. These figures have remained generally consistent over several decades, with the proportion of atheists rising slightly.[492]

Not only are these statistics disheartening, they also provide the needed segue to erase America's Christian heritage and to strip your children of your bigoted and stupid religious beliefs. We must remind ourselves that America is, in fact, a Christian nation and that she was founded upon the Judeo Christian ethic. Christianity is not only the largest religion in the world, but it's also the largest religion in America (an estimated 76.5 percent or 151,000,000 people).[493] In spite of these overwhelming numbers, the reason that atheism has been able to thrive in a Christian nation is because Naturalists have heavily congregated in the one institution where the greatest influence is found.

---

492 D'Souza, 23–24.

493 Religious Tolerance, "Religious Identification in the U.S.: How American Adults View Themselves," http://www.religioustolerance.org/chr_prac2.htm.

It's also not surprising to point out that most professors gravitate toward liberal views of religion and politics. Consider the results of a study conducted by sociologists Neil Gross of Harvard and Solon Simmons of George Mason University in 2004. The survey drew 1,417 responses from 927 colleges, and it was discovered that:

- Liberals outnumber conservatives by 11–1 among social scientists and 13–1 among humanities professors.
- 25.5 percent of those who teach sociology identify themselves as *Marxist*. Self-identified radicals accounted for 19 percent of humanities professors and 24 percent of social scientists.
- Although business school professors are believed to be predominantly conservative, professors of business voted 2–1 for John Kerry. These professors were barely more conservative than liberal.
- Only 19.7 percent of respondents identify themselves as any type of conservative, compared to 62.2 percent who say they are any type of liberal.
- At elite, Ph.D-granting schools in general, 60.4 percent of faculty members are Democrats, 30.1 percent are independents and 9.5 percent are Republicans.
- Gross and Simmons believe that liberals are losing ground to moderates among faculty, though conservatives are not gaining at all. Faculty members who are 35 or younger are less likely than their elders to be left-wing, and less likely to be conservatives as well.[494]

Again, the puzzle is not hard to piece together. When most scientists reject the possibility of God, their work naturally reflects their convictions (facts do not seem to matter). When most teachers/professors espouse liberalism, they naturally gravitate toward inculcating liberal science as well as liberal views of religion and politics. Ironically, the cards of a vast minority have been stacked against an overwhelming majority. To their credit, they have had great success in their crusade against religion. However, concerned Americans are now awake and realize the devastation that a parasite (liberalism) will inflict on the host (Christian nation). When the house is divided, it cannot stand. America will either fall back

494 John Leo, "Our Essays," Minding the Campus, http://www.mindingthecampus.com/originals/2007/10/professors_just_as_liberal_or.html.

to her Christian origin where blessings abound or she will plummet into liberalism (or socialism or progressivism) and she will reap the consequences associated with implementing an unsustainable path.

The last topic we need to discuss is a Supreme Court decision and how it relates to the propagation of religion in the classroom.

The Hypocrisy within the Schools

Supreme Court says 'No Religion in School.' *Edwards v. Aguillard* was a landmark case that rose all the way to the Supreme Court in December 1986 and was decided in June 1987. Before we examine the case and its outcome, we need to point out that the state of Louisiana tried to require balanced treatment of "Creation-Science" and "Evolution-Science" (without God) in the classroom. The intent was equal treatment so that the curriculum would provide students with information surrounding both viewpoints so that they would have a well-rounded presentation. This would enable the students to make a decision based on their own convictions regarding the origin of the universe. However, the court struck down the Balanced Treatment for Creation-Science and Evolution-Science in Public School Instruction Act (Balanced Treatment Act) because the court deemed the act to endorse a particular form of religion.

Analyzing the Rationale. The Louisiana Balanced Treatment Act was struck down by the Supreme Court on the basis that

> The Act impermissibly endorses religion by advancing the religious belief that a supernatural being created humankind. The legislative history demonstrates that the term "creation science," as contemplated by the state legislature, embraces this religious teaching. The Act's primary purpose was to change the public school science curriculum to provide persuasive advantage to a particular religious doctrine that rejects the factual basis of evolution in its entirety. Thus, the Act is designed either to promote the theory of creation science that embodies a particular religious tenet or to prohibit the teaching of a scientific

> theory disfavored by certain religious sects. In either case, Act violates the First Amendment.[495]

The Supreme Court ultimately ruled against the appeal, reasoning that Creationism was a religious belief and that it violated the First Amendment; that was the entire basis and justification for the ruling. If we were to accept the court's intent (a complete separation of church and state) and we examine today's curriculum (Naturalism, in the form of Darwinism and nontheistic evolution, is currently being taught in schools), has the court ultimately succeeded? Since Naturalism is, in fact, a religion (because it has an established belief concerning the cause of the universe) then, *No*, the Court has failed to uphold the Constitution on multiple levels.

First, the ruling states that the Balanced Treatment Act was designed to "endorse a religion by advancing the religious belief that a supernatural being created mankind." The problem is that Naturalism is also a religion, and there is no doubt that Naturalism advances a set of religious beliefs (or an opinion concerning God and the origin of the universe) as it relates to "the creation of humankind." The Constitution is being violated.

Second, the ruling states that "creation science" is unacceptable because it embraces religious teaching. Religious teaching is defined as "pertaining to, or concerned with religion."[496] Religious teaching is simply teaching a perspective that aligns with a religion. Since Naturalism is a religion and its perspective is taught in schools, teaching that perspective falls within the definition set forth by the dictionary as *religious teaching*. The Constitution is still being violated.

Third, the ruling states "the Act's primary purpose was to change the public school science curriculum to provide *persuasive advantage* to a particular religious doctrine that rejects *the factual basis* of evolution in its entirety." There are multiple problems with this statement, but we begin with the "factual basis of evolution." The theory of evolution is precisely what the title implies—a theory! Theory is defined by the dictionary as "abstract thought; speculation."[497] Although, facts (such as fossils) may lead one to believe in the possibility of evolution, it must be noted that the concept remains *speculation*, as conclusive evidence has not yet supported

495 *Edwards v. Aguillard,* 482 U.S. 578 (1987).

496 Religious. Dictionary.com. *Dictionary.com Unabridged.* Random House, Inc. http://dictionary.reference.com/browse/religious (accessed: October 21, 2009).

497 Theory. Dictionary.com. *Dictionary.com Unabridged.* Random House, Inc. http://dictionary.reference.com/browse/theory (accessed: October 21, 2009).

the theory.[498] In response to the accusation that the Act would create a *persuasive advantage*, perhaps the justices misunderstood "in its entirety"? Since Darwinism and nontheistic evolution are already taught in schools, a persuasive advantage already exists. The purpose of the Balanced Treatment Act was never to create a persuasive advantage; it attempted to remove the advantage that already existed. This is obvious because the act did not try to remove nontheistic evolution; it merely tried to offer the opposing view so that the "persuasive advantage" would be eliminated. In this debacle, we note that the Constitution is still being violated.

Fourth, the ruling states that the "Act violates the First Amendment." How does it violate the First Amendment? The Balanced Treatment Act "violated the Establishment Clause because it sought to employ the symbolic and financial support of government to achieve a religious purpose." In other words, the government is forbidden from financially supporting or endorsing any propagation of religion in the classroom (at least if the religion affirms the existence of God). If the government teaches Naturalism, in any form, it symbolically and financially supports a religious set of beliefs that we have already proven to have a very specific and precise motive. The major difference between Naturalism and every other religion is the vantage point concerning God and the creation of the universe. The Constitution is *still* being violated.

So What Did the Courts Accomplish? As we reflect on the ruling of the court, we remember the basis was to prevent religion from being propagated in the school system. Consider the effects of the court's decision:

1. If the objective was to achieve "separation of church and state" by not endorsing *any* type of religion, then the court has failed.
2. If the objective was to prevent *any* form of religious teaching in the classroom, then the court has failed.
3. If the objective was to prevent a persuasive advantage on the propagation of religion in the classroom, then the court has failed.
4. If the objective was to prevent speculation on the origin of man, or even creation, from being presented in the classroom, then the court has failed.

498 Dr. Hennry Morris, "Does Entropy Contradict Evolution?" Institute for Creation Research, http://www.icr.org/index.php?module=articles&action=view&ID=245.

5. If the objective was to prevent *all* government funding or symbolic support of any form of religion, then the court has failed.
6. If the objective was to prevent public schools from influencing a student's view on religion, then the court has failed (ask Lee Strobel about his high school experience).

When we contrast the original intent of the ruling with the curriculum that is being taught today, it appears that the *only accomplishment* was to legally allow one religion to prevail over all others. To the liberals' credit, Naturalists are currently winning the battle because Naturalism is the *only religion* that is allowed to be financially and symbolically supported by the government. This religion, alone, rests upon a pedestal where it indoctrinates your students against your will to this very day (unless, of course, you foot the bill for private school; but you still pay for the indoctrination of others students through taxes).

Should the Decision Be Upheld? The million-dollar question is whether the court's decision should be upheld. Does the fact that the government endorses one religion, and allows it to be placed on a pedestal and propagated against your will, make you feel warm and fuzzy inside?

Either way the answer is presented, we find ourselves in a catch-22 scenario. If Christians demand that Creation-Science be taught in the classroom, then we are also violating the Constitution. If Christians demand that Darwinism and all nontheistic evolution be removed from the classroom in order to uphold the Constitution, Naturalists will scream bloody murder and throw an enormous temper tantrum, on the basis that this would violate the school's duty to teach a core subject, science. There are only two directions to travel, and we must wholeheartedly embrace this one liberal principle with open arms: whatever direction is chosen, we absolutely demand fairness and equal treatment.

> *Solution #1*: If we permit the Constitution to be violated, it will be equally violated. In other words, schools will teach Creation-Science and Evolution-Science without *endorsing* or *discrediting* either.
>
> *Solution #2*: If we decide to uphold the Constitution, we demand the removal of all theories and doctrines that

assume a position concerning the existence of God or the cause of the universe. (No Darwinism, nontheistic evolution, etc.)

As the options are considered, we must remind ourselves that the Judeo-Christian ethic is the only system of morality that is able to sustain America. The founding fathers were adamant that morality was absolutely necessary—it was imperative—for the success of a government that had never before been established. The freedom Americans enjoy is truly unprecedented, but it cannot exist in the absence of religion and morality.

> *"Let us with caution indulge the supposition that morality can be maintained without religion."*
>
> —*George Washington*

> *"Our Constitution was made only for a moral and religious people. It is wholly inadequate to the government of any other."*
>
> —*John Adams*

Morality and religion are responsibilities that parents must assume. Parents are tasked with the responsibility of teaching their children about God and morality, but let us never again allow the schools to circumvent the parents or to endorse a religion on our government's dime.

The liberals have come out of the closet, and they are actually proud of everything they are doing. Nobody can deny the fact that the liberals are boldly taking a stand for that which they believe and that they are "fundamentally transforming" our nation, while the majority of Christians have remained silent as they have sat back and done nothing.

The time to act is *now*—your nation desperately needs you, and she needs you *more than she ever has before*. She is pleading with you to not let her history be stamped out—"Please! Whatever you do, just take a stand!"

Chapter 16

Steps to Restoring America

"To the pure, all things are pure, but to those who are corrupted and do not believe, nothing is pure. In fact, both their minds and consciences are corrupted. They claim to know God, but by their actions they deny Him. They are detestable, disobedient and unfit for doing anything good."

—*Titus 1:15–16*

"Do not merely listen to the word, and so deceive yourselves. Do what it says. Those who listen to the word but do not do what it says are like people who look at their faces in a mirror and, after looking at themselves, go away and immediately forget what they look like. But those who look intently into the perfect law that gives freedom and continue in it—not forgetting what they have heard but doing it—they will be blessed in what they do."

—*James 1:22–25,* TNIV

Examining the Three Priorities

'The Choice Is Up to You.' This book has undoubtedly deviated from the politically correct mantra that our society seems to be enamored with, but our deviation has been adequately supported with logic, reason, facts, and extensive supporting sources and cases but, most importantly, by biblical presuppositions that are entirely true. Believe it or not, it's actually not my desire to be abrasive in presenting this message simply because of the fact that it's not popular (who doesn't want to be liked?) and because I want to sell books (which is the only way to get the message into the hands of concerned Americans). When I bluntly reveal that liberalism, both political and religious ideologies, that they are wrong and immoral, it's not because I don't like them; it just happens to be the truth and I merely pass that knowledge along. As seekers of the truth, we must embrace the truth (wherever it may lead) because rejecting the Truth leads to destruction.[499]

However, I must be clear; I speak out against the immorality—ultimately the insanity—of liberalism because I am severely constrained by the conservative values that are taught within the *Holy Bible.* As I have systematically demonstrated, the Word of God is nothing less than a product of God. Since the Bible is conservative by nature and it makes exclusive claims, it's not possible to contradict the Scriptures with liberal theology or policies.

The Word of God is very clear on the prerequisites for salvation; it does not need anybody to add or subtract content; the Word speaks for itself. Since the Word is sufficient, it is the *duty* of all Christians to share the contents of that written revelation with all people so that they may also have the opportunity of accepting their salvation.[500] As seekers of truth, we cannot deviate from that which we know, and have proven, to be entirely true. As a result, Christians enter into controversial territory when reminding people that liberal theology is wrong, but it's an issue that must be addressed. Christians cannot—*must not*—cower in the face of opposition. Quite the contrary, Christians are expected to STAND UP! for that which they know is entirely true. Christians are expected to be the salt and the light of the world.[501] If Christians cannot stand for the Truth, who could we expect to share the Gospel or restore America? Are we really to place America's hope or the future of Christianity in government or non-Christians? That would be madness!

A simple question needs to be asked each and every time we have a impulse to *refrain* from sharing the Absolute Truth or taking a stand to restore America. Ask, "What is my priority? Whom do I desire to please more: man, myself, or Jesus?"

499 Matthew 7:13.

500 Mark 16:15.

501 Matthew 5:13; Mark 9:49–50; Luke 14:34–35; Colossians 4:6.

Prioritizing Man. If you chose "man," your priority is to try and attain political correctness. If your presentation of the Gospel is politically correct, there is a good chance the entire Gospel has not been presented. How could I be so presumptuous? The Gospel of Jesus Christ, by definition, is very exclusive (conservative) because it provides only one path to redemption.[502] If the goal is to be politically correct, then concepts such as sin, confession, repentance, and the exclusivity of the Gospel of Jesus Christ will not be entirely presented, because people, by nature, do not want to hear this message; they may not like you. The goal of political correctness is a consumer-oriented message, which is precisely what the Bible can never become. The Bible will never morph into a message that is based upon a consumer's desire.

Furthermore, we recall the very words of Jesus Christ: "Blessed are you when people insult you, persecute you and falsely say all kinds of evil against you because of me. Rejoice and be glad, because *great* is your reward in heaven, for in the same way they persecuted the prophets who were before you."[503] Jesus made it clear that Truth will be rejected, and speaking of that truth will not always be politically correct or popular. None of the major or minor prophets in the Old Testament were politically correct, but they were right and will be rewarded. What glory can one find in a spineless coward who succumbs to the approval of others?

Prioritizing man is not taught by the Bible; neither Jesus nor the prophets succumbed to political correctness. (If they had, Jesus would not have revealed His true identity or died on the cross, and the prophets would not have preached messages of repentance or punishment.) Likewise, Christians must not *conform* to what society deems acceptable or lawful but is in fact immoral. On the contrary, Christians must distinguish themselves from the world; come out and be separate so that the peace, joy, and hope Christians have in Jesus become obvious.[504] Being released from the burden of having to please others offers immense freedom, but with freedom comes responsibility. The responsibility we must assume is a continual, but accurate, presentation of the Gospel.

Prioritizing the Self. If you chose "myself," there is a good chance that the Gospel message is not being shared with family or friends at all. Why would I venture so far out on a limb? The answer is quite simple and is

502 John 14:6.

503 Matthew 5:11–12; emphasis added.

504 Isaiah 52:11; 2 Corinthians 6:17.

reduced to motive. People naturally have a tendency to avoid controversial topics such as Christianity and politics.[505] Why are these topics typically avoided with family, friends, or co-workers? It is more "self"-satisfying to be accepted and liked, rather than sharing the Gospel at the risk of being labeled as "intolerant" or "bigoted" or "exclusive." However, Christians do not have a choice as to the Gospel that we present because that was decided long before we ever set foot on earth.

We must also point out an inconvenient fact that everybody will make a choice as to their top priority. It's not possible to have multiple top priorities, just as it's not possible to serve both God and money; one is inevitably chosen and takes priority over the other.[506] Furthermore, the Bible never teaches the prioritization of the self, because when we reflect on the words of Christ, we remember, "Whoever wants to be my disciple must *deny* themselves and take up their cross and follow me. For whoever wants to save their life will lose it, but whoever loses their life for me will find it. What good will it be for you to gain the whole world, yet forfeit your soul? Or what can you give in exchange for your soul?"[507]

Clearly, Christians must not prioritize the "self." There is only one remaining priority.

Prioritizing Jesus. If your priority was Jesus, you chose the biblically correct answer. Prioritizing the King of kings and the Lord of lords should always be the highest priority of the Christian. However, we must fully understand that it's not possible to *faithfully* serve God in obedience and yet refuse to share the Gospel.[508] To prioritize God is to prioritize the non-Christian; we must not only pray for non-Christians, but also show genuine love and concern for them. (What better way than to tell them about Jesus?) Prioritizing God is achieved when Christians align their passion to His—which we know is humankind. Was God's passion for lost souls not demonstrated by Jesus' willingness to come down from the comforts of heaven to walk among mankind for the purpose of suffering on the cross so that we might have a chance in eternity? Our passion must correlate with His for us to truly be ambassadors on behalf of Jesus

505 Every other religion appears to be acceptable to discuss except for those based upon Jesus Christ as Lord and Savior. Therefore, *religion* was replaced with *Christianity*.

506 Matthew 6:24.

507 Matthew 16:24–26, TNIV; emphasis added.

508 Matthew 28:18-20.

Christ. How effective could an American ambassador be if he refused to talk about America?

Truly prioritizing God is not a walk in the park because it entails sacrificing that selfish desire within. Once again I ask: "Who is it you would rather please?" Would you rather please your eternal Judge or others (who may not like you regardless of what you say or do)? Why would you ever prioritize other people when they will not be at your side when you stand before God in judgment? Your family and friends will not be there when you stand face to face with God. You will have to give an account of your actions, but will be rewarded based on your contribution to the kingdom of God, not on the number of people you appeased.

Personally, it's unfathomable for me to even think of standing before God empty-handed. What could possibly justify a waste of our tremendous spiritual gifts, talents, or abilities? What could possibly justify refusing to spread the Gospel when *somebody* might accept it if we only cared enough to simply share? What could justify a refusal to stand for truth when it has been demonstrated time and time again that it's entirely true beyond a shadow of a doubt? *Is it even possible to fathom God's reaction to the excuses we will one day provide if we show up empty-handed?* An excuse of not defending and propagating the Gospel will undoubtedly be reduced to a motive of selfish desire; there can be no other answer, and there will be no reward (see Parable of the Talents, Mattthew 25:14–30).

As for me and this book, we *will* stand for Truth: the whole truth and nothing but the truth.[509] We will not cower in the face of opposition, and we will not stop sharing until every soul has been evangelized. We have assumed the "I can sleep when I die" mentality; but until that retirement in heaven, there is work that needs to be done. The harvest is plentiful, but the people who have a spine and are willing to share the Gospel have been few.[510] How many Christians could be counted among "the few, the proud, the faithful?"[511] How much more desirable is it to actually see a sermon lived out before your eyes and to see tangible results than to merely discuss hypothetical scenarios and the potential that could have been?

We now enter the part of the book where the rubber meets the road, the part where our action will ultimately determine whether America will be restored and our children have freedom or a future remotely as promising as ours. Unless people genuinely care enough to actualize the

509 Inspired by Joshua 24:15.

510 Inspired by Matthew 9:37.

511 Inspired by the United States Marine Corps slogan.

potential they have, results will be, at best, minimal. We will now put into action everything this book has discussed because we already know that the knowledge laid out here will be *utterly meaningless* unless it can be shared (a verb that requires action) with somebody else.

Therefore, it's my passion and my greatest desire to share a few steps that we, as Christians and *patriotic Americans*, can take in order to give our children a better future. Together we can—and we will—make a difference because Americans have never cowered in the face of danger. No mountain has ever been too tall, no river has ever been too wide, and no challenge has ever been too tough for God-fearing, patriotic Americans. We have never refused to act when the circumstances demanded action, and this time will be no different. Let us prove to the world our resilience, and let us demonstrate to the nations that are eagerly anticipating America's collapse the *power of the Christian nation.* Let us demonstrate how reliance on God brings tremendous power and blessings. Let us live out the famous words of Dr. Bruce Wilkinson, "For the Christian, dependence on God is just another word for power."[512]

Simple Steps to Profound Results

Step One: Reflect on Your Priority, then Pick One. If you are Fired Up and ready to Stand Up! and you truly have a passion—a burning desire—to see America restored, then I invite you to join me in being proactive so that we can usher in *real* "change you can believe in." In the last section, three priorities were presented, but the nature of these priorities makes them mutually exclusive as they relate to God. It's possible to simultaneously prioritize mankind and others, but choosing either of the previous two hinders a full allegiance to God. As a result, all people will inevitably choose whether or not they will prioritize God. As a result, I challenge you to make James 1:22 your life verse as we work to restore America; "Do not merely listen to the Word, and so deceive yourselves. *Do what it says.*"

In order to make James 1:22 applicable, we need to know what the Bible says. We must understand that the Word of God requires Christians to be proactive. How are Christians supposed to be proactive? First, we need to note that evangelism, as unpopular as it may be, is not only necessary to grow the faith, but that it should also be something that the

512 Bruce Wilkinson, *The Prayer of Jabez* (Sisters: Multnomah Publishers, 2000), 61.

Christian is truly passionate about. Let us revisit the Great Commission and the charge that Jesus gave to all believers (not just His apostles) with respect to Christians being proactive.

> Jesus came to them and said, "All authority in heaven and on earth has been given to me. Therefore *go* and *make* disciples of all nations, *baptizing* them in the name of the Father and of the Son and of the Holy Spirit, and *teaching* them to obey everything I have commanded you. And surely I am with you always, to the very end of the age."[513]

> He [Jesus] said to them, "*Go* into all the world and *preach* the good news to all creation. Whoever believes and is baptized will be saved, but whoever does not believe will be condemned."[514]

In the Great Commission, presented in Matthew and Mark, I have italicized the verbs that require action on the part of the Christian. It is impossible to grow the faith and restore America if we do not *go*, *make*, *baptize*, *teach*, and *preach*. When we truly have reverence for God and align our priority with His, these verbs will not be intimidating; they will become our greatest desire and an uncontainable passion. "The fear of the LORD is the beginning of wisdom."[515] Indeed, we need to fear God once again, and we need to fear the direction this nation is headed so that we will have the proper motivation to stand for that which is true and righteous. Since the Scriptures require action, we must be proactive in order to restore America. James made it clear that we must not merely acknowledge the Word; we must do what it says.

The objection usually comes when it's clear that taking a stand for Truth may make us unpopular, and we may not be politically correct, but taking a stand will never be done in vain. However, we return to priorities: what is your true priority? Surely, the words of Jesus and James mean something to the Christian! After all, they are found within the text that we have demonstrated to be entirely true, so therefore they *must* be true. If the Word promises *blessings* for taking a stand (which it does), then you will be blessed defending Truth. The blessings will not always

513 Matthew 28:18–20 (emphasis added).

514 Mark 16:15–16 (emphasis added).

515 Proverbs 9:10.

come in the physical or the material form, but they have been promised, and you will receive them. What greater blessing could one aspire to have than the *approval of God Almighty*? Could there be anything greater than to one day stand before God and hear the words "Well done, good and faithful servant" as they come from His lips? The approval of God is the most cherished blessing one could ever aspire to attain.

In addition to personal blessings, what has also been promised is that if a nation truly exalts God, then that nation will also be blessed. Recall the simple answer from the first chapter, "Blessed is the nation whose God is the LORD, the people he chose for his inheritance."[516] The promises have been made, the blessings are waiting; we simply need to receive them by living in accordance with God's moral law! After you have chosen to follow God, the next step is to persistently pray for our nation, our President, and Congress—and for wisdom and guidance.

Step Two: Pray for Wisdom and Guidance. We must communicate with God to understand God's will, teachings, and commands. God poured out His heart in the written text that we refer to as the Holy Bible. This is the primary method by which God has chosen to reveal His sovereign and moral will to mankind. However, a monologue is not the highest and best use of our relationship with God. We need to reciprocate and communicate back to God through prayer and fasting. There is unimaginable *power* in prayer—we cannot begin to understand the ways it affects us, those we pray for, and even our nation! A few verses demonstrate the power, and importance, of prayer.

- Jesus replied, "I tell you the truth, if you have faith and do not doubt, not only can you do what was done to the fig tree, but also you can say to this mountain, 'Go, throw yourself into the sea,' and it will be done. If you *believe*, you will *receive* whatever you *ask* for in *prayer*."[517]

- Confess your sins to each other and *pray* for each other so that you may be healed. The *prayer* of a righteous person is *powerful* and *effective*.[518]

516 Psalms 33:12.
517 Matthew 21:21–22 (emphasis added).
518 James 5:16 (emphasis added).

- Pray in the Spirit on all occasions with all kinds of prayers and requests. With this in mind, be alert and *always* keep on praying for the Lord's people.[519]

- This is the confidence we have in approaching God: that *if* we *ask* anything according to His *will*, he hears us. And if we know that He hears us—whatever we ask—we know that *we have* what we asked of Him.[520]

These are but a few verses, from four separate books, that all emphasize the true power in prayer. Of course we know that we cannot physically throw a mountain in the sea, but Matthew does accurately depict the incomprehensible power of genuine, persistent, and passionate prayer! Why would God be so gracious as to give us what we ask if it aligns with His will? Why would God Almighty even listen to a mere human? The answer can be found in the words of Jesus Christ.

> Ask and it will be given to you; seek and you will find; knock and the door will be opened to you. For everyone who asks receives; he who seeks finds; and to him who knocks, the door will be opened.[521]

What could be more pleasing than to see your child love you? What could be more joyful than to see your child respect you? What could be more fulfilling than to see that child actively strive toward greatness and live a moral and upright life, always seeking to do good? Would you not want to take such children and bless and spoil them (just a little)? Would you ever turn your back on your own children and give them a stone when they asked for bread? Absolutely not! You would want to encourage, honor, and bless the obedient child. This is some of what Jesus was trying to convey when He said, "If you, then, though you are evil, know how to give good gifts to your children, *how much more* will your Father in heaven give good gifts to those who ask Him!"[522]

---

519 Ephesians 6:18 (emphasis added).
520 1 John 5:14–15 (emphasis added).
521 Matthew 7:7–8.
522 Matthew 7:11 (emphasis added).

Prayer is powerful; promises have been made, and they only wait for us to receive them. We receive them through obedience to the Word. Be persistent; be patient; but above all else—pray!

Step Three: Share the Gospel. A major point that the first chapter made was that 95–97 percent of Christians do not tell their family and friends about the gift of salvation that Jesus offers. Family and friends are supposed to be the people we love and care for the most, yet Christians are somehow okay with one day seeing those family and friends suffer in hell until God wipes away the tears from our eyes.[523] Yes! There will be tears in heaven. How could there possibly be tears in heaven?

First, we know they exist because God must wipe them from our faces.[524] Second, the account of Luke 16:23 seems to indicate that people in heaven and hell can see one another. What greater pain could the Christian bear than seeing their family and friends in hell and then having the memory to reflect on the many different opportunities that they had to share with their mother, father, brother, sister, or friend about the saving grace that Jesus offers?

In that time, could there be any greater sorrow than to actually see our loved ones burn, when it was possible for us to make a difference? It is my personal opinion that those tears will be a reflection of the opportunities we disregarded in order to prioritize the self and prevent persecution rather than openly sharing the faith. Some of your family and friends perhaps have already passed away, and that opportunity is gone, but those alive still have a chance. Do you really want to add more tears and more regret? Once you have shared, the choice is up to them—but at least give them the opportunity. Are you going to let another loved one slip into eternity without doing all that you can possibly do to help?

Step Four: Vote! As Americans, we have an unusual opportunity and privilege to exercise our Constitutional right to vote for the leaders who govern our nation. Christians must also vote in order to make a difference! Christians must not only vote, but we must vote for the candidate who most reflects Christian values. Throw out the idea of parties; they make no difference. Voting Democrat or Republican is meaningless; we must vote for the candidate best aligned to the Judeo-Christian ethic.

---

523 Isaiah 25:8; Revelation 7:17.

524 Ibid.

However, before we ever cast a vote, we must know who the candidates are and the values they espouse. Even though we sometimes come across two horrible candidates, we must vote for the lesser of the two evils. One candidate will be better than the other, and we must cast our vote so that the government will best reflect our moral standards. If neither candidate is worthy of a vote, perhaps you could consider running for office. Is the Bible silent with respect to voting? Surely not! We need to read Deuteronomy 16:18–20 to see what God reveals in regard to electing government officials.

> Appoint judges and officials for each of your tribes in every town the LORD your God is giving you, and they shall judge the people fairly. Do not pervert justice or show partiality. Do not accept a bribe, for a bribe blinds the eyes of the wise and twists the words of the righteous. Follow justice and justice alone, so that you may live and possess the land the LORD your God is giving you.

Notice the word "appoint"; it is a verb and requires action (the state of being proactive). In our case, we *elect* judges and officials to judge, to enact laws, and to govern. Since we elect government officials, we must elect moral and righteous officials so that they do not pervert justice, show partiality, or engage in corruption.

I just have one question: "Is Washington perverting justice, showing favoritism, and engaging in corruption—or truly governing with godly morals?" The answer is quite clear: all three branches of our government are, in some form, violating God's moral law. Not every elected official is corrupt, but we need to look at the majority, because the majority rules and ultimately governs. Do our government officials violate God's law by supporting the murder of innocent children? Do they endorse homosexuality, gay marriage, and government theft from one group to give to another (the redistribution of wealth)? Has the Supreme Court upheld the Constitution with the separation of church and state? Has the legislative branch drafted moral laws? Has the executive branch endorsed policies that we know lead to depravity? Are there Marxists, socialists or communists in the White House?

Furthermore, we need to understand that the people who *refuse* to vote are not eligible to complain about the outcome of laws, policies, or court rulings because they have made no attempt to alter the outcome. We should consider the consequences of refusing to elect godly government officials in the verses presented below (the inverse application of the verse is to be avoided because inverse results are to be expected). If we elect morally depraved government officials, they will oppress the moral. But we must understand how a refusal to implement God's moral standards will cause us to "reap what we sow," and God will not answer. (Although the situation varies, the principles remain the same.)

First Samuel 8:18 reads, "When that day comes [oppression detailed in verses 10–17], you will cry out for relief from the king [elected officials] you have chosen, and the LORD will not answer you in that day." This is a shocking reply, and it's a warning that a nation will reap what it sows. If we sow immorality, we will reap moral oppression; if we sow ungodly government officials, we will reap ungodly laws; but if we sow morality, we will reap the blessings that accompany righteousness. They have been already been promised, and once again, they are eagerly awaiting our reception.

If you do not want to be on the immoral road that our nation is currently traveling, you need to vote—and you need to vote Christian morals and values. If you do not vote, you are not helping to restore America, and if you do not vote, you cannot complain when the nation finally reaps what it has sown. The urgency is conveyed with the law of sowing and reaping: You will reap *what* you sow, *later* than you sow and *more* that you sow. Do you really want more immorality to come later?

Step Five: Follow the News. Part of being able to vote Christian is to know what the issues are that surround each election. In order to know and understand the issues, you must be actively involved with the news. The news reports the abnormal stories of the day. You never hear in the news about how a person went to work, earned a paycheck, and provided for the family, because this is what is expected and it is normal. The news covers the *abnormal* whether it's good or bad news. Granted, most of the time the news is depressing because it covers the terrorist attacks, murders, rapes, child molestations, and the like. Ironically, the news is a reflection of our nation's morality. If all people were moral and did that which is right, there would not be any negative news! The more murders and rapes the news reports, the more our nation's morality, as a whole, is declining.

The news also reports on stories that depict the direction our nation is heading and how our government is governing. The news is your lifeline to understanding where America stands with respect to issues concerning morality and the direction our nation is heading. If you do not keep up with the news, you cannot possibly know the most important issues that surround the elections. If you do not know the issues, then how can you vote for the best candidate?

I'm not suggesting that we become obsessed with the news (because I do not want you to enter into depression), but I am suggesting that you follow it enough to grasp the state of the nation. Staying current with the news is the only way we can counter any problems. If we do not know the problems, how is it possible to solve them? Do not be ignorant and let the politicians continue to implement immoral policies and laws. Know what they are doing so you can vote accordingly.

Step Six: Get Involved (Reorganize the Organizers). In this section, we will examine one of President Obama's greatest strengths and learn how Christians can replicate the results to restore America. Since I give credit where credit is due, we will examine and commend President Obama's greatest strength. During the Presidential elections of 2008, many people made fun of Barack Obama because he was a "community organizer." He was chastised for not having any experience in governing, and only a few years of experience in the U.S. Senate, but what many people fail to understand is that he had a tremendous amount of experience in inducing change. Since we give credit where credit is due, we recognize the fact that Obama was successful in his community organizing efforts. Little did we know, there was tremendous power that accompanies community organizing! It is an undeniable fact that Obama has been tremendously successful in organizing communities in a way that induces tremendous and fundamental change. It would appear as if Obama has modeled his strategy after the "father of community organizing," Saul Alinsky.[525] Saul wrote the book *Rules for Radicals* in 1971, which became a handbook for community organizing, where he argued that a socialist revolution could not come through violence. Instead, the revolution would come by "slowly eroding principles of the Republic at the polls"—through voting."[526]

Obama, after graduating from Columbia University, was inspired by Saul Alinsky's book, and he built and guided a small network of grassroots groups.[527] Obama aligned himself with organizations and gained a lot of

---

525 Fox News, "President Obama is Still a Community Organizer," http://glennbeck.blogs.foxnews.com/2009/06/16/president-obama-is-still-a-community-organizer/.

526 Ibid.

527 Ibid.

experience "working on the ground" and instilling his principles, vision, and ideas through community organizations and voting.

Have the community organizing methods of inducing change been effective? Indeed; they have been tremendously effective. Not only was Barack Obama elected President, but many of his community organizing partners are receiving large amounts of taxpayer money that synergize one another. The government and these groups fuel each other through your tax money! If you pay taxes, your money supports ACORN (regardless of whether you agree or disagree with their political views or the fact that ACORN is involved in mass corruption) and many other community organizing groups.

Unfortunately, the scope of this book does not provide sufficient room to detail each and every single one of Barack Obama's accomplishments through his community organizing efforts or precisely how the change is taking place, but we know that they are tremendously effective to a degree that was unknown to conservatives (at least until November 4, 2008). Since we know there is tremendous power for change in "community organizing," the question now becomes: "Can the community organizing of conservative Christian morals, principles, and ideologies induce change?"

Absolutely; community organizing has tremendous potential to induce change, and the process works regardless of whether the objective is to promote liberal or conservative ideologies; the process is effective. Christians can begin reversing the devastating effects of liberalism, socialism, and progressivism by getting involved with their communities! To make a difference, Christians need to STAND UP! and essentially reorganize the organizers. If Christians expect a true restoration, we must first be proactive with respect to the solution. Christians need to demand that Christian morals and values are upheld by our local governments, school systems, courts, and institutions that receive taxpayer money; after all, America is a Christian nation!

Insanity was once defined, by Albert Einstein, as "doing the same thing over and over again and expecting different results."[528] Whether we like it or not, the conservative Christian movement has been losing momentum year after year, and it has been shrinking at an unprecedented rate. The majority of Christians have not been actively involved with methods that induce change, such as evangelism and involvement in the

528 Brainy Quote, "Albert Einstein Quotes," http://www.brainyquote.com/quotes/quotes/a/alberteins133991.html.

community. If the Christian expects different results from doing the same thing over again, they fit the definition of insanity. Let me rephrase the last sentence; if Christians expect America to be restored, but refuse to get involved—they have "lost their minds."

Step Seven: Be Outspoken! As we revisit Christianity 101, Christians must fully understand that there is *no such thing* as an obedient "closet Christian." Ironically, I found two very good definitions of closet Christian from urbandictionary.com, an entirely secular source that is often vulgar. Here are the two definitions for a closet Christian:[529]

1. A follower of the person Jesus Christ who chooses to follow His teachings, but does not feel compelled to share or propagate their personal faith among others.
2. Someone who believes in the Christian religion who is either unwilling or unable to make a public affirmation of their faith.

The sheer thought of even being considered close to the definition of a closet Christian should send chills down my spine when I compare the motive of a closet Christian with the words of Jesus. We have already established that Christians are supposed to be outspoken about their faith because Jesus commanded that Christians share the Gospel, but we need to understand the true motive of a closet Christian. Before we can accurately portray the motive, we need to first understand what accompanies being a follower of Jesus Christ. Jesus indirectly speaks to the closet Christian in Mark 8:34-38 (TNIV):

> The he [Jesus] called the crowd to him along with his disciples and said: "Whoever wants to be my disciple must deny themselves and take up their cross and follow me. For whoever wants to save their life will lose it, but whoever loses their life for me and for the gospel will save it. What good is it for you to gain the whole world, yet forfeit your soul? Or what can you give in exchange for your soul? If any of you are ashamed of me and my words in this adulterous and sinful generation, the Son of Man

529 Urban Dictionary, "Closet Christian," http://www.urbandictionary.com/define.php?term=closet%20christian.

> will be ashamed of you when he comes in his Father's glory with the holy angels."

Even though Jesus was speaking to his first-century disciples and followers, the principle is still applicable today. If you truly desire to follow Christ, He must be your priority. When Jesus is your priority, you will deny your selfish interests and metaphorically "pick up your cross" and follow Him. It is not possible to prioritize Jesus and be an obedient Christian only to turn and either refuse to share the Gospel or be unwilling to make a public affirmation of the faith. Another interesting passage is Luke 12:8–10:

> I tell you, whoever acknowledges me before men, the Son of Man will also acknowledge him before the angels of God. But he who disowns me before men will be disowned before the angels of God. And everyone who speaks a word against the Son of Man will be forgiven, but anyone who blasphemes against the Holy Spirit will not be forgiven.

From these passages, it is clear that Christians cannot be ashamed to associate themselves with Jesus Christ. How absurd is the title "closet Christian?" Is this not one of the greatest paradoxes ever known? The paradox is that Christians understand they must follow, acknowledge, support, and defend Jesus, but closet Christians are unwilling to make a public affirmation of their faith and refuse to propagate their personal faith to family and friends.

Refusing to share the faith does not mean that you are not a Christian, but it does mean you are not being obedient. Refusing to share the faith is not apostasy, but you are not defending the faith either. Refusing to share the faith does not mean the Christian will automatically go to hell, but concealing the faith does not please God, especially when we reflect on the sacrifice Jesus made for us and our unwillingness to sacrifice for Him. Put the entire picture (final judgment included) into perspective so you can make the best decision with respect to taking a stand for Jesus Christ—the King of kings and the Lord of lords.

The Hope that Became our Passion

There IS Light at the End of the Tunnel! Purposefully, this book has presented a negative view and has embraced a negative connotation because the consequences are severe and the stakes are high if America is not restored. America is truly being tested, and soon our way will be set. However, hope is not yet lost. There is light at the end of the tunnel! We can still make a difference because we are choosing our way (present tense), and the future has yet to be written. America is currently at a crossroads, and she will turn in one of two directions. Either America will fall back to God and into the comfort and the blessings associated with Christianity *or* we will fall into the depravity of socialism and the unfairness and immorality associated with the Naturalistic ideology that rejects the existence of God. This is common sense because the only two directions we can travel are either toward or away from God, but never both.

I Have a Vision. Americans are awake, people are stirring, many are taking a stand, and real change is brewing. People do not like the direction that the nation is heading, and the Tea Parties demonstrate that the masses are rejecting socialism and everything it represents. The timing is right, the people are ready, and fundamental change is upon us (just as President Obama proclaimed).

I have a vision that one day soon, we will live in a nation where the land will once again flow with milk and honey. One day soon justice will prevail over corruption; balanced budgets will prevail over deficits; earned income will prevail over government handouts and dependence; the individual will prevail over the inequality that accompanies social justice and the collective good; honesty, integrity, and morality will prevail over lies, deception, and immorality; and one day soon cherishing and preserving innocent lives will prevail over the murder of innocent children.

Indeed, one day soon Americans will see the deceptive, double-standard, backstabbing, two-tongued, corrupt, and morally depraved entity of liberalism for what it actually is. America will return to the morality she was established upon because she intuitively knows that it's the only way to survive as the greatest nation that the world has ever known. America is great, but it's not because of the government; it never has been. It's the moral people who love Jesus Christ who make this nation great because they sow the seeds that reap the blessings of God.

This great nation will accept her past, recognize her present crisis, and then forge a bright, new future—a new era of blessings and prosperity—as we venture back into Christianity. The near-death attempted venture into socialism was so horrifying that it will actually help America come back to her roots, return to her foundation, and embrace her origin with open arms.

America already has a loyalty to none other than God Himself because she was established by Christians, for God, to exalt God. America has been indoctrinated, in the beginning, by the most powerful book ever written. The truths contained within that book have been proven to be true beyond a shadow of a doubt, and only a fool could deny them. Soon—*and very soon*—America will be restored as Christians STEP UP, STAND UP, and SPEAK UP! As a nation, America will undergo a "fundamental transformation" so that our children will have a future that is filled with hope. The only question that remains: "What part will you play in the largest, and most powerful, restoration the world has ever known?"

Concluding Thoughts

We have had an incredible journey and I hope that you have thoroughly enjoyed discovering the Absolute Truth and how it pertains to America and Americans alike. I encourage you to be bold because there is no reward for being a coward. However, make your decision after knowing the potential consequences. I fully understand the consequences, and I know that most likely some critics will despise this book because it has truly taken a stand for Truth; it will undoubtedly offend people. To the immoral, there is nothing more offensive than to be confronted with Truth because they love their ways and do not want to change; their motive is ultimately reduced to selfishness and an unwillingness to submit to God.

In this section, I would like to address the critics to demonstrate how their attacks actually strengthen and ironically fulfill the Gospel. The more the critics despise truth, the more you know it is true. Because I have taken a stand for Truth, I expect personal attacks as indicated in Matthew 5:11–12. I most likely will not enjoy those attacks; who would? However, I recognize the promise of blessing(s) to those who unapologetically present and defend the faith; even though my method is unorthodox and includes a lot of sarcasm (as you may have noticed). The underlying message is entirely true, but I use humor to convey principles and ideas so that they will be remembered as I put them into a unique context. This book is not politically correct, but I have never striven to be politically correct. If not being politically correct is offensive, you need to check your premise because Jesus did not conform to the wishes of the liberal/evil mind either.

As a result of my unwillingness to conform to the liberal ideology, some of my critics will undoubtedly attack. It will be interesting to see *what* the critics attack—the Truth that I have presented, or me. Since I have presented the impossibility of trumping Absolute Truth, I think they will attack the messenger who stands for Truth. Why would they smear the messenger? Since the critic cannot entirely defend their position (the impossibility of proving a negative), many times they resort to personal attacks (similar to the way the critics tried to destroy Sarah Palin or Glenn Beck or Carrie Prejean). Why would the critics resort to personal attacks? Because they fear that person becoming influential and they will destroy, at all costs, their reputation to try and discredit the person. This is nothing new. God's prophets were persecuted, and so was Jesus. If a sinless man was persecuted, how naïve would I be in believing I am exempt?

However, we need to understand that I am merely presenting the Gospel as it was given to me. I did not write the Bible, nor do I claim to be perfect. Since I am human, I have made and will continue to make mistakes. This is not a secret because all of us are inherently sinful; are we not all human? The difference is that I recognize my sinful nature, have attempted to correct the wrong, and actively seek God. Thus, the difference is repentance and comes down to intent. My intent, although I fail, is to be moral, but the wicked have no desire to conform to God's moral standards, nor do they have a desire to submit to God.

So let me have a word with my critics and challenge them to be open-minded to the Gospel and to accept the obvious Truth. If you refuse, that's your decision, and you have a right to destroy yourself. However, let it be known that the farther you drag me down and the more you attempt to distance me from the Christian faith, the more powerful the effect the Gospel has had upon me, and the stronger my testimony will become. The worse you portray me, the more you (unintentionally) give credit to God. The more you despise the Truth, the more you prove the Truth to be entirely true. How do I know this? I presented the Absolute Truth of the Holy Bible, and contained within that *holy text* are these words:

> The righteous detest the dishonest;
> the wicked detest the upright.[530]

Those who oppose God and the Absolute Truth, flaunt their wickedness by chastising the Christian faith of those who teach morality and scorn the wicked—to them, I ask:

> *How long will you who are simple love your simple ways?*
> *How long will mockers delight in mockery*
> *and fools hate knowledge?*
> *Repent at my rebuke!*
> *Then I will pour out my thoughts to you,*
> *I will make known to you my teachings.*
> *But since you refuse to listen when I call*
> *and no one pays attention when I stretch out my hand,*

530 Proverbs 29:27.

since you disregard all my advice
and do not accept my rebuke,
I in turn will laugh when disaster strikes you;
I will mock when calamity overtakes you—
when calamity overtakes you like a storm,
when disaster sweeps over you like a whirlwind,
when distress and trouble overwhelm you.
Then they will call to me but I will not answer;
they will look for me but will not find me,
since they hated knowledge
and did not choose to fear the LORD.
Since they would not accept my advice
and spurned my rebuke,
they will eat the fruit of their ways
and be filled with the fruit of their schemes.
For the waywardness of the simple will kill them,
and the complacency of fools will destroy them;
but whoever listens to me will live in safety
and be at ease, without fear of harm."[531]

Strengthen my testimony if you dare, but always remember that it is not me whom *you* are ultimately against; think about the implications of that statement. Whether you agree with me or "hate my guts," I love and care for your soul, in the name of Jesus. I risk myself to try and reach you. Whether you agree or disagree with me, I wish you the best.

Russell A. Newman

531 Proverbs 1:22–33 (TNIV).

Index

E

F

G

H

I

J

K

L

M

T

U

V

W

LaVergne, TN USA
26 July 2010
190883LV00005B/2/P